A Research Agenda for Financial Law and Regulation

Elgar Research Agendas outline the future of research in a given area. Leading scholars are given the space to explore their subject in provocative ways, and map out the potential directions of travel. They are relevant but also visionary.

Forward-looking and innovative, Elgar Research Agendas are an essential resource for PhD students, scholars and anybody who wants to be at the forefront of research.

For a full list of Edward Elgar published titles, including the titles in this series, visit our website at www.e-elgar.com.

A Research Agenda for Financial Law and Regulation

Edited by

JOSEPH LEE

Reader in Corporate and Financial Law, University of Manchester, UK

ALINE DARBELLAY

Assistant Professor of Corporate and Capital Markets Law, University of Zurich, Switzerland

Elgar Research Agendas

Edward Elgar
PUBLISHING

Cheltenham, UK · Northampton, MA, USA

Published by
Edward Elgar Publishing Limited
The Lypiatts
15 Lansdown Road
Cheltenham
Glos GL50 2JA
UK

Edward Elgar Publishing, Inc.
William Pratt House
9 Dewey Court
Northampton
Massachusetts 01060
USA

A catalogue record for this book
is available from the British Library

Library of Congress Control Number: 2024948234

This book is available electronically in the Elgaronline
Law subject collection
https://doi.org/10.4337/9781803929996

MIX
Paper | Supporting responsible forestry
FSC® C013604

ISBN 978 1 80392 998 9 (cased)
ISBN 978 1 80392 999 6 (eBook)

Printed and bound by CPI Group (UK) Ltd, Croydon, CR0 4YY

Contents

List of contributors vii
Acknowledgments xi
List of abbreviations xiii

Introduction to *A Research Agenda for Financial Law and Regulation* 1
Joseph Lee and Aline Darbellay

1 The promise and perils of behaviourally informed bank disclosure regulation 5
Aline Darbellay

2 Empowering sustainable finance with artificial intelligence: a framework for responsible implementation 23
Georgios Pavlidis

3 From traditional to decentralized governance in the crypto environment: legal framework for decentralized autonomous organizations and decentralized finance 39
Rolf H Weber

4 The rise, fall and future of P2P lending platforms in China: the role of policy, law and enforcement 63
Joseph Lee and Yonghui Bao

5 The uncertain path towards open finance: mutual lessons from the United Kingdom and European Union regulatory approaches 83
Clara Martins Pereira

6 Developing cybersecurity in open banking and open finance: the application of blockchain technology and decentralised autonomous organisations 113

Joseph Lee and Vere-Marie Khan

7 Capital markets regulation in the age of social media: an analysis of the GameStop incident under the EU Market Abuse Regulation 139
Philipp Maume

8 Market abuse in the crypto-assets market: same risks, same activities, and same regulatory outcomes? 157
Joseph Lee and Lukas Schu

9 A European anti-money laundering supervisory authority: perspectives and challenges 179
Katia Villard

10 Traceability of crypto-asset transfers under the new EU AML/CFT regime: the crypto travel rule between challenges and open issues 197
Nadia Pocher

11 Regulation of payment systems from the perspectives of consumer protection and fraud prevention 221
Christopher Chao-Hung Chen

12 A research agenda for online dispute resolution for DLT finance 237
Pietro Ortolani

Index 251

Contributors

Yonghui Bao is a lecturer in law at Capital Normal University, Beijing. He received his PhD in Corporate and Financial Law from the University of Exeter, UK, and an LLM from the University of Hong Kong. His current research includes company law, securities and financial regulations, as well as multidisciplinary research in the area of law and economics. He is a qualified lawyer in China.

Christopher Chao-Hung Chen is currently an Associate Professor at the College of Law, National Taiwan University. Dr Chen received his PhD from the University of London (UCL). Before 2021, Dr Chen was an Associate Professor of Law at the Singapore Management University. Dr Chen specialises in corporate law and governance, financial law and regulations, and empirical legal studies. Dr Chen has publications in Taiwan, the US, the UK, Hong Kong, and Singapore.

Aline Darbellay is an Assistant Professor of Capital Markets Law at the University of Zurich, Switzerland. She was an Assistant Professor of Banking and Finance Law at the University of Geneva and a Research Associate at the University of San Diego School of Law. She holds a PhD from the University of Zurich and an LLM from the University of San Diego. She is admitted to the New York Bar. She is an Academic Fellow of the Jean Monnet Centre of Excellence on European Union Sustainable Finance and Law.

Vere-Marie Khan is an Attorney-at-Law and academic researcher from Trinidad and Tobago. Her areas of research and publications include Fintech initiatives such as blockchain, P2P lending regulations, renewable energy and commodity trading, smart technology and consumer protection, regulatory compliance, and financial regulation. She holds a Bachelor of Arts from the University of Toronto, an LLB from the University of Exeter, and is currently completing the Dual Commercial Law LLM with Queen Mary University of London and Singapore Management University.

Joseph Lee is a reader in corporate and financial law at the University of Manchester School of Law. He is the founding programme director of Manchester Online LLM Master of Laws in International Commercial and Technology Law. He is the author of the book *Crypto-Finance, Law and Regulation: Governing an Emerging Ecosystem* and the editor of the book *Data Governance in AI, FinTech and RegTech*. He is a member of the LawTech Advisory Council of the Astana International Financial Centre and of the Manchester LawTech Initiative. Dr Lee has been principal investigator of research projects funded by UKRI, the British Academy, and the British Council. He has held a number of visiting positions, including at KU Leuven and Tokyo University. He is also an attorney-at-law in New York State.

Clara Martins Pereira is Assistant Professor and Director for International Development at Durham Law School, and Invited Professor at Católica Lisbon School of Law. Her research lies at the intersection of financial regulation, technological innovation, and sustainability. Clara holds a DPhil, an MPhil, and an MJur from the University of Oxford, as well as an MSc in Law and Business and an LLB in Law from Católica Lisbon. Before moving to Durham, Clara was a Lecturer at King's College London, Stipendiary Lecturer at St Catherine's College (Oxford), and Departmental Lecturer and Tutor at Oxford Law School. Clara has been a Visiting Scholar at Columbia Law School, Sapienza Università di Roma, Max Planck Institute (Hamburg), Facultat de Dret de la Universitat de Barcelona, Tashkent State University of Law, and Mackenzie University, São Paulo. Before entering academia, she worked for a few years as a capital markets lawyer and she still does occasional work as a consultant, having previously worked with the World Bank and International Finance Corporation (ICF).

Philipp Maume is currently an Associate Professor of Law at the Technical University of Munich (TUM) School of Management. The main research areas of Professor Maume are the laws of business entities and financial markets. He is particularly interested in the influence of technology, with a focus on blockchain/distributed ledger technology (DLT). In these areas, he has advised the German government and the European Parliament. He is the editor-in-chief of one of the leading German law journals on banking and capital markets law and co-editor of the only German law journal on family firms.

Pietro Ortolani is a Full Professor in Digital Conflict Resolution at Radboud University in Nijmegen, the Netherlands. Before joining Radboud University, he was a Senior Research Fellow at the Max Planck Institute for Procedural Law and a Law Research Associate at Queen Mary, University of London. In addition to his academic activity, Professor Ortolani is also a member of the Italian Bar Association and has extensive experience in the field of cross-border commercial dispute resolution.

Georgios Pavlidis is Associate Professor of International and EU Law at the School of Law of Neapolis University Pafos (NUP) in Cyprus and holder of a UNESCO Chair and a Jean Monnet Chair. He obtained his PhD from the University of Geneva, having completed his postgraduate studies in the US (LLM, SMU Dallas) and the UK (LLM, University of Warwick). He has worked as an evaluator in EU-funded programmes, as a national expert in the evaluation of EU instruments, and as external expert for consulting and law firms in the US, UK, France, and Belgium.

Nadia Pocher is a postdoctoral researcher at the Interdisciplinary Centre for Security, Reliability and Trust (SnT), University of Luxembourg. She received her Master of Laws, summa cum laude, from the University of Trento, and her PhD in Law, Science and Technology, excellent cum laude, from the University of Bologna, jointly with a PhD in Law from the Autonomous University of Barcelona and KU Leuven. In her research, she focuses on the regulation and compliance of emerging technologies in the financial space through the lens of techno-legal design. Her main research interest lies in anti-money laundering in crypto-assets and decentralised finance.

Lukas Schu is a qualified German lawyer and currently an associate in the Frankfurt office of Noerr, focusing on issues of automotive and mobility, commerce and trade, and digital business. He graduated in law from Saarland University in Germany and received his Master of Laws (LLM) from the University of Exeter in the United Kingdom. After completing his legal clerkship at the Higher Regional Court of Frankfurt am Main with the second state examination, he was admitted to the Frankfurt Bar Association. His current research focuses on the regulation of financial instruments, and he has published an academic article on the regulation of algorithmic trading in the European Business Law Review. He also participated in a research project 'Crypto-assets: Law, Accounting and Economics' funded by UK ESRC-IAA Impact and Knowledge Exchange in collaboration with the UK Endorsement Board (UKEB).

Katia Villard is currently an Associate Professor at the Faculty of Law at the University of Geneva. She studied at the University of Geneva and the Humboldt University of Berlin. She obtained a Bachelor's degree (2007) and a Master's degree in law (2009) from the University of Geneva, followed by a Doctorate in law (2017). She also passed the Bar exam (2011). During her academic career, Katia Villard was awarded a grant from the Swiss National Science Foundation for two research periods in Freiburg im Breisgau (ten months) and London (eight months). She then worked as a researcher for the Centre for Banking and Financial Law (University of Geneva) and as a lecturer at the University of Geneva.

Rolf H Weber is Professor of International Business Law at the Law Faculty of the University of Zurich and a practising attorney-at-law in Zurich. He studied at Zurich University and Harvard Law School; he is co-founder and co-director of the Blockchain Center of Zurich University. His professional activities include the role of Visiting Professor at Hong Kong University for 16 years and serving as a legal expert for national governments and international organisations. His main fields of research encompass financial markets, information technology (including Internet and Blockchain), trade, and competition law.

Acknowledgments

We would like to thank Banu Gün at the University of Zurich for her diligence and outstanding research assistance. We are also grateful to the University of Zurich for providing financial support to cover the open access costs.

Abbreviations

ACCA	The Association of Chartered Certified Accountants
AFI	Alliance for Financial Inclusion
AI	Artificial Intelligence
AIS	Account Information Service
AISP	Account Information Service Provider
AMF	French Financial Markets Authority
AML	Anti-Money Laundering
AMLA	EU Anti-Money Laundering Authority
AMLD	EU Anti-Money Laundering Directive
AOPP	Address Ownership Proof Protocol
API	Application Programming Interface
ASPSP	Account Servicing Payment Service Provider
ATM	Automated Teller Machine
BaFin	German Federal Financial Supervisory Authority
BCBS	Basel Committee on Banking Supervision
BE	Behavioural Economics
BIS	Bank for International Settlements
BLE	Behavioural Law and Economics
BoE	Bank of England
BTC	Bitcoin
CAC	Office of the Central Cyberspace Affairs Commission
CASP	Crypto-Asset Service Provider
CBDC	Central Bank Digital Currency

CBIRC	China Banking and Insurance Regulatory Commission
CBRC	China Banking Regulatory Commission
CC	Swiss Civil Code
CDP	Carbon Disclosure Project
CDSB	Climate Disclosure Standards Board
CEPS	The Centre for European Policy Studies
CEX	Centralised Exchange
CfA	Call for Advice
CFPB	Consumer Financial Protection Bureau
CFR	Charter of Fundamental Rights of the European Union
CFT	Countering/Combating the Financing of Terrorism
CFTC	US Commodity Futures Trading Commission
CIAM	Customer Identity and Access Management
CMA	Capital Markets Authority/UK Competition and Markets Authority
CMA9	Nine Largest Banks
CO	Swiss Code of Obligations
COVID-19	Coronavirus Disease 2019
CRR	Capital Requirements Regulations
CSRC	China Securities Regulatory Commission
CSRD	European Union Corporate Sustainability Reporting Directive
DAO	Decentralised Autonomous Organisation
DApp	Decentralized Application
DdoS	Distributed Denial-of-Service
DeFi	Decentralised Finance
DEX	Decentralised Exchange
DLT	Distributed Ledger Technology
DORA	Digital Operational Resilience Act
DSS	Data Security Standard
DWF	Discount Window Facility
EBA	European Banking Authority
ECB	European Central Bank
ECMH	Efficient Capital Markets Hypothesis
EDPB	European Data Protection Board

EIOPA	European Insurance and Occupational Pensions Authority
EMD2	Electronic Money Directive No.2
ENISA	The European Agency for Cybersecurity
EPI	Electronic Payment Institution
EPI Act	Taiwan Act Governing Electronic Payment Institutions
ESA	European Supervisory Authority
ESG	Environmental, Social, and Governance
ESMA	European Securities and Markets Authority
ESVC Act	The Act Governing Issuance of Electronic Stored Value Cards
ETD	Exchange-Traded Derivatives
ETF	Exchange-Traded Funds
ETH	Ethereum
EU	European Union
EU AMLA	European Union Anti-Money Laundering Supervisory Authority
EU Data Strategy	European Commission's European Data Strategy
EU TEG	European Union Technical Expert Group on Sustainable Finance
FATF	Financial Action Task Force
FCA	Financial Conduct Authority
FDIC	Federal Deposit Insurance Corporation
FDSS	Financial Data Sharing Schemes
FIDA	Financial Data Access
FinTech	Financial Technology
FISP	Financial Information Service Provider
FIU	Financial Intelligence Unit
Forex	Foreign Exchange
FSB	Financial Stability Board
FSC	Financial Services Commission
FT	Financing of Terrorism
FTR	Fund Transfer Regulation
GCC	German Criminal Code
GDP	Gross Domestic Product
GDPR	General Data Protection Regulation
GFC	Global Financial Crisis

GHG	Greenhouse Gas
GRI	Global Reporting Initiative
HIDS	Host-Based Intrusion Detection System
HKMA	Hong Kong Monetary Authority
HSBC	The Hongkong and Shanghai Banking Corporation
IAM	Identity and Access Management
IBA	International Bar Association
ICT	Information and Communication Technology
IDS	Intrusion Detection System
IMF	International Monetary Fund
IOSCO	International Organization of Securities Commissions
IoT	Internet of Things
ISO	International Organization for Standardization
IT	Information Technology
ITO	Initial Token Offering
IVMS 101	InterVASP Messaging Standard
JROC	Joint Regulatory Oversight Committee
KIID	Key Investor Information Document
KYC	Know Your Customer
KYT	Know Your Transaction
LAO	Legal Decentralized Autonomous Organization
LEI	Legal Entity Identifier
LLC	Limited Liability Company
M&A	Mergers and Acquisitions
MAR	Market Abuse Regulation
MAS	Monetary Authority of Singapore
MEV	Maximal Extractable Value
MFA	Multi-Factor Authentication
MFF	Multiannual Financial Framework
MiCA	Regulation (EU) 2023/1114 of the European Parliament and of the Council of 31 May 2023 on markets in crypto-assets [2023] OJ L150/40
MiFID	Markets in Financial Instruments Directive
MIIT	Ministry of Industry and Information Technology

MIT	Massachusetts Institute of Technology
ML	Money Laundering
MPS	Ministry of Public Security
MRT	Mass Rapid Transport
MVTS	Money or Value Transfer Service
NFT	Non-Fungible Token
NIDS	Network-Based Intrusion Detection System
NYSE	New York Stock Exchange
OBIE	Open Banking Implementation Entity
Octopus Wallet	Octopus Online Payment Service
ODR	Online Dispute Resolution
OECD	Organisation for Economic Co-operation and Development
OTC Derivatives	Over-the-Counter Derivatives
P2P	Peer-to-Peer
PCI	Payment Card Industry
PIN	Personal Identification Number
PIS	Payment Initiation Service
PISP	Payment Initiation Service Provider
PSA 2019	Payment Services Act 2019
PSD	Payment Services Directive
PSD2	EU Second Payment Services Directive
PSD3	New Payment Services Directive
PS-G01	MAS Guidelines on Licensing for Payment Service Provider
PSN01	MAS Notice on Prevention of Money Laundering and Countering the Financing of Terrorism - Specified Payment Services
PSN07	MAS Notice on Conduct
PSP	Payment Service Provider
PSR 2017 / PSR	Payment Services Regulation 2017/Payment Systems Regulator
PSSVFO	Hong Kong Payment Services and Stored Value Facilities Ordinance
RBA	Risk-Based Approach
RegTech	Regulatory Technology
RMB/CNY	Renminbi/Chinese Yuan

RTGS	Real-Time Gross Settlement
RTS	Regulatory Technical Standard
SASB	Sustainability Accounting Standards Board
SBTI	Science Based Targets Initiative
SCA	Strong Customer Authentication
SCC	Swiss Criminal Code
SCE	European Cooperative Society
SEC	US Securities and Exchange Commission
SFDR	Sustainable Finance Disclosure Regulation
SME	Small and Medium Enterprises
SSM	Single Supervisory Mechanism
SupTech	Supervisory Technology
SVB	Silicon Valley Bank
SVC	Stored Value Card
SVF	Stored Value Facility
SWIFT	Society for Worldwide Interbank Financial Telecommunications
TBTF	Too-Big-to-Fail
TEU	The Treaty on European Union
TFEU	The Treaty on the Functioning of the European Union
TradFi	Traditional Finance
TRP	Travel Rule Protocol
UK	United Kingdom
UN	United Nations
UNODC	United Nations Office on Drugs and Crime
USA or US	United States of America
USD	US Dollar
VASP	Virtual Asset Service Provider

Introduction to *A Research Agenda for Financial Law and Regulation*

Joseph Lee and Aline Darbellay

The rapid advancement of technology has markedly accelerated the pace of societal and economic transformations, a trend that is particularly evident in the financial sector. Historically, technological innovations such as automated teller machines (ATMs), information technology (IT) systems for exchanges, and global clearing systems have played a significant role in shaping the financial industry. However, the recent wave of technological developments – such as artificial intelligence (AI), distributed ledger technologies (DLTs), and quantum computing – is poised to be revolutionary, presenting both significant challenges and opportunities.

Key among these innovations are the concepts of 'decentralisation' and 'disintermediation', which starkly contrast with the traditional models that most existing legislative frameworks are built on. These frameworks typically revolve around the principles of 'centralisation' and 'intermediation', which facilitate connectivity, growth, and service provision within the financial industry. For example, the notion of entities being 'too-big-to-fail' (TBTF) has long influenced policy-making and regulatory frameworks across various financial sectors, including banking, capital markets, cross-border payments, and investment markets.

Furthermore, market integrity measures, such as anti-money laundering, and investor protection mechanisms, such as consumer protection, have traditionally focused on the responsibilities of intermediaries. As a result, regulatory strategies often deploy multilateral approaches, relying heavily on the cooperation of these intermediaries. They act as gatekeepers or trusted partners within the global regulatory framework, an idea encapsulated in the concept of 'meta-regulation'.

This shifting landscape requires a re-evaluation of existing legal structures to address the unique challenges posed by these emerging technologies. The move towards decentralisation and disintermediation calls for an innovative and cautious approach to regulation, one that not only understands the nuances of these technologies but also investigates their potential to foster a more inclusive and efficient financial system.

Technologies are inherently neutral and require human direction to function – at least, that has been the case so far. However, the potential future scenario where AI can autonomously assign tasks and execute them poses significant risks not only to the financial sector but to humanity as a whole.

Historically, large institutions have leveraged technology to enhance growth and efficiency. Yet, the rise of financial technology (FinTech) has introduced more decentralised features and increased technology-led intermediation, or the replacement of human-operated functions with technology. Consequently, the concept of 'TBTF' is being challenged by decentralisation. This shift has exposed the inadequacies of traditional competition law tools and has led to prudential rules that impose additional operational costs on financial institutions. These costs reduce market competition and exacerbate the risks associated with decentralisation.

Moreover, decentralisation often results in less standardised operations among smaller entities or even individuals, who typically lack the know-how and resources necessary for effective gatekeeping – a function traditionally performed by intermediaries. This gap makes 'meta-regulation' – a cooperative approach involving multiple entities in public-private partnerships designed to avoid excessive state control – increasingly unworkable as a method to combat crimes such as money laundering and to advance other public policy agendas.

The challenge of disintermediation may also inadvertently strengthen state control, presenting a paradox where efforts to reduce central authority could lead to its intensification. This evolving landscape calls for a thorough understanding and a strategic regulatory response to ensure that the benefits of technological advancements are realised while mitigating their potential risks.

The aim of this edited book is to explore new research areas spurred by technological advancements, including blockchain, AI, data analytics, and other emerging fields. Through 12 chapters, this work identifies intricate legal issues arising in the financial sector in the digital age. This ground-breaking analysis offers invaluable insights into the pivotal role of law and regulation in navigating the uncharted territories that are shaping the future of finance.

Aline Darbellay's chapter examines a new theoretical approach to financial law research, advocating for the development of 'behavioural finance theory' as a guiding framework for these burgeoning topics in financial law and regulation. She highlights the promise and perils of behaviourally informed bank disclosure regulation in light of the key objectives of financial regulation.

Georgios Pavlidis delves into legal issues at the crossroads of sustainable finance and AI. In so doing, he examines the convergence of two of the most significant developments in modern financial markets. Since entrusting AI systems with sustainable finance decisions poses significant risks, emphasis is placed on the establishment of guiding principles for responsible AI.

Rolf H Weber's chapter focuses on Decentralised Autonomous Organisations (DAOs), exemplifying decentralised finance (DeFi) in action. His chapter discusses the legal frameworks necessary for this nascent area. He identifies the legal issues surrounding DeFi business models, including considerations such as selecting the appropriate legal structure under corporate law.

The chapter by Joseph Lee and Yonghui Bao draws lessons from the rise and fall of Peer-to-Peer (P2P) finance in China, highlighting the investment opportunities and financing avenues it offered before its collapse due to insufficient legal and governance structures to address systemic risks, fraud, and investor protection.

Both Weber and Lee and Bao's analyses highlight that while technologies are inherently neutral, the business models they enable must be examined to fully understand the associated activities, risks, and necessary regulatory responses.

Clara Martins Pereira's chapter compares the regulatory outcomes of open finance in the United Kingdom (UK) and European Union (EU). Open banking and open finance have catalysed financial innovation by permitting customer data sharing with third-party providers. However, these advancements also introduce significant cybersecurity risks that could undermine the benefits of innovation and competition, potentially decreasing consumer surplus.

Hence, the chapter by Joseph Lee and Vere-Marie Khan addresses the cybersecurity risks inherent in open finance and discusses how these should be integrated into regulatory frameworks. They also explore whether the concept of a data DAO – a new regulatory technology based on collaborative work – could help mitigate data breaches and hacking risks.

Philipp Maume investigates the phenomenon of social trading, highlighting the challenges in both law and policy associated with regulating this modern trading pattern. He focuses on how decentralised platforms, such as social media groups, facilitate traditional trading strategies such as the short squeeze, culminating in issues exemplified by the 'GameStop' event.

The prevalence of 'social trading' is even more pronounced in the crypto-assets markets, where participants utilise decentralised platforms to engage in market abuse. The chapter by Joseph Lee and Lukas Schu examines these market abuse activities within the crypto-market space and assesses how the newly enacted EU regulation on crypto-assets, the Regulation on Markets in Crypto-Assets (MiCA), aims to mitigate the risks associated with these activities and achieve optimal regulatory outcomes.

Katia Villard's chapter emphasises the necessity for a single regulator to coordinate anti-money laundering efforts. The cross-border nature of criminal activities poses significant challenges to oversight, especially in the digital age. Her chapter advocates for a unified regulatory authority at the EU level, exploring the challenges such an organisation may face, including resource allocation and collaboration with national authorities through information sharing and power distribution.

Nadia Pocher investigates the need for more robust anti-money laundering laws and regulations to address decentralised trading in crypto-asset markets. She clarifies specific regulations, particularly concerning the travel rule and its application to digital wallets.

The chapter by Christopher Chao-Hung Chen expands on the necessity to regulate against financial fraud, particularly within the payment services sector. It explores how laws can protect consumers against fraud, including the application of private law for redress and public law for mandating risk management procedures.

Finally, Pietro Ortolani discusses how financial disputes, particularly those involving individual consumers, could be addressed by online or smart courts facilitated by technologies such as distributed ledger technology. This chapter highlights the emerging need for a more decentralised dispute resolution forum while also pointing out the challenges, such as the off-chain enforcement of on-chain resolutions.

Overall, this edited book covers an expansive range of topics that captivate the attention of policymakers, regulators, scholars, and practitioners alike. By delving into a diverse array of subjects around the financial market, the authors aim not only to shed light on ongoing trends and challenges but also to guide future research endeavours. The 12 chapters identify significant research questions that will shape the scholarly agenda in the years to come. At the heart of the discourse lies the transformative impact of technological advancements, which continues to redefine the evolving landscape of the financial sector.

1 The promise and perils of behaviourally informed bank disclosure regulation

Aline Darbellay

I. Introduction

Disclosure is the most prominent tool of financial regulation, although it faces significant criticism from behavioural sciences. On the one hand, one strand of the literature argues that relying on disclosure as a light-touch form of substantive regulation is inadequate. Using disclosure to achieve nudging effects carries the risk of overestimating its potential. On the other hand, other scholars contend that the impact of disclosure may be rather underestimated. In particular, bank disclosure regulation may inadvertently exacerbate procyclical or herding effects within the financial system.

The mandatory disclosure paradigm serves as the cornerstone of corporate and financial markets law. Within the realm of financial markets regulation, the core function of mandatory disclosure is to provide investors with information to help them make informed investment decisions. By doing so, it may be designed to influence market behaviour. Its significance is especially pronounced in the domain of banking law and regulation.

In the context of corporate law, mandatory disclosure promotes transparent practices in the realm of corporate governance and executive remuneration. The objective here is to leverage disclosure as a tool to steer behaviour. In the field of bank governance, disclosure has partly served as a response to the abusive remuneration practices observed in the run-up to the global financial crisis of 2007–09 (GFC).

The mandatory disclosure paradigm is the bedrock of securities regulation. Disclosure obligations apply to issuers at various points in time. At the capital-raising stage, the prospectus requirement seeks to reduce asymmetries between issuers and investors. In the secondary market, mandatory periodic and ad-hoc disclosure obligations ensure that information keeps flowing in the market on an ongoing basis, bolstering disclosure as a tool for supporting an efficient price mechanism.[1] This assumes that publicly available information is swiftly incorporated into market prices.

Furthermore, disclosure is essential in the financial services sector. Contractual relationships between banks and their customers are preceded by comprehensive disclosures and rules requiring that the client is informed about their ongoing relationship with the financial intermediary.[2] Conduct-of-business rules encompass, for instance, the disclosure of conflicts of interest. In addition, particular concerns apply to financial institutions such as banks. The additional disclosure regulation reflects the unique characteristics of the banking business, for instance, relating to risk management. At any rate, the significance of trust is essential among financial institutions, especially banks, which are susceptible to bank runs. This renders disclosure and communication particularly sensitive.

This chapter emphasises the importance of designing behaviourally informed bank disclosure regulation. It highlights the intricate evolution of bank disclosure regulation being shaped by the pursuit of multiple objectives. The chapter outlines a research agenda drawing upon insights from the behavioural sciences. A central and complex issue tackled herein is the design of effective bank disclosure regulation. Part II explores the multifaceted goals of bank disclosure regulation, emphasising the importance of assessing its desirable outcomes. Part III delves into the challenges surrounding regulatory design and discusses what policy instruments help achieve the outcomes. In particular, the question arises as to whether the desirable outcomes are achieved or whether unintended consequences reinforce behavioural issues. Part IV concludes.

II. The multiple objectives of bank disclosure regulation in the light of behavioural sciences

A. Investor protection and market efficiency as the traditional objectives of bank disclosure regulation

The initial inquiry revolves around identifying the key objectives of bank disclosure regulation to assess what the desirable outcomes are. Broadly speaking, the mandatory disclosure paradigm has become one of the central regulatory instruments

---

1 Konstantinos Serdaris, 'Behavioural Economic Influences on Primary Market Disclosure – The Case of the EU Regulation on European Crowdfunding Service Providers' (2021) 3(18) European Company and Financial Law Review 428, 433.

2 Luca Enriques and Sergio Gilotta, 'Disclosure & Financial Market Regulation' in Niamh Moloney, Eilis Ferran, and Jennifer Payne (eds), *The Oxford Handbook of Financial Regulation* (Oxford University Press 2015) 512.

of financial markets law. 'Disclosure, again disclosure, and still more disclosure.'[3] This regulatory concept is the bedrock of United States (US) securities regulation, which has always followed a disclosure philosophy for regulating capital markets.[4] Subsequently disclosure provisions became a key tool in the EU.[5]

Within the sphere of securities regulation, disclosure pursues two pivotal objectives: safeguarding investors and enhancing market efficiency. Traditionally, the mandatory disclosure paradigm strives to provide investors with information so that they can make informed investment decisions. The underpinning rationale for mandatory disclosure is rooted in the belief that without compulsory requirements, there would be an undersupply of information. Consequently, disclosure requirements are designed to ensure that the optimal amount of information is readily accessible to all market participants.

The mandatory disclosure framework benefits investors owing to the fact that market forces are inadequate to generate the optimal supply of information.[6] This arises from inherent market failures. Banks are disproportionately affected by agency problems, necessitating measures to mitigate information asymmetries.[7] There is a societal interest in fostering allocatively efficient capital markets.[8] Coffee, in his analysis, concluded that the most compelling arguments in favour of a mandatory disclosure system may be efficiency-based.[9]

B. The stakeholder orientation of bank disclosure regulation

From the corporate law perspective, behavioural insights have shed light on how disclosure influences managerial decision-making. This prompts the question of whether disclosure, in itself, can serve as a light-touch form of substantive regulation for shaping corporate behaviour. Mandatory disclosure, as a regulatory tool, can be harnessed to steer managerial conduct. At any rate, the scope of mandated disclosure hinges on who the intended beneficiaries of the information are. This matter is intertwined with the view of the corporation and the ongoing debate between shareholder primacy and stakeholder orientation. In particular, the approach to bank corporate governance should reflect the distinctiveness of the banking business. Overall, bank corporate governance is characterised by the need to address high information asymmetries as well as negative externalities.

---

3 Louis Loss, *Securities Regulation* (2nd edn, Volume 21, Little Brown and Company 1961) 21.

4 Hendrik Brinckmann, 'Disclosure System: Foundations' in Rüdiger Veil (ed), *European Capital Markets Law* (3rd edn, Hart Publishing 2022) 261.

5 Ibid.

6 John C Coffee, Jr, 'Market Failure and the Economic Case for a Mandatory Disclosure System' (1984) 70(4) Virginia Law Review 717, 728.

7 Kern Alexander, *Principles of Banking Regulation* (Cambridge University Press 2019) 35.

8 Coffee (n 6) 737.

9 Ibid 751.

First, with respect to corporate governance issues in the banking sector, the shareholder primacy model fails to work due to the fact that banks are high information asymmetry firms.[10] The information conveyed through market prices can be misleading. Decision-making by managers based on shareholder expectations is not considered an optimal governance structure.[11] Given the opacity of business models and resulting information asymmetries, the governance structure cannot focus exclusively on the interests of shareholders.[12] Accordingly, distinctive corporate governance issues arise in the banking sector and are only partly addressed by bank disclosure regulation. The traditional securities regulation model, centred on providing investors with information, falls short of adequately addressing the intricacies of the sector. Simply furnishing more information may not sufficiently mitigate persistent information asymmetries.

Second, there is a need to recognise the external effects of corporate conduct in the public domain owing to the high risk of negative externalities.[13] Past banking scandals have illustrated that flawed corporate cultures can inflict harm upon stakeholders, even if such misconduct appears to benefit shareholders.[14] Consequently, corporate governance frameworks should factor in these externalities. The banking industry, by its very nature, involves systemic risks. Banks that are too-big-to-fail (TBTF) pose significant threats to financial stability. Moreover, even smaller banks may be too interconnected to fail, thus also contributing to systemic risk. Concentrating exclusively on shareholder interests would amplify these risks, offering returns during prosperous times while shifting the burdens onto other stakeholders during downturns. Let us suppose now that the agreed-upon objective is to actively discourage specific types of behaviour.[15] Traditional economic theory would regard this as a laudable goal, at least if fully informed consumers would abstain from the behaviour in question; this objective becomes even more compelling when the said behaviour generates adverse externalities.[16]

---

10 William W Bratton and Michael L Wachter, 'The Case Against Shareholder Empowerment' (2010) 158 University of Pennsylvania Law Review 653.

11 Ibid.

12 Aline Darbellay, 'Algorithm-Driven Information Gatekeepers' in Joseph Lee and Aline Darbellay (eds), *Data Governance in AI, Fintech and LegalTech, Law and Regulation in the Financial Sector* (Edward Elgar 2022) 87.

13 Jennifer G Hill, 'Corporations, Directors' Duties, and the Public/Private Divide' in Arthur B Laby and Jacob Hale Russell (eds), *Fiduciary Obligations in Business* (Cambridge University Press 2021) 289–90.

14 Ibid 292.

15 Cass R Sunstein, Christine Jolls, and Richard Thaler, 'A Behavioral Approach to Law and Economics' (1998) 50 Stanford Law Review 1471, 1536.

16 Ibid.

It is worth mentioning that similar issues arise more generally in the realm of sustainability.[17] Corporate activities generate negative externalities whenever they jeopardise sustainability objectives. Information disclosure may seek to achieve a policy goal in the case of externalities.[18]

A recurring problem arises whenever a public good is produced. Information is a public good. The key characteristic is the non-excludability of users who have not paid for it owing to the fact that the use of a piece of information by someone does not prevent that same piece of information from being used by someone else.[19] This leads to a market failure causing insufficient information production and dissemination.[20] Information would be underproduced in the absence of mandatory disclosure requirements. Accordingly, a traditional argument for establishing mandatory disclosure rests upon the public goods-like nature of information.[21]

Bank disclosure regulation shall moreover be shaped by the fact that bank corporate governance requires the pursuit of the interests of multiple stakeholders. This consists of a multistakeholder approach to banking regulation.[22] As compared to other corporate entities, banks are therefore subject to a wider range of mandatory rules in the public interest.

C. Financial stability as an objective of bank disclosure regulation

Disclosure is a challenging topic in light of financial stability concerns. In principle, financial stability should benefit from transparency. Disclosure regulation is thus an essential pillar of bank prudential regulation. The banking sector is prone to systemic risk and financial instability. Improving risk management practices has become a specific objective of bank disclosure regulation. Changing conceptions as to the regulatory ends of public disclosure have contributed to disrupting the classic foundations of disclosure.[23] The bank regulator public disclosure system that emerged in the wake of the GFC is directed at the well-being of the entities themselves and the stability of the financial system.[24]

---

17 Aline Darbellay, 'A Behavioral Law and Economics Approach to Sustainability Information' (2024) 17(1) Law and Financial Markets Review 4, 7.

18 Sunstein, Jolls and Thaler (n 15) 1533.

19 Enriques and Gilotta (n 2) 521.

20 Coffee (n 6) 725–27.

21 Enriques and Gilotta (n 2) 521.

22 Andrea Perrone, 'Banking Regulation and Multistakeholder Corporate Law' (forthcoming).

23 Henry T C Hu, 'The Disclosure Paradigm, Conventional Understandings and Modern Divergence' in Danny Busch, Guido Ferrarini and Jan Paul Franx (eds), *Prospectus Regulation and Prospectus Liability* (Oxford University Press 2020) 100.

24 Henry T C Hu, 'Disclosure Universes and Modes of Information: Banks, Innovation, and Divergent Regulatory Quests' (2014) 31(3) Yale Journal on Regulation 565, 569; Hu (n 23) 118 and 122.

The system developed by bank regulators, under the auspices of the Basel Committee on Banking Supervision (BCBS), has reshaped bank disclosure regulation by factoring in the minimisation of systemic risk as a regulatory end. In particular, the market discipline approach of Pillar 3 has developed a set of disclosure requirements with a view to ensuring that investors learn the risks to which banks are exposed.[25] Regarding banks, the BCBS identified a non-exhaustive list of risks, including credit risk, liquidity risk, market risk, concentration risk, country risk, transfer risk, operational risk, and reputational risk.[26] Transparency regarding risk is considered a necessary prerequisite for effective risk management by individual banks as well as for effective supervision by financial market authorities in order to assess the riskiness of individual banks and the systemic risk in the financial system as a whole.[27] Furthermore, the market discipline approach hinges on establishing a comprehensive set of disclosure requirements which provide market participants with key pieces of information to assess the amount and quality of capital, risk exposures, risk-assessment processes, and hence the overall capital adequacy of the institution.[28] Therefore, requiring extensive disclosure has become an important tool in the prudential toolkit.[29]

In addition, the market discipline pillar of Basel III could also play an important role in enhancing risk management in respect of systemic environmental risks.[30] By providing disclosures to the capital markets, investors should learn of the risks to which banking institutions are exposed – including the bank's exposure to systemic environmental risks.[31] Nevertheless, public disclosure of these risks prompts the question of whether or not the public is able to comprehend the long-term effects of their investment choices.[32] emergency liquidity assistance from central banks. From a behavioural perspective, the fear of stigma has played a crucial role in this context. Empirical evidence has shown that banks are reluctant to ask for liquidity when they suffer a liquidity shock because of the fear that the markets will react negatively to the information being disclosed.[33] Accordingly, the problem is that banks may wait until it is too late. The question has arisen as to what extent legal and regulatory frameworks can reduce the stigma effect. Withholding unfavourable information may be

---

25 Alexander (n 7) 160.

26 Kern Alexander, 'The Role of Capital in Supporting Banking Stability' in Niamh Moloney, Eilis Ferran, and Jennifer Payne (eds), *The Oxford Handbook of Financial Regulation* (Oxford University Press 2015) 369–70.

27 Ibid 386.

28 Ibid 358.

29 Ibid 386.

30 Kern Alexander, 'Stability and Sustainability in Banking Reform: Are Environmental Risks Missing in Basel III?' (*CISL & UNEP FI*, 2014) 20, <https://www.unepfi.org/fileadmin/documents/StabilitySustainability.pdf> accessed 1 May 2024.

31 Ibid.

32 Ibid.

33 Olivier Armantier, Eric Ghysels, Asani Sarkar, and Jeffrey Shrader, 'Discount Window Stigma During the 2007–2008 Financial Crisis' (2015) 118(2) Journal of Financial Economics 317, 318.

tempting to prevent a financial crisis. As a response, policymakers and regulators have adapted their frameworks to make the recourse to emergency liquidity assistance less visible to the markets. For instance, in the UK the Bank of England (BoE) sought to reduce the financial stability risks posed by the premature disclosure of discount window facility (DWF) drawings by extending its own disclosure lag to five quarters.[34] Moreover, the BoE has argued the case for ensuring that national and international disclosure regimes do not increase financial stability risks through other channels.[35] In Switzerland, the stigma question has surfaced in relation to the demise of Credit Suisse in March 2023.[36] Nevertheless, it is permissible to cast doubt on whether reducing transparency is an appropriate regulatory response to solve the stigma problem. At any rate, this topic gives rise to concerns and warrants further attention from the scientific community.

D. Investor confidence as an objective of bank disclosure regulation

Other arguments supporting bank disclosure regulation are based on investor confidence. These arguments relate to market integrity, the promotion of fair markets, and the deterrence of fraud. The promotion of fair markets enhances the confidence of investors in the market, thereby preserving the well-functioning of financial markets.[37] Banks depend on reputational constraints. Trust is key. Investors' reactions may lead to the creation of bubbles and may also result in bank runs.

First, financial markets are prone to bubbles with detrimental effects whenever they burst. Tulip bulbs were the issue in the 1600s, dot.com companies were the issue in the 2000s, and subprime mortgages were the issue in the GFC.[38] While the details of each

---

34 Bill Winters, 'Review of the Bank of England's Framework for Providing Liquidity to the Banking System' (*Presented to the Court of the Bank of England*, October 2012) <https://www.bankofengland.co.uk/-/media/boe/files/news/2012/november/the-banks-framework-for-providing-liquidity-to-the-banking> accessed 25 April 2024 (Winters Report); Bank of England, 'Liquidity Insurance at the Bank of England: Developments in the Sterling Monetary Framework' (Bank of England, October 2013) 6, <https://www.bankofengland.co.uk/-/media/boe/files/markets/sterling-monetary-framework/liquidity-insurance-at-the-boe.pdf> accessed 25 April 2024.

35 Ibid.

36 Expert Group on Banking Stability, 'Report of the Expert Group on Banking Stability 2023: The Need for Reform After the Demise of Credit Suisse' (*Expert Group on Banking Stability*, 1 September 2023) 47 <https://www.efd.admin.ch/efd/en/home/the-fdf/nsb-news_list.msg-id-97593.html> accessed 25 April 2024; Federal Council of Switzerland, 'Federal Council Report on Banking Stability, Including an Evaluation in Accordance with Article 52 of the Banking Act' (Federal Council of Switzerland, April 2024) 34 <https://www.newsd.admin.ch/newsd/message/attachments/87002.pdf> accessed 25 April 2024.

37 Enriques and Gilotta (n 2) 513.

38 Frank Partnoy, 'Financial Systems, Crises, and Regulation' in Niamh Moloney, Eilis Ferran, and Jennifer Payne (eds), *The Oxford Handbook of Financial Regulation* (Oxford University Press 2015) 73.

crisis vary, the cognitive error school argues that there is a certain pattern to crises, fuelled by investor irrationality, displacement, credit expansion, mania, panic, and crash.[39] Minsky has developed the Financial Instability Hypothesis and modelled how financial markets are prone to booms and crashes.[40]

Information is at the core of the rise and burst of bubbles. A story develops, and then it generates feedback, leading to a price increase. Yet when the price drops, the agreement also falls, generating negative feedback.[41] Accordingly, feedback reinforces market trends. In fact, stock market prices are not only driven by fundamentals but also by how people are thinking.[42] While irrational behaviour is a central concept in many of the models explaining the initial formation of bubbles, it is important to underscore that rational behaviour can also play a pivotal role.[43] For instance, even in the presence of unsustainable market prices, it may, under some circumstances, be rational for investors not to bet against the bubble.[44]

Second, the banking industry is prone to bank runs. Diamond and Dybvig have modelled bank runs.[45] In the banking literature, opaque, difficult-to-value assets increase the possibility of bank runs because they create uncertainty about how other depositors will evaluate solvency.[46] There is a pattern of time-varying relative bank opacity.[47] In the wake of the GFC, the law and regulation were amended to seek to head off the bank runs motivated by potentially self-fulfilling beliefs about bank solvency.[48]

Communication and reputation are intricately intertwined. In the banking industry, where reputational risks loom large, firms are particularly sensitive as their communication acutely affects investors' perception of their activities. Overall, the banking business hinges on investor confidence and trust. Behavioural finance plays a key role in explaining investors' reactions to information. The role of communication is paramount given the potential of herd behaviour.[49] The efficient markets theory does not

---

39 Ibid.

40 Hyman P Minsky, *Can 'It' Happen Again? Essays on Instability and Finance* (Routledge 2016).

41 Robert J Shiller, *Irrational Exuberance* (3rd edn, Princeton University Press 2015).

42 Ibid.

43 Markus K Brunnermeier and Stefan Nagel, 'Hedge Funds and the Technology Bubble' (2004) 59(5) Journal of Finance 2013, 2030–2032; Erik F Gerding, *Law, Bubbles, and Financial Regulation* (Routledge 2014) 5.

44 Brunnermeier and Nagel (n 43) 2030–32.

45 Douglas W Diamond and Philip H Dybvig, 'Bank Runs, Deposit Insurance, and Liquidity' (1983) 91(3) Journal of Political Economy 401, 401.

46 Mark J Flannery, Simon H Kwan, and Mahendrarajah Nimalendran, 'The 2007–2009 Financial Crisis and Bank Opaqueness' (2013) 22 Journal of Financial Intermediation 55, 82.

47 Ibid 83.

48 Ibid 82.

49 David S Scharfstein and Jeremy C Stein, 'Herd Behavior and Investment' (1990) 80(3) The American Economic Review 465; Kenneth A Froot, David S Scharfstein, and

fully explain price movements when banks' stock prices are affected by a confidence crisis. Informational cascades or herding effects in collective action occur when people's decisions to adopt a behaviour are interdependent over time.[50]

Herd behaviour manifests whenever irrational thinking is similar over large numbers of investors, thereby potentially causing stock market booms and busts.[51] In fact, not only irrational behaviour, but also rational behaviour may occur in a bank run. It is worth mentioning that individual behaviour may be rational and still produce irrational group behaviour.[52] This phenomenon is partly attributed to investors reacting to the same publicly available information, although this is not the sole factor.[53] As investors aggregate information, collective action serves as a signalling phenomenon.[54]

III. Challenges in designing behaviourally informed bank disclosure regulation

A. The limits of the mandatory disclosure paradigm in the light of behavioural sciences

Behavioural sciences have implications for legal theory. After determining the objectives of bank disclosure regulation, the question arises as to whether the rules achieve the desirable outcomes.

Concern has been raised about the fact that the multiple objectives of bank disclosure regulation cannot always be achieved simultaneously. Although the multiple objectives add up and even overlap to some extent, they may also be conflicting. While securities regulation is essentially concerned with investor protection, bank prudential regulation gives particular attention to risk management and financial stability. Different regulators may supervise the same entities from different perspectives. Under the sectoral model, there is a different authority for bank prudential supervision and another for the securities business. Also, in the partially integrated model, that is to say, the Twin Peaks model, two different supervisors are responsible for

---

Jeremy C Stein, 'Herd on the Street: Informational Inefficiencies in a Market with Short-Term Speculation' (1992) 47(4) The Journal of Finance 1461; Abhijit V Banerjee, 'A Simple Model of Herd Behavior' (1992) 107(3) The Quarterly Journal of Economics 797; Russ Wermers, 'Mutual Fund Herding and the Impact on Stock Prices' (1999) 54(2) Journal of Finance 581.

50 Susanne Lohmann, 'Collective Action Cascades: An Informational Rationale for the Power in Numbers' (2008) 14(5) Journal of Economic Surveys 655, 657.

51 Shiller (n 41) 175.

52 Ibid 177–78.

53 Ibid 175.

54 Lohmann (n 50) 676.

prudential oversight and the conduct of business.[55] Both viewpoints entail different disclosure obligations depending on the regulatory activity.

In terms of securities regulation, relating to market integrity, market egalitarianism remains popular among regulators and courts, which is reflected in case law on insider trading and ad-hoc disclosure obligations.[56] Accordingly, public investors should be able to make investment decisions on the basis of the same information. This triggers the necessity to disclose relevant information to the financial markets. For instance, the obligation to disclose on an ongoing basis relates to the key objectives of investor protection, fair and efficient markets, and market egalitarianism. Such an obligation may conflict with financial stability.[57] In fact, the duty of disclosure may trigger an obligation to disclose adverse information. The resulting market reaction, due to the behavioural effect, may precipitate a downward spiral and even cause a bank run. Therefore, the question arises as to how the various bank disclosure obligations are intertwined.

Compelled disclosure has long served as the traditional tool of legal intervention. Policymakers and regulators typically rely on mandatory disclosure as a response to market failures because it is often the least controversial measure. There is almost a consensus about the fact that voluntary disclosure is insufficient. The least obtrusive method of legal intervention relies on disclosure.[58] Mandatory disclosure, often seen as the most viable solution, aligns with the idea of free markets and the autonomy principle, which are deeply rooted principles of Western societies.[59] Interest groups typically prefer this approach to more invasive solutions aimed at directly constraining behaviour, as it fits with these fundamental principles.

However, scholarship has cast significant concerns regarding the efficacy of mandatory disclosure.[60] A large body of research has demonstrated the constrained impact

---

55 Daniel Calvo, Juan Carlos Crisanto, Stefan Hohl, and Oscar Pascual Gutiérrez, 'FSI Insights on Policy Implementation No 8, Financial Supervisory Architecture: What has Changed after the Crisis?' (Bank for International Settlements 2018) 7.

56 Case ECJ C-45/08, *Spector Photo Group NV and Chris Van Raemdonck v Commissie voor het Bank-, Financie- en Assurantiewezen (CBFA)*; Case ECJ C-19/11, *Marcus Geltl v Daimler AG*; Enriques and Gilotta (n 2) 516.

57 For further detail relating to the potential for conflicting objectives, see Veerle Colaert, 'The Changing Nature of Financial Regulation: Sustainable Finance as a New Policy Goal' (April 2022) KU Leuven Working Paper No.2022/04 <https://papers.ssrn.com/sol3/papers.cfm?abstract_id=4087166> accessed 23 October 2023.

58 Oren Bar-Gill, 'Seduction by Plastic' (2004) 98(4) Northwestern University Law Review 1373.

59 Omri Ben-Shahar and Carl E Schneider, 'The Failure of Mandated Disclosure' (2011) 159 University of Pennsylvania Law Review 647, 681–84; Enriques and Gilotta (n 2) 512–13.

60 Troy A Paredes, 'Blinded by the Light: Information Overload and its Consequences for Securities Regulation' (2003) 81(2) Washington University Law Quarterly 417.

of mandated disclosure on behaviour.[61] While designing disclosure obligations, policymakers and regulators typically fail to take into account the costs for the regulated entities.[62] Furthermore, the disclosure system essentially relies on a traditional approach to information that is structurally insufficient to address the informational challenges posed by financial innovation.[63]

The design of meaningful disclosure must take into account behavioural biases.[64] First, behavioural insights may be used to improve disclosure techniques by identifying not only which information should be disclosed, but also how it should be disclosed.[65] Second, behavioural studies have highlighted the limited effectiveness of disclosure duties in certain contexts, calling for other, more effective regulatory means.[66] Third, behaviourally informed regulation relies on a more nuanced comprehension of human behaviour than the classical rational actor model would predict and is cognisant of the role of psychological factors that influence how people behave.[67]

Due to the exaggeration of its implications, the market efficiency theory has long faced considerable criticism, particularly from insights stemming from behavioural finance.[68] The limits of the market efficiency theory are particularly acute in the case of banks. In light of the disclosure system, the most troubling aspect is that beliefs about the opaqueness of major banks persist even though banks provide massive amounts of information to the public.[69] In accordance with the market efficiency theory, securities should be accurately priced based on the publicly available information. This theory builds on the rational investor model. However, behavioural sciences have challenged this assumption. According to Gerding, behavioural finance connects experimental evidence and theory on the cognitive limitations of individual investors

61 Omri Ben-Shahar and Carl E Schneider, *More Than You Wanted To Know: The Failure of Mandated Disclosure* (Princeton University Press 2014) 33–54; Yannis Bakos, Florencia Marotta-Wurgler, and David R Trossen, 'Does Anyone Read the Fine Print? Consumer Attention to Standard-Form Contracts' (2014) 43(1) The Journal of Legal Studies 1; Debra Pogrund Stark and Jessica M Choplin, 'A Cognitive and Social Psychological Analysis of Disclosure Laws and Call for Mortgage Counseling to Prevent Predatory Lending' (2009) 16(1) Psychology, Public Policy & Law Journal 85, 101; Eyal Zamir and Doron Teichman, *Behavioral Law and Economics* (Oxford University Press 2018) 175.

62 Bar-Gill (n 58) 49.

63 Hu (n 24) 569.

64 Bar-Gill (n 58) 49.

65 Eyal Zamir and Doron Teichman, *Behavioral Law and Economics* (Oxford University Press 2018) 172.

66 Ibid.

67 Michael S Barr, Sendhil Mullainathan, and Eldar Shafir, 'Behaviorally Informed Regulation' in Eldar Shafir (ed), *The Behavioral Foundations of Public Policy* (Princeton University Press 2013) 457.

68 See further Brinckmann (n 4) 261.

69 Hu (n 24) 571.

to market events.[70] Hence, emotions play a pivotal role in driving human decisions. 'Behavioral finance itself builds off evidence from psychological experiments that document how individuals suffer from various behavioral biases and cognitive limitations. These biases and limitations cause individuals to make decisions that deviate from the predictions of economic models that assume individuals are rational actors who maximize their self-interest.'[71] 'Behavioural economics has identified several instances where individual behaviour departs from the rationality predictions of neoclassical economics. Alongside these developments in behavioural economics, the concept of nudging was introduced as an intervention able to steer individual behaviour in welfare-enhancing directions without using coercion or incentives.'[72]

In sum, the presence of a behavioural market failure signals a potential role for legal intervention.[73] The question arises as to how to incorporate behavioural models into the economic analysis of law. This contributes to integrating more realistic insights. The approach to regulation reflects the importance of academic literature applying insights from behavioural sciences to legal policy.[74]

---

70 Gerding (n 43) 5.

71 Nicholas Barberis and Richard Thaler, 'A Survey of Behavioral Finance' in George M Constantinides, Milton Harris, and Rene M Stulz (eds), *Handbook of the Economics of Finance* (Volume 1B, Elsevier Science BV 2003) 1054; Gerding (n 43) 4–5.

72 Mark Whitehead, Rhys Jones, Rachel Howell, Rachel Lilley, and Jessica Pykett, 'Nudging All Over the World: Assessing the Global Impact of the Behavioural Sciences on Public Policy' (*Economic & Social Research Council (ESRC)*, 2014) <https://www.researchgate.net/publication/271826328_Nudging_all_over_the_World_Assessing_the_Global_Impact_of_the_Behavioural_Sciences_on_Public_Policy> accessed 1 May 2024; Maria C de Campos, *Behavioural Economics and Regulation: The Design Process of Regulatory Nudges* (Routledge 2022) 1.

73 Bar-Gill (n 58) 66.

74 Ryan Bubb and Prasad Krishnamurthy, 'Regulating Against Bubbles: How Mortgage Regulation Can Keep Main Street and Wall Street Safe – From Themselves' (2015) 163(6) University of Pennsylvania Law Review 1539, 1544; Oren Bar-Gill and Ryan Bubb, 'Credit Card Pricing: The Card Act and Beyond' (2012) 97(5) Cornell Law Review 967; Bar-Gill (n 58) 1373; Ryan Bubb and Alex Kaufman, 'Consumer Biases and Mutual Ownership' (2013) 105 Journal of Public Economics 39; Sunstein, Jolls and Thaler (n 15) 1471; Christine Jolls and Cass R Sunstein, 'Debiasing through Law' (2006) 35(1) The Journal of Legal Studies 199; Russell B Korobkin and Thomas S Ulen, 'Law and Behavioral Science: Removing the Rationality Assumption from Law and Economics' (2000) 88(4) California Law Review 1051; Russell B Korobkin, 'The Endowment Effect and Legal Analysis' (2003) 97 Northwestern University Law Review 1227; Donald C Langevoort, 'Taming the Animal Spirits of the Stock Markets: A Behavioral Approach to Securities Regulation' (2002) 97(1) Northwestern University Law Review 135; Jeffrey J Rachlinski, 'The Psychological Foundations of Behavioral Law and Economics' (2011) University of Illinois Law Review 16.

B. The diversity of responses to the limits of mandatory disclosure

Although the mandatory disclosure paradigm is subject to criticism, the diversity of responses to the problem gives rise to serious challenges. On the one hand, some scholars conclude that disclosure is insufficient and cannot replace substantive regulation.[75] As a response to the limited effect of mandatory disclosure, more regulation would be needed. This is already the case in the banking sector, where not only the disciplining effects of capital markets but also far-reaching regulatory intervention play a significant role. On the other hand, others contend that disclosure has a behavioural effect and that it may be detrimental. They typically refer to the problem of information overload, the incapacity of the unsophisticated investor to process large amounts of information, whereby mandatory disclosure may even make matters worse.[76] According to them, the results of the behavioural analysis would support a deregulation agenda.

In addition, behaviourally informed regulation involves a careful consideration of how disclosure is portrayed. This presentation hinges on the regulatory objectives as well as the users of the information. The informational needs of various actors, such as retail investors, sophisticated investors, and regulatory bodies, must be taken into account. In the EU, there are regulatory instruments aimed at protecting less informed financial services participants. The classification of clients as retail investors involves additional mandatory rules to avoid the adoption of irrational investment decisions, including more extensive and more comprehensible investment information provided by financial services providers, for example, the key investor information document (KIID).[77]

This approach provides an example of behaviourally informed disclosure regulation. Instead of full disclosure of complex information, the idea is to give access to concise and comprehensible information.[78] Given individuals' limited ability to grasp large quantities of complex information, disclosures should be timely, brief, and salient.[79] In addition, disclosures should not include lengthy wording in complex language or be presented in a way that draws attention away from important information.[80]

---

75 Lucian Arye Bebchuck and Jesse M Fried, 'Executive Compensation as an Agency Problem' (2003) 17(3) Journal of Economic Perspectives 71, 79–81; Enriques and Gilotta (n 2) 530.

76 Paredes (n 60) 417.

77 Pieter Van Cleynenbreugel, 'Conduct of Business Rules in EU Financial Services Regulation: Behavioural Rules Devoid of Behavioural Analysis?' in Alberto Alemanno and Anne-Lise Sibony (eds), *Nudge and the Law, A European Perspective* (Hart Publishing 2015) 259–60.

78 Serdaris (n 1) 428–63.

79 Zamir and Teichman (n 65) 173.

80 Ibid.

Apart from that, a second strand of disclosure pertains to sophisticated actors, for instance intermediaries who can optimise choices for end-investors.[81] While disclosures aimed at sophisticated actors need not be simple or brief, they should be comprehensive and standardised to increase comparability, thereby facilitating a competitive process that enables boundedly rational actors to make better choices.[82] Further, Coffee has laid emphasis on the importance of institutional investors, who are key users of financial disclosure.[83] Arsalidou contends that institutional investors are not always rational.[84]

The transmission mode also matters. Regulators primarily use the descriptive mode of information according to which the reporting entity analyses the reality and, relying on depiction tools, crafts a description on which market participants rely.[85] Technological innovation has made a new approach possible, the transfer mode of information, which does not rely on intermediary depiction: the entity is no longer standing between the reality and market participants, market participants can download pure information reflective of objective reality, they can bring their own analytical skills, and the accessed information is less structured and more granular.[86] There is thus a possibility of crowdsourcing on the part of market participants.[87]

Apart from that, not only the quantity of information delivered to the markets but also the quality of the information matters. The question arises as to how to ensure the quality of disclosure. An important part depends on the effectiveness of enforcement. Both public and private enforcement matter. 'Indeed, the larger the amount of information released to the public and the more frequently disclosures have to be made, the higher the probability of issuing an incomplete or misleading statement and the greater the liability risk.'[88]

Insights from behavioural sciences are practically absent from EU public and private enforcement initiatives.[89] Private law has consistently relied on rationality-orientated legal approaches and downplayed the behavioural considerations.[90]

---

81 Ibid.
82 Ibid.
83 John C Coffee, Jr, 'The Future of Disclosure: ESG, Common Ownership, and Systematic Risk' (2022) 2 Columbia Business Law Review 602.
84 Demetra Arsalidou, 'Institutional Investors, Behavioural Economics and the Concept of Stewardship' (2012) 6(6) Law and Financial Markets Review 410, 410.
85 Hu (n 24) 637.
86 Ibid 640.
87 Daren C Brabham, 'Crowdsourcing as a Model for Problem Solving' (2008) 14(1) Convergence: The International Journal of Research into New Media Technologies 75.
88 Enriques and Gilotta (n 2) 531.
89 Van Cleynenbreugel (n 77) 266.
90 Ibid 270.

Conduct-of-business rules involve disclosure requirements. Even in the event of compliance with *ex ante* disclosure regulation, civil courts may still find *ex post* that the disclosure was insufficient by resorting to the backdoor method of the transparency requirement; merely complying with disclosure obligations does not mean that the transparency requirement was not breached.[91]

On the one hand, according to the enforcement theory, shareholder litigation ensures the quality of corporate disclosure by serving as an important check on management, thereby complementing regulatory efforts.[92] On the other hand, according to the strike-suit theory, firms may face the opportunistic behaviour of plaintiffs who sue regardless of merits. Regardless of their conduct, firms will be sued if their stock price plummets. In this view, firms face potential litigation in the event of a stock price drop, potentially reducing their incentive to proactively provide additional information to investors.[93]

Another typical problem arises with after-the-fact determination. In securities fraud litigation, issues may arise owing to the fact that courts must determine whether an *ex ante* standard was met while armed with the knowledge that a negative event has in fact materialised.[94] For instance, whenever disclosure prompted the fall of the stock price, the court is required to assess whether a particular issue facing the company should have been disclosed at an earlier stage.[95] This determination is difficult to make.

In terms of public enforcement, compliance with the rules is paramount. However, lower compliance with financial laws designed to protect the safety and soundness of financial institutions causes a deterioration in the effectiveness of those rules.[96] Negative feedback loops form in the event that deteriorating compliance with laws combating fraud or restraining investment and lending may exacerbate a bubble, which, in turn, can further vitiate obedience to financial law.[97]

---

91 Danny Busch, 'The Future of EU Financial Law' (2022) 17(1) Capital Markets Law Journal 52, 91.

92 James Bohn and Stephen Choi, 'Fraud in the New-Issues Market: Empirical Evidence on Securities Class Actions' (1996) 144(3) University of Pennsylvania Law Review 903, 935–40, 979–80, 907–08.

93 Ibid 972.

94 Sunstein, Jolls and Thaler (n 15) 1532.

95 Ibid.

96 Gerding (n 43) 10–11.

97 Ibid.

IV. The risk of procyclical regulation and herd-promoting regulation relating to bank disclosure regulation

Procyclical regulation and herd-promoting regulation may be precipitating factors in the run-up to financial crises.[98] In many instances, financial law appears to have contributed to the expansion of bubbles and to the severity of their implosion.[99] Bubbles arise because of the herding of investors into particular asset classes. Financial regulations may reinforce this trend by promoting dangerous collective behaviour by financial institutions.[100] For instance, regulation may lead to homogenous market reliance on the same information. Indeed, the risk occurs that financial regulation homogenises the information that market participants rely on to make their investment decisions. A prominent example of this behavioural phenomenon is provided by regulatory over-reliance on credit ratings.[101] Whenever ratings are used for regulatory purposes, financial institutions are incentivised to massively invest in highly rated instruments. In the event of a rating downgrade, there is an expectation that investors will react to such an announcement, even when no additional information about the financial situation of the company is conveyed, because the fact that a rating downgrade has occurred is perceived as autonomous information.[102] Regulations requiring that investors react to rating downgrades – for instance by selling assets that are downgraded below investment grade, or by holding more capital against downgraded assets – have procyclical effects. They prompt investors to sell off at the same time, leading to a downward spiral.

The issue as to whether there is a legal obligation to reveal adverse information to the markets varies between the US and the EU. In the US, pursuant to Securities and Exchange Commission (SEC) Rule 10b-5, omissions to state a material fact may be misleading.[103] With respect to the state of mind, scienter is required.[104] In the EU, the duty to disclose adverse information stems from ad-hoc disclosure obligations pursuant to Article 17 of the Market Abuse Regulation.[105]

---

98 Ibid 12–13.

99 Ibid 2.

100 Diamond and Dybvig (n 45) 401; Gerding (n 43) 13.

101 Frank Partnoy, 'Overdependence on Credit Ratings was a Primary Cause of the Crisis' (2009) University of San Diego Legal Studies Research Paper Series No 09-015, 10 <https://papers.ssrn.com/sol3/papers.cfm?abstract_id=1430653#> accessed 1 May 2024; Aline Darbellay, *Regulating Credit Rating Agencies* (Edward Elgar 2013) 179.

102 Claire A Hill, 'Regulating the Rating Agencies' (2004) 82(1) Washington University Law Quarterly 4, 68.

103 SEC Rule 10b-5, 17 CFR 240.10b-5.

104 Zamir and Teichman (n 65).

105 Council, Regulation (EU) No 596/2014 of the European Parliament and of the Council of 16 April 2014 on market abuse (market abuse regulation) and repealing Directive 2003/6/EC of the European Parliament and of the Council and Commission Directives 2003/124/EC, 2003/125/EC and 2004/72/EC [2014] OJ L 173/1 of 12.06.2014, Art. 17.

Unfavourable information, if material, is likely to lead to a significant decline in market prices. Unfavourable information may consist of adverse information about the issuer or of corrective disclosure in the sense of the revelation of the truth after false or misleading information was disclosed to the markets. In any case, the revealed information can lead to a sharp decline in market prices. To make matters worse, public statements may become self-fulfilling prophecies.[106] In the realm of banking, events like bank runs can be triggered by rational actions relating to herding effects, where investors follow the crowd. In fact, there is some rationality in the herding behaviour of market participants, for instance when bank runs occur as self-fulfilling prophecies or in the event of information cascades.[107]

In the banking sector, the fact that a bank has suffered a liquidity shock is a prime example of adverse information. Owing to the fear of stigma, banks are reluctant to seek emergency liquidity assistance from central banks. As explained in Section II.C., policymakers and regulators may attempt to solve the stigma problem by creating frameworks enabling banks to make their recourse to emergency liquidity assistance less visible to the markets. However, withholding unfavourable information has its weaknesses. This causes opacity in the markets. In the event information is not disclosed in a timely manner, it could erode investor confidence in the disclosure system, leading to dramatic consequences in the financial markets. In the complex financial landscape, bank balance sheets are often perceived as opaque. The intricacies of the rules and the occurrence of off-balance-sheet activities make it even more challenging to assess the risks accurately. In addition, even financial market authorities may be reluctant to intervene early, fearing the risk of triggering a financial crisis. This may result in an illusion of safety and soundness. Any revelation to the contrary could potentially trigger a bank run, raising questions about the credibility of the system. If the uncertainty is exacerbated, financial stability may be jeopardised.

In sum, this topic provides more questions than answers. Every strategy has its merits and weaknesses. Consequently, it is crucial for legal scholars to consider behavioural economic analysis. This concept is not novel. Starting from the late 1970s, economic analysis has gained prominence as the predominant cross-disciplinary approach to law and legal theory.[108] Furthermore, proponents of Behavioural Economics (BE), Behavioural Law and Economics (BLE), and non-economic behavioural analyses of law typically employ behavioural insights as correctives for economic and other perspectives on legal and policy issues rather than as substitutes for them.[109] They do not call for abandoning the tools of traditional economic analysis, but rather advocate for

106 Costas Azariadis, 'Self-Fulfilling Prophecies' (1981) 25(3) Journal of Economic Theory 380, 380–96; Robert P Flood and Robert J Hodrick, 'On Testing for Speculative Bubbles' (1990) 4(2) Journal of Economic Perspectives 85, 85–101.

107 Gerding (n 43) 43.

108 Richard A Posner, *Economic Analysis of Law* (9th edn, Aspen Publishing 2014) 7–18; Zamir and Teichman (n 65) 141.

109 Zamir and Teichman (n 65) 153.

refining them by adopting more accurate assumptions about human behaviour.[110] The variation in behavioural economics models and the characteristics of the scientific method hold significant implications for legal scholars who import economic theory into legal settings.[111]

V. Conclusion

This chapter has shed light on multiple issues relating to bank disclosure regulation. In light of the intricacies of behavioural analysis, there are still many unanswered questions. In so doing, this provides a roadmap for future research in the field of law and finance. A crucial aspect relates to the difficulties arising from how securities regulation and bank prudential regulation are intertwined. While securities regulation revolves around providing investors with information, bank prudential regulation may occasionally prioritise financial stability over transparency. This is best illustrated by the regulatory responses to the stigma problem. However, this topic raises significant concerns that warrant further attention from the scientific community. The issue is that the various objectives of financial regulation may to some extent be conflicting. Banks face particular risks, including the possibility of bank runs. Accordingly, trust is essential. Disclosure plays a key role in investor confidence. Publicly available information, such as bad news or corrective disclosures, may quickly lead to a downward spiral, which may have a detrimental impact on financial stability. If information is however not timely disclosed, investors may lose confidence in the disclosure regime, which would have dramatic effects on the financial markets. Therefore, it is crucial to recognise all these issues and to further develop behaviourally informed bank disclosure regulation.

---

110 Ibid.

111 Joshua C Teitelbaum and Kathryn Zeiler, 'Introduction' in Joshua C Teitelbaum and Kathryn Zeiler (eds), *Research Handbook on Behavioral Law and Economics* (Edward Elgar 2018) 1.

2

Empowering sustainable finance with artificial intelligence: a framework for responsible implementation

Georgios Pavlidis

I. Introduction

The global economy and societies around the world are facing a once-in-a-lifetime situation, as two major developments are underway and becoming collinear. On the one hand, financial markets are rapidly entering the era of environmental, social, and governance (ESG) investing. Market participants predict that investors' demand for more diverse instruments, such as green and ESG-linked loans, will increase in the coming years.[1] On the other hand, the artificial intelligence (AI) industry is experiencing close to exponential growth, and the impact of this new technology on business and society has already become visible. Indeed, the estimated value of the global AI market was $387.45 billion in 2022, and it is projected to reach $1,394.30 billion in 2029, with a compound annual growth rate of 20.1 per cent in this period.[2]

The aim of this chapter is to examine how these two processes – the rise of ESG investing (Section II) and the ascendance of AI technological innovation (Section III) – could be aligned and which risks and opportunities would emerge from this alignment. We argue that AI can help markets identify and price climate risks as well as set more ambitious ESG goals, yet there are serious risks in delegating sustainable finance

1 United Nations Environmental Program, 'State of Finance for Nature 2022' (UNEP Report, 1 December 2022) <https://www.unep.org/resources/report/state-finance-nature-2022> accessed 7 February 2024.

2 Fortune Business Insights, 'AI Market Size to Reach USD 1394.30 Billion by 2029' (Market Research Report, April 2023) <https://www.fortunebusinessinsights.com/industry-reports/artificial-intelligence-market-100114> accessed 7 February 2024. According to other estimates, the market size of the AI industry was USD $93.5 billion in 2021 and is projected to expand at a compound annual growth rate of 38.1 per cent from 2022 to 2030; see Grand View Research, 'Artificial Intelligence Market Size, Share & Trends Analysis Report' (Market Analysis Report, April 2022) <https://www.grandviewresearch.com/industry-analysis/artificial-intelligence-ai-market> accessed 7 February 2024.

decisions to AI. We further argue that developing new principles and rules for AI and ESG investing is necessary but prone to ambiguities and practical obstacles that could undermine norm-setting initiatives (Section IV). We conclude that implementing changes such as the use of AI in non-financial reporting requires a new sense of responsibility and the fine-tuning of the principles of legitimacy, oversight and verification, transparency, and explainability, along with international coordination in the context of AI and ESG investing (Section V).

II. Unlocking the potential of sustainable finance and navigating the pitfalls of responsible investing

The first trend worth examining is the increase in global awareness about sustainable investing – in particular, ESG, which extends the notion of sustainability beyond the need to protect the environment and mitigate climate change. The environmental component of ESG may include climate policies and policies governing energy use, waste, pollution, greenhouse gas (GHG) emissions, natural resource conservation, and so on.[3] The social component of ESG may include policies on diversity, inclusion, a community focus, social justice, and corporate ethics, such as ethical supply chains and prevention of questionable labour practices domestically and overseas.[4] The governance component may include the use of accurate and transparent accounting methods, corporate transparency, diversity in leadership, and accountability to shareholders.[5] In the ESG context, both policymakers and the markets shift from an exclusive focus on financial factors towards non-financial aspects when identifying risks and growth opportunities. Indeed, the importance of non-financial information in establishing a company's reputation and influencing the decisions made by investors is growing rapidly.[6]

ESG investing has become a clearly detectable and increasingly widespread trend in business, finance, and policymaking. According to Bloomberg, global ESG assets surpassed $35 trillion in 2020, and they may surpass $41 trillion by 2022 and $50 trillion

---

3 Sachini Supunsala Senadheera et al., 'Scoring Environment Pillar in Environmental, Social, and Governance (ESG) Assessment' (2021) 7(1) Sustainable Environment 1.

4 Elizabeth Pollman, 'Corporate Social Responsibility, ESG, and Compliance' in Benjamin van Rooij and D Daniel Sokol (eds), *The Cambridge Handbook of Compliance* (Cambridge University Press 2021) 662–672.

5 Julie Linn Teigland, 'How can boards strengthen governance to accelerate their ESG journeys?' (EY Long-Term Value and Corporate Governance Survey, February 2022) <https://assets.ey.com/content/dam/ey-sites/ey-com/en_gl/topics/attractiveness/ey-long-term-value-and-corporate-governance-survey-february-2022.pdf> accessed 7 February 2024.

6 Muhammad Naveed et al., 'Role of Financial and Non-Financial Information in Determining Individual investor Investment Decision: A Signaling Perspective' (2020) 9 South Asian Journal of Business Studies 261.

by 2025.[7] This will represent one-third of the assets under management globally. With regard to bond markets, there is already a sizeable $4 trillion ESG global debt market, which could swell to $15 trillion by 2025. ESG debt markets are dominated by European private and public issuers and investors, and this trend will be strengthened by the implementation of the colossal Green Deal of the European Union (EU).[8] With regard to ESG exchange-traded funds (ETF), cumulative assets in this category reached over $360 billion in 2021. This represents a small part (4 per cent) of global ETF assets, but the share of ESG in ETF annual flows is increasing rapidly, and investors expect that this expansion will continue in 2023 and beyond.[9] However, the trend in favour of ESG investment could be halted due to unforeseen events. For example, amid the Coronavirus Disease 2019 (COVID-19) pandemic, environmental protection and the fight against climate change were sidelined temporarily, as is often the case in times of crisis.[10] Nevertheless, as policymakers set in motion the recovery of national economies, green and sustainable development became a key element of economic recovery plans, especially at the level of the EU, with its Green Deal.[11]

The trend in favour of ESG investment is undoubtedly a positive one and paved with good intentions. However, the transition towards ever-stronger ESG performance contains some serious pitfalls. The three main ones are the lack of definitive, universal ESG metrics, the risk of so-called 'greenwashing', and the labour-intensiveness of ESG reporting.

---

7 Bloomberg, 'ESG May Surpass $41 Trillion Assets in 2022, But Not Without Challenges, Finds Bloomberg Intelligence' (Bloomberg Press Announcement, 24 January 2022) <https://www.bloomberg.com/company/press/esg-may-surpass-41-trillion-assets-in-2022-but-not-without-challenges-finds-bloomberg-intelligence/> accessed 7 February 2024.

8 In summer 2020, the European Council adopted the EU recovery plan and multiannual financial framework (MFF) for 2021–2027 with the objective of ensuring 'that the next MFF as a whole contributes to the implementation of the Paris Agreement'; Conclusions of the Special Meeting of the European Council (17–21 July 2020) 14. The EU intends to borrow €750 billion under NextGenerationEU, 30 per cent of which will be raised through green bonds.

9 BNP Paribas Asset Management, 'ESG ETF Barometer shows strong shift in investor expectations' (BNP Press Release, February 2023) <https://mediaroom-en.bnpparibas-am.com/news/bnp-paribas-asset-management-european-esg-etf-barometer-shows-strong-shift-in-investor-expectations-26f5-0fb7a.html> accessed 7 February 2024.

10 Charlotte Burns, Peter Eckersley, and Paul Tobin, 'EU Environmental Policy in Times of Crisis' (2020) 27(1) Journal of European Public Policy 1; Yves Steinebach and Christoph Knill, 'Still an Entrepreneur? The Changing Role of the European Commission in EU Environmental Policymaking' (2017) 24(3) Journal of European Public Policy 429.

11 Of course, there are significant risks and shortcomings. For example, the EU Green Deal does not focus on the social dimensions of sustainable development, and it fails to make sufficiently clear the cost-benefit effects for citizens. See Sanja Filipović, Noam Lior, and Mirjana Radovanović, 'The Green Deal – Just Transition and Sustainable Development Goals Nexus' (2022) 168 (13) Renewable and Sustainable Energy Reviews 112759.

First, ESG investing requires predetermined, commonly accepted, and uniformly applied ESG metrics. Currently, there is no definitive, universal set of ESG metrics, although there are various distinct frameworks and certifications that differ in scope, methodology, and acceptance by markets, for instance the Global Reporting Initiative (GRI), the Sustainability Accounting Standards Board (SASB) Standards, the Carbon Disclosure Project (CDP), and the International Organization for Standardization's ISO 14001 for environmental management systems. The variety of ESG business projects does not help, since different metrics will be relevant for numerous types of projects, from renewable energy and green infrastructure projects to payments for ecosystem services, biodiversity offsets, and pro-biodiversity and adaptation businesses. Depending on the project, ESG metrics may include carbon footprints, GHG emissions, year-over-year energy, waste variance, community impact, and pay gap, not all of which can be easily measured, and surely not with the same methodology. The volume of data and the complexity of the metrics are likely to increase, as will the variety of green projects that receive financing. Therefore, ensuring convergence will be a serious challenge for ESG metrics,[12] given the growing demand of investors for extra-financial data, including 'sustainable performance' and 'green performance' data, which are required to meet the fragmented international and regional standards.[13]

A second pitfall is the risk of 'greenwashing', that is to say, misleading information regarding how a product or service is environmentally sound.[14] A characteristic example of greenwashing was the 'Dieselgate' scandal in which the car giant Volkswagen admitted to cheating emissions tests by using proprietary software (the 'defeat device') and altering the performance of engines undergoing testing.[15] At the same time, the company was advertising the low-emissions features of its products through marketing campaigns.[16] In the specific context of ESG investing, greenwashing is the use of misinformation to gain investor confidence around a company's ESG claims.[17] Several cases of greenwashing have been reported in the financial industry, such as the recent

---

12 Luluk Widyawati, 'A Systematic Literature Review of Socially Responsible Investment and Environmental Social Governance Metrics' (2020) 29(2) Business Strategy and the Environment 619.

13 United Nations Environment Program, 'Driving Meaningful Data: Financial Materiality, Sustainability Performance and Sustainability Outcomes' (UNEP Finance/United Nations Global Compact, September 2020) 3.

14 Maria J Bachelet, Leonardo Becchetti, and Stefano Manfredonia, 'The Green Bonds Premium Puzzle: The Role of Issuer Characteristics and Third-Party Verification' (2019) 11(4) Sustainability 1098.

15 Edin Mujkic and Donald Klingner, 'Dieselgate: How Hubris and Bad Leadership Caused the Biggest Scandal in Automotive History' (2019) 21(4) Public Integrity 365.

16 Regulators in multiple countries reacted and began investigating Volkswagen. As a result, the stock price of the company fell in value, and key executives were suspended.

17 This term is rather broad, and there is a lack of shared understanding about its definition and taxonomy; see Soh Young In and Kim Schumacher, 'Carbonwashing: ESG Data Greenwashing in a Post-Paris World' in Thomas Heller and Alicia Seiger (eds), *Settling Climate Accounts* (Palgrave Macmillan 2021) 39–58.

advertising campaign of HSBC, which was banned by the United Kingdom (UK)'s advertising regulator for being 'misleading' about the company's contribution to the fight against climate change; the campaign in question outlined the bank's efforts to help its customers achieve 'net zero' emissions, but it omitted significant information about its role in financing fossil fuel firms and new oil and gas production.[18] In a troubling study conducted in 2021, the Economist examined the holdings of the world's 20 biggest ESG funds[19] and found that each of them held investments in fossil fuel producers, while others held stakes in oil producers, coal mining, gambling, alcohol, and tobacco.[20] The extensive range of ESG reporting enables corporations to prioritise one ESG metric over another, focussing on improving reported ESG metrics while ignoring unreported ones, thus masking or hiding the negative impacts of their actions.[21] To prevent greenwashing in ESG investing, reduce informational asymmetries, and ensure the accuracy and quality of extra-financial reporting, investors need to demand and markets need to develop reliable labels, certifications, and verifications to be carried out by independent third parties. The adoption of regulations imposing transparency and high standards in non-financial reporting can accelerate this development, as we will examine in Section IV of this study.

A third challenge to ESG investing is the fact that extra-financial reporting is labour intensive.[22] Reporting on ESG projects requires collecting, analysing, and publishing information on ESG impacts, leading to complex and technical metrics. The costs of extra-financial reporting are recurring and, under current market practices, extend to the entire lifecycle of the project, as reporting takes place periodically, usually

18 Annabelle Liang, 'HSBC climate change adverts banned by UK watchdog' *BBC* (19 October 2022) <https://www.bbc.com/news/business-63309878> accessed 7 February 2024.

19 The Economist, 'Sustainable finance is rife with greenwash. Time for more disclosure' (22 May 2021) <https://www.economist.com/leaders/2021/05/22/sustainable-finance-is-rife-with-greenwash-time-for-more-disclosure> accessed 7 February 2024.

20 See also Tim Espiner, 'Big banks fund new oil and gas despite net zero pledges' *BBC* (14 February 2022) <https://www.bbc.com/news/business-60366054> accessed 7 February 2024. According to this article, big banks continue to fund oil and gas projects despite their net zero pledges and being part of the United Nations-led Net Zero Banking Alliance.

21 Robert S Kaplan and Karthik Ramanna, 'How to Fix ESG Reporting' (2021) Harvard Business School Accounting & Management Unit Working Paper No. 22–005, <https://www.hbs.edu/ris/Publication%20Files/22-005revised_ed6ac430-c3ca-4ba6-b0be-ca48c549aaf2.pdf> accessed 7 February 2024. An interesting example given by these authors is a company that reports a decrease in GHG emissions from its truck fleet, which is an ESG metric that is measured and reported on; however, the same company does not report on another ESG metric, namely the use of indentured labour in mining minerals for electric vehicles' batteries, which may have worsened as a result of its actions.

22 EU Technical Expert Group on Sustainable Finance, 'Report on EU green bond standard' (TEG Report Proposal for an EU Green Bond Standard, June 2019) 22.

annually, prior to the full allocation of proceeds.[23] Moreover, several jurisdictions have enhanced reporting requirements, further increasing the costs. The increased workload and costs associated with ESG investing may deter investors, but new and promising methods and technologies, such as AI, have the potential to alleviate most of these constraints and even allow for the use of alternative data as an objective and reliable data source.

The rise of ESG investing is associated with risks, like all new trends in the worlds of business and finance. Not surprisingly, there have been several proposals and norm-setting initiatives, but most are still under development, and they have still not matured into a comprehensive, coherent, and universally applied framework of rules and principles. Currently, principles and rules for ESG investing can be found at three levels: a) global goals, such as the United Nations (UN) Sustainable Development Goals, Principles for Responsible Investment, Greenhouse Gas Protocol, and Paris Climate Agreement; b) voluntary reporting frameworks, as in the context of the GRI, the ISO, the Science Based Targets Initiative (SBTI), the Climate Disclosure Standards Board (CDSB), the SASB, and the CDP; c) mandatory regulations at the national and EU levels, such as the EU Corporate Sustainability Reporting Directive (CSRD), Sustainable Finance Disclosure Regulation (SFDR), and EU Taxonomy.[24] The challenge for policymakers and standard-setting bodies will be to promote the global consolidation of ESG reporting governance by overcoming the differences between their respective reporting philosophies.[25] Until this happens, the challenge for issuers and investors will be navigating the complex landscape and finding the sweet spots between ESG reporting initiatives that are relevant to their projects.

23 Deloitte, 'Thinking Allowed: The future of corporate reporting' (Deloitte, July 2016) 8 <https://www2.deloitte.com/content/dam/Deloitte/ch/Documents/audit/ch-en-audit-thinking-allowed-future-corporate-reporting.pdf> accessed 7 February 2024.

24 Directive (EU) 2022/2464 of the European Parliament and of the Council of 14 December 2022 amending Regulation (EU) No 537/2014, Directive 2004/109/EC, Directive 2006/43/EC and Directive 2013/34/EU, as regards corporate sustainability reporting [2022] OJ L 322/15 of 16.12.2022; Regulation (EU) 2019/2088 of the European Parliament and of the Council of 27 November 2019 on sustainability-related disclosures in the financial services sector [2019] OJ L 317/1 of 09.12.2019; Regulation (EU) 2020/852 of the European Parliament and of the Council of 18 June 2020 on the establishment of a framework to facilitate sustainable investment, and amending Regulation (EU) 2019/2088 [2020] OJ L 198/13 of 22.06.2020.

25 Adam Sulkowski and Ruth Jebe, 'Evolving ESG Reporting Governance, Regime Theory, and Proactive Law: Predictions and Strategies' (2022) 59(3) American Business Law Journal 449.

III. The rise of artificial intelligence, its impact on finance, and the risks of hype in the absence of regulation

According to the Organisation for Economic Co-operation and Development (OECD), 'an AI system is a machine-based system that can, for a given set of human-defined objectives, make predictions, recommendations, or decisions influencing real or virtual environments ... with varying levels of autonomy'.[26] Almost identically, the EU defines an AI system as 'software that ... can, for a given set of human-defined objectives, generate outputs such as content, predictions, recommendations, or decisions influencing the environments they interact with'.[27] AI refers to the ability of a computer to accomplish tasks that require human intelligence and discernment and, for this reason, are usually executed by humans. AI encompasses subfields, such as machine learning and deep learning, in which the algorithms use input data to learn, draw inferences, and adapt without explicit instructions.[28] Numerous AI applications have already been developed and many others are underway, from manufacturing robots, self-driving cars, smart assistants, and marketing chatbots to AI applications in healthcare, agriculture, and finance.[29]

These exciting prospects have attracted the fervent interest of investors worldwide, and as a result, global spending on AI systems reached $118 billion in 2022 and is expected to surpass $300 billion in 2026, which will represent a massive compound annual growth rate of 26.5% over this period.[30] The banking and retail industries are expected to make the most significant investments in AI, collectively comprising around 25 per cent of all AI expenditure globally.[31] It is also projected that by 2030, AI will have the potential to add approximately $15.7 trillion to the global economy (a 14

---

26 OECD, 'Recommendation of the Council on Artificial Intelligence' (OECD Recommendation of the Council on Artificial Intelligence OECD/LEGAL/0449, 2019); See also IBM, 'What is Artificial Intelligence?' (3 June 2020) <https://www.ibm.com/topics/artificial-intelligence#anchor-1174800854> accessed 7 February 2024, according to which 'artificial intelligence is a field that combines computer science and robust datasets to enable problem-solving'.

27 Article 3 par. 1, Proposal for a Regulation laying down harmonised rules on artificial intelligence (Artificial Intelligence Act), COM(2021) 206 final.

28 Several classifications have been proposed: AI can be reactive, have limited memory, have a theory of mind, and be self-aware. Authors also distinguish between artificial narrow intelligence, artificial general intelligence, and artificial super intelligence. Among numerous interesting works, see Stuart Russell and Peter Norvig, *Artificial Intelligence: A Modern Approach* (4th edn, Pearson Education 2021).

29 Nicole Radziwill, *Connected, Intelligent, Automated: The Definitive Guide to Digital Transformation and Quality 4.0* (Quality Press 2020) 49.

30 International Data Corporation, 'Worldwide Artificial Intelligence Spending Guide' (IDC Spending Guide, September 2022). According to the IDC, 27 per cent of the growth in AI by 2023 will be in hardware, which includes devices such as AI-powered smart speakers; 38 per cent of the growth in AI will be in services, such as information technology; and 35 per cent will be in software.

31 Ibid.

per cent increase in global GDP), which is more than the combined output of China and India at present. Out of this total amount, an estimated $6.6 trillion is expected to result from a boost in productivity, while approximately $9.1 trillion is expected to result from the consumption side.[32]

In the field of finance, AI can be used both for portfolio management and client enablement, as well as for improving front-, middle-, and back-office efficiency. For example, AI applications can help evaluate management sentiment by reading earnings transcripts and generating automated insights. AI can also help identify non-intuitive relationships between assets, market indicators, and alternative datasets, such as social media, weather forecasts, and container ship movements. Furthermore, AI can automate functions in financial operations intelligence, monitor suspicious transactions, generate reports, and respond to employee or investor queries using machine learning and chatbots.[33]

Moreover, applications can combine all elements of the so-called 'BIA Trinity', that is, blockchain, the Internet of Things (IoT), and AI, to revolutionise numerous aspects of our lives, including the world of sustainable finance.[34] This will allow data from the real economy (e.g., data from sensors) in a sustainable project to be uploaded to the blockchain directly and in real time.[35] Impact reports could then be compiled with the use of AI to analyse complex data to be ultimately delivered to the digital wallet of the investor, an independent certification agency, or the oversight authorities. This will constitute a shift from manual to automated reporting by harvesting recognised metrics from assets, codifying them as data tokens, and communicating them to multiple stakeholders. Automatic reporting will increase the reliability and traceability of projects' performance. Moreover, it has been estimated that such digitalisation could reduce the average cost of data gathering (including the cost of IoT

---

32 PwC, 'Sizing the prize: What's the real value of AI for your business and how can you capitalise?' (PWC Global Artificial Intelligence Study, 2017) <https://www.pwc.com/gx/en/issues/analytics/assets/pwc-ai-analysis-sizing-the-prize-report.pdf> accessed 7 February 2024.

33 Deloitte, 'Artificial Intelligence: The next frontier for investment management firms' (Deloitte, 2022) <https://www.deloitte.com/global/en/Industries/financial-services/perspectives/ai-next-frontier-in-investment-management.html> accessed 7 February 2024.

34 Darius Nassiry, 'The Role of Fintech in Unlocking Green Finance: Policy Insights for Developing Countries' (2018) Asian Development Bank Institute, ADBI Working Paper Series No. 88310 <https://www.adb.org/sites/default/files/publication/464821/adbi-wp883.pdf> accessed 7 February 2024.

35 Wanli Chen and Qianxia Wang, 'The Role of Blockchain for the European Bond Market' (2020) Frankfurt School Blockchain Center, FSBC Working Paper, 11 <http://explore-ip.com/2020_The-Role-of-Blockchain-for-the-European-Bond-Market.pdf> accessed 7 February 2024.

devices), data aggregation, and reporting for the full lifecycle of a sustainable project by up to ten times.[36]

It is a positive sign that many economic sectors, such as transport, energy, and water, already employ IoT devices and harvest data automatically, which can be useful for extra-financial reporting.[37] Nevertheless, the exact metrics for automated reporting must be determined – that is, which specific data are to be collected, analysed, and reported. Once this has been determined, it will be possible to generate impact indexes for one or more projects by combining relevant indicators, such as measurements of air quality or CO_2, from multiple monitoring points over time. To deal with the lack of well-structured data formats and the huge volume of datasets gathered automatically, AI tools and advanced analytics can be employed to organise and evaluate data volumes. For example, an application developed by Global Mangrove Trust uses AI to monitor forest density, a particularly complex set of data, and combines it with TreeCoin rewards, which are exchangeable for goods.[38] AI can be deployed in similarly large and complex datasets, from the evapotranspiration necessary for the preservation of wetlands ecosystems[39] to geoinformatics in smart, sustainable agriculture.[40] The use of AI and digitalisation in sustainable finance has the potential to economise time and costs, facilitate the scaling-up of sustainable investments, improve the quality of reporting, and facilitate aggregating reporting, allowing for follow-up innovations, such as the fragmentation of green asset ownership and the aggregation of smaller assets and projects into a bond.

---

36 HSBC Sustainable Digital Finance Alliance, 'Blockchain: Gateway for Sustainability Linked Bonds' (HSBC Centre of Sustainable Finance, September 2019) 17 <https://www.sustainablefinance.hsbc.com/-/media/gbm/reports/sustainable-financing/blockchain-gateway-for-sustainability-linked-bonds.pdf> accessed 7 February 2024.

37 Sandro Nizetic et al., 'Internet of Things (IoT): Opportunities, Issues and Challenges towards a Smart and Sustainable Future' (2020) 274 Journal of Cleaner Production 274; In Lee and Kyoochun Lee, 'The Internet of Things (IoT): Applications, Investments, and Challenges for Enterprises' (2015) 58(4) Business Horizons 431–40; HSBC Sustainable Digital Finance Alliance, 'Blockchain: Gateway for Sustainability Linked Bonds' (HSBC Centre of Sustainable Finance, September 2019) 20 <https://www.sustainablefinance.hsbc.com/-/media/gbm/reports/sustainable-financing/blockchain-gateway-for-sustainability-linked-bonds.pdf> accessed 7 February 2024.

38 TreeCoin, *Tree Coin White Paper* (White Paper, November 2020) 23.

39 Francesco Granata, Rudy Gargano, and Giovanni de Marinis, 'Artificial Intelligence Based Approaches to Evaluate Actual Evapotranspiration in Wetlands' (2020) 703 Science of The Total Environment 135653.

40 Abhishek Singh et al., 'Geoinformatics, Artificial Intelligence, Sensor Technology, Big Data: Emerging Modern Tools for Sustainable Agriculture' in Pavan Kumar et al. (eds), *Sustainable Agriculture Systems and Technologies* (John Wiley & Sons Ltd 2022) 295–313.

Nevertheless, faced with the near-exponential pace of progress in AI, including AI used for sustainability, serious concerns have been voiced regarding potential risks[41] and the need for more regulation and oversight, which we will examine in the following section.

IV. Developing new principles and rules for AI: a journey in unchartered territory

In 2014, the billionaire investor Elon Musk told an audience at the Massachusetts Institute of Technology (MIT) the following: 'I'm increasingly inclined to think that there should be some regulatory oversight, maybe at the national and international level, just to make sure that we don't do something very foolish. I mean with artificial intelligence, we're summoning the demon.'[42] The deployment of AI raises legitimate concerns about cyber resilience; data security, quality, consistency, completeness, and privacy; the risk of bias; and several other risks.[43] For this reason, new sets of principles and rules have been proposed to mitigate risks and guide responsible digital innovation in AI.

Among several other interesting initiatives introduced by governments, industry, and other stakeholders,[44] we can look at the OECD's 'Recommendation' on AI.[45] This non-binding instrument treats AI as a general-purpose technology – that is, not in the specific context of ESG investing – and puts forward five key principles,[46] which are worth discussing. Principle 1 (inclusive and sustainable growth) highlights the potential for trustworthy AI to contribute to overall growth and prosperity for all – individuals, society, and the planet – and advance global development objectives. In the ESG context, this means ensuring that the development and use of AI tools align with sustainability goals, social inclusivity, and environmental responsibility. Therefore, Principle 1 aims to enhance the contribution of AI to long-term value creation, sustainable development, and positive societal impacts. Principle 2 (fairness and rule of

---

41 Rohit Nishant, Mike Kennedy, and Jacqueline Corbett, 'Artificial Intelligence for Sustainability: Challenges, Opportunities, and a Research Agenda' (2020) 53 International Journal of Information Management 102104.

42 Gregory Wallace, 'Elon Musk warns against unleashing artificial intelligence "demon"' *CNN Business* (26 October 2014) <https://money.cnn.com/2014/10/26/technology/elon-musk-artificial-intelligence-demon/> accessed 7 February 2024.

43 Matthew U Scherer, 'Regulating Artificial Intelligence Systems: Risks, Challenges, Competencies, and Strategies' (2016) 29(2) Harvard Journal of Law & Technology 353.

44 Jessica Morley et al., 'From What to How: An Initial Review of Publicly Available AI Ethics Tools, Methods and Research to Translate Principles into Practices' (2020) 26 Science and Engineering Ethics 2141.

45 OECD, 'Recommendation of the Council on Artificial Intelligence' (OECD Recommendation of the Council on Artificial Intelligence OECD/LEGAL/0449, 2019).

46 Roger Clarke, 'Principles and Business Processes for Responsible AI' (2019) 35(4) Computer Law & Security Review 410.

law) states that AI systems should be designed in a way that respects the rule of law, human rights, democratic values, and diversity, and should include appropriate safeguards to ensure a fair and just society. The main difficulty in this situation is creating efficient systems for informed oversight. Principle 3 (transparency and explainability) aims to ensure transparency and responsible disclosure around AI systems so that people understand when they are engaging with them and can challenge outcomes. In the context of ESG, this requires that the methodology and outcomes of an AI model be properly explained and communicated to the oversight authorities and/or independent certification agencies. Principle 4 (safety) provides that AI systems must function in a robust, secure, and safe way throughout their lifetimes, and potential risks should be continually assessed and managed. This concept closely resembles the EU's more intricate, risk-based approach, as outlined in the EU AI Act. In the ESG context, understanding and mitigating risks associated with AI technologies is crucial for ensuring alignment with sustainability goals and avoiding negative impacts on stakeholders and the environment. To illustrate, consider the hypothetical situation where an investment firm utilises an AI-powered trading algorithm designed to prioritise investments in companies with high ESG scores. The algorithm is programmed to buy or sell stocks based on real-time ESG data and market trends. However, due to a technical glitch or unforeseen data irregularity, the algorithm mistakenly interprets negative news about a socially responsible company as positive, leading it to heavily invest in that company's stocks. Such scenarios and risks must be mitigated promptly and effectively. Finally, Principle 5 (accountability) proposes that organisations and individuals developing, deploying, or operating AI systems should be held accountable for their proper functioning. In the ESG context, any organisation that undertakes ESG reporting remains responsible for ensuring compliance with the applicable legislative provisions and reporting standards, and it cannot invoke the use of an AI system to shield itself against liability.

These principles have influenced national and regional norm-setting initiatives, the most prominent and comprehensive of which is the AI Act of the EU. This legislation, adopted in December 2023, has yet to be published in the Official Journal of the European Union as of February 2024. This is a 'horizontal' rather than sector-specific piece of legislation, and it may overlap with several legislative provisions, such as those related to cybersecurity and data protection.[47] As a result, inconsistencies may emerge that negatively affect legislative quality and regulatory certainty. The EU Act follows a risk-based approach to AI, where legal intervention is tailored to levels of risk.[48] To that end, the AI Act distinguishes between AI systems posing (i) unacceptable risk,

47 Arthur Bogucki et al., 'The AI Act and emerging EU digital acquis: Overlaps, gaps and inconsistencies' (CEPS In-Depth Analysis, September 2022) <https://cdn.ceps.eu/wp-content/uploads/2022/09/CEPS-In-depth-analysis-2022-02_The-AI-Act-and-emerging-EU-digital-acquis.pdf> accessed 7 February 2024.

48 Luciano Floridi, 'The European Legislation on AI: A Brief Analysis of Its Philosophical Approach' in Jakob Mökander and Marta Ziosi (eds), *The 2021 Yearbook of the Digital Ethics Lab* (Springer 2022) 1–8.

(ii) high risk, (iii) limited risk, and (iv) low or minimal risk.[49] Under this approach, AI applications would be regulated only as strictly necessary to address specific levels of risk. Like the OECD Principles, the EU AI Act aims to ensure the transparency and explainability of AI. Datasets must be free of errors, and humans must be able to 'fully understand' how AI systems work. Nevertheless, sometimes even AI creators do not fully understand how AI programs arrive at their conclusions, while tech companies are uncomfortable about giving external auditors or regulators access to their source code and algorithms. Despite some loopholes and exceptions (e.g., facial recognition by the police is banned unless the images are captured with a delay or the technology is being used to find missing children), the EU AI Act could be used as a template for other jurisdictions,[50] as was the EU General Data Protection Regulation (GDPR) – the block's most famous tech export – which has been copied everywhere from California to India.

With the adoption of the EU AI Act, a significant transition has occurred from relying on soft-law principles to implementing hard-law regulations. This shift is deemed timely and fitting, especially in light of the numerous risks associated with the rapid advancement of AI technologies. As society increasingly integrates AI into various sectors, including sustainable finance, there is a necessity for robust oversight. Therefore, the next logical progression involves the creation of a comprehensive supranational authority dedicated to overseeing AI. This authority would be vested with powers and responsibilities, encompassing policy development, threat assessment, risk management, standard-setting, monitoring, and enforcement. Such an entity is essential to ensure that AI is deployed in a manner that prioritises ethical considerations and mitigates potential harms in many areas, including sustainable finance. The EU AI office or European AI Board, as part of their broader mandate, will play a key role in overseeing AI applications within this realm too, thus preventing potential negative impacts such as biased decision-making, unsustainable investments, and environmental degradation. Furthermore, the supranational AI authority will promote the establishment of clear guidelines and common standards for AI applications, including in sustainable finance, fostering trust and confidence among stakeholders, investors, and consumers.

Of course, not all jurisdictions will follow the model of the EU AI Act.[51] In the United States of America (USA), the National Artificial Intelligence Initiative Act of 2020

49 Under Art. 5, unacceptable risk, such as the use of AI for social scoring, is prohibited. Under Art. 6 & ss, high risk, such as the use of AI in education, justice, or immigration, requires a conformity assessment. Under Art. 52, limited risk, such as the use of chatbots and deepfakes, requires respect for transparency. Under Art. 69, low or minimal risk, such as the use of AI in video games and spam filters, requires the adoption and implementation of a code of conduct.

50 Anu Bradford, *The Brussels Effect: How the European Union Rules the World* (Oxford University Press New York 2020).

51 Corinne Cath et al., 'Artificial Intelligence and the "Good society": The US, EU, and UK Approach' (2018) 24(2) Science and Engineering Ethics 505.

follows a non-interfering approach to AI with the goal of fostering research and design in this area.[52] One should not expect the US Congress to act anytime soon on AI regulation, since there is little chance such action would garner support from US Senators or House Representatives, although this risks creating 'conditions for a race to the bottom in irresponsible AI' in the US.[53] Indeed, a 2022 report by the US Federal Trade Commission raised serious concerns that even well-intended AI uses can be inaccurate, biased, and discriminatory, enabling increasingly invasive forms of surveillance.[54] In October 2023, President Biden issued an Executive Order on AI outlining seven principles for the development and use of AI across the federal government.[55] These principles emphasise fairness, non-discrimination, accountability, and public participation, but don't directly impose regulations, and it is not clear how and when federal agencies will extend their authority into the AI space under the Executive Order. In the UK, the 2021 National AI Strategy and the 2022 AI Regulation Policy Paper aimed to promote innovation and establish a risk-based approach to AI.[56] The UK does not have specific laws designed to regulate AI, but it is partially regulated through a combination of legal and regulatory requirements created for other purposes that also apply to AI technologies. Based on these requirements, some regulators in the UK, such as the Information Commissioner's Office and the Equality and Human Rights Commission, have taken steps to promote responsible AI use by making AI a strategic priority in their plans and issuing guidance on how existing legislation governs the use of new technologies, such as AI, in automated decision-making.[57]

---

52 There is also an EU–US tech partnership (the Trade and Technology Council) designed for mutual understanding of the principles underlying trustworthy and responsible AI; see <https://commission.europa.eu/strategy-and-policy/priorities-2019-2024/stronger-europe-world/eu-us-trade-and-technology-council_en> accessed 7 February 2024.

53 Andrew Ross Sorkin et al., 'Why lawmakers aren't rushing to police AI' *New York Times* (3 March 2023) <https://www.nytimes.com/2023/03/03/business/dealbook/lawmakers-ai-regulations.html> accessed 7 February 2024.

54 Federal Trade Commission, 'Combatting Online Harms Through Innovation' (Federal Trade Commission Report to Congress, September 2022) <https://www.ftc.gov/reports/combatting-online-harms-through-innovation> accessed 7 February 2024.

55 Joseph R Biden Jr, 'Executive Order on the Safe, Secure, and Trustworthy Development and Use of Artificial Intelligence' (The White House, 30 October 2023) <https://www.whitehouse.gov/briefing-room/presidential-actions/2023/10/30/executive-order-on-the-safe-secure-and-trustworthy-development-and-use-of-artificial-intelligence/> accessed 7 February 2024.

56 Department for Digital, Culture, Media & Sport and Damian Collins MP, 'UK sets out proposals for new AI rulebook to unleash innovation and boost public trust in the technology' (UK Government Press Release, 18 July 2022) <https://www.gov.uk/government/news/uk-sets-out-proposals-for-new-ai-rulebook-to-unleash-innovation-and-boost-public-trust-in-the-technology> accessed 7 February 2024. See also Data Protection and Digital Information Bill 143 2022–23 (HL Bill 30, as introduced).

57 For example, UK data protection law includes requirements for 'automated decision-making' and the processing of personal data that cover the development and training

V. Putting it all together: implementing changes and a new sense of responsibility

AI can foster the growth of ESG investing in multiple ways. It can help analyse the performance of sustainable investments in different asset classes using novel and alternative datasets. It can be combined with new technologies, including distributed ledgers, the IoT, and smart contracts, to ensure greater data quality, consistency, and comparability. AI can also measure and track ESG-related risks and impacts facing companies and investor portfolios. Nevertheless, serious risks remain, such as the risk of greenwashing, challenges to cybersecurity and privacy, the lack of coordination between regulators, and the use of adversarial AI. For these reasons, we argue in favour of a new sense of responsibility and for respecting some core principles governing the use of AI in the context of ESG investing. By merging established ESG principles and standards with emerging standards and principles specific to AI, such as those outlined by the OECD and EU frameworks, we arrive at the following core principles.

First, legal provisions and rigorous standards should apply both to AI processes and ESG decision-making. Second, external oversight and verification mechanisms need to ensure respect for regulations and standards, both for AI and ESG. Third, ESG decisions made by AI tools should be intelligible and explicable to investors, regulators, and oversight mechanisms in accordance with the principles of transparency and explainability. Fourth, regulation, oversight, and verification must function both at the national and international levels to cover cross-border cases. Indeed, regulating technological and financial innovation and imposing restrictions at the national level alone would be ineffective, since companies would simply opt for investing, doing research, and developing their products and services in jurisdictions that lack such restrictions.[58] In any event, regulatory intervention requires consultation with and the involvement of all major stakeholders (big tech companies, start-ups, financial markets, as well as academic institutions, non-governmental organisations, and civil

---

of AI; the Online Safety Bill (HL Bill 87, 2022-23(Rev)) also contains provisions relating to the design and use of algorithms. See the UK Secretary of State for Digital, Culture, Media and Sport, 'Establishing a pro-innovation approach to regulating AI' (UK Government Policy Paper, 18 July 2022) <https://www.gov.uk/government/publications/establishing-a-pro-innovation-approach-to-regulating-ai/establishing-a-pro-innovation-approach-to-regulating-ai-policy-statement> accessed 7 February 2024.

58 In an interview with the Washington Post in 2015, Dr Peter H Diamandis, pioneer in the field of innovation and incentive competitions, correctly pointed out that 'the notion that the government can regulate against [technological innovation] is a fallacy. If the government regulates against use of drones or stem cells or artificial intelligence, all that means is that the work and the research leave the borders of that country and go someplace else'; see Jena McGregor, 'How to go after big, bold goals' *Washington Post* (19 February 2015) <https://www.washingtonpost.com/news/on-leadership/wp/2015/02/19/the-xprize-founders-how-to-guide-for-going-after-big-bold-goals/> accessed 7 February 2024.

society) in the development of new principles and rules. By working collaboratively to establish clear principles and standards for AI in the context of ESG investing, we can ensure that these technologies are used to create positive social and environmental outcomes, mitigate potential risks, and foster a new era of responsible and sustainable finance powered by AI.

3 From traditional to decentralized governance in the crypto environment: legal framework for decentralized autonomous organizations and decentralized finance

Rolf H Weber

I. Introduction

New business models based on decentralized infrastructures such as distributed ledger technology (DLT) have caused the creation of the buzzword "decentralization". The technological advances allowing decentralized governance mainly concern challenges to corporate law and financial market regulations.

This contribution addresses the decentralized autonomous organizations (DAOs) and the decentralized finance (DeFi) business models and develops the contours of the legal environment for these new appearances. Since the traditional normative framework is based on centralized structures, regulations are addressed to the market participants. In a world in which intermediaries do not play any important role anymore, such a concept is ill-driven. Moreover, the services as such do not comply with the quality and security requirements. Therefore, regulators of financial markets have begun to develop new, more appropriate rules.

Organizational rules should also be adapted. The existing legal provisions design a hierarchical corporate structure with individuals conducting business governance. In the future, automated and autonomous procedures within horizontal networks will gain importance; therefore, company law needs to be partly redesigned.

II. Technical design of a decentralized environment

A. Decentralized structures of networks

The decentralized architectures are based on the distributed ledger technology (DLT) infrastructure having a large number of so-called nodes.[1] These nodes are interconnected in order to form a network, but they run independently representing the participants on the platform. In other words, the nodes that include interests, values, perceptions, knowledge, and legal sources interact with each other and build those ties that shape the network structure.[2]

According to economic theory, centralized networks are arguably the most efficient structures; centralization leads to positive network externalities.[3] Nevertheless, it cannot be overlooked that centralized networks are also vulnerable if the hub fails (for example, in case of a heavy cyberattack).[4] Therefore, decentralized networks based on the DLT infrastructure do have some operative advantages; however, the decentralized access structure also offers potential access points for any kind of cyberattack.

For technical reasons, a given network is suitable to be divided into clusters (subnetworks). The different types of networks can be described as follows:[5]

- *Centralized structure*: All nodes are directly linked to the central node.
- *Decentralized structure*: The nodes are linked to other nodes that in turn are linked together, building a star structure.
- *Distributed structure*: Each node has a link to two or more other nodes, building a trellis structure.

The decentralized network structure is the most common form of the yet existing DAOs; this structure, even if less efficient, has the advantage of enhanced resilience since the network does not depend on a single network or node.[6] But theoretically, the

1 This subsection is based on Rolf H Weber, 'Global Financial Architecture and Decentralized CBDC Regimes' in Christos V Gortsos and Rolf Sethe (eds), *Central Bank Digital Currencies* (EIZ Publishing 2023) 13, 17–18.

2 See also Burkard Eberlein and others, 'Transnational Business Governance Interactions: Conceptualization and Framework for Analysis' (2013) 8(1) Regulation and Governance 1 et seq.

3 Andrew Sheng, 'Financial Crisis and Global Governance: A Network Analysis' (2010) World Bank Commission on Growth and Development Working Paper No. 67, 1, 4 <https://documents1.worldbank.org/curated/en/143071468174883223/pdf/577660NWP0Box353767B01PUBLIC10gcwp067web.pdf> accessed 26 February 2024.

4 For a general overview, see Rolf H Weber and Okan Yildiz, '*Cybersicherheit und Cyber-Resilienz in den Finanzmärkten*' (EIZ Publishing 2022) 7 et seq.

5 See also the charts of Sheng (n 3), 4.

6 Heng Wang and Simin Gao, 'The Future of the International Financial System: The Emerging CBDC Network and its Impact on Regulation' (2024) 18(1) Regulation & Governance 1, 5, also include the notion of ties in their description of networks.

form of the distributed network would also be an option even if it is less probable that such a network will be implemented. At any rate, however, the network structure will be flat or multipolar.[7]

For the time being, it appears to be uncertain how exactly the different decentralized networks will be linked to each other on a cross-border scale, that is, how the interoperability is globally established. This aspect depends on the number of nodes, how often those nodes interact, and the network structure (i.e., the network "density"); in addition, clusters (subgroups) may not necessarily be based on a model of hubs if interoperability can be guaranteed otherwise.[8]

B. Smart contracts as transactional mechanisms

Transactions on decentralized network structures cannot be executed in the traditional way, for example by concluding oral or written contracts. Moreover, the transactional mechanism is based on so-called smart contracts. According to an often-used saying, smart contracts are neither smart nor contracts.[9]

From a technical perspective, smart contracts are computerized transaction protocols capable of autonomously running the transactions upon the triggering of certain conditions. They automate the formation and/or execution of contractual obligations, or more precisely, of their operational (as opposed to purely normative or non-operational) components.[10] Since their contents are reflected in the chosen computer program logic, smart contracts are seen as computer routines that automatically execute the contractual terms without the intervention of third persons.[11]

Even if the program code of a smart contract can encompass a wide variety of contractual relations and obligations, its technical characteristics are rigid, encompassing the following typical elements:[12]

- *Self-execution*: The smart contract is executed based on the chosen program logic and the cryptographic protocols.
- *Self-determination*: Since the smart contract is determined by the code (transactional logic), interventions by third parties are in principle not possible and the counterparty is usually not known (anonymous program).

---

7 See Thomas Oatly and others, 'The Political Economy of Global Finance: A Network Model' (2013) 11(1) Perspectives on Politics 133, 135–137.

8 For additional details see Wang and Gao (n 6), 6.

9 See Rolf H Weber, 'Smart Contracts: Do We Need New Legal Rules?' in Alberto de Franceschi and Reiner Schulze (eds), *Digital Revolution – New Challenges for Law* (Beck and Nomos 2019) 299, 301.

10 Primavera De Filippi and Aaron Wright, *Blockchain and the Law* (Harvard University Press 2019) 72 et seq.

11 Max Raskin, 'The Law and Legality of Smart Contracts' (2017) 1 Georgetown Law and Technology Review 305, 311.

12 Weber (n 9), 302.

- *Unchangeability*: Because transactions on the blockchain cannot be reversed, it is correspondingly impossible to change the terms of a smart contract.
- *Digital performance*: Smart contracts allow the "transfer" of digitally referenced goods and services, not a performance in the real world.

The key characteristics relevant for decentralized business models are the anonymity (self-determination) and the unchangeability of transactions. These two elements substantially deviate from the well-known characteristics in company law (for example, the personalization of membership) and in financial market law (for example, the regulation of institutions, not of services).

C. Impact of the decentralization on governance structures

For the time being, decentralized business models are mainly discussed in the context of financial markets or the application of financial regulation, specifically DeFi.[13] However, it should not be underestimated that similar normative challenges are also occurring in the area of company law, particularly in the design of corporate forms (within the given normative types). The corresponding new legal questions merit being addressed by academic circles around the globe; legal certainty is needed at the global level (in view of the many regulations governing finance law) as well as at the national level (containing the main normative foundations for company law at present).

Decentralized and distributed systems allow decentralized governance with transparent on-chain mechanisms. Neither a representative nor a central organization empowered to make decisions is needed. But on-chain governance has the potential to disrupt the way businesses are organized and may lead to IT-based decision-making processes.[14] Particularly, on-chain governance is seen as an appropriate model that, for example, provides an adequate system (i) for managing and implementing changes to the DLT infrastructure or the network design, (ii) for encoding new elements into the protocols, and (iii) for updating nodes of participants.[15] See Table 3.1 on page 43.

The new technological (decentralized and distributed) infrastructures, as well as the corresponding organizational models, will have a remarkable impact on company law and financial market regulation.[16] (i) The existing numerus clausus of corporate forms is no longer easily suitable for new business models, such as the differently implemented DAOs; in view of the needs given in reality, flexible governance forms need to be developed and implemented. (ii) In the field of financial law, regulators have

---

13 A very extensive analysis has been undertaken by David Meirich, *Regulatorische Einordnung von Decentralized Finance* (Schulthess 2023); for further details, see section IV below.

14 Therefore, the new legal challenges caused by decentralization are an important issue in the research agenda pursued by the book.

15 For a general description of the governance processes, see Meirich (n 13), 89 et seq.

16 Company law is discussed in section III below.

begun to consider alternative regulatory designs, but the respective efforts have not yet advanced very far.[17]

Table 3.1 Traditional and on-chain governance

Traditional governance is characterized by the following elements	On-chain governance encompasses the following designs
Hierarchical	Horizontal and not structured
Based on specific roles	Only very few fixed roles
Static power structure	Quite fluid power structure
Trust related to humans	Trust related to technology
Political impact possible	Mostly apolitical

Source: Own elaboration.

D. Consequences for the legal framework

Decentralized structures lead to fragmentation at first instance. A central body coordinating the activities of the market participants does not exist anymore and the traditional intermediaries in financial markets are losing their coordinating function. However, fragmentation does not mean that coherence and interoperability do not play an important role anymore; in contrast, standardization is an important tool in the decentralized environment.[18] For good reasons, Central Banks around the globe are developing, testing, and implementing interoperability mechanisms that allow – at least in wholesale, not yet in retail markets – the circulation of Central Bank Digital Currencies (CBDCs).[19]

The recent technological developments have a major impact on company and financial law, both of which are based on centralized legal and regulatory designs. Companies are organized in hierarchical structures leading to a governance model that flows

17 Financial market regulations are discussed in section IV below.

18 For a general overview of the importance and function of standardization, see Won Sang Lee and So Young Sohn, 'Effects of Standardization on the Evolution of Information and Communications Technology' (2018) 132 Technological Forecasting and Social Change 308 et seq.

19 Weber (n 1), 25–26.

from the top to the bottom. Similarly, in financial law, the legal framework attaches regulation and supervision to the services' providers, who are the intermediaries for financial transactions. However, this approach is confronted with the fact that the ongoing decentralization of services' offerings makes the function of intermediaries evanishing. In particular, the difficulties in adequately implementing the well-known principle of "same business, same risks, same rules" are increasing.

Two consequences can be drawn from these observations: (i) Company law has to develop possibilities that enable "group members" interested in joining their forces to agree on a corporate form that reflects the decentralized structure in the governance of legal bodies; (ii) forward-looking financial market regulations should focus more on the services themselves instead of the service providers.

Even if authorities are struggling with such a new approach, it should be acknowledged that academics have begun to analyze and assess potential normative solutions. However, additional efforts need to be invested in order to design a new regulatory framework. These issues build a research agenda for the future.

III. New legal "cloth" for decentralized autonomous organizations?

The first topic to be addressed in the research agenda concerns the challenges caused by the newly established "decentralized autonomous organizations" (DAOs) for corporate law.[20]

A. Characteristics of decentralized autonomous organizations

So far, a unanimously agreed-upon definition for a DAO does not yet exist. Often, a DAO is described as a new form of an open, scalable, and self-organized network that is coordinated through crypto-economic incentives and self-executing codes on the DLT infrastructure with the objective of reaching jointly agreed objectives.[21] In an ideal setting, the management and organization of a DAO are implemented into smart

20 Assessing corporate law means, at first instance, analyzing which national law is applicable. This legal question is answered by the conflict of laws rules (international private law). The respective analysis cannot be done herein, but the author deals with the conflict of laws rules in a separate article (Rolf H Weber, 'Is There a Need for DAO Regulation in Switzerland?' in Florence Guillaume (ed.), *Decentralized Autonomous Organizations in the Legal Landscape: From Decentralized Governance to Legal Frontiers* (Edward Elgar 2025) forthcoming). Hereinafter, Swiss law serves as the main references point (see n 25).

21 Biyan Mienert, *Dezentrale autonome Organisationen (DAOs) und Gesellschaftsrecht*, Thesis Marburg (Mohr Siebeck 2022), 52.

contract programs, resulting in algorithms executing, surveilling, and enforcing the decisions, thus eliminating the need for directors/managers of the entity.[22]

A DAO realizes the self-determination characteristic of smart contracts[23] by providing for DLT-based voting and managing rights. Therefore, most DAOs issue a membership or participation token which can be used for cooperation in the governance mechanisms and for voting. However, at present, completely autonomous DAOs do not seem to exist in reality; usually, at least a certain influence of natural persons is foreseen in the decision-making processes. Nevertheless, a DAO must have a certain autonomy, even if the organizational structures are complex, so that it is able to hold and transfer digital assets.[24] In addition, decentralization makes it difficult for a single person or a single group to control a DAO since majority decisions are taken in a transparent, "controllable" process, which also excludes the occurrence of the well-known principal-agent problem as seen in traditional companies.

B. Numerus clausus of available legal forms

1. *Basic criterion of legal personality*

Most legislations around the globe, including Swiss law, only acknowledge a limited number of forms that can be used if a company is to be incorporated, i.e., new forms not foreseen in the legislation cannot be "invented" due to the so-called "numerus clausus" of legal forms.[25] Therefore, members of a DAO are not necessarily in a position to implement the governance structures potentially best suited for the intentions and needs of the involved participants.

The closed number of legal forms concerns companies with legal personality, making the company a subject of law and limiting the liability of its members. Swiss law, like most Western jurisdictions, not only recognizes companies with legal personality after incorporation but also company-like "groups" normatively based on the (individual) personality of the involved members.[26]

---

22 Mienert (n 21), 53; for a general overview, see also Aaron Wright, 'The Rise of Decentralized Autonomous Organizations: Opportunities and Challenges' (2021) 4(2) Stanford Journal of Blockchain Law & Policy 1, 4 et seq.

23 See above subsection II.B.

24 Stephan D Meyer, 'Dezentrale Autonome Organisationen (DAOs) und das Gesellschaftsrecht der Zukunft' [2023] Aktuelle Juristische Praxis 319, 322–323.

25 Contrary to financial market regulations, company law still is national law to a large extent, even if, for example, several EU Directives are in force and the accounting rules are fairly harmonized through international standardization organizations. As a Swiss law expert, therefore, the author has to rely on Swiss law and Swiss legal sources in section III; nevertheless, it may be said that most civil law countries have similar legal provisions in the company law field.

26 Meyer (n 24), 328–329.

The main form of a "group" without legal personality is the simple partnership. The establishment of a legal partnership is easy, and its members do not have to fulfill formalities. The governance can be agreed upon by the partners. The main disadvantage of this form consists of the fact that each partner is fully liable for the obligations, particularly the debts, of the partnership, even if entered into by another partner.[27] Consequently, most members of a DAO might not be inclined to build a partnership but rather to make a choice between any of the forms with legal personality.

2. *Stock corporation*

The most common capital company in Switzerland is the stock corporation ("Aktiengesellschaft").[28] But this form appears unsuitable for DAOs for several reasons: (i) The incorporation requires the fulfillment of extensive formal requirements; (ii) many provisions are of a mandatory nature and cannot be waived, in particular regarding the management and governance of the company by directors and officers; (iii) management by a member-controlled algorithm is legally not possible.[29]

3. *Company with limited liability*

The alternative type, namely the company with limited liability ("Gesellschaft mit beschränkter Haftung")[30] causes similar problems. Even if the formal requirements are less extensive and the flexibility for the governance structure is greater, a relatively tied "cloth" exists. Insofar, at least under Swiss law, this corporate type is not a recommendable form for DAOs.

Such an appreciation does not overlook the fact that, on the international level, certain examples of the model of a limited liability company do exist in legislative instruments. After Vermont had introduced a Blockchain-Based Limited Liability Company in 2018[31] and OpenLaw presented a concept of a Legal DAO (LAO) in Delaware,[32] it was Wyoming that offered the opportunity to be officially registered and recognized as a DAO Limited Liability Company (LLC) since 1 July 2021, being the first legal framework for DAOs.[33] In contrast to the traditional LLC, the management can be

---

27 Arthur Meier-Hayoz and Peter Forstmoser, *Schweizerisches Gesellschaftsrecht* (13th edn, Stämpfli 2023), § 12 n 37 and n 90.

28 Art. 620 of the Swiss Code of Obligations (CO).

29 Mienert (n 21), 125 et seq.

30 Art. 772 CO.

31 See Vermont General Assembly, 'The Vermont Statutes Online: § 4173 Authority; requirements, Title 11 Corporations, Partnerships and Associations, Chapter 25 Limited Liability Companies, Subchapter 12 Blockchain-Based Limited Liability Companies' <https://legislature.vermont.gov/statutes/section/11/025/04173> accessed 26 February 2024.

32 See 'The LAO: A For-Profit, Limited Liability Autonomous Organization' (*Medium*, 3 September 2019) <https://medium.com/openlawofficial/the-lao-a-for-profit-limited-liability-autonomous-organization-9eae89c9669c> accessed 26 February 2024.

33 See Decentralized Autonomous Organizations Bill 2021 (Supplement to the Wyoming Limited Liability Company Act: Decentralized Autonomous Organizations) SF0038

assumed not only by individuals but also by a combination of individuals and self-executing algorithmic programs. An online setup is possible; thereby, the "identifier" of the used smart contract must be indicated, and the manner in which algorithmic processes work must be described; however, as a traditional element, a "registered agent" is required to be appointed in Wyoming.[34]

The Wyoming Statute requires that several elements be regulated in the Articles of Organization and that all smart contracts used by the DAO must subsequently be renewable or adaptable ("capable of being updated, modified or otherwise upgraded").[35] The Articles of Association of the LLC need to state the nature of the processes for adjusting and revising the smart contracts and the rules for dispute resolution. Furthermore, it is possible to implement a so-called Operating Agreement containing more extensive provisions in the form of a smart contract.[36] The entry into and the exit from the DAO LLC automatically happen with the acquisition or the disposal of a right of ownership, a membership interest, or other property. In the meantime, Utah and New Hampshire introduced similar DAO Statutes based on the limited liability company concept.

Theoretically, the provisions of the Wyoming Statute could also be introduced into Swiss law. However, on the one hand, the number of amendments would be quite substantial; on the other hand, some formal requirements, such as the registration of an agent, limit the flexibility of DAOs as a centralizing element. Therefore, the Wyoming LLC does not seem to be the most suitable model for Swiss law.

4. *Cooperative*

A further potential form is the cooperative, being an association organized as a legal entity of an unaffiliated number of persons (but at least seven) or commercial enterprises whose main objective is to promote or safeguard the economic interests of its members by way of mutual self-help or for charitable purposes.[37] Unlike the partnership, the cooperative is independent of the entry and departure of its members. Looking from the purpose and the investment possibilities angle, the cooperative would often fit the needs of DAO members.

But as a disadvantage, the formal requirements for its incorporation can constitute a remarkable hurdle; in addition, some mandatory tasks are imposed on the corporate bodies, specifically the administration, limiting decentralized governance.[38] This

<https://www.wyoleg.gov/Legislation/2021/SF0038>; for additional information, see also the FAQ list of the government <https://sos.wyo.gov/Business/Docs/DAOs_FAQs.pdf> both accessed 26 February 2024.

34 Wyoming Statutes, Section 17-31-106.

35 Wyoming Statutes, Sections 17-31-106 and 17-31-109.

36 Wyoming Statutes, Section 17-31-108.

37 Art. 828 CO.

38 Meyer (n 24), 331.

problem can also not be overcome with the European Cooperative Society (SCE) as recently proposed by European Union (EU) representatives.[39] Furthermore, since a cooperative cannot issue certificated shares (in the same way as a corporation), the new provisions of the Swiss DLT Act in respect to the transfer and, in particular, of the cancellation of securities do not apply.[40]

5. *Foundation*

Since the time when Vitalik Buterin incorporated the Ethereum Foundation, this legal form has been judged as the ideal vehicle for the execution of blockchain activities.[41] Parallels to a DAO can be seen insofar as the assets are tied due to the principle of non-alteration.[42] Even if the purpose of a foundation can be changed, following a formal procedure including some caveats,[43] the assets are largely protected against misuse or unintended modification of the purpose. Furthermore, the liability is centralized in the foundation since it is a legal person, that is, the beneficiaries cannot become legally liable.[44] Insofar, the form of the foundation is well suited for decentralized blockchain-based projects (and has therefore, subsequent to Ethereum, often been used by large protocols and applications projects).

However, the form of the foundation also bears several disadvantages for DAOs. Tensions exist between the management by the board and the use of algorithms for decision-making. Furthermore, since the foundation does not have any members in conceptual terms, it is not to be excluded that additional counterparts (persons and companies) are acting as DAO members and could become subject to personal liability.[45] Consequently, even if the foundation as a structuring form is conceivable, it might often not satisfy the requirements of a DAO.

6. *Association*

The most suitable legal form, even if some adaptations to the DAO's needs are necessary, appears to be the association, being flexible as far as governance is concerned and having a basic democratic character; therefore, this legal form will be discussed in more detail hereinafter.

---

39 See BTC ECHO, 'Home Page' <https://www.btc-echo.de/> accessed 26 February 2024.

40 Federal Council of Switzerland, Dispatch to the Distributed Ledger Technology Act of 27 November 2019, Bundesblatt 2020, 233, 277.

41 Art. 80 of the Swiss Civil Code (CC).

42 Meyer (n 24), 330.

43 Art. 86 CC.

44 A further advantage for the trustworthiness of foundations can consist of supervision by a special Federal authority with respective surveillance functions (Art. 84 CC).

45 Meyer (n 24), 330.

C. Suitability and adaptation of association law

1. *Basic suitability*

According to Swiss law, an association is composed of members and has legal personality. The purposes of associations can be very broad[46] and encompass the main objectives aimed at by a DAO. The formalities in connection with the foundation are quite slim (for example, no formal notarization). The entry into the Commercial Register is (only) required if a business is conducted or (since 2023) if assets abroad are directly or indirectly collected or distributed;[47] the new requirement could be relevant for DAOs. However, legal doctrine is of the opinion that deposited membership fees or issued tokens do not qualify as asset collection or distribution.[48]

The structure of an association is quite flexible, and the organization can be adapted to the needs of a DAO as specifically outlined hereinafter and partly seen in practice.[49] A major advantage of an association consists in the possibility of excluding any liability of its members (in contrast to the simple partnership), that is to say, in establishing a "legal wrapper".[50]

Two different structures are available for the implementation of the relations between an association and a DAO: On the one hand, a DAO can exist as a vehicle next to an association; on the other hand, the DAO can act as an organ of the association.[51] The limitation of personal liability is more effective if a close identity between the legal structure and the members of the joint entity is designed. However, in such a case, the complexity is increased,[52] since membership in the DAO and in the association must be achieved and reflected in the applicable smart contract.

2. *Desirable adaptations*

The DAO as a peer-to-peer organization should be structured as decentralized as possible, that is to say, the tasks of the legal bodies of an association must be designed in a way that centralization is only applicable if mandatory law so requires. The flexibility of the rules governing the general assembly and the governance by administrators of an association is relatively high; however, some adaptations to the specific needs of a DAO should be implemented. Depending on the concrete circumstances,

46 Art. 60 CC; for more details see Rolf H Weber, 'Neues "Kleid" für Dezentrale Autonome Organisationen?' [2024] Weblaw Jusletter, 3 June, nos 24 et seq.

47 Art. 61 para. 2 no. 3 CC.

48 Meyer (n 24), 331.

49 For a project which was launched in practice in 2016, see Andreas Glarner, Thomas Linder, and Luka Müller, 'Decentralized Autonomous Association (DAA)' (*MME*, 4 May 2020) <https://www.mme.ch/de-ch/magazin/artikel/decentralized-autonomous-association-daa> accessed 26 February 2024.

50 Art. 71 CC.

51 Meyer (n 24), 332 with a respective graph.

52 The complexity is caused by the fact that membership in the DAO, as well as in the association, must be achieved and reflected in the applicable smart contract.

it is recommendable to consider the following aspects when preparing the Articles of Association:[53]

- To the extent feasible, meetings of the general assembly should be conducted in a digital or peer-to-peer manner. A respective possibility consists of the realization of on-chain voting mechanisms. If properly organized with the right to submit motions, express voices, etc., and with a method to establish a safe voting system, such digital assemblies are widely accepted. The general meeting can be replaced by blockchain-based peer-to-peer structures; even if the ballot vote ("Urabstimmung") is not provided for by law, it is acknowledged in legal practice.[54]
- In the decentralized environment of a DAO, the powers of the executive board and potential management need to be limited. The flexibility is broad since the board of an association does not have mandatory and inalienable powers. A certain problem for DAOs could only be caused by the new Article 69a CC requiring the board of directors to keep accounts.[55]
- A special issue concerns the question of whether the one-person/one-vote system governing an association could and/or should be replaced by a voting system based on the number of tokens held by a person. According to Article 67 paragraph 1 CC, all members of an association have the same voting rights at a general meeting. However, legal doctrine accepts a deviation from this principle; that is to say, the Articles of Association can provide for multiple and plural voting rights. Therefore, the aspect of introducing voting rights differentiations in DAOs becomes a relevant issue to be discussed by its founding members, since the respective rules need to be clearly stated (and reflected in the smart contracts);[56] a similar solution could also be foreseen for the liquidation proceeds.
- Finally, the ongoing "identity" between the members of the association and the members of the DAO in a double-tier structure must be secured. If somebody becomes a member of the association, the holding of a DAO token should be attached to the respective process. The solution might be technically difficult, but it can be implemented since compliance with a specific form is not required.[57]

In a nutshell, the legal form of an association does not solve all problems of each DAO; however, depending on the concrete circumstances, several possibilities exist to adapt this legal "cloth" to the practical needs. Insofar, the main purpose of the legal drafting

---

53 The following text is based on the detailed considerations of Meyer (n 24), 332–335 and of Weber (n 46), nos 27–38.

54 See Hans Michael Riemer, *BK (Berner Kommentar) zum schweizerischen Privatrecht: Die Vereine Art. 60–69 ZGB, Art. 712m Abs. 2 ZGB* (2nd edn, Stämpfli 2023) Art. 66 n 42 et seq.

55 Meyer (n 24), 333 and Weber (n 46), no 36.

56 Riemer (n 54), Art. 67 n 10 et seq.

57 See Urs Scherrer and Rafael Brägger, 'Die Vereine Art. 60-79' in Thomas Geiser and Christiana Fountoulakis (eds), BSK (Basler Kommentar) *Zivilgesetzbuch I* (7th edn, Helbing 2022) Art. 70 n 33.

in the smart contract should consist of bringing the technically implemented DAO governance in line with the legal association governance.[58]

D. New legal forms

Theoretically, it would also be possible that legislators create a new legal form that meets the needs of DAOs. Wyoming has done so with a legal entity that is close to a company with limited liability.[59] Switzerland could also try to be innovative and develop completely new rules.

In 2021, a "Model Law for Decentralized Autonomous Organizations" was published by a group of internationally eminent experts under the auspices of the Coalition of Automated Legal Applications.[60] This Model Law, containing 20 Articles with corresponding comments thereto, is based on the concept of a DAO with legal personality ("a legal entity separate and distinct from its Members", Article 2) that meets its liabilities through its on-chain and off-chain assets. The formal requirements for its incorporation are relatively low, and generally open-source formats are preferred (Article 4). A DAO may have multiple classes of participation rights (Article 7). The internal organization of a DAO can be flexible without mandatory requirements to convene a general meeting or to have physical in-person meetings (Article 12). In addition, a DAO is not required to have administrators, including a board of directors or a trustee (Article 13). Furthermore, persons who make discretionary decisions are not subject to an implicit fiduciary status (Article 15).

This academic "Model Law" contains many provisions reflecting the needs of DAOs. As long as the legislators in Europe are not inclined to introduce a new legal form into a formal statute by extending the existing "numerus clausus" of legal forms, which is not likely to happen in the near future, the "Model Law" can serve as inspiration for the designers of Articles of Association applicable in the context of a DAO. Since the respective design of rules is complicated and legal doctrine has not yet advanced its research by deepening the challenging legal questions, ample room remains for further activities in the research agenda.[61]

---

58 Meyer (n 24), 335.

59 See above subsection III.B.3.

60 Coalition of Automated Legal Applications, 'Model Law for Decentralized Autonomous Organizations' (*coala*, 2021) <https://coala.global/wp-content/uploads/2022/03/DAO-Model-Law.pdf> accessed 26 February 2024.

61 Since March 2022, the experts who drafted the DAO Model Law have continued their work in further developing the proposed provisions, but a new version of the Model Law is not yet available. Very recently, Swiss academics proposed to introduce a specific DAO Statute based on the DAO Model Law in Switzerland: Nina Reiser and Basil Wälchli, 'Rechtliche Erfassung von Dezentralen Autonomen Organisationen' [2024] 120 (16/17 and 19) Schweizerische Juristen-Zeitung 755 et seq. and 863 et seq. (872–876).

IV. New regulatory framework for decentralized finance?

A. Technological and legal challenges

In recent practice, decentralization has mainly become a discussion topic in the financial markets' context. The DLT serves as the cornerstone for DeFi models. Generally speaking, DeFi is a concept that employs public blockchain and smart contract platforms to create more open, robust, transparent, and non-custodial financial infrastructures.[62] The traditional approach of imposing regulation and supervision on financial services providers reaches its limits since decentralization attempts to make financial intermediaries obsolete.

In particular, the value chain becomes very fragmented due to the special design of the so-called decentralized applications (DApps) being a software application offering an interface for the use of the DeFi infrastructure.[63] DApps have four characteristics, namely (i) functioning by way of a direct mediation of value units, (ii) execution of transactions based on a public, permission-free blockchain, (iii) final control of the users over the assets through the existence of non-custodial wallets, and (iv) availability of a transparent and programmable architecture of combined elements. Therefore, providers can hardly rely on any measures implemented by other providers acting ahead or in parallel with each other; in such a situation, decentralization makes it very difficult to allocate regulatory requirements and responsibilities to the market participants.[64]

Not surprisingly, legislators around the globe have so far not implemented DeFi rules. As an example, the recent EU Markets in Crypto-Assets Regulation (MiCAR) does not at all address DeFi as a business model.[65] Since MiCAR is a rules-based normative

---

62 For more details see Fabian Schär, 'Decentralized Finance: On Blockchain- and Smart Contract-based Financial Markets' (2021) 103(2) Federal Reserve Bank of St. Louis Review 153 et seq.; Thomas Dünser, 'DeFi and Financial Market Regulation' (*Medium*, 22 September 2022) <https://medium.com/@tduenser/defi-and-financial-market-regulation-4ec8843619b8> accessed 26 February 2024.

63 See World Economic Forum (WEF) and Wharton Blockchain and Digital Asset Project, *Decentralized Autonomous Organization Toolkit, Insight Report* (January 2023), 3–4 and 6, <https://www.weforum.org/reports/decentralized-autonomous-organization-toolkit> accessed 26 February 2024, and Meirich (n 13), n 271.

64 For a general overview, see Dirk A Zetzsche, Douglas W Arner, and Ross P Buckley, 'Decentralized Finance' (2020) 6 Journal of Financial Regulation 172 et seq.; Katrin Schuler, Ann Sofie Cloots, and Fabian Schär, 'On DeFi and On-Chain CeFi: How (Not) to Regulate Decentralized Finance' (2024) Journal of Financial Regulation, 1, 7 et seq. <https://ssrn.com/abstract=4422473> accessed 26 February 2024; see also Meirich (n 13), nos 1395 et seq.

65 Council Regulation (EU) 2023/1114 of the European Parliament and of the Council of 31 May 2023 on markets in crypto-assets, and amending Regulations (EU) No 1093/2010 and (EU) No 1095/2010 and Directives 2013/36/EU and (EU) 2019/1937 [2023] OJ L 150/40 of 9 June 2023.

framework (with no fewer than 149 Articles), the existing provisions would have to be amended if DeFi should be included in the regulatory framework. The Swiss legal environment, being mainly principles-based, is more flexible and could assess DeFi business models by interpreting existing rules by analogy. In view of the given legal uncertainties, the regulatory challenges occurring in the DeFi context will be addressed hereinafter; two main bodies of possible rules need to be addressed, namely the self-regulatory regime and the governmental regulation.

B. Self-regulation

Self-regulation is a generally accepted and widely recognized regulatory instrument in financial markets.[66] Self-regulation is efficient since it usually responds to real needs, mirrors the technology, and provides the opportunity to flexibly adapt the legal framework to a changing environment.[67] A further benefit consists in the fact that this regulatory model develops and establishes the rules independently of the territorial implementation, that is to say, at least in principle, self-regulation has a global reach being of major importance in the DLT and financial markets' context.

1. *Protocol standards and governance*

A major area for self-regulation is the development of and the agreement on technical protocol standards, as already realized in the electro-technical field for many decades. Internationally, the World Bank[68] and the European Union[69] advocated for the self-regulation model in the blockchain context. Apart from the protocols, harmonized technical standards are also relevant for the design of DApps.[70] For example, centralized administration must be avoided in the DeFi environment, and alternative modification variations should be possible.

---

66 For an early detailed analysis, see Rolf H Weber, 'Overcoming the Hard Law/Soft Law Dichotomy in Times of (Financial) Crises' (2012) 1(1) Journal of Governance and Regulation 8, 10–13; in the past, self-regulation has particularly been relevant in the KYC/AML context.

67 Rolf H Weber, 'Sectoral Self-Regulation as Viable Tool' in Klaus Mathis and Avishalom Tor (eds), *Law and Economics of Regulation* (Springer 2021) 25, 28–29.

68 IMF, 'The rapid growth of fintech: vulnerabilities and challenges for financial stability' (*IMF*, Global Financial Stability Report, April 2022) 82 <https://www.imf.org/en/Publications/GFSR/Issues/2022/04/19/global-financial-stability-report-april-2022> accessed 26 February 2024.

69 EUBOF, 'Legal and regulatory framework of blockchains and smart contracts' (*EUBOF*, 27 September 2019) 34–35, <https://www.eublockchainforum.eu/sites/default/files/report_legal_v1.0.pdf> accessed 26 February 2024.

70 For further details, see Schuler, Cloots, and Schär (n 64), 28 et seq., and Meirich (n 13), n 1409.

Another area of self-regulation concerns the governance encompassing the involved network participants, usually organized in and administered through a DAO.[71] Relevant issues in this context are:[72]

- A DeFi protocol must be designed in a way that a broad allocation of voting rights and adequate participation of the DAO members is made possible. The transferability of governance tokens could jeopardize this objective; therefore, non-transferable tokens should be issued to reach a higher degree of decentralization.
- If a system is implemented in which each vote is tied to a specific token (allowing the collection of many votes), the introduction of voting restrictions would be appropriate in order to avoid a potential dominance of an important token-holder and a long-term risk for the decentralization.[73]
- Furthermore, loyalty tokens could incentivize the holding of tokens over a longer period of time.
- Special transparency requirements should be foreseen, allowing verification that the implementation of rights and obligations as foreseen in the "corporate documentation" (i.e., the smart contracts) of the DAO is actually executed and that the agreed governance is applied in practice.[74]

The mentioned examples are not concluding; moreover, they show that governance is an important issue for self-regulation (and less so for governmental regulation).

2. *Certification*

The certification of protocols is another typical area for self-regulation. Private organizations (as already functioning today, for example in the electro-technical field) could act as developers and supervisors of compliance with certification standards.[75] For example, assessment bodies could certify the quality and appropriateness of DApps; with such an assessment, trust and confidence in the functionality of the respective DApps would be increased.[76]

Assessment bodies must be able to verify the reliability and the risk mitigation measures of a DApp. The protocols providing the functionalities could become the basis for

---

71 For the DAO, see section III above.

72 Meirich (n 13), nos 1418 et seq.

73 See also Ryosuke Ushida and James Angel, 'Regulatory Considerations on Centralized Aspects of DeFi Managed by DAOs' in Matthew Bernhard, Andrea Bracciali, Lewis Gudgeon, Thomas Haines, Ariah Klages-Mundt, Shin'ichiro Matsuo, Daniel Perez, Massimiliano Sala, and Sam Werner (eds), *Financial Cryptography and Data Security: FC 2021 International Workshops* (Springer 2021), 21, 34.

74 See also Claude Humbel, 'Decentralized Finance: A New Frontier of Global Financial Markets Regulation' (2022) 1 Schweizerische Zeitschrift für Gesellschafts- und Kapitalmarktrecht sowie Umstrukturierungen 9, 14.

75 Meirich (n 13), nos 1435 et seq.

76 De Filippi and Wright (n 10), 192.

quality labels. The contents of the assessments should be developed and implemented by a standardization organization accepted in the given market segment.[77]

In the form of a so-called co-regulatory approach, the financial markets supervisory authority could be partly involved in the certification mechanism. For example, it would be possible to foresee that the authority has a whitelist of accepted assessment bodies guaranteeing the necessary review quality.[78] Furthermore, the authority can be empowered to state some minimum requirements (e.g., covering modification rights for smart contracts, audits of smart contracts, financial volumes of certain DApps, reductions of complexity regarding complicated DApps, etc.) which must be met by the assessment bodies when executing the review.[79]

3. *Alternative compliance mechanisms*

Self-regulation is also suitable for the implementation of alternative compliance mechanisms to be imposed on developers of DApps. As examples, the following compliance measures can be considered:

- *Transaction analyses*: Financial market laws impose strict regulatory requirements in respect of know your customer/anti-money laundering (KYC/AML) compliance; special procedures are needed in cases of online identification. Soft law standards could develop the notion of "know your transaction" (KYT).[80]
- *Restrictions*: Access limitations could be desirable; the relevant measure is the whitelisting of acceptable wallets and the blacklisting of suspicious or even sanctioned wallets.[81] Such kinds of white- or blacklisting can technically also be implemented with respect to the immutable registered securities (Art. 974d CO).[82]
- *Custody*: The decentralized custody of the identity becomes an increasingly important need in DeFi business models. Self-regulatory standards could address topics like self-sovereign identities,[83] the zero-knowledge-proof-KYC procedures (if possible, in compliance with the applicable law),[84] and the so-called "Soulbound

77 See also Yves Mauchle, 'Die regulatorische Antwort auf Fintech: Evolution oder Revolution? Eine Verortung aktueller Entwicklungen' (2017) 6 Schweizerische Zeitschrift für Wirtschafts- und Finanzmarktrecht 810, 830.

78 See also Meirich (n 13), nos 1436–1438.

79 See also Benedikt Maurenbrecher and Benjamin Leisinger, 'Decentralized Finance (Teil 2): Ansätze einer rechtlichen Einordnung' (2022) 14 Schweizerische Juristenzeitung 704, 717.

80 For a detailed analysis, see Meirich (n 13), nos 1446 et seq.

81 See Iwa Salami, 'Challenges and Approaches to Regulating Decentralized Finance' (2021) 115 American Journal of International Law Unbound 425, 428.

82 See Swiss Blockchain Federation, Circular 2021/01 Ledger-based Securities, Updated Version of September 2021, published on 12 October 2021, no 2.2.2; see also Meirich (n 13), nos 1453 et seq.

83 For further details, see Meirich (n 13), nos 1461 et seq.

84 For further details, see Magdalena Boškić and Sebastian Hepp, 'zkKYC in Decentralized Finance (DeFi): Unter besonderer Berücksichtigung des Geldwäschereigesetzes'

Tokens" (being tokens which are issued by DApps or DAOs in the form of non-transferable "non-fungible tokens" [NFT]).[85]

C. Governmental regulation

If the self-regulatory instruments do not suffice, that is to say, if undesirable market developments occur, governmental regulation must be put in place to guarantee compliance of individual behavior with public interests. In financial markets, the delegation of responsibilities to private actors is increasingly assessed as insufficient due to the risks caused by inappropriate market conduct (misuse of economic freedom). As a consequence, a move to more governmental regulation at the cost of self-regulation can be diagnosed.

Notwithstanding this development, the distinction between hard law and soft law has become blurred during the last decade. Many forms of "coordinated" regulation (for example, co-regulation) have shown that the dichotomy between hard law and soft law must be overcome.[86] Thereby, a graduated regulatory approach calls for regimes that consider the fast-moving technological advances and the corresponding need to provide for flexibility and adaptability.[87]

1. Sandbox and experimental regulation

Since a few years ago, legislators mainly in the United Kingdom and in Switzerland, but now also on the EU level, have introduced so-called sandbox regulations in the FinTech field. Such an approach can be seen as an experimental exercise to let market forces drive the business processes within a largely designed governmental regime.[88] In the meantime, quite different sandbox regimes in several countries do exist;[89] related to the MiCAR framework in the EU, the notion of a "pilot regime" as foreseen in a separate Directive has been coined.[90]

After some time, based on a regulatory lookback, it is possible to decide whether any regulation is needed and/or which regulation should be implemented subject to an identified risk occurrence.[91] From a theoretical perspective, sufficient time should be

(2023) 2 Schweizerische Zeitschrift für Gesellschafts- und Kapitalmarktrecht sowie Umstrukturierungen 209 et seq.

85 For further details, see Meirich (n 13), nos 1477 et seq.

86 Weber (n 67), 10–13.

87 Rolf H Weber and Rainer Baisch, 'Cryptoassets: Taxonomy and Regulatory Approaches' (2023) 39 Banking and Finance Law Review 467, 476.

88 Weber and Baisch (n 87), 477 and 479.

89 See Digital Financial Services Working Group (DFSWG), 'Innovative Regulatory Approaches Toolkit' (*Alliance for Financial Inclusion (AFI)*, 7 April 2021) 14 <https://www.afi-global.org/publications/innovative-regulatory-approaches-toolkit/> accessed 26 February 2024.

90 See Dirk A Zetzsche and Jannik Woxholth, 'The DLT Sandbox under the Pilot-Regulation' (2022) 17(2) Capital Markets Law Journal 212 et seq.

91 Weber and Baisch (n 87), 479.

allocated to the sandbox (or pilot) regulation, enabling the legislator to thoroughly analyze the need for regulatory certainty and to develop a coordinated approach.[92]

In the DeFi context, it could be considered to introduce a "DeFi Sandbox" that would carve out a protected field for partial decentralization. Apart from stating an adequate time limitation, it appears to be reasonable to develop a roadmap that would strengthen the confidence in the new market and increase its transparency.[93] As limiting factors for the sandbox, the regulatory approach could provide for a maximum balance of smart contracts (leading to restrictions for liquidity pools, lending pools, and vaults) as well as a maximum number of interactive wallets. Furthermore, the implementation of alternative compliance mechanisms can be foreseen as another regulatory requirement.[94]

Any kind of sandbox, pilot, or experimental regulation makes it necessary to implement a cooperative approach between the governmental legislator and the market participants in order to continuously monitor the outcome of the chosen DeFi business models.[95]

2. *Safe harbor*

As an alternative to the sandbox regulation, the legislator could introduce safe harbor rules which allow DeFi providers to exercise their businesses without a license and without supervision for a certain period of time if potentially applicable conditions are complied with. Insofar, safe harbor rules can complement a sandbox regime.

After the given time period has elapsed, a license regime could become applicable except if the DeFi services do not reach the level requiring the application of a governmental regulatory regime.[96] In order to allow an assessment of the DeFi business activities (for example, through smart contract audits), the most important information related to the project must be made publicly available (for example, on the website) and transparency with respect of governance processes and controlling power within a DAO needs to be secured. Partly, it is also proposed that developers have to agree on some representations and warranties with regard to the technological advances and

---

92 Zetzsche and Woxholth (n 90), 23 et seq.

93 Meirich (n 13), no 1503 and nos 1506 et seq.

94 See also Christoph Krönke, 'Sandkastenspiele – "Regulatory Sandboxes" aus der Perspektive des Allgemeinen Verwaltungsrechts' (2021) 76(9) Juristen Zeitung 434, 436, and 440.

95 Stephanie Volz, 'KI Sandboxen für die Schweiz' (2022) 1 Schweizerische Zeitschrift für Wirtschafts- und Finanzmarktrecht 51, 61.

96 Meirich (n 13), nos 1516 et seq.

the maintenance of DApps.[97] Finally, appropriate data security measures and business limitations regarding liquidity risks must be implemented.[98]

3. *Extended regulatory regime*

3.1 Regulatory objectives

Due to the (desirable) interoperability of the manifold DApps, an increased intra-systemic risk can occur. The higher the deposited capital on a protocol is, the more system-relevant the protocol will be.[99] The risks concern the so-called functional or systemic protection of the financial markets. If DeFi applications should spread out and more individuals take advantage of them, the respective structural challenges will increase.[100] Furthermore, transparency is a general regulatory objective in financial markets. However, on the one hand, over-regulation should be avoided to avoid arbitrage measures by experienced market participants and, on the other hand, the regulatory mechanism should not be rigid since technological developments must be reflected by the applicable rules.[101]

But an important normative guideline in the crypto environment field is the principle of technology-neutral regulation. The notion of "same business, same risks, same rules" can only unfold if comparable services are regulated by comparable legal provisions.[102] The principle of technology-neutrality has become prominent in the crypto environment (and, for example, is often reinstated by the Swiss regulator), but daily reality is not always in line with the political statements.[103]

As already outlined, the main challenge for the regulation of DeFi consists in the fact that due to decentralization, a clear addressee for the rules, usually in the person of an intermediary, does not exist; therefore, the traditional point of contact does not function anymore.[104] This fact requires moving from an entity-based approach to an activity-based approach.

---

97 Hester M Peirce, 'Token Safe Harbor Proposal 2.0' (SEC Statement, 13 April 2021) <https://www.sec.gov/news/public-statement/peirce-statement-token-safe-harbor-proposal-2.0> accessed 26 February 2024.

98 Meirich (n 13), no 1517 and nos 1522 et seq.

99 Maurenbrecher and Leisinger (n 79), 710 and 714.

100 See also Zetzsche, Arner, and Buckley (n 64), 210 et seq.

101 Meirich (n 13), no 1486 and WEF and Wharton Blockchain and Digital Asset Project (n 63), 25.

102 Federal Council of Switzerland, DLT Act (n 40), 245, 246, 248, 251, 259, 260, 272, 279, 299.

103 See Hans Kuhn and Rolf H Weber, 'Zur Umsetzung des Basler Krypto-Standards in der Schweiz' [2024] Weblaw Jusletter IT, 13 February, nos 61–64; see also Dünser (n 62), no 4.2.2.

104 See subsection IV.A above and Dünser (n 62), no 3.

3.2 Analogous application of traditional instruments?

Theoretically, traditional instruments used in financial market regulation can also be "activated" in the DeFi context. The most restrictive approach would be a prohibition regulation, as done, for example, in respect of cryptocurrencies in China and South Korea, which would not allow the use of DApps, non-custodial wallets, or of mixers.[105] Apart from major difficulties in successfully enforcing such kind of prohibitions (for example, by way of network access controls), this regulatory regime does not correspond to the philosophy of legislators in business-friendly open societies. A less stringent normative instrument would be the requirement of obtaining a license for the DeFi business (similar to the regime for other financial market participants) or to limit the DeFi business to already licensed financial market participants, having the consequence that unregulated DeFi service providers would be forced to cooperate with an already regulated financial intermediary.[106]

In the sense of moving from an entity-based to an activity-based approach, the license requirement could be tied to the programming of DApps. Insofar, the difficulty consists of properly balancing between the protection of innovation and the protection of consumers.[107] Furthermore, the programming of DApps is not really a financial market activity; that is to say, the knowledge of the respective authorities might not be sufficient to judge the technological achievements, and the access to a public permission-less blockchain can hardly be controlled.[108]

At least theoretically, alternatives would be available even if partly difficult to implement. The relatively "easiest" vehicle suitable being obliged to apply for a license appears to be a DAO; the decentralized structure usually does have a point of contact, possibly the registration of the association or the domicile of a key member of the DAO.[109] The disadvantage of this approach consists in the fact that a certain centralization effect, which is untypical for DAOs, is caused. Another possibility consists in the imposition of obligations on service providers performing the on- and off-ramp procedures of fiat currencies into the DeFi system;[110] potential actors are offerors of wallets, issuers of stablecoins, and centralized trading platforms.[111] Such an approach would have to extend the licensing regime to a new type of services rendering, namely the on- and off-ramp procedures.

105 To understand the prohibition regulation concept, see Weber and Baisch (n 87), 478; for a discussion in the DeFi context, see Meirich (n 13), nos 1467 et seq.

106 Meirich (n 13), nos 1546/47.

107 See Zetzsche, Arner, and Buckley (n 64), 192.

108 For further aspects, see Maurenbrecher and Leisinger (n 79), 715; Zetzsche, Arner, and Buckley (n 64), 203; WEF and Wharton Blockchain and Digital Asset Project (n 63), 22.

109 Meirich (n 13), nos 1552 et seq.

110 EUBOF (n 69), 17; Maurenbrecher and Leisinger (n 79), 713 and 716; Meirich (n 13), nos 1558–1559.

111 Meirich (n 13), nos 1561 et seq.

3.3 Supervision and enforcement

The enforcement of any kind of regulation, and in particular of a license regime, is highly complex in the DeFi context, as already stated in the discussion of the substantive issues several times.[112] A key challenge is the pseudonymity of participants in DeFi transactions; nevertheless, possible tracking could be done through the wallet addresses.[113] Over the next few years, potential supervisory instruments will have to be developed.

Another transparency door might be the "traditional" procedure known from the FinTech business, allowing the providers of a new service to ask the supervisory authority for a non-action letter. In Switzerland, such a procedure is often used in cases of legal uncertainties. Such a non-action letter will only be issued if the service provider submits a filled-in questionnaire on a full name disclosure basis; if later this provider engages in an identical critical DeFi business, the supervisory authority might be in a position to identify the concerned market participant.[114]

V. Outlook

The new technological infrastructures leading to decentralized governance regimes cause major normative challenges in at least two legal fields, namely (i) in company or group organization law and (ii) in financial market regulation.

DAOs do not nicely fit into any of the available forms of regulated entities with legal personality, including the company with limited liability and the foundation. The partnership model is not suitable due to the unlimited liability risks for partners. The best legal "cloth" is offered by the association; in addition, most of the applicable provisions are not of a mandatory nature, and the articles of incorporation can be drafted in a tailor-made way. Theoretically, it would also be possible to design a completely new legal form along the lines of a proposed Model Law; however, this approach would cause legal uncertainties at least at the beginning.

DeFi requires the implementation of a new regulatory approach. The decentralization makes the financial intermediaries disappear, and the key elements for regulatory compliance are reflected in the services rendered. As a first reaction, self-regulation

112 See above subsections IV.C.3.1 and IV.C.3.2.
113 See Bruno Pasquier, 'Anonymisierungstechniken bei Blockchains: Chancen und Herausforderungen in rechtlicher Hinsicht' (2022) 118(7) Schweizerische Juristen-Zeitung 357 et seq.
114 See WEF and Wharton Blockchain and Digital Asset Project (n 63), 30; Meirich (n 13), nos 1586 et seq.

is an instrument that could cope with many issues such as standardization, certification, governance, and compliance framework. If this approach is not sufficient, governmental regulation, starting with sandbox models and safe harbor provisions, can step in.

In a nutshell, the discussed problems spread out a broad number of legal challenges that offer room for innovative ideas and fresh research agenda points.

4

The rise, fall and future of P2P lending platforms in China: the role of policy, law and enforcement

Joseph Lee and Yonghui Bao

I. Introduction

Peer-to-peer (P2P) lending platforms are a decentralised system of micro-finance providing financial services in limited amounts to low-income individuals as well as small and informal businesses.[1] Micro-finance has been advocated by Nobel Peace Laureate, Professor Muhammad Yunus, founder of the Grameen Bank, as a means of supporting entrepreneurs and social inclusion. In 2006, Professor Yunus visited China to talk about the success of micro-finance and called for China to allow micro-credit institutions as a means of alleviating poverty.[2] As the internet is widely accessible in China, using it to expand micro-finance was seen as an innovative, inclusive, and sustainable initiative. With the prospect of e-commerce, the internet finance industry has expanded dramatically in China,[3] and P2P lending platforms have enabled individuals to obtain micro-credit or small loans from other individuals without involving a traditional financial institution as intermediary.[4]

During the golden era of Fintech between 2013 and 2019,[5] P2P lending flourished in China to such an extent that its volume surpassed that of the US and the EU, and it

---

1 Bank for International Settlements (BIS), 'Microfinance Activities and the Core Principles for Effective Banking Supervision' (*Basel Committee on Banking Supervision Consultative Document*, February 2010) <https://www.bis.org/publ/bcbs167.pdf> accessed 18 April 2024.

2 Zining Zhen, 'The Development of Microcredit in China under the Microfinance' (2019) 9 American Journal of Industrial and Business Management 1486.

3 Michael Chiu, 'Money, Technology and Banking: What Lessons can China Teach the Rest of the World?' (2019) BIS Working Papers No 947 <https://www.bis.org/publ/work947.pdf> accessed 18 April 2024.

4 Shuai Shao and Hong Bo, 'Behavioural Aspects of China's P2P Lending' (2022) 28(1) The European Journal of Finance 30, 45.

5 Marco Marsans, 'China's Fintech Revolution' (*Center for Strategic & International Studies*, 12 January 2021) <https://www.csis.org/blogs/new-perspectives-asia/chinas

was on track to become a national alternative system for access to finance.[6] Although recently the EU and US P2P lending markets have been growing steadily, supported by regulation and supervision,[7] in China they have dwindled and show little sign of recovery or even of remaining an accepted market model.[8] In this chapter, we investigate China's P2P lending market in the context of global Fintech development by analysing the reasons for its rise and fall. We focus on the business models that were developed, along with the regulatory policy and intervention prevalent during its heyday. We analyse the risks these business models have posed and how regulatory intervention, such as the Joint Guiding Opinions,[9] has affected the market. In the context of the Joint Guiding Opinions and the current state of the internet market, along with developments in the EU and the US, we assess the outlook for the market in the future and the extent to which law and regulation can strike the right balance to transform this micro-finance market.[10]

II. Some characteristics of P2P lending platforms in China

The most common operating modes of P2P platforms in China are pure online mode, pure offline mode, and hybrid mode. Pure online and hybrid modes have developed more rapidly than pure offline mode through the advantages they bring to the acquisition of capital and to risk control. In essence, the pure online mode is the same as traditional private lending, but online. Pai Pai Dai is a typical example that was

-fintech-revolution> accessed 18 April 2024.

6 Yingdong Wang et al., 'The Statistical Analysis of the Transaction Volume of Peer-to-Peer Lending in China' (2020) 214 E3S Web of Conferences 1.

7 Joseph Lee, 'Crowdfunding Platforms on Blockchain and Investor Protection' in P Ortolani and M Louisse (eds), *Crowdfunding and the Law: The Crowdfunding Regulation and Beyond* (OUP 2021) <https://papers.ssrn.com/sol3/papers.cfm?abstract_id=3968572> accessed 18 April 2024.

8 Joe Zhang, 'Collapse of China's Disgraced P2P Sector Offers Important Lessons' (*NIKKEI Asia*, 10 February 2020) <https://asia.nikkei.com/Opinion/Collapse-of-China-s-disgraced-P2P-sector-offers-important-lessons> accessed 25 November 2022; *see also* Derin Cag, 'The FinTech Revolution in China: Opportunities and Threats' (*FinTech Magazine*, 06 December 2021) <https://fintechmagazine.com/financial-services-finserv/fintech-revolution-china-opportunities-and-threats> accessed 25 November 2022.

9 Hung-Yi Chen and Chang-Hsien Tsai, 'Changing Regulations of Peer-to-Peer Lending in China' (2017) 36(11) Banking & Financial Services Policy Report 13, 25; *see also* Robin Hui Huang, 'Online P2P Lending' in Robin Hui Huang, *Fintech Regulation in China: Principles, Policies and Practices* (Cambridge University Press 2021) 14–51.

10 Qian Zhou, 'A Close Reading of China's Fintech Development Plan for 2022-2025' (*China Briefing*, 20 January 2022) <https://www.china-briefing.com/news/a-close-reading-china-fintech-development-plan-for-2022-2025/#:~:text=To%20be%20more%20detailed%2C%20in,channel%20for%20China's%20financial%20services> accessed 25 November 2022.

established in 2007[11] when both the credit reporting system and the online market in China were in their infancy.[12] It is an information intermediary for online unverified information that matches lenders and borrowers who gain online access, while investors bear any risk that may result.[13] The hybrid mode, by contrast, acquires capital from investors online while borrowers' credit status is obtained offline. Since in pure online mode all risks are borne by investors and the credit information system is unreliable, in order to meet the financing needs of small and micro-enterprises, online lending companies tend to prefer the hybrid mode by setting up offline stores and marketing teams.[14]

In P2P lending, capital is lent to borrowers without a financial institution acting as an intermediary. Borrowing is achieved through online platforms matching lenders with potential borrowers. In essence, the role of a P2P platform is as an information intermediary, which is fundamentally different from that of traditional financial institutions such as commercial banks who act as credit intermediaries, performing the function of maturity transformation.[15] Originally devised in Europe and the United States,[16] P2P platforms receive applications from potential borrowers, assess the risk of lending to them, and then decide the appropriate rate of interest. Borrowers make periodic interest payments and repay the full principal amount at an agreed maturity date.[17] Compared with traditional bank deposits, P2P lending normally gives a higher return rate to lenders (investors), yet the entry criteria for investing on the platforms are significantly lower than for other types of investment due to often no requirement

---

11 Haifeng Li, Yuejin Zhang, and Ning Zhang, 'Evaluating the Well-Qualified Borrowers from PaiPaiDai' (2017) 122 Procedia Computer Science 775, 779.

12 ibid.

13 Shuai Shao and Hong Bo (n 4), 45.

14 Qiwei Liang, 'On Chinese Online Lender's Model Building on the Macro, Micro and Industry Level' in Marcus Aaron (ed), *Design, User Experience, and Usability: Design Discourse* (Springer 2015) 315–327.

15 Mark Carney, 'The Promise of FinTech – Something New Under the Sun?' (*Bank of England Speech*, 25 January 2017) <https://www.bis.org/review/r170126b.pdf> accessed 18 April 2024; Calebe de Roure, Loriana Pelizzon, Paolo Tasca, 'How Does P2P Lending Fit into the Consumer Credit Market?' (*Deutsche Bundesbank Discussion Paper No 30/2016*, 2016) <https://www.bundesbank.de/resource/blob/704046/b53dc281b4666672e6d526a35e50fd50/mL/2016-08-12-dkp-30-data.pdf> accessed 18 April 2024; European Banking Authority (EBA), 'Final Report on response to the non-bank lending request from the CfA on digital finance' (*EBA*, 8 April 2022) <https://www.eba.europa.eu/sites/default/documents/files/document_library/Publications/Reports/2022/1032199/Report%20on%20response%20to%20the%20non-bank%20lending%20request%20from%20the%20CfA%20on%20Digital%20Finance.pdf> accessed 18 April 2024.

16 Tetyana Balyuk, 'Financial Innovation and Borrowers: Evidence from Peer-to-Peer Lending' (*Federal Deposit Insurance Corporation (FDIC)*, 2019) <https://www.fdic.gov/bank/analytical/fintech/papers/balyuk-paper.pdf> accessed 25 November 2022.

17 Robin Hui Huang (n 9).

for a minimum investment or for opening a bank account.[18] For borrowers, especially individuals or owners of small businesses, P2P lending has the advantage over traditional bank loans of not requiring collateral, since the majority of P2P loans are unsecured.

III. The historical development of P2P platforms and China's intervention

A. The UK and US experiences

The world's first P2P platform, Zopa, originated in the UK,[19] where the banking industry is monopolised by five giants in a way that makes it hard for individuals and smaller enterprises to get bank loans. To alleviate this problem, in 2005, Zopa, the world's first P2P lending platform, set itself up as an information intermediary to match lenders and borrowers at a charge to both parties. Subsequently, Zopa's business operation model was replicated worldwide by platforms such as Lending Club and Prosper in the US.[20]

There are two kinds of P2P model: direct lending and platform lending. In the former, either institutional or qualified investors issue loans directly to borrowers through the platform, which acts merely as an information intermediary. But in the platform lending model, cooperating banks issue loans, and the P2P platform turns them into creditors' rights, which can be sold to investors – a form of securitisation.[21] In the US, the P2P model retains the function of an information intermediary, and the platform does not guarantee returns nor bear credit risks. The Chinese model differs here, as explained below.

To explain the original mode of operation of P2P platforms in the US and Europe, we will take Lending Club as an example. Lending Club's business model[22] has developed through three phases.

18 Robin Hui Huang and Christine Meng Lu Wang, 'The Fall of Online P2P Lending in China: A Critique of the Central-Local Co-regulatory Regime' (2021) 36(3) Banking & Finance Law Review 481–515.

19 Jan Bednorz, 'The History of P2P Lending' (*P2PMarketData*, 6 June 2023) <https://p2pmarketdata.com/articles/p2p-lending-history/> accessed 25 November 2022.

20 Tania Ziegler and Rotem Shneor, 'Lending Crowdfunding: Principles and Market Development' in Shneor Rotem, Zhao Liang and Flaten Bjorn-Tore (eds), *Advances in Crowdfunding: Research and Practice* (Palgrave Macmillan 2020) 63–92.

21 Ming Gao, Jerome Yen, and Matthew Liu, 'Determinants of Defaults on P2P Lending Platforms in China' (2021) 72 International Review of Economics and Finance 334, 348.

22 Paul Jeffery, 'Why the Lending Club IPO Matters' (*Think at London Business School*, 10 September 2014) <https://www.london.edu/think/why-the-lending-club-ipo-matters> accessed 25 November 2022.

In phase one around 2007,[23] Lending Club acted as an intermediary for the loan and provided post-loan services for the loan business, yet did not take the loan risk. In phase two around 2008,[24] the platform issued loans to borrowers and became the lender of funds. Hence, Lending Club needed to obtain lending licences, and this restricted the expansion of its business. In order to circumvent this problem and to avoid interest rate caps, Lending Club cooperated with WebBank, which had a licence. Loans were issued by WebBank and then assigned to Lending Club as non-recourse loans. After Lending Club obtained the transferred borrower's loans, it sold the loan to investors either directly or in the form of a certificate of creditor's rights and income. In phase three around 2008,[25] the US Securities and Exchange Commission (SEC) strengthened supervision in October 2008, requiring P2P operations in the US to comply with relevant legal standards in the securities industry. Lending Club then officially entered the asset securitisation model by registering with the SEC. The difference between this model and the platform lending model (phase two) is that the investor purchased the bonds issued by the platform, making investors unsecured creditors of Lending Club. Here again, China differs from the US (see following paragraph).

Lending Club's profit comes primarily from the transaction fees charged to borrowers, which accounts for between 75 per cent and 90 per cent of its net income.[26] Each time a borrower successfully obtains a loan, a transaction fee of between 1 per cent and 6 per cent is paid to the platform.[27] There is also a service fee charged to investors of between 10 per cent and 15 per cent of the net income.[28] Each time the borrower pays the principal and interest to the investor, Lending Club deducts 1 per cent of the service fee from the investor's account. In addition, institutional investors are charged an annual account management fee of between 0.7 per cent and 1.25 per cent.[29] At the end of 2019, Lending Club's transaction fees amounted to 599 million USD (78.9 per cent of its total revenue).[30] However, once Lending Club was listed, it ceased to be profitable. In 2013, it made a profit of 7.31 million USD,[31] but this was followed by losses of over 100 million USD in both 2016 and 2018.[32] The reason for this is that to make

23 PYMNTS, 'A Brief History of Lending Club' (*PYMNTS*, 13 May 2016) <https://www.pymnts.com/news/alternative-financial-services/2016/lending-club-timeline/> accessed 25 November 2022.

24 Ibid.

25 Ibid.

26 *See* Lending Club Corporation, 'Annual Report pursuant to Section 13 or 15(d) of the Securities Exchange Act of 1934' (*SEC*, 2021) <https://www.annualreports.com/HostedData/AnnualReportArchive/l/NYSE_LC_2021.pdf> accessed 18 April 2024; *see also* SEC Filing on <https://ir.lendingclub.com/financials/Docs/> accessed 25 November 2022.

27 Lending Club, 'Moving Forward Together' (*Lending Club*, 2022) <https://www.lendingclub.com/investing/peer-to-peer> accessed 25 November 2022.

28 Ibid.

29 Ibid.

30 *See* Lending Club's Annual Report 2019.

31 *See* Lending Club's Annual Report 2013.

32 *See* Lending Club's Annual Reports 2016 and 2018.

a profit sustainably by charging a service fee requires consistent rapid growth in the scale of transactions in order to cover the considerable expense involved in management and marketing. We will see how the Chinese P2P platforms operated differently from this model in the following sections.

B. The Chinese experience

P2P lending was originally a niche business model for a specific range of lenders and borrowers in China.[33] The historical development of P2P platforms in China can also be divided into three phases.[34]

1. *Phase one (2006–2011)*

In 2006, CreditEase was the first P2P platform that came into the market[35] and in 2008, Pai Pai Dai launched the first official domestic website for microcredit loans. At this stage, P2P platforms were merely information intermediaries that published borrowers' loan information. Each loan had a credit limit set by the platform, and investors were invited to make their investment directly. By the end of 2011, there were about 60 online P2P lending platforms in China, and average monthly transactions amounted to 500 million Renminbi (RMB) from some 10,000 investors.[36]

2. *Phase two (2011–2015)*

After its introduction to China in 2006, P2P lending platforms evolved through financial innovation, but its business model was difficult to sustain as we have seen in the US Lending Club's fee-based model. Between 2012 and 2015, market demand stimulated growth in the number of P2P platforms to a peak of about 5,000,[37] but the regulatory regime did not keep pace. Indirect financing was the dominant source of finance in China and this limited investors' investment outlets. At the same time, small and micro enterprises found it hard or impossible to obtain bank loans due to

---

33 The Association of Chartered Certified Accountants (ACCA), 'The Rise of Peer-to-Peer Lending in China: An Overview and Survey Case Study' (*ACCA Think Ahead*, October 2015) <https://www.accaglobal.com/content/dam/ACCA_Global/Technical/manage/ea-china-p2p-lending.pdf> accessed 18 April 2024.

34 Ibid.

35 Paolo Danese, 'CreditEase Reaps Rewards of Transition from P2P Lending Platform to All-Round Wealth Manager' (*Euromoney*, 29 June 2017) <https://www.euromoney.com/article/b13n61d80mnklt/creditease-reaps-rewards-of-transition-from-p2p-lending-platform-to-all-round-wealth-manager> accessed 17 November 2022;

36 Jason Jones, 'The Most Important Chinese P2P Lending Companies' (*Fintech Nexus*, 2 May 2014) <https://news.fintechnexus.com/the-most-important-chinese-p2p-lending-companies/> accessed 17 November 2022; Geran Tian and Weixing Wu, 'Mismatch between Investor Preferences and Financial Services/Products' (2022) 35(1) Economic Research 4437, 4456.

37 Jiefei Liu, 'The Dramatic Rise and Fall of Online P2P Lending in China' (*TC*, 2 August 2018) <https://techcrunch.com/2018/08/01/the-dramatic-rise-and-fall-of-online-p2p-lending-in-china/?guccounter=1> accessed 25 November 2022.

a lack of sufficient collateral.[38] As a result of this, P2P lending platforms thrived to fill this financing gap. Then, in 2012 and 2013, monetary policy became tighter,[39] making it even harder for small and medium enterprises with low credit qualifications to obtain finance. At this stage, the operating model of P2P platforms gradually changed from being information intermediaries to credit intermediaries. They began to ask borrowers to provide collateral and promised to protect the repayment of both principal and interest to investors.[40] This new model meant that platforms became credit intermediaries who bore the credit risk of default for the borrowers.

After 2012, the P2P lending industry experienced two waves of failure. Economic growth in China slowed down, and this increased credit risk. Many borrower companies failed, and some investors withdrew capital from the platforms because they felt that regulation was weak.[41] In 2013, the macro-economic downturn caused further failure of some platforms. Between 2014 and 2016,[42] an array of regulations was introduced to prevent malpractice in the P2P lending industry.[43] This, along with the rising stock market, led to the shift of capital from the P2P industry to the stock market, resulting in the failure of many P2P platforms that had been active in illegal fundraising and fraud. In order to further tighten control in the P2P lending market, in April 2016, the China Banking Regulatory Commission issued its Plan for Rectification of P2P Online Lending Risks,[44] with the result that 65 per cent of P2P platforms were assessed as 'problematic'.

3. *Phase three (2016–2020)*

The year 2016 saw the introduction of strict governance of the P2P lending industry. In March, the Internet Finance Association was established, and in August,[45] the China Banking Regulatory Commission and other ministries jointly issued the 'Interim Measures for the Administration of the Business Activities of Online Lending

---

38 Ibid.

39 Wang Yang-Chao, Tsai Jun-Jung, and Xu Jingsi, 'The Impact of Monetary Policy on China's Stock and Bond Markets' (2022) 20(2) China: An International Journal 134–159.

40 ACCA (n 33).

41 Ming Gao, Jerome Yen, and Matthew Liu (n 21).

42 Qing He and Xiaoyang Li, 'The Failure of Chinese Peer-to-Peer Lending Platforms: Finance and Politics' (2021) 66 Journal of Corporate Finance 929.

43 Robin Hui Huang (n 9).

44 The 15 Ministries and Commissions of China, 'Notice of 15 Ministries and Commissions including the China Banking Regulatory Commission on Issuing the Implementation Plan for the Special Rectification of Risks concerning Online Peer-to-Peer Lending' (中国银行业监督管理委员会等十五部委关于印发《P2P网络借贷风险专项整治工作实施方案》的通知), <https://www.pkulaw.com/chl/1850eof59b4f0847bdfb.html> accessed 18 April 2024.

45 Chen Ding, Anil Savio Kavuri, and Alistair Milne, 'Lessons from the Rise and Fall of Chinese Peer to Peer Lending' (2021) 22(2) Journal of Banking Regulation 133, 143.

Information Intermediary Institutions'.[46] Since then, three major policies relating to information disclosure have been implemented. This regulatory activity caused a wave of defaults in the P2P lending industry. Multiple factors, such as the strengthening of online lending supervision and the reduction of investor confidence, forced the industry to reconsider its business models. The macro-economy was depressed, and financial deleveraging continued. Credit risk was increasing, and the overdue rate also increased during this period. As platforms reconsidered their operation, many went out of business: 1,071 in 2018 and a further 344 in 2019.[47] Illegal platforms were continuously being removed, as regulations require P2P lending platforms to act as information intermediaries only. The number of P2P platforms dropped from a peak of about 5,000 to three by the end of 2020.[48] With the arrival of strong supervision, every P2P platform in China has been closed.[49]

The average duration of maturities of P2P lending has been continuously extended since 2014, and the trend has become more obvious since the end of 2017. As of June 2018, the average duration of maturities has exceeded 12 months and reached its peak. Judging from the loan situation, the amount of small loans is more significant. The per capita investment amount remains at the level of 460,000 RMB, but the per capita loan amount reached more than 300,000 RMB at the beginning of 2014, and then continued to drop to 40,000 RMB per capita, mainly because the introduction of industry supervision measures stipulated the upper limit of the amount of small loans for individuals and enterprises.

Combined with the revenue of P2P platforms in 2013–14, due to the relatively small scale of the P2P lending industry, the average borrowing period was mostly short-term, up to six months in 2013–14, and the risk-free interest rate was relatively high at that time, resulting in the overall industry's rate of return being relatively high. However, the overall rate of return dropped to about 10 per cent afterward, which gradually met the requirements of regulatory policies. Furthermore, the long-term return rate of large platforms is relatively low.

---

46 China Banking Regulatory Commission (CBRC), Ministry of Industry and Information Technology (MIIT), Ministry of Public Security (MPS), and Office of the Central Cyberspace Affairs Commission (CAC), 'Interim Measures for the Administration of the Business Activities of Online Lending Information Intermediary Institutions' (《网络借贷信息中介机构业务活动管理暂行办法》), <http://www.gov.cn/xinwen/2016-08/24/content_5102029.htm> accessed 18 April 2024.

47 PYMNTS, 'Tighter Reg Shrinks China's P2P Lending Mkt by 50 Pct in 2018' (*PYMNTS*, 2 January 2019) <https://www.pymnts.com/news/regulation/2019/chinese-government-p2p-lending-market/> accessed 17 November 2022.

48 CBNEditor, 'China's P2P Lending Sector Crushed Out of Existence Completely' (*China Banking News*, 30 November 2020) <https://www.chinabankingnews.com/2020/11/30/chinas-p2p-lending-sector-crushed-out-of-existence-completely/> accessed 17 November 2022.

49 Chen Ding, Anil S Kavuri, and Alistair Milne, 'Lessons from the Rise and Fall of Chinese Peer to Peer Lending' (2021) 22(2) Journal of Banking Regulation 133, 143.

IV. Business models and potential risks exposed by P2P lending platforms in China

As discussed, there are two main types of P2P business models in China. In the first, the platform acts solely as an information intermediary that matches borrowers with lenders. In the second, the platform acts as a credit intermediary and, in effect, operates like a traditional commercial bank by taking deposits and issuing loans in capital pool mode, that is, maturity transformation. If a P2P lending platform is to operate in this way, it needs regulatory approval.[50] When commercial banks operate in capital pool mode, they normally apply protective measures such as forming a risk reserve, but when P2P platforms operate in capital pool mode, they pool investors' funds which are then lent to borrowers. This means that the platform bears risks when there is a maturity mismatch between lenders and borrowers, and can easily incur liquidity and credit risks. In addition, under this mode, the platform provides guarantees for borrowers using its own credit.

If a P2P platform acts solely as an information intermediary, investors bear the risks of the investment. The policy paper 'Guiding Opinions of the People's Bank of China, the Ministry of Industry and Information Technology, the Ministry of Public Security on Promoting the Sound Development of Internet Finance'[51] defines P2P lending as direct lending between lenders and borrowers through the internet platform. Therefore, P2P lending is seen as a form of private lending and is subject to laws and regulations such as Contract Law[52] and the General Principles of Civil Law,[53] as well as judicial interpretation by the Supreme People's Court.[54] By this definition, the functions of a P2P lending platform include providing an information exchange, matching lenders with borrowers, assessing the credit status of the borrowers and carrying out other information intermediary services.

50 See Capital Requirements Regulations (CRR).

51 People's Bank of China, 'Guiding Opinions of the People's Bank of China, the Ministry of Industry and Information Technology, the Ministry of Public Security, et al., on Promoting the Sound Development of Internet Finance' (人民银行等十部门发布《关于促进互联网金融健康发展的指导意见》), <http://www.gov.cn/xinwen/2015-07/18/content_2899360.html> accessed 18 April 2024.

52 See Contract Law of the People's Republic of China of 1999, Arts 196–211.

53 See Contract Law of the People's Republic of China of 2009, Art 90; the Civil Code of the People's Republic of China of 2020, Arts 667–680.

54 The Supreme People's Court of China, 'Provisions of the Supreme People's Court on Several Issues concerning the Application of Law in the Trial of Private Lending Cases (2020 Second Amendment)' (中华人民共和国最高人民法院，《最高人民法院关于审理民间借贷案件适用法律若干问题的规定》2020).

A. Type one: information intermediary

Pure P2P lending platforms only carry out information matching. The platforms use their ability to control risk, such as by deploying big data[55] to identify qualified and creditworthy borrowers and by publishing their information on the investment platform. As an information intermediary, the platform is only responsible for reviewing borrower qualifications, disclosing relevant information, matching transactions, and charging a service fee. Investors are responsible for their investment outcomes, whether losses or gains.

Pai Pai Dai is a Chinese information intermediary platform which was established in Shanghai in 2007 and successfully listed on the New York Stock Exchange in November 2017.[56] As of 2020, the number of borrowers on the platform since its inception amounted to about 16.5 million and of lenders, seven million, with a transaction volume of 180 billion RMB.[57] The platform cooperates with well-known third-party payment platforms such as Alipay and WeChat Pay, which are licensed by the China Banking and Insurance Regulatory Commission (CBIRC), and this allows it to realise the collection and payment of capital by lenders and borrowers. The platform then uses big data for asset screening and fraud detection.[58] It applies a unique risk pricing model to collect information about borrowers and uses it to detect fraud. Information obtained is shared with authorities such as the Ministry of Public Security. The platform also forms a risk reserve by requiring borrowers to provide additional capital. Target projects for investment are required to meet certain conditions to ensure that investments are prudent and reasonable.

Pai Pai Dai's profit model is mainly based on the fees charged to borrowers. As a pure information platform, 76% of its income is from loan and post-loan service fees.[59] This profit model has meant slower growth in the scale of Pai Pai Dai's transactions than for its peers. Since 2012, the P2P lending industry expanded greatly, but unlike Pai Pai Dai, most P2P platforms provided finance to borrowers through the internet and promised the return of both principal and interest to investors.[60] This limited the appeal of Pai Pai Dai to investors, but when in 2016 strong supervision of online lending was introduced and the information intermediary nature of P2P platforms

---

55 Zhiqing Li, 'The Application of Big Data in Preventing Financial Risks of P2P Network Loan' (2021) Proceedings of the 2021 International Conference on Enterprise Management and Economic Development (ICEMED 2021), DOI: <http://doi.org/10.2991/aebmr.k.210601.035> accessed 30 April 2024.

56 Ying Li, Jacky So, and Jia Yuan, 'Voluntary Verifiable Information Disclosure and Loan Funding Performance: Evidence from Paipaidai in China' (2020) 65(2) The Singapore Economic Review 419, 441.

57 Daniel Slotta, 'Market Size of the P2P Lending Industry in China 2014–2020' (*Statista*, 13 October 2022) <https://www.statista.com/statistics/1261276/china-size-of-the-p2p-lending-market/> accessed 17 November 2022.

58 Qing He and Xiaoyang Li (n 42).

59 Ibid.

60 Haifeng Li, Yuejin Zhang, and Ning Zhang (n 11).

was clarified, Pai Pai Dai once again achieved profitability. According to Pai Pai Dai's website, in the 37 days after the release of the 'Interim Measures for the Administration of the Business Activities of Online Lending Information Intermediary Institutions', transaction volume on the platform increased by 39 per cent, the amount of new loans increased by 34 per cent, and investment increased by 31 per cent.[61] However, stricter regulation of the industry as a whole has led to a decrease in market participation, and since 2016 the rate of growth of the platform has declined. In 2019, Pai Pai Dai changed its name to Xinye Technology,[62] reduced its P2P lending services, and closed its online loan business. Pai Pai Dai, as Xinye, now links funds from traditional financial institutions with investors. It has transformed itself into a loan assistance institution and cooperates with banks to carry out its loan business.

B. Type two: credit intermediary

In the second type of business model, the platform guarantees both the principal and the interest, and this gives it the characteristics of indirect financing, similar to a bank loan. The function of the P2P platform is now not limited to screening borrowers' information; it has become a financial institution in its own right that can provide guarantees and match funds, and it takes on the triple function of an information, credit, and risk intermediary by operating in capital pool mode.

However, unlike traditional financial institutions, these credit intermediary platforms lack the reserves to be able to cover risks, which most are weak at controlling. In essence, platforms operating in this way create a Ponzi scheme where they release new products to generate revenues that are used to pay for the promises of the old products in order to maintain their operation.[63] This can initiate a chain reaction since products in the capital pool cannot be risk-isolated from one another, and exposure to the risk of one product endangers all the others.

It gives an incentive to investors by guaranteeing the principal and interest, and it then amasses all the capital from investors to form a capital pool for the platform. Because payment is guaranteed, investors have no incentive to intervene in the operation of the business, hence increasing the risk of moral hazard. In the event of a borrower's default on repayment, the platforms cover the loss by introducing new products to attract new investors and using the funds raised from the new investors to repay the principal and interest to previous investors.

---

61 Jiefei Liu (n 37).

62 See Paipaidai, 'Announcement on Completion of Clearance', (拍拍贷，《关于清退完成的公告》)， accessed 8 November 2024.

63 Charlie Custer, 'Fall of $7.6b Ponzi Scheme Ezubao is Bad for All of China's P2P Lending Companies' (*TechinAsia*, 2 February 2016) <https://www.techinasia.com/fall-76b-ponzi-scheme-ezubao-bad-chinas-p2p-lending-companies> accessed 17 November 2022.

All the top P2P cases that shocked the industry for their illegal fundraising were credit intermediaries. One of the most notorious is the case of Ezubao[64] which was launched in 2014 and rapidly rose in the industry for the scale of its transactions. By the end of 2015, its accumulated transactions amounted to 70.3 billion RMB,[65] ranking it fourth in the industry. But its fortunes changed when, in 2015, the public security agencies filed a case against Ezubao.[66] Although it had once served as an industry benchmark, Ezubao now became notorious for its illegal fundraising of more than 50 billion RMB from more than 900,000 victims.[67] It transpired that 95% of Ezubao's financing originated from fake projects fabricated by its founder.[68] The police investigation showed that the platform bought information from other enterprises and used it to build fake financing projects, and to continuously raise funds in a Ponzi scheme that produced its 70 billion RMB transaction volume.[69] From its inception, Ezubao advertised in major media and capitalised on individual investors' lack of financial knowledge by promising them an annualised return of between 9 per cent and 14.6 per cent,[70] far outstripping that of bank wealth management products.

C. Type three: asset-backed securities business

Under the third model, the controllers of P2P platforms themselves assume the role of third-party professional lenders. They provide borrowers with funds directly, and then package, split, and transfer their account receivables to investors, similar to the US Lending Club's model. However, in China, many platforms attract investors with promises of high yields, falsely stating that funds have been invested in projects, such as real estate and other capital-intensive ventures, while in reality, most of this information is fake.[71] Behind the high returns expected, there were no real assets to support the projects. The platforms could only rely on borrowing more to pay the existing investors. The funding gap increased constantly along with the operational risk.

---

64 Matthew Miller, 'Leader of China's $9 billion Ezubao Online Scam Gets Life; 26 Jailed' (*Reuters*, 12 September 2017) <https://www.reuters.com/article/us-china-fraud-idUSKCN1BN0J6> accessed 17 November 2022; *Also see* Guo Yiming, 'Ezubao: a US$7.6b Dollar Ponzi Scheme' (*China.org.cn*, 2 February 2016) <http://www.china.org.cn/business/2016-02/02/content_37716726.htm> accessed 23 April 2024.

65 Neil Gough, 'Online Lender Ezubao Took $7.6 Billion in Ponzi Scheme, China Says' (*The New York Times*, 1 February 2016) <https://www.nytimes.com/2016/02/02/business/dealbook/ezubao-china-fraud.html> accessed 25 November 2022.

66 Ibid.

67 Ibid.

68 Matthew Miller (n 64); *Also see* Guo Yiming (n 64).

69 Ibid.

70 Richard Macauley, 'Nearly One Million iInvestors May Have Been Fleeced in China's Latest Ponzi Scheme' (*Quartz*, 31 January 2016) <https://qz.com/606786/nearly-one-million-investors-were-fleeced-in-chinas-latest-ponzi-scheme> accessed 17 November 2022.

71 Qing He and Xiaoyang Li (n 42).

Based on the fund pool model, the P2P platform has changed from a direct financing mode to an indirect financing mode, and the types of underlying assets are more diversified. The asset securitisation business, which involves splitting and repackaging securitised assets, trust assets, and fund shares, and transferring to investors on the platform, bypasses the formal process of securitisation. This includes asset transfer, overall subscription, equity arrangement, and listing on the exchange in the process of asset securitisation. Essentially, it becomes the way for online lending institutions to operate licensed financial institutions' businesses, resulting in cross-industry risk accumulation. Due to the lack of industry supervision at the early stage, it was not uncommon to establish a large-scale P2P platform by means of asset securitisation.

D. Potential risks exposed by P2P lending platforms

The announcement of an array of joint guiding opinions made the intention of the regulatory authorities very clear: P2P lending platforms can only be used as an information intermediary and for matching transactions. In practice, the business model of the majority of P2P platforms was broader than that of an information intermediary, and this carried great potential risk.

1. *Risks posed by asset pool and maturity mismatch*

A large number of businesses on P2P platforms involved transferring creditors' rights, as discussed in the last section. From the perspective of investors, creditors' rights are products with a low initial investment and a short lock-up period. Most lenders who take advantage of this kind of opportunity are professionals, and it is not a case of transferring creditors' rights between individuals.[72] Through the platform, professional lenders first lend to borrowers, thus obtaining the creditors' rights which they accumulate for transfer (sale) to investors through repackaging, segmentation and securitisation.[73] This is one of the most common modes in the online lending industry, as seen in the Lending Club's model.[74] From the point of view of a P2P platform, this business mode can improve the efficiency of matching funds between borrowers and lenders, and also of repackaging creditors' rights. This business model, however, is not sustainable as there is severe risk of maturity mismatch, because borrowers normally need a much longer time before maturity than investors, who pay more attention to short-term investment returns. Because of this, platforms often split the borrowers' debts and repeatedly pay the last batch of investors' principal and interest with finance from new investors. Should there be a problem in obtaining finance from new investors, the capital chain is broken, putting the business at risk.

---

72 Xiao Man, 'The Basics of China's P2P Lending Bust' (*China Change*, 9 August 2018) <https://chinachange.org/2018/08/09/the-basics-of-chinas-p2p-lending-bust/> accessed 17 November 2022.

73 Robin Hui Huang (n 9).

74 Ibid.

2. *Regulatory uncertainty*

The decrease in the number of P2P platforms has been closely connected with regulation. In 2016–17, a regulatory framework was set up by the industry and then implemented by regional financial regulatory agencies, normally at the provincial level.[75] However, the enforcement of supervision has been weak, and as of 2018, more than half of the platforms still in operation had not obtained licences in accordance with the new regulations. Continuing to operate without a licence after the due date is regarded as an illegal operation, and as a result, a large number of platforms either left the online lending industry, were taken over, or absconded with investors' capital.

3. *Investor's confidence*

Negative public comments on the online lending industry led to investors losing confidence in it, and as a result, some relatively stable P2P platforms also faced the risk of a large number of withdrawals by investors in a short time, with great consequential risks to the industry.

V. Regulatory frameworks

A. Phase one: before 2014

Before 2015, there was little supervision of the online lending industry, and the regulatory authorities showed a generally supportive attitude towards internet finance. However, in 2014, the regulators published their first joint guidelines, which set out four red lines to bring order to the chaos in the P2P lending industry.[76] There were, however, no supporting documents to prescribe specific measures. In the first place, red lines for P2P lending platforms clarified the intermediary nature of the P2P platform. Second, they forbade platforms themselves from providing guarantees for borrowers. Third, they made clear that collected funds from investors must not be pooled together. And fourth, they stated that funds must not be illegally absorbed from the public. In 2015, the CBIRC was identified as the regulatory body for the online lending industry[77] while, at the same time, it was made clear that the legal nature of the P2P platform was as a private lender, subject to relevant laws and judicial interpretations.

75 Hung-Yi Chen and Chang-Hsien Tsai (n 9).

76 Opinions of the Supreme People's Court, the Supreme People's Procuratorate and the Ministry of Public Security on Several Issues Concerning the Application of Law in the Handling of Illegal Fund-Raising Criminal Cases Issued on 25th March 2014.

77 The 10 Ministries of China, 'Guiding Opinions of the People's Bank of China, the Ministry of Industry and Information Technology, the Ministry of Public Security, et al., on Promoting the Sound Development of Internet Finance', (人民银行等十部门发布《关于促进互联网金融健康发展的指导意见》), <http://www.gov.cn/xinwen/2015-07/18/content_2899360.htm> accessed 18 April 2024; Simmons and Simmons, 'China Releases Draft Rules to Tighten P2P Lending Business' (2016) <https://www.simmons-simmons.com/en/publications/ckod9vc3bdrfkob943al5e0g1/06-china-releases-draft-rules-to-tighten-p2p-lending-business> accessed 17 November 2022.

Despite all this, no specific regulatory rules relating to P2P lending were set out at that time.

B. Phase two: 2015–2017

In November 2015, China's 13th Five-Year Plan explicitly mentioned the importance of regulating internet finance.[78] Over 500 P2P platforms closed because of the difficulties investors faced in withdrawing their invested principal and interest. As a result, in 2016, the CBIRC, the Ministry of Information Technology, and the Ministry of Public Security jointly announced 'Interim Measures for the Administration of the Business Activities of Online Lending Information Intermediary Institutions',[79] which became the first detailed regulatory rules for the online lending industry. In October that year, the China Internet Finance Association also published self-regulation documents for the industry entitled 'Peer-to-Peer Lending for Individual Internet Financial Information Disclosure'[80] and China Internet Finance Association's 'Self-Discipline Management Model for Information Disclosure'.[81]

C. Phase three: 2017 onwards

Since 2017, in addition to the various regulatory guidelines issued by the CBIRC, banking regulatory authorities at the provincial level have also issued local regulatory and rectification rules and strengthened filing and registration requirements.[82] From 2016 to mid-2017, the entire P2P lending industry established a regulatory framework which largely consisted of the 'one method and three guidelines' principle.[83] This involved the 'Interim Measures for the Administration of the Business Activities of Online Lending Information Intermediary Institutions,'[84] the 'Notice of

78 Katherine Koleski, 'The 13th Five-Year Plan' (US-China Economic and Security Review Commission Staff Research Report, 14 February 2017) <https://www.uscc.gov/sites/default/files/Research/The%2013th%20Five-Year%20Plan_Final_2.14.17_Updated%20(002).pdf> accessed 17 November 2022.

79 Martin Chorzempa, 'Massive P2P Failures in China: Underground Banks Going Under' (*PIIE*, 21 August 2018) <https://www.piie.com/blogs/china-economic-watch/massive-p2p-failures-china-underground-banks-going-under> accessed 25 November 2022.

80 China Internet Finance Association, 'The Group Standard of "Internet Finance Information Disclosure for Peer-to-Peer Online Lending"' (T/NIFA1-2017) (《互联网金融信息披露个人网络借贷》).

81 China Internet Finance Association, 'Self-Discipline Management Norms for Information Disclosure of the China Internet Finance Association' (2016). (《中国互联网金融协会信息披露自律管理规范》).

82 Robin Hui Huang (n 9).

83 China Securities Regulatory Commission (CSRC), 'The Completion of 1+3 Institutional System in the Online Lending Industry' ('中国银监会：网贷行业"1+3"制度体系完成'), <http://www.flr-cass.org/newsitem/278014742> accessed 18 April 2024.

84 China Internet Finance Association, 'Interim Measures for the Administration of the Business Activities of Online Lending Information Intermediary Institutions'

the General Office of the China Banking Regulatory Commission, the General Office of the Ministry of Industry and Information Technology and the General Office of the State Administration for Industry and Commerce on Issuing the Guidelines for the Administration of Recordation and Registration of P2P Lending Information Intermediary Institutions",[85] the 'Notice of the General Office of the China Banking Regulatory Commission on Issuing the Guidelines for the Online Lending Fund Depository Business'[86] and the 'Notice of the General Office of the China Banking Regulatory Commission on Issuing the Guidelines for the Disclosure of Information on the Business Activities of Online Lending Information Intermediary Institutions'.[87] These form a regulatory system to provide supervision of P2P platforms whose action was limited to that of an information intermediary. As a result, the majority of P2P platforms that had conducted business as credit intermediaries closed.

D. Enforcement

In terms of the macro-environment, financial deleveraging continued to advance, and market liquidity shrank greatly after 2017. As a result, credit risk pressure increased, and the overdue rate increased as well, which aggravated the platform repayment crisis. In terms of industry supervision, in December 2017, the 'Notice on the Special Rectification and Revision of Risks of the P2P Industry', required every P2P platform to pass the rectification and revision process and file a record with the authorities. Platforms were to orderly carry out the rectification, revision, filing, and registration of online lending institutions. During the filing period, platforms were required to strictly cooperate with the supervision and its suggestions for rectification. They did not use the capital from renewing the old products to pay off unexpired assets, although the old assets had not yet expired, and the income of old investors still needed to be paid. Once the investors redeem their shares, the platform needed to

(《网络借贷信息中介机构业务活动管理暂行办法》), <http://www.gov.cn/gongbao/content/2017/content_5181095.htm> accessed 18 April 2024.

85 CBIRC, 'Notice of the General Office of the China Banking Regulatory Commission, the General Office of the Ministry of Industry and Information Technology and the General Office of the State Administration for Industry and Commerce on Issuing the Guidelines for the Administration of Recordation and Registration of P2P Lending Information Intermediary Institutions'（《中国银监会办公厅、工业和信息化部办公厅、工商总局办公厅"关于印发网络借贷信息中介机构备案登记管理指引的通知》）, <http://cietac.chinalawinfo.com/fulltext_form.aspx?Gid=313198&Db=chl> accessed 18 April 2024.

86 CBRC, 'Notice of the General Office of the China Banking Regulatory Commission on Issuing the Guidelines for the Online Lending Fund Depository Business', (中国银监会办公厅关于印发网络借贷资金存管业务指引的通知), <http://www.cac.gov.cn/2017-02/24/c_1120521333.htm> accessed 18 April 2024.

87 CBRC, 'Notice of the General Office of the China Banking Regulatory Commission on Issuing the Guidelines for the Disclosure of Information on the Business Activities of Online Lending Information Intermediary Institutions', (中国银监会办公厅关于印发网络借贷信息中介机构业务活动信息披露指引的通知), <https://www.cebnet.com.cn/20170828/102420549.html> accessed 18 April 2024.

advance the income of old investors on the one hand and make up the fund gap of the investors' redemption on the other hand, which caused pressure on the capital chain of P2P platforms. In terms of investor confidence, risk spillover had a significant impact on investor confidence, further crowding out the operation of non-compliant platforms. In July 2018, the total number of problematic platforms in a single month surged to 171, of which 86.5 per cent found it difficult to withdraw cash.

In 2016, 15 ministries and commissions, including the CBIRC, issued the 'Implementation Plan for the Special Rectification of Risks concerning Online P2P Lending',[88] which requires regulatory authorities to conduct a thorough investigation of the industry and set a time schedule for rectification. Right after, the CBIRC, the Ministry of Industry and Information Technology, the Ministry of Public Security, and the State Internet Information Office jointly announced the 'Interim Measures for the Administration of the Business Activities of Online Lending Information Intermediary Institutions'.[89] The aim of these interim measures is to strengthen the supervision and administration of the business activities of online lending information intermediary institutions, and to promote the sound development of the online lending industry. In addition, CBIRC implemented specific regulatory rules, which became special governing rules for the online lending industry, and adopted negative list management, putting forward 13 prohibited activities, including acting as credit intermediaries by P2P lending platforms, and emphasised in-process supervision and ex post supervision. In the same year, regulatory authorities also announced the rules for establishing the registration management system of information intermediaries and standardising the business activities of fund depository and information disclosure in P2P lending. In 2018, the 'Notice on Conducting Compliance Inspections for P2P Network Lending Institutions'[90] and 'Lists of P2P Compliance Inspection Issues'[91] were introduced, unifying the rectification standards and solving the regulatory arbitrage problems caused by different local standards. These notices also required that compliance inspections, including institutional self-inspection, self-discipline inspection, and administrative verification, be completed in an orderly manner before the

88 CBRC, 'Notice of 15 Ministries and Commissions including the China Banking Regulatory Commission on Issuing the Implementation Plan for the Special Rectification of Risks concerning Online Peer-to-Peer Lending', (《P2P网络借贷风险专项整治工作实施方案》), (2016).

89 The China Banking and Insurance Regulatory Commission (CBIRC), the Ministry of Industry and Information Technology (MIIT), the Ministry of Public Security (MPS), and the Office of the Central Cyberspace Affairs Commission (CAC), 'Interim Measures for the Administration of the Business Activities of Online Lending Information Intermediary Institutions', (《网络借贷信息中介机构业务活动管理暂行办法》), (2016).

90 Leading Group for Special Rectification of P2P Online Loan Risks, 'Notice on Conducting Compliance Inspections for P2P Network Lending Institutions', (《关于开展P2P网络借贷机构合规检查工作的通知》), (2018).

91 Leading Group for Special Rectification of P2P Online Loan Risks, 'List of P2P Compliance Inspection Issues', (《P2P合规检查问题清单》), (2018).

end of December 2018. In 2019, the regulatory authorities also issued 'The Opinion on the Classified Disposal and Risk Prevention of Online Loan Institutions'.[92] It outlined that: first, for the institutions that have been filed and investigated because of fraud or failure of repayments to investors, the objective of regulatory bodies is to improve the level of recovery rate and stabilise investor sentiment; while for the institutions that have failed but have not been put on file, the objective is to control risks orderly under supervision. The objectives for the disposal of non-operating institutions are to clear those entities from the online lending industry as soon as possible and to resolutely promote the clearing process of small-sized online lending institutions and provide guidance about exit from the industry with lower risk. For institutions in operation with high risk, the objective is also to steadily promote the clearing process of these online lending institutions. As of November 2020, there were no operating P2P platforms in China.

VI. Looking forward

At present, China's P2P platforms are in a transitional phase. Looking to the future, using their accumulated international experience, some may be able to cooperate with traditional financial institutions to break the limitations of the existing business model.

A. Industry level

At the industry level, there are three possible pathways for P2P platforms to transform. The first is to become a licensed lending institution such as a small loans and consumer finance company. This pathway has not been popular as there is a relatively high threshold for applying for a consumer finance company licence.[93] So far, few platforms have transformed in this way.

The second pathway is to become a loan assistance institution.[94] Platforms can apply their technology and assets to carry out a loan assistance business by listing bank loans on their platforms and conducting borrowers' credit checks. Their role will be to reduce the risk of information asymmetry between financial institutions and borrowers. At present, the most representative of this mode is Pai Pai Dai, whose online loan

---

92 The Office of the Leading Group for the Special Rectification of Internet Financial Risks, The Leading Group for the Special Rectification of P2P Online Loan Risks, 'The Opinion on the Classified Disposal and Risk Prevention of Online Loan Institutions', (《关于做好网贷机构分类处置和风险防范工作的意见》) (2019).

93 Sina Finance, 'The Dilemma of License for Consumer Finance' (《消费金融牌照困局》), (2017) <http://finance.sina.com.cn/money/bank/bank_hydt/2017-03-24/doc-ifycstww1007110.shtml> accessed 25 November 2022.

94 *See* Weiyang Net, 'Loan Assistance Business: Realistic Dilemma, Social Values, and Regulatory Suggestions', (《助贷业务：现实困境、社会价值与监管建议》), (2022) <https://www.weiyangx.com/412172.html> accessed 25 November 2022.

business has stopped and transformed into a loan assistance institution.[95] In 2019, Pai Pai Dai changed its name to Xinye Technology,[96] shifting its business focus to financial technology and reducing its P2P services.

The third pathway is to become a comprehensive wealth management platform,[97] cooperating with funds companies and banks to carry out marketing and advisory services, such as recommending asset management products to investors.

B. Supervisory level

At the supervisory level, the credit reporting system needs improvement.[98] Since 2019, the regulatory authorities have begun to expand the scope of credit reporting,[99] including collating and transferring borrowers' information on malicious debt evasion platforms into the credit reporting system, and establishing a market-orientated personal credit reporting agency.[100] However, the People's Bank of China's personal credit information system includes 930 million individuals, of whom only 460 million have credit business records. Hence, the coverage of credit information data is still relatively low.[101] Furthermore, the protection of investors' interests must be enhanced. Up to now, P2P investors have lacked the ability to appreciate the risks of investing. For high-risk investments, a higher investment threshold and a sound investor asset protection mechanism should be set to protect the interests of investors.

---

95 Yan Li, Cungang Li, and Yijun Gao, 'Voluntary Disclosures and Peer-to-Peer Lending Decisions: Evidence from the Repeated Game' (2020) 14(7) Frontiers of Business Research in China <https://fbr.springeropen.com/articles/10.1186/s11782-020-00075-5> accessed 17 November 2022.

96 Michael, 'Paipaidai Changed its Name, Changed its Type, and Quietly Disbanded its Auto Finance Team' (*DayDayNews*, 2 February 2020) <https://daydaynews.cc/en/technology/295751.html> accessed 17 November 2022.

97 Souhu Net, 'Actively Transforming P2P Platforms: Multiple Platforms Transforming into Investment and Wealth Management Platforms' (《P2P平台积极转型：多家平台转型为投资理财平台》), (2015) <https://www.sohu.com/a/32990550_120797> accessed 25 November 2022.

98 Nicole Kobie, 'The Complicated Truth about China's Social Credit System' (*WIRED*, 7 June 2019) <https://www.wired.co.uk/article/china-social-credit-system-explained> accessed 25 November 2022.

99 Ibid.

100 Theresa Krause et al., 'China's Corporate Credit Reporting System: A Comparison with the United States and Germany' (2022) 17(3) Regulation & Governance 755, 771.

101 The People's Bank of China, 'PBC Work Conference on Credit Information Reference' (*The People's Bank of China*, 16 March 2009) <http://www.pbc.gov.cn/english/130721/2842034/index.html> accessed 17 November 2022.

VII. Conclusion

The advent of the internet and recent technological developments have allowed P2P lending services in China to provide an alternative financial market that enhances access to finance and provides more investment targets for retail investors. As in the EU, the P2P financial market was intended to provide access to finance for smaller businesses that did not have sufficient credit or adequate collateral to secure bank loans. Coupled with strict lending policies after the global financial crisis in 2008, the global rise of P2P platforms was seen as a positive financial innovation. In China's large single market, the convenience of internet finance propelled by smart technology caused exponential growth of P2P platforms that surpassed that of the Western markets. The lax regulatory attitude towards P2P platforms played an important role in this development. The light (or even no) touch approach, coupled with the escalating requirement for access to finance and for investment returns, drove this remarkable growth. However, the lack of adequate regulation and supervision has resulted in problems in financial stability, investor protection, and market integrity. In particular, the outflow of capital from the traditional banking system to the light or unregulated P2P lending sector caused concerns among policymakers. The Joint Guiding Opinions epitomise such a fear, and their enforcement has swiftly caused the P2P market to shut down almost completely.

The EU's legal solution of providing a comprehensive crowdfunding regulation may help sustain the development of the P2P lending platforms in China.[102] It provides both ex-ante and ex-post measures to give investor protection. Yet, P2P lending platforms may draw capital from bank depositors and lower the banks' reserves, giving rise to the risk of financial instability. The EU has avoided this experience, but the volume of activity was much smaller than it was in China. Nevertheless, the current situation in China, with the collapse of Evergrande, the problems of regional banks, and the low economic growth during the continuing COVID-19 lockdowns, may lead to even tighter control of the credit services sector.

102 Joseph Lee (n 7).

5

The uncertain path towards open finance: mutual lessons from the United Kingdom and European Union regulatory approaches

Clara Martins Pereira

I. Introduction

Recent years have seen a new dawn in finance. First, with the popularisation of Open Banking—a framework of technologies and standards that allow consumers and businesses to give third parties access to banking data and authorisation to initiate payments on their behalf[1]—and, more recently, with a gradual transition into Open Finance—which builds on Open Banking[2] to encompass a wider range of data-driven products and services[3]—we have been witnessing a radical paradigm shift in how financial data is shared and transmitted across the financial system, making its way from 'data holders' to 'data users'.[4]

---

1 For a definition of Open Banking, *see*, ia, Joint Regulatory Oversight Committee, 'Recommendations for the Next Phase of Open Banking in the UK' (*FCA and PSR*, 2023) <https://assets.publishing.service.gov.uk/media/643e608e22ef3b000c66f3bf/JROC_report_recommendations_and_actions_paper_April_2023.pdf> accessed 15 December 2023.

2 For a description of how Open Banking frameworks can transition into Open Finance frameworks, *see*, ia, The Organisation for Economic Co-operation and Development, 'Shifting from Open Banking to Open Finance - Results from the 2022 OECD Survey on Data Sharing Frameworks' (*OECD*, 2023) <https://www.oecd-ilibrary.org/docserver/9f881c0c-en.pdf?expires=1701120835&id=id&accname=guest&checksum=C4ECECD791A3372F1B9DA54B1037B2FF> accessed 15 December 2023.

3 The significant variety of Open Finance use cases has been illustrated, for example, *in* Expert Group on European Financial Data Space, 'Report on Open Finance' (*European Commission*, 2022) <https://finance.ec.europa.eu/system/files/2022-10/2022-10-24-report-on-open-finance_en.pdf> accessed 15 December 2023.

4 A note on terminology is necessary because different Open Banking/Open Finance regulatory frameworks use different expressions to refer to the agents interacting within those frameworks. In this chapter, the expression 'data holders' is used to refer to the agents required or encouraged to share data under an Open Banking/Open Finance framework, while the expression 'data users' is used to refer to the agents that

Around the world, most nations have embraced Open Banking[5] and begun to navigate the seemingly inevitable path leading to Open Finance and beyond.[6] However, different economies have been taking markedly different roads towards developing Open Banking and Open Finance frameworks, and regulatory approaches to these phenomena can look radically dissimilar across jurisdictions.[7]

Differences in approaches include both differences in *substance* and differences in *process*. When it comes to *substance*, different jurisdictions have come—or are coming—to distinctive conclusions in terms of who should be subject to their Open Banking and Open Finance frameworks, which kinds of data ought to be shared and transmitted to data users, and how data sharing and transmission should be governed. In terms of *process*, there is also significant disagreement over who should take the lead in developing these frameworks—namely, whether the initiative should be left to the market, or whether a top-down approach is preferable—and whether the transition into Open Banking and Open Finance should be staggered or occur more quickly.

The variety of regulatory approaches to Open Banking and Open Finance—and, crucially, the asynchronous nature of regulatory reform in this area—creates room for fascinating analysis of interactions between economies, and how policymakers in some geographies are variously influenced by legislative developments in others. In this context, a particularly noteworthy comparison can be made between the United Kingdom (UK) and the European Union (EU).

---

use that data in the provision of financial products and services. In many frameworks, data holders can also be data users (and vice versa), depending on which side of the data sharing relationship they are in (and regardless of whether such frameworks are ruled by a principle of reciprocity in data sharing).

5 For a list of Open Banking regulatory initiatives around the world, which also showcases the variety of regulatory approaches to Open Banking adopted across jurisdictions, *see* the database maintained by Matthias Biehl at <http://www.openbankingmap.com> accessed 15 December 2023.

6 The future of Open Finance might take the shape of Open Data, a framework of technologies and standards that will allow parties to access, share, transmit, and reuse data across increasingly varied domains of modern life. For a brief discussion, *see* Linda Jeng, 'Inception to Open Banking' in Linda Jeng (ed.), *Open Banking* (Oxford University Press 2022) 1–11.

7 For discussions of these different regulatory approaches, *see*, ia, Douglas W. Arner, Ross P. Buckley, and Dirk A. Zetzsche, 'Open Banking, Open Data, and Open Finance: Lessons from the European Union' in Linda Jeng (ed.), *Open Banking* (Oxford University Press 2022) 147–172; Dan Awrey and Joshua Macey, 'The Promise and Perils of Open Finance' (2022) European Corporate Governance Institute Working Paper 632/2022 <https://chicagounbound.uchicago.edu/cgi/viewcontent.cgi?article=2605&context=law_and_economics> accessed 15 December 2023; and Nydia Remolina, 'Open Finance: Regulatory Challenges of the Evolution of Data Sharing Arrangements in the Financial Sector' (2023) Singapore Management University for AI & Data Governance Research Paper No. 2019/05 <https://papers.ssrn.com/sol3/papers.cfm?abstract_id=3475019> accessed 15 December 2023.

There are two reasons why such a comparison is especially interesting. First, because the UK and the EU have both positioned themselves as leaders in this area: indeed, the UK has been widely credited with spearheading the Open Banking revolution, creating a blueprint for other countries to follow[8] (with the remainder of Europe falling somewhat behind);[9] more recently, it could be argued that the tables have turned, with the EU advancing a legislative proposal for a framework for Financial Data Access (FIDA)[10] at a time when the UK is still in the process of refining its Open Banking framework in preparation for the country's seemingly inevitable transition into Open Finance.[11]

A second reason why a comparison between the approaches adopted by the UK and the EU regarding Open Banking and Open Finance is interesting has to do with the history that unites both jurisdictions, namely with the fact that the UK was, until recently, a Member State of the EU, having withdrawn from the Union only in 2020—in the culmination of the long-drawn-out process that came to be known as 'Brexit'.[12] Brexit has created inevitable tension between the UK and the EU: on the one hand, the rationale behind the UK's withdrawal from the EU was ostensibly a desire to 'actively diverge' from EU policy and law, so that divergence of UK financial regulation from EU financial regulation is 'almost a given outcome following Brexit';[13] on the other

8 For a detailed examination of the UK's 'butterfly effect' on Open Banking regulations around the world, *see*, ia, Gavin Littlejohn, Ghela Boskovich, and Richard Prior, 'United Kingdom: The Butterfly Effect' in Linda Jeng (ed.), *Open Banking* (Oxford University Press 2022) 173–200.

9 *See* the opinion of the EU's own European Banking Authority, as stated *in* European Banking Authority (EBA), 'Opinion of the European Banking Authority on Its Technical Advice on the Review of Directive (EU) 2015/2366 on Payment Services in the Internal Market (PSD2)' (2022) EBA/Op/2022/06 of 23 June 2022 <https://www.eba.europa.eu/sites/default/files/document_library/Publications/Opinions/2022/Opinion%20od%20PSD2%20review%20(EBA-Op-2022-06)/1036016/EBA%27s%20response%20to%20the%20Call%20for%20advice%20on%20the%20review%20of%20PSD2.pdf> accessed 15 December 2023. For a different opinion, which casts the EU as taking the leading role in this area, *see* Arner, Buckley, and Zetzsche (n 7).

10 *See* Commission, 'Proposal for a Regulation of the European Parliament and of the Council on a Framework for Financial Data Access and Amending Regulations (EU) No 1093/2010, (EU) No 1094/2010, (EU) No 1095/2010 and (EU) 2022/2554' COM(2023) 360 final <https://eur-lex.europa.eu/legal-content/EN/TXT/?uri=CELEX:52023PC0360> accessed 15 December 2023 ('proposed FIDA').

11 Joint Regulatory Oversight Committee (n 1).

12 There are multiple sources illustrating the complexity of Brexit. For a brief description of the timeline leading up to Brexit, *see* European Union, 'Brexit: EU-UK Relationship' <https://eur-lex.europa.eu/content/news/Brexit-UK-withdrawal-from-the-eu.html> accessed 15 December 2023; the complete agreement on the withdrawal of the UK of Great Britain and Northern Ireland from the EU and the European Atomic Energy Community can be found at <https://www.legislation.gov.uk/eut/withdrawal-agreement/contents/adopted> accessed 15 December 2023.

13 *See* Christy Ann Petit and Thorsten Beck, 'Recent Trends in UK Financial Sector Regulation and Possible Implications for the EU, Including Its Approach to Equivalence'

hand, EU policymakers have been left with the challenge of having the most important financial centre in Europe now sitting firmly outside their regulatory framework,[14] all while openly nurturing a growing desire to challenge the UK's financial hegemony.[15]

In the end, we have two jurisdictions that justifiably see themselves as financial regulation influencers, while also finding themselves in the delicate position of having to strike the right balance between—on the one hand—regulatory autonomy and competitiveness goals, and—on the other hand—equivalence, cooperation, and financial stability goals. The areas of Open Banking and Open Finance then become fertile ground for analysis that can illuminate not just the future of regulation in this area, but also the future of the broader relationship developing between UK and EU policymakers in a post-Brexit world.

This piece embraces this challenge by analysing the UK and EU current and proposed approaches to Open Banking and Open Finance, by determining whether signs of convergence or divergence of approaches can already be identified at this stage, and by highlighting the importance of both jurisdictions learning lessons from each other: both the UK, as it continues its transition into Open Finance, and the EU, as it finalises its FIDA framework[16] and begins the process of guiding Member States through its implementation. Specifically, it argues that the EU should reconsider the initial timeline and process for implementing its Open Finance framework, namely by reflecting on the benefits of setting up an entity that can help with the phased implementation of a system of true standardisation—and it should also consider the importance of reciprocity to address the uneven playing field seemingly created by the proposed FIDA. The UK, on the other hand, should look at developments in the EU Open Finance scene for an indication of how broad standardisation requirements can be operationalised, as well as for inspiration on how mandatory compensation arrangements can be used to unlock the full potential of the country's burgeoning Open Finance ecosystem.

This chapter is organised as follows: first, it discusses the nature of Open Banking and its transition into Open Finance, highlighting the variety of regulatory approaches that might govern that process (Section II); second, it focusses on the approaches specifically adopted by the UK and the EU in this area, comparing them (Section III); and third, it highlights mutual lessons to be learnt by both jurisdictions as they walk their distinctive paths into Open Finance and beyond (Section IV). Section V concludes.

(European Parliament, ECON Committee, February 2023), 8 <https://www.europarl.europa.eu/RegData/etudes/STUD/2023/740067/IPOL_STU(2023)740067_EN.pdf> accessed 15 December 2023.

14 ibid.

15 *See* the 'competitiveness and growth' objective recently attributed to the UK's Financial Conduct Authority and Prudential Regulation Authority under the new UK Financial Services and Markets Act 2023.

16 *See* Proposed FIDA.

II. The uncertain path from open banking to open finance

A. A changing financial system

The only constant thing about financial systems is that they keep changing.[17] The functions that we expect them to perform in relation to the real economy are broadly the same as they have always been, but their building components—the players, intermediaries, and structures through which those functions are performed—have been undergoing radical change in the last decades, leaving the world of finance transformed almost beyond recognition.[18]

The most significant drivers of change in financial systems are arguably technology, regulation, and competition,[19] and, in the last few years, many jurisdictions—particularly in Europe—have seen these factors combine to create the phenomenon that has come to be known as 'Open Banking'. Open Banking is a technology-fuelled financial innovation that has been (or is being) allowed to develop in certain jurisdictions within or through existing (or proposed) regulatory frameworks. It has been significantly shaped by the stances adopted by both the new players entering the markets, as well as by the incumbents that have long dominated them. And while Open Banking is broadly restricted to the area of 'banking', its influence is rapidly extending to other branches of finance and beyond, prompting regulators around the world—namely in the UK and the EU—to adopt regulatory approaches that can guide them through an (uncertain) path into Open Finance.

B. Open banking, open finance, and beyond

The analysis of novel financial technology (FinTech) innovations often requires engaging with novel concepts and enquiring into the nature of these innovations—and it is worth considering what Open Banking is and how it can be distinguished from neighbouring concepts like Open Finance and Open Data.

Open Banking refers to the set of technologies and standards whereby consumers and businesses are given the necessary tools for granting access to banking data and authorisation to initiate payments to particular third-party providers (data users)

---

17 John Armour and others, *Principles of Financial Regulation* (illustrated edition, OUP 2016), 44.

18 ibid, 23.

19 *See* Fox *et al.*, noting that equity markets are 'very dynamic, with changes driven by innovations in technology, market participants' strategies, and regulation itself' in Merritt B. Fox, Lawrence R. Glosten, and Gabriel V. Rauterberg, *The New Stock Market: Law, Economics, and Policy* (Columbia University Press 2019), 34. Crucially, competition is not always seen as an independent driver of change: for instance, Schwartz *et al.* see competition instead as a product of technology and regulatory developments (*see* Robert A. Schwartz, John Aidan Byrne, and Antoinette Colaninno, *Technology and Regulation: How Are They Driving Our Markets?* (Springer Science & Business Media 2009)).

through the cooperation of banks (data holders).[20] An example helps illustrate the potential of Open Banking. A consumer with multiple bank accounts scattered across multiple institutions may have trouble keeping track of their financial situation and spending—indeed, there is wide literature demonstrating consumers' vulnerability to narrow bracketing and their consequent tendency to take decisions in isolation, focussing on particular assets instead of considering their portfolio as a whole.[21] Such a consumer would benefit from access to bank account aggregation services—often made available by small FinTech[22] providers—but such services hinge on these providers having access to the consumer's banking data, which has traditionally been locked away deep in the vaults of banks. Under an Open Banking framework, these vaults become unsealed: upon consumer consent, banks are forced or encouraged to share this data with certain third parties.

In practice, this 'unsealing' is powered by Application Programming Interface (API) technology, a type of software that connects the functions of different applications and allows them to communicate, broadly reducing transaction costs:[23] in layman's terms, a common language that different software applications can use to talk to each other.[24] There are different types of APIs, depending on their level of 'openness', or, in other words, on whether they are used internally, between partners, or to facilitate communication with third parties. Open APIs—which create the infrastructure required for communications with third parties—have become particularly popular in recent years,[25] effectively providing the necessary technological backbone to the collaborative ecosystem that in many countries has fuelled the Open Banking revolution.[26]

In the UK, Open Banking has now flourished into a framework where over seven million consumers and businesses—including around 750,000 Small and Medium Enterprises (SMEs)—are able to use Open Banking-enabled products and services to manage their money and make payments. Open Banking-powered payments, in

20 Joint Regulatory Oversight Committee (n 1).

21 *See*, ia, Financial Conduct Authority (FCA), 'Applying Behavioural Economics at the Financial Conduct Authority' (April 2013) Occasional Paper 1 <https://www.fca.org.uk/publication/occasional-papers/occasional-paper-1.pdf> accessed 26 November 2023; and Clara Martins Pereira, 'Reviewing the Literature on Behavioural Economics' (2016) 11(3) Capital Markets Law Journal 414.

22 The expression 'FinTech' has multiple meanings for a discussion; *see*, ia, Howell E. Jackson and James S. Reid, 'The Nature of the Fintech Firm' (2020) 61 Washington University Journal of Law & Policy 9. Here, it is being used to refer to the new players in the financial system whose core business involves using technology in the provision of financial services—whereas previously it was used to describe the innovative use of modern technologies in the provision of these types of services.

23 Yuanbo Qiu, 'The Openness of Open Application Programming Interfaces' (2017) 20(11) Information, Communication & Society 1720, 1721.

24 Remolina (n 7), 8.

25 Qiu (n 23), 1720.

26 Remolina (n 7), 13.

particular, amounted to over 68 million in 2022 (compared to 25 million in 2021).[27] There is no comparable data available to characterise the evolution of Open Banking in the rest of Europe, but the general consensus is that its development has generally lagged behind the UK's;[28] still, a recent report conducted by MasterCard predicts significant growth in this area in a number of key EU Member States.[29]

Crucially, Open Banking has also laid down a more ambitious path towards Open Finance, which is often described as the next step for Open Banking. Indeed, while Open Banking is typically limited to personal and SME banking, Open Finance has a much broader scope, applying to a significantly wider range of financial products and services, including pensions, insurance, and asset management.[30] In the future, it is expected that an Open Data framework—sometimes also referred to as an 'Open Everything' framework—will stretch the boundaries of Open Banking even further, potentially culminating in a utopia where everyone owns and controls both the data that they supply and the data created on their behalf,[31] and can freely enlist such data in the service of their own interests.[32]

Ultimately, the concepts of Open Banking, Open Finance, and Open Data do not fit neatly into confined boxes—and distinguishing between them involves considering multiple factors, including, in particular, the nature of the products and services from which the data originates, and the nature of the data holders required or encouraged to share data under a particular framework.[33] It is also worth considering the relationship between them: they are often seen as sequential stages in the road towards 'Open Everything', but Open Finance should not be seen as replacing Open Banking (while setting itself up to be replaced by Open Data); rather, Open Banking should be seen as

27 A complete picture of the UK Open Banking ecosystem can be found *in* Joint Regulatory Oversight Committee (n 1), 3.

28 *See* EBA (n 9). For a different perspective, *see* Arner, Buckley, and Zetzsche (n 7).

29 Specifically, the analysis conducted by Mastercard in September 2023 projects usage of Open Banking among adults to grow significantly between 2021 and 2027 in several European countries: from 7% to 29% in the Netherlands, from 8.5% to 36% in France, and from 9.8% to 41% in Spain (*see* Mastercard, 'Four European Takes on Open Banking' (Mastercard Report, September 2023) <https://go.mastercardservices.com/four-european-takes-on-open-banking> accessed 15 December 2023, 11–20).

30 For a discussion of the scope of Open Finance, *see*, ia, Arner, Buckley, and Zetzsche (n 7); and Remolina (n 7).

31 Arner, Buckley, and Zetzsche (n 7).

32 Brad Carr, 'From Open Banking to Open Data and Beyond: Competition and the Future of Banking' in Linda Jeng (ed), *Open Banking* (OUP 2022); and Jeng (n 6).

33 This is a particularly challenging task in a world where the boundaries of the banking system (*vis-à-vis* the remainder of the financial system), and the boundaries of the financial system itself, are by their own nature somewhat uncertain. For a discussion, *see*, ia, Armour and others (n 17), 23ff and 433ff.

an aspect of Open Finance (with Open Finance being seen as an aspect of Open Data) that can be subject to specific rules even within a broader regulatory framework.[34]

And this brings another key point to light: crucially, Open Banking, Open Finance, and Open Data are as much a product of technological innovation as they are a product of regulatory forces.[35] The extent to which Open Banking has been allowed to flourish in the first place—and the extent to which, in many jurisdictions, it is now being allowed to develop into Open Finance—is significantly determined by the regulatory framework that surrounds it. A close analysis of the regulatory framework that applies to Open Banking and Open Finance in a particular jurisdiction is therefore crucial to understanding what those concepts mean in that specific context.

Notably, there is little consensus over what constitutes the 'right' legal and regulatory environment for Open Banking and Open Finance, leading different jurisdictions to adopt markedly different regulatory approaches in this field. As such, the next section continues its characterisation of Open Banking and Open Finance by outlining the main categories of regulatory approaches that have been identified by commentators in the area and that have played different roles in shaping the evolution of these phenomena around the world. Additionally—and given this piece's central goal of comparing the UK and EU regulatory approaches to Open Banking and Open Finance—these approaches will also be situated within the categories outlined below.

C. Regulatory approaches in the path towards open banking and open finance

Few phenomena illustrate how technology and regulation can combine to generate financial innovation better than Open Banking and Open Finance.

At its core, Open Banking is just the 'opening' up of banking systems to third parties willing to directly provide banking products and services to customers—much like Open Finance is just the broader 'opening' up of financial systems to third parties looking to directly provide financial products and services to customers. But it is

---

34 A good example is provided by the EU Open Banking/Open Finance frameworks—with Open Banking continuing to be regulated under the EU Second Payment Services Directive (PSD2) (and, in the near future, under PSD3 and PSR), whereas the framework for Open Finance will be the new FIDA. As a result of this separation, Open Banking will (at least for the time being) continue to be subject to special rules (under PSD2); an example of one such rule is that Open Banking data users are able to initiate payments (upon customer consent) under PSD2 (*see* PSD2, recital (93)), even though data users under the proposed FIDA are generally unable to initiate transactions on the customer's behalf.

35 According to Arner *et al.*, 'open banking is the regulatory response to the anticompetitive tendencies of the data economy' (*see* Arner, Buckley, and Zetzsche (n 7), 150). Similarly, Remolina observes that Open Banking—and presumably Open Finance—cannot be seen as pure 'technology-based' concepts because the conversation around these phenomena 'started from a regulatory perspective' (*see* Remolina (n 7), 13).

intuitively easy to understand that the extent to which the regulatory framework in a particular jurisdiction encourages, facilitates, regulates, or even mandates data sharing (in general or within a particular context) can fundamentally shape the nature and evolution of these phenomena within the legal space where they apply.

Faced with the popularisation of data-scraping and other data-sharing technology[36]—and their application within finance—each jurisdiction around the world has (or has had) a fundamental choice to make: to intervene or not to intervene. This choice has resulted in two fundamental types of regulatory approaches to Open Banking and Open Finance: *(i)* compulsory approaches,[37] and *(ii)* market-led approaches,[38] respectively. Next to these categories, it is also possible to identify a third type of *(iii)* hybrid approaches that see regulators collaborate closely with the market to develop Open Banking/Open Finance frameworks, in particular by setting up regulatory sandboxes where innovations can be tested before being deployed, or by incentivising market players to adhere to Open Data environments without explicitly mandating them to do so.[39]

In more detail, *(i)* compulsory approaches are embodied by regulatory frameworks that require particular data-holding institutions—banks, in the case of Open Banking, and other financial institutions like insurance companies and pension providers, in the case of Open Finance—to provide and facilitate immediate access to financial data

36 Data-scraping technology, in particular, refers to the technology tools used to extract and import data from the web. For a discussion of the concept of 'data scraping' and its impact on the banking industry, *see* Natalia Jevglevskaja and Ross P. Buckley, 'Screen Scraping of Bank Customer Data: A Lamentable Practice' (2023) University of New South Wales Faculty of Law and Legal Studies Research Paper 23–3 <https://papers.ssrn.com/sol3/papers.cfm?abstract_id=4382528#> accessed 15 December 2023.

37 Jurisdictions that are often noted for having adopted compulsory approaches to Open Banking include the UK, the European Union, Mexico, Hong Kong, and Australia.

38 Countries that are commonly said to have embraced market-driven approaches to Open Banking include the US, India, Japan, and South Korea (although it could be argued that India and Japan, for example, represent instances of a hybrid approach to Open Banking).

39 Arner *et al.* divide regulatory approaches to open banking into three categories: 'mandatory', 'voluntary', and 'collaborative', essentially corresponding to the 'compulsory', 'market-led', and 'hybrid' approaches listed in this chapter (*see* Arner, Buckley, and Zetzsche (n 7)). Similarly, Remolina also suggests that there are three regulatory models, including a 'sandbox approach' whereby regulators intervene to incentivise an open data environment and to connect technology developers with traditional financial institutions; she then gives Singapore—sometimes seen as adopting a market-led model—as an example of a jurisdiction adopting a sandbox approach (*see* Remolina (n 7), 5 and 21). Under the terminology adopted by this chapter, this 'sandbox approach' would fall under the category of 'hybrid approaches' that sees regulators variously collaborating with industry members and other stakeholders to develop Open Banking/Open Finance frameworks, although not necessarily by way of setting up regulatory sandboxes.

by third-party developers and service providers (upon consumer consent). By contrast, *(ii)* market-led approaches allow relationships between data holders—typically market incumbents—and data users—typically new players—to develop organically, on the back of individual data-sharing agreements facilitated by data aggregators and other such intermediaries.[40] Such market-led approaches rely on market participants identifying a business opportunity in Open Banking and Open Finance, and on incumbents understanding the importance of entering into partnerships with new FinTechs in order to remain competitive.[41] Finally, *(iii)* hybrid approaches recognise that additional incentives and collaboration might be necessary before incumbents, in particular, adhere or are required to adhere to data-sharing environments.

An in-depth analysis of the reasons that might motivate a particular jurisdiction to select one of these approaches over the others far exceeds the scope of this piece, as do discussions of which approach might be better, particularly as much might hinge on jurisdiction-specific factors. However, it is worth acknowledging that this is a complex choice—likely shaped, in each case, by the consideration of the benefits and risks inherent in Open Banking and Open Finance and how such benefits and risks might materialise in a particular geography.

Briefly, the shift in paradigm towards Open Banking and Open Finance might be welcomed by a particular jurisdiction to the extent that it represents: *(i)* an opportunity for increasing competition in finance, namely by facilitating access to relevant financial data by third-party entities and allowing them to compete with incumbent financial institutions in the provision of products and services that they would otherwise be unable to provide;[42] *(ii)* a potential path to financial inclusion, with the opening of new channels for serving underbanked and underfinanced segments of the population; *(iii)* an incentive for innovation and the creation of one-stop shops for the provision of financial services and products, in line with potential consumer demand for seamless interactions with the financial system; and *(iv)* an opportunity for encouraging incumbent firms to modernise legacy systems and find paths towards collaboration with more agile (typically FinTech)[43] third parties.[44]

---

40 *See* Littlejohn, Boskovich, and Prior (n 8), 174. The most important data aggregator in the US is Plaid; for a discussion of concerns over the dominant market position arguably achieved by Plaid, *see* Awrey and Macey (n 7).

41 In the absence of individual agreements, third-party providers may have to rely on screen-scraping (*see* n 36 above).

42 Indeed, this has been the main driving force behind the development of Open Banking in the UK, where the push towards Open Banking was conducted by the Competition and Markets Authority upon identifying competition problems within the UK banking market (for a discussion, *see* below at III.C).

43 Littlejohn, Boskovich, and Prior (n 8), 175.

44 For a more in-depth discussion of the benefits inherent in an Open Banking/Open Finance framework, *see*, ia, Arner, Buckley, and Zetzsche (n 7); Awrey and Macey (n 7); and Remolina (n 7).

At the same time, policymakers justifiably fear that Open Banking and the move towards Open Finance might result in: *(i)* significant transition costs derived, in particular, from mandated investment in technology by smaller players, magnified in systems without standardisation requirements (resulting in added barriers to entry into the financial sector); *(ii)* an effective decrease in competition, to the extent that lack of reciprocity in data-sharing obligations and the search for one-stop shops create an uneven playing field that disproportionately favours third-party providers, in particular, 'BigTech' platforms entering the financial services arena;[45] *(iii)* access to data by third-party entities that fall outside of the regulatory perimeter of (financial) regulators, and which include not just data users, but also data aggregators and other intermediaries; *(iv)* added financial instability and systemic risk, particularly to the extent that unregulated entities are allowed to build up significant market power within existing frameworks;[46] *(v)* added threats to consumer privacy due to increased circulation of data and the creation of pockets of cyber risk lodged in unregulated players;[47] *(vi)* added risk of financial exclusion due to combinations of data creating more accurate consumer profiles; and *(vii)* excessive reliance on consumer consent as the cornerstone of Open Banking/Open Finance frameworks, in circumstances when true consent may be difficult to ensure.[48]

All things considered, it is clear that designing the right Open Banking/Open Finance framework is a difficult challenge for regulators that involves: first, recognising that such a framework might pose both benefits and risks to users of the financial system—and the stability of that system—and that any regulatory approach leads to inevitable trade-offs; and, second, acknowledging that opting for a compulsory approach (or even a hybrid approach) in the path towards Open Finance is just the first of many steps that will need to be taken in designing that system. As a result, other

---

45 BigTechs are large technology firms with high customer bases and access to rich customer datasets; examples of BigTechs include Alphabet, Amazon, Apple, Meta, and Microsoft. For a discussion of BigTechs and their impact on the European financial sector, *see*, ia, Elisabeth Noble, 'The Next Generation of Financial Conglomerates: BigTech and Beyond' [2020] Butterworths Journal of International Banking and Financial Law <https://papers.ssrn.com/sol3/papers.cfm?abstract_id=3693870> accessed 15 December 2023.

46 A thorough discussion of the specific risk that certain Open Finance frameworks—namely the US Open Finance framework—may favour the emergence of a market where a handful of (broadly unregulated) data aggregators have significant market power, potentially creating a new source of systemic risk, can be found *in* Awrey and Macey (n 7).

47 For a discussion of the applications of cybersecurity within the context of Open Banking and Open Finance, *see* Joseph Lee and Vere-Marie Khan, 'Developing Cybersecurity in Open Banking and Open Finance: The Application of Blockchain Technology and Decentralised Autonomous Organisations' *in* Joseph Lee and Aline Darbellay (eds), *A Research Agenda for Financial Law and Regulation* (Edward Elgar 2024).

48 The risks arising from Open Banking/Open Finance environments are also discussed, ia, *in* Arner, Buckley, and Zetzsche (n 7); Awrey and Macey (n 7); and Remolina (n 7).

criteria—in addition to who initiates the development of a particular Open Banking/Open Finance framework—can then be used to distinguish and compare regulatory approaches adopted by different jurisdictions in this field.

Indeed, the UK and EU Open Banking/Open Finance frameworks offer a great example of variety within the traditional categories of regulatory approaches identified in this area. Even though, as will be demonstrated below, both jurisdictions have traditionally been seen as adopters of a compulsory approach, similarities between them hide important regulatory differences. It is those differences that ought to be examined by both the UK and the EU in search of mutual lessons that can help them complete their transition from Open Banking into Open Finance—and it is to those differences that this chapter now turns.

III. The UK and EU regulatory approaches to open banking and open finance

A. UK and EU: same but different

The UK is widely recognised as having pioneered the adoption of Open Banking globally,[49] in a process that started with an investigation of the retail banking market by the UK's Competition and Markets Authority (CMA), which found that incumbent banks were not competing hard enough for customers, at a time when smaller and newer banks were also struggling to enter the market.[50] Following the publication of these findings, a wide-reaching package of reforms was adopted requiring the bulk of the UK banking sector to embrace Open Banking by 2018.[51] Such a package was comprised, in particular, of the Competition Markets Authority (CMA) Retail Banking Market Investigation Order 2017[52] and by the Payment Services Regulations 2017 (SI 2017/75)—which at the time transposed the EU Second Payment Services Directive (PSD2)[53] into national law—and led, in particular, to the creation of a new

49 *See* Littlejohn, Boskovich, and Prior (n 8). For a different view—which casts the EU as having taken the leading role in compulsory approaches to Open Banking—*see* Arner, Buckley, and Zetzsche (n 7).

50 *See* Competition and Markets Authority (CMA), 'CMA Paves the Way for Open Banking Revolution' (*CMA Press release*, 9 August 2016) <https://www.gov.uk/government/news/cma-paves-the-way-for-open-banking-revolution> accessed 15 December 2023. For a more detailed discussion of the UK's journey into Open Banking, *see* Littlejohn, Boskovich, and Prior (n 8), 181ff.

51 CMA (n 50).

52 CMA, 'Retail Banking Market Investigation: The Retail Banking Market Investigation Order 2017' (CMA, 2017) <https://assets.publishing.service.gov.uk/media/5a759cc7ed915d506ee80283/retail-banking-market-investigation-order-2017.pdf> accessed 15 December 2023.

53 Council Directive (EU) 2015/2366 of the European Parliament and of the Council of 25 November 2015 on payment services in the internal market, amending Directives

entity—the Open Banking Implementation Entity (OBIE),[54] entrusted with building and developing the country's burgeoning Open Banking ecosystem.[55]

In the EU, the transition into Open Banking arguably developed a bit later, but was ultimately encouraged by PSD2, which created a regulatory framework whereby banks were required to facilitate safe access to payments data by third parties, including account information service providers (AISPs) and payment initiation service providers (PISPs)[56]—and complemented by other important cross-sector digital market initiatives, like the EU General Data Protection Regulation (GDPR).[57]

More recently, both jurisdictions have been trying to determine the best road into Open Finance—and here it could be argued that the EU is taking the lead.[58] Indeed, the UK is still designing the next phase for Open Banking, which will involve the creation of a new supervisory entity and the establishment of a long-term regulatory framework[59]—and, in time, the building of a new 'smart data' framework that can transpose the success of Open Banking to other sectors (like the energy sector).[60]

2002/65/EC, 2009/110/EC and 2013/36/EU and Regulation (EU) No 1093/2010, and repealing Directive 2007/64/EC [2015] OJ L 337/35 of 23.12.2015.

54 The OBIE is an entity created by the CMA to deliver the APIs, data structures, and security architectures needed to enable developers to harness the technology needed to share data across the UK banking system. The standards and guidelines that apply to the OBIE also comprise the UK Open Banking regulatory framework, together with the CMA Retail Banking Market Investigation Order 2017 and the Payment Services Regulations 2017 (SI 2017/75).

55 For a summary of the UK's road into Open Banking, *see* Joint Regulatory Oversight Committee (n 1); and Littlejohn, Boskovich, and Prior (n 8), 181ff.

56 European Commission, 'Payment Services: Revised Rules to Improve Consumer Protection and Competition in Electronic Payments' (*European Commission, Questions and Answers*, 28 June 2023) <https://ec.europa.eu/commission/presscorner/detail/en/qanda_23_3544> accessed 15 December 2023.

57 *See* Council Regulation (EU) 2016/679 of the European Parliament and of the Council of 27 April 2016 on the protection of natural persons with regard to the processing of personal data and on the free movement of such data and repealing Directive 95/46/EC (General Data Protection Regulation). However, it is worth noting that the GDPR and PSD2 were developed separately, and although they share similar goals in terms of data safety and portability, their provisions can be difficult to reconcile in practice (*see*, below, at n 135).

58 *See*, for example, a comment made recently by the Global Head of Government Affairs at Revolut, noting that 'other jurisdictions are now leapfrogging [the UK]—doubling down on Instant Payments and expanding to Open Finance and Open Data' (*see* Isabelle Castro Margaroli, 'In Global Shift to Open Finance Can the UK Remain a Leader?' (*FinTech Nexus News*, 2023) <https://www.fintechnexus.com/in-global-shift-to-open-finance-can-the-uk-remain-a-leader/> accessed 15 December 2023).

59 *See* the next steps described *in* Joint Regulatory Oversight Committee (n 1), 42.

60 The UK's new Smart Data framework is being designed by a 'Smart Data Council' on the back of a proposed new Government Bill (the Data Protection and Digital Information Bill). This framework is meant to specify which data holders are covered

The EU, on the other hand, has identified the 'absence of clear rules' as the reason for the slow development of Open Finance solutions in Europe,[61] and has already taken two combined initiatives to accelerate its transition into the next stage of Open Banking. First, the European Commission has advanced a series of targeted amendments to its Open Banking framework, namely by proposing a new Regulation on Payment Services (PSR) and a significant modernisation of PSD2 (which will predictably become PSD3).[62] Second, the European Commission has also put forward a new legislative proposal for a financial data access regulation—the aforementioned FIDA—which is set to extend the obligation to provide access to financial data beyond payment account data.[63]

Ultimately, a perfunctory examination of these initiatives suggests that both the UK and the EU have adopted, or are adopting, a similar approach to regulating Open Banking/Open Finance—namely, a compulsory approach whereby, upon consumer consent, data-holding institutions are required to share data with third-party providers. This common preference for a compulsory approach is unsurprising for two reasons. First—when it comes to Open Banking—it is worth noting that even though the UK has now left the EU, at the time that both the UK and later the EU started embracing Open Banking, it was still very much an EU Member State, and therefore aligned with the EU in matters of competition and financial regulation. Second—when it comes to Open Finance—it is significant that the impressive uptake of Open Banking in the UK (cementing the country's position as a leader in this field) has been interpreted by some as a sign that compulsory approaches to regulation in this area are superior to market-led approaches,[64] which have caused countries like the United States (US) to lag behind in this area.[65] Ultimately, it is unclear whether pure

by the scheme, what data will be shared under the scheme, and how (*see* n 13). For more information about the Smart Data Council and the new Data Protection and Digital Information Bill, *see*, respectively, the information available *in* Open Banking, 'Smart Data Council' (2023) <https://www.openbanking.org.uk/glossary/smart-data-council/> accessed 15 December 2023 and *in* UK Parliament, 'Data Protection and Digital Information Bill - Government Bill' (*Parliamentary Bills*, 16 April 2024) <https://bills.parliament.uk/bills/3430> accessed 16 April 2024.

61 European Commission, 'Framework for Financial Data Access' (*Digital Finance*, 2023) <https://finance.ec.europa.eu/digital-finance/framework-financial-data-access_en> accessed 15 December 2023.

62 ibid.

63 *See* European Commission (n 56). *See* also, Proposed FIDA, Art. 2(1).

64 Indeed, this should also explain why the UK took an early lead on Open Banking (when compared to the rest of Europe), since the work of the CMA allowed the UK to identify the importance of creating an Open Banking framework, and its nine largest banks were required to have standardised APIs in place by January 2018 (in contrast to elsewhere in Europe).

65 This is set to change with the Personal Financial Data Rights Rule proposed by the US Consumer Financial Protection Bureau on 19 October 2023, which aims to introduce an open banking framework to the United States (*see* Consumer Financial Protection Bureau (CFPB), 'CFPB Proposes Rule to Jumpstart Competition and

compulsory approaches are actually preferable,[66] but it would be understandable if both the UK and the EU were seeking to secure their status as regulatory leaders in this area by having their Open Finance frameworks draw inspiration from the UK Open Banking framework, in an attempt to replicate its earlier success.[67]

At the same time, other reasons exist for expecting a degree of divergence in how the UK and the EU approach regulation in the areas of Open Banking and Open Finance, particularly pertaining to tensions resulting from Brexit, and the UK's appetite for creating a competitive new financial framework—as showcased by the recent trend towards revoking retained EU financial regulation and requiring financial regulators like the Financial Conduct Authority (FCA) to place an added focus on the international competitiveness of their rules and guidance.[68] And while the regulation of Open Banking and Open Finance will by no means be the only area where the UK and the EU might go in different directions, it is an area where we can already witness signs of divergence.

In the end, identifying both signs of convergence and divergence as the UK and the EU transition into Open Finance requires a nuanced look into their regimes that cannot be satisfied by their superficial characterisation as examples of the compulsory approach to regulating Open Banking/Open Finance. First, because it could be argued that the UK's approach to Open Finance is actually gearing up to be more 'hybrid' than purely 'compulsory' (like the EU's); and, second, because there are multiple other factors—beyond whether regulation is top down or bottom up—that can be used to distinguish between both frameworks. A more detailed look into both regimes is then the only way to distil both similarities and differences as a first step towards discussing whether there are any mutual lessons that these jurisdictions can learn from each other.

For reasons of simplification, these factors will be grouped into two categories, depending on whether they illustrate convergence/divergence in the *process* of adopting or developing new Open Banking/Open Finance frameworks, or in the *substance* of those frameworks. In other words, the following sub-sections discuss the 'who' and

---

Accelerate Shift to Open Banking' (CFPB Newsroom, 19 October 2023) <https://www.consumerfinance.gov/about-us/newsroom/cfpb-proposes-rule-to-jumpstart-competition-and-accelerate-shift-to-open-banking/#:~:text=The%20proposed%20Personal%20Financial%20Data%20Rights%20rule%20would%20protect%20the,agree%20to%20certain%20important%20conditions.> accessed 15 December 2023).

66 For a discussion, *see* Remolina (n 7).

67 According to the 2023 JROC Recommendations, the UK is trying to determine 'the joint actions required to successfully transition to the next phase of open banking and maintain the UK's international leadership' (*see* Joint Regulatory Oversight Committee (n 1), 3).

68 *See* Financial Services and Markets Act 2013.

the 'when' of the EU and UK approaches to Open Banking and Open Finance (*process*) before diving into an analysis of the 'what' and the 'how' (*substance*).[69]

B. Convergence and divergence in process

In terms of *process*, a comparative analysis of the UK and EU approaches to Open Banking—and, more recently, to Open Finance—can be boiled down to the answers given by both jurisdictions to two questions. First, *(i) who* takes the lead in developing these approaches? And, second, *(ii) when* did their transition into Open Banking and Open Finance start?

When it comes to *(i) who* is taking the lead in developing the UK and EU regulatory approaches to Open Banking/Open Finance, a surface-level analysis of both frameworks would reveal only convergence: as noted previously, both the UK and the EU have long been seen as prime examples of a compulsory approach, where the rules and requirements applicable to data holders are externally imposed by regulatory authorities from the top down.[70] But there are fundamental differences lurking under the surface.

In particular, it is worth noting that both jurisdictions give very different answers to the question of *who exactly* should be responsible for promoting and overseeing each jurisdiction's Open Banking/Open Finance ecosystem. In the UK, an industry-funded special entity, the OBIE, was created to drive the country's transition into Open Banking.[71] As the country prepares its transition into Open Finance, the OBIE is now expected to transform into an entity that can guide that transition while ensuring 'fair and effective representation of the interests of relevant industry and end user stakeholders', and while under the regulatory oversight of a Joint Regulatory Oversight Committee (JROC) comprising, in the first instance, the UK's FCA and Payment Systems Regulator as co-chairs, and the country's Treasury and CMA as members.[72] The EU, on the other hand, has refrained from creating a special-purpose entity for governing and overseeing its transition into Open Finance, noting that such tasks already fall within the existing mandates of the European Supervisory

---

69 Often referred to as 'the Five Ws', 'who', 'what', 'when', 'where', and 'why' are a series of questions that form a framework that can guide understanding of a particular phenomenon; such a framework is often traced back to Hermagoras of Temnos or Aristotle (for a discussion, *see* Michael C. Sloan, 'Aristotle's *Nicomachean Ethics* as the Original Locus for the *Septem Circumstantiae*' (2010) 105(3) Classical Philology 236). Whereas the analysis in this section is split into, on the one hand, the 'whos' and 'whens' and, on the other hand, the 'whats' and 'hows', the 'whys' are also analysed throughout.

70 *See*, ia, the discussions *in* Arner, Buckley, and Zetzsche (n 7); Littlejohn, Boskovich, and Prior (n 8); and Remolina (n 7).

71 Open Banking, 'The OBIE' <https://www.openbanking.org.uk/wp-content/uploads/OB_MediaPDF_FINAL.pdf> accessed 15 December 2023.

72 Joint Regulatory Oversight Committee (n 1).

Authorities (ESAs),[73] and that 'implications in terms of costs and administrative burden for national competent authorities' should remain 'limited'.[74] Additionally, the EU has refrained from tasking any specific regulators or industry bodies with setting up general standards under the data-sharing schemes that are set to form the backbone of its Open Finance ecosystem.[75]

The question of *(ii) when* the transition into Open Banking/Open Finance was/is to take place has also elicited different answers from the UK and the EU. While both jurisdictions already enjoy a fairly developed Open Banking framework—particularly compared to other geographies around the world—the transition from Open Banking into Open Finance is set to occur at a very different pace in the UK and the EU.

Indeed, while the EU has already proposed a new Open Finance framework—spearheaded by the new proposed FIDA—the UK is still working on developing its open banking framework so that it can 'support potential future data sharing schemes', in a process that involves, in particular, strengthening its existing Open Banking ecosystem, putting in place effective measures for consumer protection, and designing a new entity capable of governing and overseeing the move into Open Finance.[76] Throughout this process, the JROC has announced its intention to continue working with participants and users of the Open Banking ecosystem by organising workshops and sprints, and by adopting a use case-driven approach that can allow new business models with potential impact on Open Banking and Open Finance to be developed, tested, and fine-tuned.[77]

Comparing between both jurisdictions, it is not necessarily true that the EU is rushing its transition from Open Banking into Open Finance; indeed, the EU itself has acknowledged that it will take some time before the 'FIDA framework [is] up and running'—and before the legal framework that applies to Open Banking can be integrated into the FIDA framework.[78] Additionally, it is worth noting that data sharing under the new framework will depend on the approval of generally recognised standards to be jointly developed by data holders and data users—and this is likely to take a while. However, it is significant that the EU has already attempted to take legislative action in this area, particularly by means of a Regulation that will become directly applicable within a mere two years after it is published,[79] and in Member States that have made varied progress in this area. And this stands in notable contrast

73 The ESAs are currently comprised of the EBA, the European Securities and Markets Authority (ESMA), and the European Insurance and Occupational Pensions Authority (EIOPA).
74 Proposed FIDA, Budgetary Implications.
75 Although the European Commission might be required to step in if such standards fail to emerge (Proposed FIDA, Art. 11).
76 Joint Regulatory Oversight Committee (n 1).
77 For a discussion of these initiatives, *see* ibid.
78 European Commission (n 56).
79 *See* Proposed FIDA, Art. 36.

to hesitations experienced in the UK, where the FCA has explicitly endorsed a phased implementation of the country's new Open Finance framework.[80]

Ultimately, the statement that the UK and the EU have both adopted a compulsory approach to regulating Open Banking and Open Finance is thus somewhat deceiving: looking closely at the *process* through which both jurisdictions are transitioning into Open Finance, it is evident that the UK is on a different timeline from the EU. Additionally, it is clear that the UK sees the development of a hybrid entity for governing and overseeing the transition into an Open Finance ecosystem—as well as the development of partnerships with industry members—as playing an absolutely essential role in the future of Open Banking. To that extent, when comparing between the UK and EU approaches to regulation in this area, it is perhaps more accurate to characterise the EU's as being closer to a 'pure' compulsory approach'[81]—while the UK's looks more like a 'hybrid' approach, with an ethos centred around the importance of close collaborations between regulatory authorities and the market, in a slow, staggered march towards Open Finance.

C. Convergence and divergence in substance

When it comes to *substance*, a comparison between the UK and EU approaches to Open Banking and Open Finance comes down to analysing the answers given by both jurisdictions to two questions. First, *(i) what* should fall under the scope of an Open Banking/Open Finance framework? And second, *(ii) how* should data sharing and transmission under such framework occur—under what rules?

In terms of *(i) what* should fall under the scope of Open Banking/Open Finance frameworks it is worth looking at both subjective scope (*what* entities falls under those frameworks) and objective scope (*what* data is to be shared between those entities).

Currently, both jurisdictions enjoy well-defined Open Banking frameworks that give clear—if somewhat different—answers to these questions. When it comes to objective scope, the UK's Open Banking framework broadly covers all data pertaining to personal and SME banking,[82] whereas the EU's corresponding framework applies only to payment services data.[83] In terms of subjective scope, the UK's Open Banking framework is comprised of two main categories of regulated participants: *(i)* account providers (which include banks, building societies and payment companies); and *(ii)*

---

80 FCA, 'Open Finance' (FCA Feedback Statement FS21/7, March 2021) <https://www.fca.org.uk/publication/feedback/fs21-7.pdf> accessed 15 December 2023.

81 At the same time, it is worth noting that the full implementation of the EU's Open Finance framework relies somewhat on data holders and data users working together to develop Financial Data Sharing Schemes (FDSS) that provide parties with generally recognised standards for data sharing—although the European Commission is expected to step in and directly establish compensation limits, common standards, and liability frameworks if no FDSS emerges (*see* Proposed FIDA, Art. 11).

82 CMA Retail Banking Market Investigation Order 2017, Background.

83 PSD2, Art. 1.

third-party providers offering customers new ways to make use of their banking data, and make/receive payments directly from their bank accounts. Out of these players, only the nine largest banks and building societies included in the category of account providers—that is, Allied Irish Bank, Bank of Ireland, Barclays, Danske, HSBC, Lloyds Banking Group, Nationwide, RBS Group and Santander (jointly known as the CMA9)—have been required by the CMA Retail Banking Market Investigation Order 2017 to work together with OBIE to develop common open API standards and, crucially, only these CMA9 are required to follow them; other institutions are welcome to adopt the same standards but are not mandated to do so.[84] Similarly to the UK, the EU's Open Banking framework also applies to both data holders and data users; notably, the EU requires all data holders—namely, all banks and other account servicing payment service providers—to adopt and implement open standards that can 'ensure the interoperability of different technological communication solutions',[85] but has not imposed specific standards on any players.

As both countries prepare to transition into Open Finance, the extent to which the UK's current Open Banking framework will be extended beyond personal and SME banking data—and the extent to which the requirements currently applicable to the CMA9 will extend beyond these institutions—remain unclear.[86] The EU, on the other hand, has already shed light on its ambitious vision for Open Finance, setting out fairly broad definitions for both 'data holders' and 'data users' under its proposed new framework.[87] Indeed, the concept of 'data holders' under the proposed FIDA is set to include every financial institution (other than account information service providers) that collects, stores and otherwise processes financial data[88]—from credit and payment institutions to asset managers, insurance companies, and pension providers[89]—and the concept of 'data users' will also include Financial Information Service Providers (FISPs, instead of just PISPs), in addition to AISPs (from PSD2), as well as all institutions that can (also) act as data holders.[90] Correspondingly, the objective scope of the new EU Open Finance framework similarly extends far beyond payment services data (which will continue to be regulated under the Union's PSD)[91] and will

84 *See* CMA Retail Banking Market Investigation Order 2017, Background, Part 1, 3. *See* also Littlejohn, Boskovich, and Prior (n 8), 186–187.

85 PSD2, recital (93).

86 For clues into what the future of UK Open Finance might look like, *see*, in particular, FCA (n 80); and Joint Regulatory Oversight Committee (n 1).

87 For a discussion of the EU's proposed new Open Finance framework, *see* above at III.A.

88 Proposed FIDA, Art. 3(5).

89 For a complete list of the entities subject to the proposed FIDA—both as data holders and as data users—*see* its Art. 2(2).

90 For a discussion, *see* Eugerta Muçi, 'The EU Open Finance Proposal: Opening the Gates to Financial Services Data' (*Oxford Business Law Blog*, 15 December 2023) <https://blogs.law.ox.ac.uk/oblb/blog-post/2023/12/eu-open-finance-proposal-opening-gates-financial-services-data> accessed 15 December 2023.

91 *See* proposed FIDA, Art. 2(1)(a). The current version of the EU Payment Services Directive—PSD2—is currently under review and set to be replaced by a new Payment

include, in particular, data pertaining to mortgage credit agreements, insurance-based investment products, and pension rights.[92]

The analysis of the *substance* of the UK and EU Open Banking and Open Finance frameworks requires answering a second question: *(ii) how* do both frameworks regulate the sharing and transmission of data? Without making any pretence to an exhaustive treatment of the matter,[93] the UK Open Banking regime is fundamentally characterised by five features: first, relative standardisation (resulting, in particular, from the CMA9 being required to agree on a single open banking standard implemented and enforced by the OBIE); second, broad access to data, typically including both 'read' and 'write' access (ie, both account information access and payment initiation access); third, authorisation/registration requirements for third-party providers; fourth, lack of reciprocity (in the sense that only account providers are strictly required to share data under the framework, without any corresponding obligation from third-party providers); and, finally, absence of mandatory compensation arrangements for data providers, coupled with requirements to make data available to third-party providers free of charge.[94]

Much like the UK, the EU's Open Banking framework also requires authorisation/registration by data users—namely PISPs and AISPs[95]—who can enjoy both 'read' and 'write' access[96] to the framework without any obligation to reciprocate the data

---

Services Directive—PSD3—and Payment Services Regulation—PSR—which will, in particular, look to 'improve the functioning of open banking, by removing remaining obstacles to providing open banking services and improving customers' control over their payment data, enabling new innovative services to enter the market' (*see* European Commission, 'Modernising Payment Services and Opening Financial Services Data: New Opportunities for Consumers and Businesses' (*European Commission, Press release*, 2023) <https://ec.europa.eu/commission/presscorner/detail/en/ip_23_3543> accessed 15 December 2023).

92 Proposed FIDA, Art. 2(1).

93 Another notable feature that can be used to characterise and distinguish between regulatory approaches to Open Banking/Open Finance pertains to the regimes for the liability of the entities involved in making the customer data available (for a discussion on the various features that can be used to illustrate variation in compulsory models, *see* Remolina (n 7), 18). Other rules that typically comprise these frameworks include provisions pertaining to privacy, data protection, cybersecurity, licensing and organisational requirements for data holders and users, and enforcement and penalties.

94 For a detailed description of these various features and how they have been implemented in practice, *see* CMA Retail Banking Market Investigation Order 2017—in particular, Background and provisions 9 and 10.

95 *See* PSD2, Title II—with Art. 33 applying specifically to account information service providers.

96 PSD2, recital (93).

sharing,[97] and without any requirement to compensate data holders for the costs inherent in data sharing. Crucially, however, the EU's Open Banking framework has never required the level of (relative) standardisation imposed by the UK regime; instead, the EU chose to embrace differences in technological communications solutions, demanding only the interoperability and safety of the different systems[98]—and abiding by strict technology neutrality principles.[99]

Beyond Open Banking, it appears that the proposed EU Open Finance framework is set to diverge from PSD2 in two fundamental ways: first, it does not look like it will allow data users to initiate transactions on behalf of customers, granting them only 'read' access;[100] second, it gives data holders the tools required to ask for reasonable compensation for the costs inherent in sharing data with prospective users.[101] When it comes to 'standardisation', the new EU Open Finance framework does encourage the development of common standards—explicitly taking things further than PSD2—but it is presently unclear how such standards will be developed and how effective they can become, particularly since data holders and data users are meant to take the initiative in developing them without meaningful involvement from any public authorities,[102] at least in first instance.[103] As for reciprocity, the EU's new Open Finance Framework continues to rely on the GDPR, which fails to create truly reciprocal data-sharing

97 The GDPR does contemplate a right to 'data portability' (*see* EU GDPR, Art. 20), but such a right is not subject to any technical or timing requirements—the absence of which is fundamentally incompatible with the ethos of the data-sharing ecosystem underlying the concept of Open Banking (or the concept of Open Finance, for that matter). Also noting that 'data portability' in Open Finance and 'data portability' under the GDPR are 'not identical' *see* Arner, Buckley, and Zetzsche (n 7), 157).

98 *See* PSD2, recital (93). For a discussion, *see* EBA (n 9), 86ff. As a result, different API standards have developed in the EU, including the Berlin Group NextGenPSD2, the Polish API, the Stet, and the Slovak Banking API Standard; for further discussion, *see* Anne-Sophie Morvan, 'Open Finance: EU & UK on the Same Path, What About Standards?' (AGEFI Luxembourg) <https://papers.ssrn.com/sol3/papers.cfm?abstract_id=3844101> accessed 15 December 2023.

99 For a comprehensive discussion of the reasons why the EU failed to anchor its Open Banking framework in principles of standardisation, *see* Littlejohn, Boskovich, and Prior (n 8), 187–189.

100 Proposed FIDA, Title II.

101 Proposed FIDA, Title IV.

102 Proposed FIDA, recital (28) and Title IV.

103 *See* Proposed FIDA, Art. 11, noting that 'in the event that a financial data sharing scheme is not developed for one or more categories of customer data listed in Art. 2(1) and there is no realistic prospect of such a scheme being set up within a reasonable amount of time, the Commission is empowered to adopt a delegated act in accordance with Art. 30 to supplement [the] Regulation', in particular by developing common standards for the sharing of that particular category of data and the technical interfaces needed to allow customers to request data sharing under the proposed FIDA.

obligations;[104] indeed, although EU financial institutions can be both data holders and data users under the new framework—which arguably creates a degree of reciprocity within the FIDA—EU non-financial institutions acting solely as FISPs (which can only act as data users), foreign institutions and BigTech companies[105] all evade the sharing requirements imposed by the EU's newly proposed framework.[106]

As for the UK, its path towards Open Finance remains partially shrouded in mystery, but it is largely expected that the country will stick to the same fundamental principles that have guided its Open Banking regime—and which have cast it in the eyes of UK policymakers as 'a leader in the field'.[107] In particular, it is worth noting the preference expressed by these policymakers for the centralised developed of 'standards and guidelines for all data holders and data users with a view to ensuring consistent user experience and interoperability across use cases',[108] although only time will tell how this ambitious plan will be implemented. At the same time, early signs of departure from the current Open Banking regime can also be detected in a recent statement by the FCA, which notes that the UK Open Finance ecosystem 'will best flourish if the right commercial incentives exist for firms to invest and participate on a sustainable, and probably reciprocal basis',[109] expressly endorsing both the importance of

104 *See* n 97 above: while the EU GDPR does include a right to 'data portability', the lack of strict technical and timing requirements means that it does not mandate true reciprocity.

105 Notably, many BigTechs will fall under the definition of 'gatekeepers' put forth by the new Council Regulation (EU) 2022/1925 of the European Parliament and of the Council of 14 September 2022 on contestable and fair markets in the digital sector and amending Directives (EU) 2019/1937 and (EU) 2020/1828 [2022] OJ L 265/1 of 12.10.2022 (the EU Digital Markets Act). Indeed, according to Art. 3(1) of the new EU Digital Markets Act, entities will be classed as gatekeepers so long as they have 'significant impact on the market', '[provide] a core platform service which is an important gateway for business users to reach end users', and '[enjoy] an entrenched and durable position, in its operations, or it is foreseeable that it will enjoy such a position in the near future'—which are features generally found in BigTechs (for a discussion, *see* Noble (n 45)). Under the EU Digital Markets Act, gatekeepers (and BigTechs) are required to 'provide (…) third parties authorised by an end user, at their request and free of charge, with effective portability of data provided by the end user or generated through the activity of the end user in the context of the use of the relevant core platform service, including by providing, free of charge, tools to facilitate the effective exercise of such data portability, and including by the provision of continuous and real-time access to such data', which does appear to meet the criteria for reciprocity (*see* Art. 6 (9); *see* also recital (59))—so that even though BigTechs are not strictly subject to reciprocity obligations under the new FIDA, such reciprocity might nevertheless result from compliance with the EU Digital Markets Act.

106 Muçi (n 90).

107 Joint Regulatory Oversight Committee (n 1), 3.

108 ibid, 18.

109 FCA (n 80), 30.

compensating those required to share data under the system, as well as the need to anchor data sharing in principles of reciprocity.

All things considered, it is clear that even though the UK and the EU have long been grouped together as jurisdictions with similar approaches to Open Banking there are important ways of distinguishing between them. Their Open Banking frameworks do contain significant resemblances, but the many differences between them illustrate the danger of using closed categories and making inferences from rigid classification systems. As the UK and EU start moving forward from Open Banking, it is worth continuing the discussion of whether they might drift further apart—and it is worth determining if there are any mutual lessons to be learned as both jurisdictions continue navigating into Open Finance and beyond.

IV. Mutual lessons from the UK and EU approaches to open banking and open finance

A. UK and EU: a complicated relationship

There are multiple reasons why the UK and EU's approach to Open Banking has been perceived as being rather similar: under classification systems that distinguish between jurisdictions that have let Open Banking/Open Finance develop organically within them, on the one hand, and jurisdictions that have been actively encouraging the transition of their economy into an Open Data ecosystem, on the other hand, there is no question that both the UK and the EU belong to the latter. This is hardly surprising, given the early success of the UK's pioneering approach to Open Banking—which many countries have attempted to replicate, particularly in Europe—and the historical links that traditionally tied together the UK and the EU, namely before Brexit.

At the same time, the previous section listed a number of differences lurking beneath these similarities. Two main points of divergence separate the Open Banking frameworks found in the UK and in the EU: one pertaining to *process* and one pertaining to *substance*. When it comes to *process*, the UK and the EU have both enacted regulatory measures to foster the development of their Open Banking ecosystems, but while the EU has adopted a 'pure' top-down approach to Open Banking (and Open Finance)—heavily reliant on the work developed by existing regulatory authorities—the UK has anchored its transition into Open Banking and beyond on industry-funded special-purpose entities that will oversee the development of these ecosystems through a staggered approach built on key use cases and growing market demand for Open Finance. In terms of *substance*, the only main difference that has traditionally separated the EU and UK Open Banking regimes has to do with degree of standardisation: while the UK early on mandated the development of common API standards to be adopted by the largest data holders within its ecosystem, the EU chose to accept the differences in technological communications solutions adopted by different players across the Union.

As both the EU and the UK start transitioning into Open Finance—with the EU seemingly taking the lead—it appears clear that a few of these differences will remain or grow, even as others might fade. While both jurisdictions are naturally looking to adopt the best Open Finance framework in the best way possible, Open Finance (much like Open Banking) comes with both promise and peril and different jurisdictions are bound to make different trade-offs and weigh in different jurisdiction-specific factors when designing and implementing their own regime.[110] Additionally, the UK and the EU have complicated history together that might help explain lack of coordination in this area: Brexit was professedly justified by a desire to 'actively diverge' from EU policy,[111] and the EU may be keen to capture the competitive advantages often bestowed upon first-movers.[112]

Still, there are lessons that both jurisdictions can learn from each other as they take the first steps towards Open Finance—the UK as it continues its efforts to modernising its Open Banking framework, and the EU, as it finalises FIDA, begins the process of complementing it with regulatory technical standards and delegated acts,[113] and starts guiding its Member States through its ambitious implementation calendar.[114]

B. Mutual lessons in the path towards open finance

The fact that the UK and the EU might feel inclined to diverge in some aspects of their transition from Open Banking and Open Finance—both in terms of *process* and in terms of *substance*—does not mean that they are unwilling to learn from each other's perceived successes and mistakes. Indeed, the UK is widely seen as a hugely influential jurisdiction in the area of Open Banking, and, while considering its transition into Open Finance, the EU was made keenly aware that its underdeveloped EU digital financial market has been struggling to compete with countries like the UK.[115] Similarly, the UK has also expressed a willingness to '[look into] how other countries have adopted data-sharing initiatives'.[116]

---

110 As noted by Remolina, 'the desirability of each model depends on a variety of country-specific factors. Therefore, none of these models can automatically be considered superior to others' (*see* Remolina (n 7), 5).

111 Petit and Beck (n 13), 8.

112 Morvan (n 98).

113 Proposed FIDA, recital (53).

114 The proposed FIDA is meant to apply between 18 and 24 months after the date of its entry into force.

115 European Parliament, 'Open Financial Data Implications - Impact Assessment (SWD(2023) 224, SWD(2023) 230 (Summary)) Accompanying a Commission Proposal for a Regulation of the European Parliament and of the Council on a Framework for Financial Data Access and Amending Regulations (EU) No 1093/2010, (EU) No 1094/2010, (EU) No 1095/2010 and (EU) 2022/2554' (Initial Appraisal of a European Commission Impact Assessment, November 2023) <https://www.europarl.europa.eu/RegData/etudes/BRIE/2023/753178/EPRS_BRI(2023)753178_EN.pdf> accessed 15 December 2023.

116 Joint Regulatory Oversight Committee (n 1), 16.

So, what lessons does the EU appear to have learned from the UK as it begun its transition into Open Finance—and what lessons might it want to keep in mind as it refines its newly proposed Open Finance framework? Most obviously, the EU is now aware of the importance of standardisation, as made possible by recent developments in open API technologies.[117] As noted by the EBA during the process of reviewing the EU Open Banking framework, 'the absence of a single API standard [led] to the emergence of different API solutions across the EU', creating 'significant challenges' for data users—and the EU has promptly accepted recommendations to increase the level of standardisation in its Open Finance framework.[118] Indeed, the proposed FIDA explicitly encourages the development of common standards by data holders and data users,[119] and membership of standard-setting financial data-sharing schemes will be a pre-condition to participating in the new EU Open Finance ecosystem. At the same time, there is no denying that the path towards standardisation—particularly as Open Banking is extended into Open Finance—is a complex one, and it remains unclear how these requirements will be operationalised.

Going forward, the EU might then consider implementing two lessons from the UK. First, the EU should consider revising its calendar for implementing its Open Finance framework, mitigating its 'big bang' approach to Open Finance[120] and favouring a slower, staggered implementation model built on industry collaboration and driven by developing use cases. Second, the EU should examine the merits of designing a single specialised regulatory/supervisory entity that could support markets' efforts in developing the level of standardisation demonstrably required for a flourishing Open Finance ecosystem.[121]

Additionally, the EU would also be well advised to follow future UK developments when it comes to reciprocity. In this area, the EU has chosen to continue to rely on the GDPR to ensure data portability, but the GDPR does not require entities to respond in real-time to data portability requests, preventing it from ensuring true reciprocity.[122] In the UK, however, the FCA has stated its preference for a reciprocal Open Finance framework[123]—and while it is currently unknown how UK reciprocity requirements will be designed and implemented, future developments might inspire the EU to find the solutions needed to level the playing field between EU financial institutions, on

117 Littlejohn, Boskovich, and Prior (n 8), 186–187.
118 *See*, ia, EBA (n 9); European Parliament (n 115).
119 *See* Proposed FIDA, recital (28) and Title IV.
120 Alexander Lehmann and J. Scott Marcus, 'Open Finance: What Can an Enabling Framework Look Like?' (European Parliament, Econ Committee, October 2023) <https://www.europarl.europa.eu/RegData/etudes/STUD/2023/754188/IPOL_STU(2023)754188_EN.pdf> accessed 15 December 2023.
121 For a discussion of what this future entity might look like, *see* Joint Regulatory Oversight Committee (n 1).
122 *See* GDPR, Art. 20.
123 FCA (n 80), p30.

the one hand, and EU non-financial institutions and foreign institutions, on the other hand.[124]

Finally, the EU should keep these lessons in mind not only during the process of implementing its Open Finance framework, but also as it begins to update its Open Banking framework, namely by reviewing PSD2 (set to become PSD3) and by approving a new PSR. This is particularly important as the European Commission has acknowledged the merits of transferring the Open Banking framework to the FIDA framework—and is only waiting for a time when 'the FIDA framework will be up and running' and 'conditions for a smooth transfer are considered appropriate'.[125]

And what about the UK? What can it learn from examining the road taken by the EU towards Open Finance? There is something to be said for EU's demonstrated ambition, even if some caution is also advisable. On the one hand, the importance of anchoring Open Finance on common standards has become clear—both looking at the early success of the UK's Open Banking framework and at the EU's willingness to build its Open Finance framework on the back of common standards developed under financial data-sharing schemes.[126] As such, the UK should not backtrack on its goal to develop general data-sharing standards beyond banking—and it is hoped that the transition from Open Banking to Open Finance will see the UK extend the requirement to compulsorily join a nascent standard-based financial data-sharing ecosystem beyond the CMA9. On the other hand, the UK should not underestimate the difficulty of developing these common standards and it will be worth keeping a close eye on the EU as it tries to operationalise its new standardisation requirements under FIDA. And particularly when it comes to determining who should be required to follow the common standards that will anchor its new Open Finance framework, the UK might want to consider establishing different tiers of requirements for players with different degrees of market power.[127]

Another ambitious feature of the EU's Open Finance framework is its approach to compensation. Neither the EU's Open Banking framework nor the UK's require the compensation of the data holders participating in their respective ecosystems; more recently, however, a consensus has emerged that—absent regulatory

124 Muçi (n 90).

125 European Commission (n 56).

126 Indeed, the importance of standardisation has been recently recognised by UK regulatory authorities as they noted that 'enforcing a single open banking standard for the largest Account Servicing Payment Service Providers (ASPSPs) through an implementation entity has allowed the ecosystem to overcome challenges faster than in other jurisdictions, establishing the UK's international standing as a leader in open banking' (*see* Joint Regulatory Oversight Committee (n 1), 3).

127 For a discussion about the possibility of regulators imposing different open data requirements 'on firms with a potentially dominant position, regardless of whether they are financial institutions or tech firms', *see* Arner, Buckley, and Zetzsche (n 7, 152).

intervention—commercial incentives for open finance-type arrangements lead to partial initiatives that fail to fully unlock the potential benefits of Open Banking and Open Finance. As a result, the EU's proposed FIDA now requires that data holders are 'able to request reasonable compensation from data users for putting in place [APIs]'.[128] Going forward, the UK's FCA has already expressed support for the idea that 'open finance will best flourish if the right commercial incentives exist'[129]—and it is hoped that UK policymakers will look to the data-sharing schemes developed within the EU over the next few years as a source of inspiration for designing the compensation-related standards that will eventually be implemented by the OBIE successor as the country transitions into Open Finance.

At the same time, there are also a number of ways in which the EU's proposed Open Finance framework can be seen as falling short of what the UK could achieve in this area, particularly considering the country's many unique advantages in this field: the fact that the UK's journey towards standardisation started with Open Banking (in contrast to the EU's, which only started with Open Finance);[130] the fact that the UK enjoys a unified financial regulation framework (which can be contrasted with the cross-border regulatory differences between Member States as the EU continues its progress towards the Capital Markets Union);[131] the fact that the UK financial markets remain much less fragmented than the EU's;[132] the fact that UK regulators and financial industry members enjoy a deeply close relationship fostered through regulatory innovations like sandboxes and tech/policy sprints;[133] and, finally, the fact that the UK already has a specialised Open Banking entity which can more easily be redesigned to help the country transition into Open Finance.[134]

---

128 Proposed FIDA, recital (29) and Art. 10(1)(h).

129 FCA (n 80), 30.

130 *See* the discussion above at III.C.

131 For an up-to-date account of progress made in this regard, *see* European Commission, 'Capital Markets Union' (*Financial Markets*, 2023) <https://finance.ec.europa.eu/capital-markets-union-and-financial-markets/capital-markets-union_en> accessed 15 December 2023.

132 Indeed, the European Commission itself has noted that 'EU capital markets remain fragmented, hampering companies' ability to raise capital across the EU' and that 'the EU's global competitiveness is weakened by the fragmentation of its capital markets' (*see* European Commission, 'Communication from the Commission to the European Parliament, the Council, the European Economic and Social Committee and the Committee of the Regions: Capital Markets Union - Delivering One Year after the Action Plan' COM(2021) 720 final <https://eur-lex.europa.eu/legal-content/EN/TXT/HTML/?uri=CELEX:52021DC0720> accessed 15 December 2023).

133 A few of these regulatory innovations are detailed, for example, in the latest FCA Business Plan (*see* FCA, 'FCA Business Plan 2023/24' (*FCA*, 2023) <https://www.fca.org.uk/publication/corporate/business-plan-2023-24.pdf> accessed 15 December 2023).

134 For a discussion of the difficulties faced by EU policymakers *vis-à-vis* UK policymakers in this area, *see*, i.a., Littlejohn, Boskovich, and Prior (n 8), 197.

In truth, all these comparative advantages put the UK in a unique position to put forward a bolder Open Finance framework than the EU's—namely, one that continues to offer broad access to data, including both 'read' and 'write' access. Indeed, something is being (partly) lost in the EU's transition from Open Banking to Open Finance, as the proposed FIDA framework does not explicitly contemplate the possibility of allowing data users to initiate transactions on behalf of customers—and while this should help tame the complexity of a significantly ambitious framework, it is also bound to hamper the development of potential use cases, like accounts comparison and switching services. By retaining 'write' access within its Open Finance framework—while also extending uniform standards beyond the CMA9—the UK will be in a better position than the EU to take complete advantage of the promises of Open Finance.

Finally, the UK should be ready to go further than the EU when it comes to reciprocity. Early criticism levelled at FIDA has already noted how the proposed regime creates an uneven playing field between EU financial institutions, on the one hand, and EU non-financial institutions and foreign institutions, on the other hand—and the UK faces additional challenges arising from the fact that it does not currently impose reciprocal data-sharing obligations on BigTechs.[135] Notably, the FCA has already expressed a preference for a reciprocal Open Finance framework, but the devil is in the details and the shortcomings of the EU regime in this regard should inform any regulatory actions taken to integrate reciprocity principles into the UK's future Open Finance ecosystem.[136]

V. Conclusion

The world of finance is changing, leaving the UK and the EU at a crossroads. The move from Open Banking to Open Finance is not a question of 'whether' but of 'when', and both jurisdictions must make wise use of the time and resources available to them to

135 The regulatory challenges arising from the activity developed by BigTechs in the financial system are bound to be somewhat mitigated by the Digital Markets, Competition and Consumers Bill currently making its way through the House of Lords, but—even then—it remains to be discussed whether even the new requirements imposed on these entities will be enough to ensure true reciprocity under an Open Finance framework. The latest version of the Digital Markets, Competition and Consumers Bill is available at <https://bills.parliament.uk/bills/3453> accessed 15 December 2023.

136 At the end of the day, both jurisdictions might also have something to learn from one another when it comes to reconciling Open Banking/Open Finance/Open Data frameworks and Data Protection frameworks—which are often approved in isolation and which tend to attach particular importance to values that might be difficult to reconcile in practice: on the one hand, data openness, and, on the other hand, data privacy. For a discussion of this difficult challenge, *see* Arner, Buckley, and Zetzsche (n 7).

prepare their inevitable transition into Open Finance—namely by embracing the lessons that they can learn from each other.

The EU has already taken the first steps in the direction of Open Finance, but the road ahead remains perilous, and much can still happen on the way towards, on the one hand, updating its Open Banking framework, and, on the other hand, approving and implementing its newly proposed Open Finance framework. In this regard, the timeline for the applicability of the proposed FIDA—set to apply only two years after entering into force—is nothing short of ambitious, and a degree of scepticism is warranted about the system's dependence on common standards that the EU expects data holders and users to develop without initial intervention from public authorities. If the EU has been right to learn the importance of common standards from the UK's Open Banking framework, it is also advised to consider the importance of adopting a staggered, industry-supported approach—as well as the crucial role that a special-purpose entity like the OBIE played in the UK's Open Banking success story.

The UK, on the other hand, finds itself in an unfamiliar position: while the country pioneered the development of Open Banking, it has been delaying its transition into Open Finance by adopting a careful, phased approach that will start by strengthening its Open Banking regime before enabling its scope to expand to potential Open Finance initiatives. This is not necessarily cause for concern: while there are undeniable first-mover advantages in this area—as demonstrated, most notably, by the UK's own cemented position as a global leader and influencer in Open Banking regulation—there is value in getting things right the first time around, particularly as the success of Open Banking and Open Finance hinges on building customer trust and confidence in these nascent ecosystems.[137]

In the end, both the UK and the EU have everything to gain by keeping an eye on each other as they both walk the road from Open Banking to Open Finance. Their broad regulatory approaches to Open Banking—both examples of compulsory approaches—have their fair share of similarities, so that any points of divergence, particularly as both jurisdictions take their own individual paths into Open Finance, should be seen as opportunities for learning how to tinker with and improve their regulatory ecosystems without endangering their fundamental principles and identities. In this regard, the EU has much to learn by reconsidering the initial timeline and process for implementing is Open Finance framework, namely by setting up an entity like the UK's OBIE that can help in the path towards true standardisation, and by exploring reciprocity solutions. The UK, on the other hand, has everything to gain by paying attention to the latest EU Open Finance developments as the Union operationalises its standardisation and mandatory compensation requirements under the proposed FIDA.

137 Joint Regulatory Oversight Committee (n 1), 13.

Tensions between the UK and the EU have arguably been at an all-time high after Brexit—and few other fields are able to showcase such tensions as expressively as financial regulation—but the pressures of regulatory competition should encourage the UK and the EU to look for lessons that they can learn from each other's experience with Open Banking and Open Finance, rather than force them into rushed action. There is danger in inaction, but slow and steady can often win the race.

6 Developing cybersecurity in open banking and open finance: the application of blockchain technology and decentralised autonomous organisations

Joseph Lee and Vere-Marie Khan

I. Introduction

This chapter will discuss and examine the application of blockchain technology to open banking and open finance from the perspective of cybersecurity. Open banking and open finance are revolutionary concepts that foster collaboration amongst financial institutions and third-party service providers. Considering this, this chapter will delve into the principles underpinning these ecosystems and the potential for blockchain-based initiatives to provide enhanced cybersecurity practices and mechanisms.

Furthermore, this chapter will also explore innovative governance measures such as decentralised autonomous organisations (DAOs) where blockchain technology and data governance converge. Overall, this chapter will navigate the complexities and potential opportunities developing in open banking and open finance and how blockchain-based solutions present a disruptive and revolutionary approach to cybersecurity systems in consideration and alignment with different regulatory advancements and requirements.

II. Open banking

Directly resulting from the evolving global financial landscape, the functional operations of traditional banking ecosystems are undergoing a fundamental shift through the integration of smart technology. The modern utilisation of open banking and open finance systems in consumer services is creating space for essential and efficient third-party financial service providers. However, despite the mounting use and popularity of these different types of digital financial application systems, at present there is no universal definition of open banking.[1] Overall, the functionality of open banking can be described as the sharing of banking data with third-party financial service providers through the use of open Application Programming Interfaces (APIs).[2] These APIs serve as a digital medium for the communication and data exchange between two distinct applications.[3]

These activities are reliant upon the acknowledgement and consent of traditional banking consumers, and they also provide the foundational framework to enhance competition and innovation within the financial sphere by streamlining systems of collaboration with traditional financial industries.[4] Therefore, consumer and institutional trust are integral aspects of achieving collaboration, facilitating secure data-sharing processes, and providing seamless integration between multiple financial institutions and third-party service providers.[5] Furthermore, numerous independent studies have surveyed and assessed the positive impact of the appropriate application of these open banking systems on consumers' experiences and autonomy within the financial sector. This impact can be credited to the facilitation of data portability and encouragement of collaboration among diverse financial stakeholders, allowing greater financial freedom and market competition.[6]

A. Operations of open banking

General data governance within the European Union (EU) is influenced by the principle of consumer autonomy and established fundamental principles of human rights.[7] Therefore, in light of this overarching ethos, statutory and guidance documents seek to provide guidelines for consumers to exercise control over their personal data while

---

1 Hunter Dorwart, Daniel Berrick, and Dale Rappaneau, 'Developments in Open Banking: Key Issues from a Global Perspective' (*Future of Privacy Forum*, March 2022) <https://fpf.org/wp-content/uploads/2022/08/FPF-Open-Banking-Report-R2-Singles.pdf> accessed 3 March 2024.

2 Basel Committee on Banking Supervision, 'Report on open banking and application programming interfaces' (*Bank for International Settlements (BIS)*, November 2019) <www.bis.org/bcbs/publ/d486.pdf> accessed 1 September 2023.

3 Markos Zachariadis and Pinar Ozcan, 'The API Economy and Digital Transformation in Financial Services: The Case of Open Banking' (2017) SWIFT Institute Working Paper No. 2016-001, <http://dx.doi.org/10.2139/ssrn.2975199> accessed 10 January 2024.

4 Ibid.

5 Ibid.

6 Joint Regulatory Oversight Committee, 'Recommendations for the next phase of open banking in the UK Joint Regulatory Oversight Committee 17 April 2023' (Financial Conduct Authority (FCA) and Payment Systems Regulator (PSR), 17 April 2023) <https://assets.publishing.service.gov.uk/government/uploads/system/uploads/attachment_data/file/1150988/JROC_report_recommendations_and_actions_paper_April_2023.pdf> accessed 8 January 2024.

7 Alexander Bernier, Fruzsina Molnar-Gabor, and Bartha Maria Knoppers, 'The International Data Governance Landscape' (2022) 9(1) Journal of Law and the Biosciences 1.

ensuring privacy protection and facilitating the promotion of financial inclusion. This aim serves as a key aspect of the foundation for creating a thriving environment for financial service competition.[8] Furthermore, the implementation of the Second Payment Services Directive (PSD2) created an obligation and requirement for banks to ensure consent-based access to client data by authorised third parties to further promote this competitive environment.[9] However, to comply with PSD2, authorised third parties and established financial institutions are required to meet specific criteria when dealing with digital financial services and mobile payments.[10]

The criteria for authorised third parties under the PSD2 regulation require the acquisition of a Payment Initiation Services (PISP) or Account Information Service Providers (AISP) licence, the implementation of a third-party specific customer identity and access management (CIAM) system for the facilitation of strong customer authentication (SCA),[11] Know Your Customer (KYC) requirements, identity proofing through secure application systems that require explicit consumer consent, and access controls that oversee specific data access points.[12] Additionally, banks and other financial institutions are required to enact identity and access management (IAM) systems for employees, and CIAM for consumers, as well as utilise APIs that grant third parties access to transactional payment data.[13]

Open banking systems are focused on the provision of access and standardised reading of financial data across institutions through respective API tools.[14] These specific APIs enable authorised third parties to obtain account information, such as consumers' bank account balance and transactional information, as well as additional account features such as interest rates and charges.[15] These account features are known as Account Information Services (AISs)[16] which are defined in Article 4 (16) of the PSD2. This aggregation of data allows consumers to consolidate their payment and

8 Douglas W Arner, Giuliano G Castellano, and Eriks K. Selga, 'Financial Data Governance' (2023) 74(2) Hastings Law Journal 235.
9 Ibid.
10 Council Directive (EU) 2015/2366 of the European Parliament and of the Council of 25 November 2015 on payment services in the internal market, amending Directives 2002/65/EC, 2009/110/EC and 2013/36/EU and Regulation (EU) No 1093/2010, and repealing Directive 2007/64/EC [2015] OJ L 337/35 of 23.12.2015, Art. 98.
11 Ibid, Art. 4 (30).
12 Ibid, Art. 14.
13 Ibid, Art. 47.
14 Marianna Gounari, George Stergiopoulos, Kosmas Pipyros, and Dimitris Gritzalis, 'Harmonising Open Banking in the European Union: An Analysis of PSD2 Compliance and Interrelation with Cybersecurity Frameworks and Standards' (2024) 5 International Cybersecurity Law Review 79–120.
15 Gorka Koldobika Briones de Araluze and Natalia Cassinello Plaza, 'Open Banking: A Bibliometric Analysis-driven Definition' (2022) 17(10) PLoS One.
16 Council Directive (EU) 2015/2366 (n 10) Art. 4 (16).

account data for third parties to provide specific services in relation to the provided financial information.[17]

Furthermore, other APIs enable the initiation of payments on the customer's behalf, with the customer's consent,[18] through a Payment Initiation Service (PIS), which is defined in Article 4 (15) of the PSD2. Recital 27 states that the PIS establishes a software bridge between merchant websites and online banking platforms of financial institutions to provide seamless credit transfers.[19] Recital 29 refers to the aforementioned services as the enabling of PISP to assure that payment has been initiated and therefore there is no delay or uncertainty in the delivery of transactions.[20]

PSD2 served as a statutory guideline for the implementation and governance of potential open banking systems within the EU. In the United Kingdom (UK), the governing bodies initiated and integrated the development of digital payment regulations through a more investigative approach. In 2016, a study was conducted by the UK's Competition and Markets Authority (CMA)[21] and this was carried out with the intention of developing strategies to enhance competition in the banking sector through market research. As a result, in 2017, following that investigation, the Open Banking Implementation Entity (OBIE) was established,[22] and in 2018, the UK implemented the mandatory requirement for Account Servicing Payment Service Providers (ASPSPs) to have open banking systems regulated under the Payment System Regulations 2017 (as amended) (PSR 2017).[23] In addition to this, further instruction for the incorporation of supplementary PISP provisions from PSD2 into national legislation was also implemented as a response.[24]

---

17 Ibid; Marianna Gounari, George Stergiopoulos, Kosmas Pipyros, and Dimitris Gritzalis (n 14).

18 Ibid, Art. 64.

19 Ibid, Recital 27.

20 Ibid, Recital 29.

21 Competition and Markets Authority (CMA), 'Retail banking market investigation final report' (*CMA*, 2016) <https://assets.publishing.service.gov.uk/media/57ac9667e5274a0f6c00007a/retail-banking-market-investigation-full-final-report.pdf> accessed 25 October 2023.

22 Open Banking, 'What is Open Banking?' (*openbanking.com*) <https://www.openbanking.org.uk/wp-content/uploads/OB_MediaPDF_FINAL.pdf> accessed 6 January 2024.

23 Financial Conduct Authority (FCA), 'Payment Services and Electronic Money – Our Approach: The FCA's role under the Payment Services Regulations 2017 and the Electronic Money Regulations 2011' (*FCA.org.uk*, November 2021) <https://www.fca.org.uk/publication/finalised-guidance/fca-approach-payment-services-electronic-money-2017.pdf> accessed 19 January 2024.

24 Ibid.

In light of these investigations and implemented strategies, following the 2016 investigation, the CMA issued an Order[25] which detailed the requisite technical and operational requirements to be applied to the nine largest retail banks within the UK at that time, as determined by the CMA and referred to as the CMA9, as part of the open banking initiative.[26] Banks that were included in the CMA9 were: Lloyds Banking Group, together with Bank of Scotland and Halifax; HSBC Group, which included First Direct and M&SNationwide Building Society; AIB Group UK, which also included the First Trust Bank in Northern Ireland; Bank of Ireland, Barclays Bank; the NatWest Group, which included NatWest, Royal Bank of Scotland, and Ulster Bank NI; Northern Bank Limited, also known as Danske Bank; and Santander UK.[27]

Under the aforementioned Order, these banks were mandated to grant access to customer data using secure data protocols for the use of third-party service providers.[28] Additionally, it was mandated that ASPSPs were required to allow access to customers' payment account data without contract, without charge, and without restriction or discrimination.[29] As a result, open banking in the UK allowed customers the opportunity to utilise a singular application or platform to manage and view multiple bank accounts, which may have been held with different institutions.[30] For example, through the use of a singular personal finance assistance application, the API would gather data from various banks to provide users with a comprehensive overview of their financial data in a more convenient and streamlined manner.[31]

Thus, through open banking mechanisms, consumers can benefit from personalised services derived from personal financial aggregation applications. Demonstratively, this ecosystem is inherently reliant upon adherence to robust security, privacy, and regulatory frameworks, which contribute to the assurance of consumer data protection and maintenance of trust in the existing financial ecosystem.[32]

B. Benefits of open banking

The implementation of open banking has unequivocally provided numerous benefits for consumers associated with digital banking systems, including the ability for consumers to possess the ability to revoke consent at any time with respect to the

25 CMA, 'Retail Banking Market Investigation: The Retail Banking Market Investigation Order 2017' (*CMA*, 2017) <https://assets.publishing.service.gov.uk/media/5893063bed915d06e1000000/retail-banking-market-investigation-order-2017.pdf>
26 Ibid.
27 Ibid.
28 Ibid.
29 Ibid.
30 Christoph Frei, 'Open Banking: Opportunities and Risks' in Thomas Walker, Elaheh Nikbakht, and Maher Kooli (eds), *The Fintech Disruption: How Financial Innovation is Transforming the Banking Industry* (Palgrave Macmillan 2023) 167–189.
31 Ibid.
32 Ibid.

application's access to their data.[33] As another benefit of open banking, consumers are not required to provide their banking credentials to the third-party service provider directly to gain access and enjoy the benefits of using open banking; consumers are given the option to determine which type of data they are willing to share versus granting full and unlimited access to the application.[34] Therefore, practically, open banking enables the further development of personal financial management applications and tools, which would allow consumers to gain insight into spending habits and budgeting, and assist with long-term financial planning within the parameters of the consumers' consent.[35]

Overall, this process is beneficial to consumers through the compiled centralisation and automated aggregation of financial information, which provides the relevant stakeholders with an avenue and a medium to comprehensively assess their financial circumstances and options. Furthermore, the average consumer can additionally consolidate the majority of their banking data, which may be stored across multiple financial institutions, to appropriately manage personal debt, payments, and loans.[36] Therefore, as a result, this open banking system allows consumers to make more informed financial decisions and ensures that consumers retain greater control of their financial data, which remains in line with the overarching ethos of consumer autonomy, choice, and financial freedom.

Furthermore, open banking has facilitated an increase in innovation as well as enhanced client experience since most large financial institutions have created digital applications to streamline their services on a digital platform.[37] Through these digital platforms, third-party service providers are able to provide additional benefits to the users of open banking, which include permitting third-party payment providers to initiate transactions directly from a customer's bank account through online retailers and websites.[38] Therefore, as a result, the open banking system bypasses traditional payment methods and provides a secure system for the integration of e-commerce

---

33 Joint Regulatory Oversight Committee (n 6).

34 EMEA Centre for Regulatory Strategy, 'Open Banking around the World' (*Deloitte*, 2023) <https://www.deloitte.com/an/en/Industries/financial-services/perspectives/open-banking-around-the-world.html> accessed 13 October 2023.

35 Ibid.

36 European Commission, 'Keynote speech by Commissioner McGuinness at an event in European Parliament 'From open banking to open finance: what does the future hold?' (*European Commission Speech*, 21 March 2023) <https://ec.europa.eu/commission/presscorner/detail/en/SPEECH_23_1819> accessed 15 January 2024.

37 Basel Committee on Banking Supervision (n 2).

38 Global Payments, 'Open banking - Overview: Global payments developer portal - open banking - Overview | Global Payments Developer Portal' (*globalpay.com*) <https://developer.globalpay.com/ecommerce/open-banking> accessed 13 November 2023.

for consumer benefit, which, in turn, promotes competition and consumer spending through convenience and access.[39]

Moreover, another benefit associated with open banking is the utilisation of APIs to assist loan and mortgage applications.[40] Third-party lenders and banks would possess the ability to effectively and comprehensively assess an applicant's financial history to determine their creditworthiness.[41] This aggregation of an applicant's financial history and spending habits would streamline the decision-making and approval process for loans while ensuring increased accuracy and accountability in the allocation of financial assistance. Finally, open banking offers a basis for increased innovation through greater collaboration between financial technology (FinTech) start-ups and financial institutions, where supplementary, advanced financial products and services are provided for consumer benefit.

As such, these examples demonstrate that secure data-sharing and integration mechanisms provided by open banking ecosystems allow consumers greater security, ensure financial autonomy when dealing with personal financial management, provide efficient access to lending processes, and overall create a space for personalised benefits from third-party innovations and competition.[42]

C. Challenges of open banking

Despite the many benefits associated with the application of open banking, the nature of data-sharing systems presents numerous risks. These risks include data vulnerabilities, potential gaps in consumer protection regulation, data privacy issues, and potential cyberattacks that could leave consumers vulnerable to identity theft and other digital risks. For example, open banking involves the sharing of sensitive financial data with third-party service providers. Therefore, this system for the sharing of data

39 Danete Higgins Zandamela, 'The Benefits of Open Banking to Consumers, Banks and FinTech Companies' (Degree of Doctor of Business Administration, Thesis of Sheffield Hallam University and Business School Netherlands, September 2021) <10.7190/shu-thesis-00441> accessed 18 February 2024.

40 Olivia White and others, 'Financial Data Unbound: The Value of Open Data for Individuals and Institutions' (*Mckinsey Global Institute*, 24 June 2021) <https://www.mckinsey.com/industries/financial-services/our-insights/financial-data-unbound-the-value-of-open-data-for-individuals-and-institutions> accessed 13 November 2023.

41 Lars Ole Hjelkrem, Petter Eilif de Lange, and Erik Nesset, 'The Value of Open Banking Data for Application Credit Scoring: Case Study of a Norwegian Bank' (2022) 15(12) *Journal of Risk Financial Management* 597.

42 Ashraf Khan and Majid Malaika, 'Central Bank Risk Management, Fintech, and Cybersecurity' (2021) IMF Working Papers WP/21/105 <https://www.imf.org/en/Publications/WP/Issues/2021/04/23/Central-Bank-Risk-Management-Fintech-and-Cybersecurity-50278> accessed 30 April 2024.

creates significant data security and privacy concerns due to the nature of forming pathways to access to private, financial information.[43]

Further to this, open banking presents the risk of potential data breaches, unauthorised access, and the misuse of personal information given to third-party service providers in the event there are errors or vulnerabilities within the coding of the APIs and storage servers.[44] These challenges lead to potential fraud and identity theft risks where a data breach may exploit vulnerabilities within the open banking system to gain unauthorised access to accounts, manipulate transactions, or impersonate customers.[45]

As a result of these potential risks to consumers utilising the open banking ecosystem, consumer trust is another potential hurdle in the universal adoption of these mechanisms. Open banking is a relatively new concept that has emerged over recent years and, as such, it is vital to build confidence and trust with consumers to drive adoption and ensure the success of open banking initiatives for the relevant stakeholders. To ensure stakeholder trust within these systems, open banking applications are required to be in compliance with requisite, implemented legislation and regulations. For example, various regulatory requirements and frameworks which revolve around data protection, privacy, and consumer protection rights are monumental in the safeguarding of consumer trust and the appropriate operation of open banking mechanisms.[46] These requirements can become complex due to the cross-border and international nature of the transactions and financial information.

Finally, there are technological challenges that must be addressed with open banking systems, such as ensuring that the technical infrastructure behind the ecosystem is resilient against cyberattacks or malfunctions, and that the implemented standardised APIs are secure and can fulfil the requisite obligations set out by the stakeholders involved. Additionally, the systems must be compatible with a multitude of different financial institutions and jurisdictional requirements and can manage large amounts of data processing, which would require significant processing power. As such, the crucial aspects to be considered in overcoming these technological hurdles include ensuring that the infrastructure behind open banking is continuously monitored,

43 The Organisation for Economic Co-operation and Development (OECD), 'Data Portability in Open Banking: Privacy and Other Cross-cutting Issues' (OECD Digital Economy Papers, No. 348, OECD Publishing, 2023) <https://doi.org/10.1787/6c872949-en> accessed 19 January 2024.

44 Ibid.

45 Ibid.

46 Ilesh Dattani Assentian and Nuria Ituarte Aranda, 'Overview of Applicable Regulations in Digital Finance and Supporting Technologies' in John Soldatos and Dimosthenis Kyriazis (eds), *Big Data and Artificial Intelligence in Digital Finance* (Springer 2022).

the upkeep of system resilience is consistently maintained, and that collaboration between banks and third-party providers is up to date with the requisite guidelines.[47]

However, as the technology and implementation of open banking progress, open finance presents new challenges and opportunities for the evolving data-driven financial sector.

III. Open finance

As previously discussed, while open banking is primarily focused on the sharing of banking data through APIs, open finance encompasses a broader scope by incorporating other financial sectors and data sources beyond traditional banking.[48] In essence, the aim of open finance is to facilitate the secure sharing of financial data between the financial industry and other external sectors. For example, external sectors would include insurance companies, investment businesses, and money-lending institutions, to promote interoperability and collaboration between the various stakeholders to enhance services to consumers.[49]

In light of these aims, plans for a unified financial information space will be constructed in accordance with the European Commission's European Data Strategy (EU Data Strategy) by the end of 2024.[50] Within the proposal, a few initiatives included are providing real-time digital access to all regulated financial information, as well as the usage of Regulatory Technology (RegTech) and Supervisory Technology (SupTech) tools,[51] and the promotion of 'authority-to-authority and business-to-business data-sharing'[52] within the EU financial sector.[53] However, the term open finance refers to an extension and evolution of the principles and concepts behind open banking.

---

47 Ibid.

48 Dan Awrey and Joshua Macey, 'The Promise & Perils of Open Finance' (2023) 40 Yale Journal on Regulation 1.

49 Ibid.

50 European Commission, 'A European strategy for data' (*European Commission*, 2024) <https://digital-strategy.ec.europa.eu/en/policies/strategy-data> accessed 11 February 2024.

51 Commission, 'Communication from the Commission to the European Parliament, the Council, the European Economic and Social Committee, and the Committee of the Regions on a Digital Finance Strategy for the EU' (Communication) COM (2020) 591 final.

52 Gudula Deipenbrock, 'Digital Finance and Beyond in the Third Decade of the 21st Century – Observations with a Focus on the EU Policy and Legal Perspective' (2022) 33(3) European Business Law Review 309–330.

53 Commission (n 51).

A. Operation of open finance

In essence, with respect to consumers' consent and data portability, the operations of open finance function upon the same principles as open banking.[54] These principles empower stakeholders and ensure that consumers have greater autonomy over their financial data.[55] Furthermore, there are greater benefits for consumers from the innovative ecosystem of services provided and the personalised overview of their financial data through leveraging the data-sharing capabilities. For example, as demonstrated with the application of open banking, through a singular and centralised application or platform, consumers can manage their banking and credit information, investment portfolios, insurance policies, and loan management held by different providers.

Therefore, much like open banking, open finance allows consumers to have control over the amount of data that is shared, as well as presents opportunities for third-party service providers to develop and integrate new services for personalised financial advice, risk assessment, and other automated services. Moreover, while open banking focuses more on financial data between banks, consumers, and third-party service providers, open finance serves as the progression of the same system. The main principle of open finance stems from the depth of data accessibility for the consumer.[56] While open banking emphasises the centralisation of data, open finance prioritises the consumers' ability to view the entirety of personal and transactional data held and produced by a financial institution based on the consumer.[57] Furthermore, another feature of open finance is the consumers' access to data portability, which is defined as the 'ability to easily transfer data from one system to another without being required to re-enter data'.[58] As such, open finance enhances open banking to a broader scope and application. Furthermore, the concept encourages the sharing of financial data and information with other products and services within the digital finance ecosystem.

B. Benefits of open finance

Considering the above, it is clearly demonstrated that open finance presents an array of advantages that challenge and reshape the traditional banking sector. Firstly, open finance significantly contributes to the concept of financial inclusion through the

---

54 Ibid.

55 Ibid.

56 Emma Leong and Jodi Gardner, 'Open Banking in the UK and Singapore: Open Possibilities for Enhancing Financial Inclusion' (2022) NUS Centre for Banking & Finance Law Working Paper 22/01 <https://law.nus.edu.sg/wp-content/uploads/2022/08/CBFL-WPS-2201.pdf> accessed 11 January 2023.

57 Ibid.

58 International Organization for Standardization (ISO), 'ISO/IEC 22123–1:2023: Information Technology–Cloud Computing–Interoperability and Portability' (*ISO*, 2023) <https://www.iso.org/obp/ui#iso:std:iso-iec:22123:-1:ed-2:v1:en:term:3.5.1> accessed 30 April 2024.

offering of services to previously marginalised or unbanked individuals.[59] Further to this, through the expansion of accessibility to loans, savings, and investment products, open finance also facilitates a more inclusive financial ecosystem by supporting a wider and broader demographic in engaging with financial services. Furthermore, the framework of open finance cultivates an environment of innovation and heightened competition as it encourages both established financial institutions and emerging FinTech and RegTech companies to introduce novel and innovative financial products and services.

This competition fosters a diverse market with a range of choices for consumers, enhancing the quality and variety of available services. Another notable advantage of open finance lies in the improvement of the overall customer experience. As previously established, the seamless and secure sharing of financial data among various service providers, outside of the traditional banking and retail systems, allows for a more tailored and personalised approach to financial services. Therefore, these tailored services cater to unique customer preferences, significantly enhancing customer satisfaction, loyalty, and trust.

The empowerment of consumers regarding their financial data constitutes another key benefit. Open finance affords individuals greater control over their financial information, enabling them to selectively share data with different institutions or third-party service providers. This controlled and transparent approach to data sharing offers users a new level of command over their financial information. Furthermore, open finance streamlines processes, enhancing efficiency and reducing costs. By implementing automated and standardised data-sharing protocols, it minimises administrative complexities for both consumers and financial institutions, resulting in an overall more efficient system.

The overall potential for open finance is significant in terms of economic development, consumer trust, and autonomy. In addition to offering increased accessibility to financial and third-party services, open finance fosters economic growth and contributes to potential fraud prevention mechanisms and enhanced security measures across a multitude of industries because of its standardised nature. However, despite the numerous benefits associated with the implementation and future impact of open finance, it is imperative that the accompanying challenges be addressed.

These challenges include data privacy and protection issues, regulatory considerations, and consumer rights and protection. In addressing these challenges, stakeholders will be able to foster and ensure the successful and sustainable integration of open finance into the current landscape between financial institutions and third-party service providers.

---

59 Massimo Preziuso, Franziska Koefer, and Michel Ehrenhard, 'Open Banking and Inclusive Finance in the European Union: Perspectives from the Dutch Stakeholder Ecosystem' (2023) 9 Financial Innovation 1.

C. Challenges of open finance

As established previously with open banking, there are numerous challenges related to consumer data protection, secure infrastructure, and consumer trust with respect to regulatory frameworks and safeguards against data breaches.[60] Furthermore, due to the high level of industry fragmentation, there is a massive issue with coordination, which may result in difficulties for financial institutions to develop the requisite standardised API to fulfil the absolute potential of open finance procedures.[61]

However, despite these challenges, open finance fosters an environment of technological and entrepreneurial collaboration across a multitude of sectors to deliver improved and customer-centric financial experiences. Therefore, it is clearly demonstrated that many of the challenges of open finance stem from potential cybersecurity threats and digital risks associated with technological infrastructure.

IV. Cybersecurity and open banking

In consideration of the above, to address the aforementioned challenges presented in open banking and open finance, both the physical infrastructure and digital platforms require a robust and flexible approach to cybersecurity within the data-sharing ecosystem. In terms of definition, there is no universal definition of cybersecurity.[62] However, it can be referred to as a collection of digital and physical practices which form the infrastructure of security and protection for digitally-based networks, systems, software, and data, against unauthorised or malicious access, attacks, or disruption.[63] Therefore, the practice of cybersecurity is an amalgamation of various procedures that intersect diverse digital and physical mechanisms and technologies for the purpose of hardware and software data protection.

Due to the modern, evolving digital landscape, cybersecurity serves as a crucial form of defence in terms of safeguarding financial data.[64] Within the context of open banking and open finance, the protection of consumers' financial data ensures the trust and integrity of the system, which would lead to further adoption and integration into traditional financial institutions and other potential uses. Furthermore, another integral purpose of cybersecurity is the mitigation of risks associated with digital infrastructures through security protocols, specifically targeted protocols and policies,

60 Ibid.
61 Dan Awrey and Joshua Macey (n 48).
62 Chris Florackis and others, 'Cybersecurity Risk' (2023) 36(1) The Review of Financial Studies 1, 351–407.
63 Ibid.
64 Marianna Gounari, George Stergiopoulos, Kosmas Pipyros, and Dimitris Gritzalis (n 14).

digital and physical tools focused on data protection, and the creation of relevant departments and regulatory instruments to respond to cyber threats.[65]

A. Operations of cybersecurity

Therefore, in considering the circumstances, cybersecurity includes the establishment of procedures and systems to mitigate, as well as manage, the aftermath of any potential cyber threats or attacks. This is achieved through ensuring the establishment of roles and responsibilities associated with the institutions involved in the data-sharing systems and third-party service providers.[66] As such, cybersecurity requires a multifaceted and flexible approach to protect the data privacy of consumers, the integrity and reliability of stored data, and the verification process of authorised consumers.[67]

Consequently, established cybersecurity measures include the implementation of secure computer networks through firewalls, detection systems, and encryption protocols.[68] Furthermore, additional aspects of cybersecurity require the employment of data loss prevention policies and the implementation of strategies for the purpose of data retention, backup, and recovery mechanisms, to protect against any loss or theft.[69] For example, systems such as Intrusion Detection Systems (IDS) encompass Host-Based Intrusion Detection Systems (HIDS), Network-Based Intrusion Detection Systems (NIDS), and hybrid combinations of the two aforementioned systems.[70] The purpose of these systems is to monitor digital network traffic, from host networks or external connections, by detecting suspicious or malicious activity and then identifying, isolating, and mitigating any potential threats that may be harmful to the digital ecosystem.[71]

In addition to these, a more popular cybersecurity mechanism is the use of firewalls, which are utilised to safeguard against unauthorised access or alteration of data by Trojan viruses or ransomware. Firewalls also filter potentially malicious programs or

---

65 Ibid.

66 Christopher Wilson, Tamas Gaidosch, Frank Adelmann, and Anastasiia Morozova, *Cybersecurity Risk Supervision* (IMF, 2019).

67 Ibid.

68 Usman Tariq, Irgan Ahmed, Ali Kashif Bashir, and Kamran Shaukat, 'A Critical Cybersecurity Analysis and Future Research Directions for the Internet of Things: A Comprehensive Review' (2023) 23(8) Sensors (Basel) 4117.

69 Olivér Gulyás and Gábor Kiss, 'Impact of Cyber-Attacks on the Financial Institutions' (2023) 219 Procedia Computer Science 84–90.

70 Ansam Khraisat, Iqbal Gondal, Peter Vamplew, and Joarder Kamruzzaman, 'Survey of Intrusion Detection Systems: Techniques, Datasets, and Challenges' (2019) 2 Cybersecurity 20.

71 Safana Hyder Abbas, Wedad Abdul Khuder Naser, and Amal Abbas Kadhim, 'Subject Review: Intrusion Detection System (IDS) and Intrusion Prevention System (IPS)' (2023) 14(2) Global Journal of Engineering and Technology Advances 155–158.

network traffic, which may disguise itself to infiltrate a digital system for the purpose of corruption or exploitation.[72]

Additionally, another established cybersecurity practice is the use of encryption to encode information in an unreadable format, ensuring that the sensitive details are inaccessible to unauthorised users.[73] By essentially scrambling data, encryption protects sensitive data during transmission or storage within a data-sharing system.[74] Further to this, the practice of encryption also aids with Multi-Factor Authentication (MFA) security practices, which require users to provide multiple forms of authentication before being granted access to a system or being provided data.[75]

Typically, MFA security systems require verification of personal data or confirmation from a specific medium, such as a personal cellular phone, to ensure the identity of the user requesting access.[76] For example, a combination of biometric data, passwords, authentication tokens (where confirmation comes directly from users' cellular phones without requiring login credentials each time), or email passwords is used as part of the MFA system to ensure that authorised consumers are accessing specific data from specific databases.[77]

As a result, these established protection mechanisms are regarded as being a component of Security Information and Event Management Systems,[78] which gather and evaluate logged data from each point of protection. Institutions use these practices to guarantee that the integrity of their system is not jeopardised and that customers maintain faith in digital systems. Financial institutions use these specialised practices to support the necessary security of financial data, with an emphasis on the prevention and mitigation of cyber threats and data breaches to protect consumers as well as financial institutions' infrastructure.[79]

---

72 Ibid.

73 Jagpreet Kaur and K.R. Ramkumar, 'The Recent Trends in Cyber Security: A Review' (2022) 34(8) Journal of King Saud University - Computer and Information Sciences 5766–5781.

74 Ibid.

75 Chalee Vorakulpipat, Sasakorn Pichetjamroen, and Ekkachan Rattanalerdnusorn, 'Usable Comprehensive-Factor Authentication for a Secure Time Attendance System' (2021) 7 Peer J Computer Science.

76 Federico Sinigaglia, Roberto Carbone, Gabriele Costa, and Nicola Zannone, 'A Survey on Multi-Factor Authentication for Online Banking in the Wild' (2020) 96 Computers & Security 101745.

77 Vassilis Papaspirou and others, 'A Novel Authentication Method that Combines Honeytokens and Google Authenticator' (2023) 14(7) Information 386.

78 Igor Kotenko, Diana Gaifulina, and Igor Zelichenok, 'Systematic Literature Review of Security Event Correlation Methods' (2022) 10 IEEE Access 43387–43420.

79 Joseph Goh and others, 'Cybersecurity Risk Surveillance: A Case Study of Singapore' (2020) IMF Working Papers WP/20/28.

This is because these financial institutions have access to a large amount of personal and compiled groups of data for both individuals and corporations, and it is imperative that any possibility of unauthorised access or data breaches be mitigated. Since financial institutions' success is directly correlated with consumers' trust, robust cybersecurity procedures and mechanisms are vital. Therefore, adequate cybersecurity practices and protection measures ensure that consumer and institutional confidentiality remains secure and inaccessible to unauthorised breaches or accidental access.[80] As such, these cybersecurity practices require a level of fraud prevention procedures and mitigation mechanisms in order to identify and alleviate any suspicious or potentially malicious activities.[81] Common examples of this, with respect to commercial and individual cybersecurity concerns, are potential phishing attacks or identity theft.

Further to the above, as previously elaborated, firewalls and intrusion detection and prevention systems are examples of these prevention and mitigation mechanisms, and they work to prevent network-based attacks such as distributed denial-of-service (DDoS)[82] attacks and network breaches. These infrastructures are governed by guidelines established under the regulatory compliance instruments in regional data protection law. For example, Article 5(1)(f) of the General Data Protection Regulation (GDPR) outlines that personal data collected and processed must be done with adequate security through proportionate and appropriate technical or organisational measures. Furthermore, the GDPR requires compliance to consider the risks of data processes and implement measures to ensure that technical data protection mechanisms are reviewed and kept up to date.[83]

Further security measures for data processing are addressed in Article 32, which outlines potential levels of security depending on the proportional circumstances. For example, pseudonymisation and encryption of personal data,[84] and the regular testing and assessment of technical measures for security to protect against the risk of loss, unauthorised access, or destruction of data.[85] As such, the GDPR provides flexibility to determine necessary data protection and cybersecurity measures to be implemented through regular evaluations and assessments based on the potential risks in each industry.

---

80 Ibid.

81 Francesco De Pascalis, 'The Journey to Open Finance: Learning from the Open Banking Movement' (2022) 33(3) European Business Law Review 397–420.

82 Muhammad Ahsan Raza and others, 'Analyzing the Behaviour of DDoS Cyber Attack' (2022) 26(4) Technical Journal 46–55.

83 Council Regulation (EU) 2016/679 of the European Parliament and of the Council of 27 April 2016 on the protection of natural persons with regard to the processing of personal data and on the free movement of such data, and repealing Directive 95/46/EC [2016] OJ L 119/1 of 04.05.2016 (General Data Protection Regulation), Art. 24.

84 Ibid, Art. 32 (1) (a).

85 Ibid, Art. 32 (1) (d); Art. 32 (2).

Additionally, Article 95 of the PSD2 outlines that member states are required to establish appropriate mitigation measures for security risks and create an adequate framework for the assessment and reporting of cyber incidents. Furthermore, the Payment Card Industry (PCI) Data Security Standard (DSS) (PCI DSS) created and enforced specific standards for the PCI security requirements. These standards also apply to entities which "store, process, or transmit" sensitive authentication data.[86] As such, it also applies to third-party service providers, which would include merchants, data processors, and card issuers within the market. However, specific brands follow their own requirements with respect to requisite compliance procedures.[87]

Finally, with respect to third-party service providers, financial cybersecurity requires financial institutions to assess and implement third-party risk management systems when sharing sensitive data between the parties.[88] This requires the establishment of obligations and specific codes of conduct governing the performance of requisite due diligence to ensure that third parties maintain adequate security measures.[89] Due to the nature of cybersecurity and the consistently evolving nature of technological security systems and threats, financial institutions are required to remain proactive in combating emerging industry practices.[90]

B. Cybersecurity risks in open banking and open finance

In light of the aforementioned discussions on open banking, open finance, and cybersecurity, it is clearly demonstrated that the enhanced data-sharing practices within the financial space create numerous cybersecurity risks for institutions and individual stakeholders operating within this ecosystem.[91] Therefore, as a result, these risks may place consumers' financial data at risk where account details, transaction history, or identification security checks such as Personal Identification Numbers (PINs) are vulnerable to cyberattacks. This is because as the number of stakeholders and users of open finance and open banking services increases, so do the potential areas of risk and vulnerabilities.[92]

These vulnerabilities and risks create gaps within the operating infrastructure, which would be ripe for exploitation and cyberattacks that would result in loss or corruption of consumer data, impersonation and identity theft of consumers, unauthorised

86 Payment Card Industry (PCI) Security Standards Council, 'Payment Card Industry Data Security Standard' (*PCI*, 2022) <https://www.commerce.uwo.ca/pdf/PCI-DSS-v4_0.pdf> accessed 10 January 2024.

87 Ibid.

88 Council, General Data Protection Regulation (n 83), Art. 32 (1) (d); Art. 32 (2).

89 Ibid, Art. 40.

90 Deloitte United Kingdom, 'Achieving robust cyber-security in a connected banking environment' (*Deloitte UK*, 2021) <https://www2.deloitte.com/uk/en/pages/financial-services/articles/achieving-robust-cyber-security-in-connected-banking-environment.html> accessed 13 November 2023.

91 Francesco De Pascalis (n 81).

92 Ibid.

transactions, and potential loss of funds, as well as the manipulation of financial data held by third-party service providers or banking institutions.[93] As such, these gaps stem from the operation of open banking and open finance being heavily reliant upon APIs to facilitate data-sharing practices between financial institutions and third-party providers. Therefore, potentially flawed or unmonitored, authentication and authorisation practices present opportunities for exploitation, which would compromise the integration of the platforms established for financial data and access information exchanges.[94]

Cybercriminals would utilise these compromised systems to hack and compromise the infrastructure through Trojan viruses, malware, or phishing attacks that target individuals or organisations involved in systematic, interconnected operations, especially those involved in open finance and open banking API regimes.[95] Phishing attacks are a result of manipulating or defrauding users to access malicious links or attachments, which allow hackers to access personal information through false login pages, gain access to authentication credentials, or access the system through a backdoor exploitation and install malicious software to destroy the security of the entire operating system.

As such, these risks demonstrate that there are significant risks associated with open banking and open finance systems that would affect the operational stakeholders contributing to the system.[96] As such, it is vital that adequate due diligence through digital and physical cybersecurity measures is established to manage, prepare, mitigate, and protect against potential cyber threats in accordance with requisite legislation and guidelines.[97]

Furthermore, Article 95 of the PSD2 states and outlines requisite security measures and protocols to be enforced in connection with the mitigation of risks and vulnerabilities associated with open banking and open finance, as well as to protect

---

93 Usman Tariq, Irgan Ahmed, Ali Kashif Bashir, and Kamran Shaukat (n 68).

94 Abduvahobov Shohruh Xolmo'min o'g'li, 'API in Open Banking' (2023) 22 World Economics and Finance Bulletin 193.

95 Moatsum Alawida and others, 'A Deeper Look into Cybersecurity Issues in the Wake of COVID-19: A Survey' (2022) 34(10) Journal of King Saud University - Computer and Information Sciences 8176–8206.

96 Jo Ann Barefoot, 'Digital Technology Risks for Finance: Dangers Embedded in Fintech and Regtech' (2020) M-RCBG Associate Working Paper No. 151 <https://www.hks.harvard.edu/centers/mrcbg/publications/awp/awp151> accessed 30 April 2024.

97 Council, 'Regulation (EU) 2019/881 of the European Parliament and of the Council of 17 April 2019 on ENISA (the European Union Agency for Cybersecurity) and on information and communications technology cybersecurity certification and repealing Regulation (EU) No 526/2013 (Cybersecurity Act)' [2019] OJ L 151/15 of 07.06.2019.

stakeholders such as banking networks and institutions, third-party service providers such as insurance companies, FinTech companies or business corporations, and consumers.[98]

V. Blockchain technology and cybersecurity in open banking

A. Defining blockchain technology

Despite the cybersecurity risks associated with open finance and open banking, there are potential solutions available in smart technology implementation. Blockchain technology can offer several cybersecurity benefits in the context of open banking, open finance and GDPR compliance.[99] Blockchain technology can be defined as a technological database operating as a distributed ledger which utilises cryptographic security combined with validating consensus mechanisms.[100]

This system ensures that transactional activities remain transparent and immutable, due to the decentralised nature of blockchain, which enables each node on the chain to access records of transactions on the relevant platforms.[101]

B. Blockchain technology in open banking and open finance

The immutable nature of blockchain technology enforces an additional layer of security and protection for stored financial information, which is relevant to open banking and open finance. Therefore, the implementation of blockchain technology creates a more robust environment for cybersecurity strategies and procedures when confronted with malicious cyber threats aimed at altering or tampering with stored data. This is achieved by the technology's inherent defence mechanisms for protecting data integrity and promoting greater trust among participants in the open banking ecosystem.[102] Furthermore, blockchain's employment of cryptographic algorithms and consensus mechanisms enables secure and transparent transactions, reducing the risk of unauthorised modifications or fraudulent activities within open banking and open finance.

---

98 Marianna Gounari, George Stergiopoulos, Kosmas Pipyros, and Dimitris Gritzalis (n 14).

99 Prasanth Varma Kakarlapudi and Qusay H. Mahmoud, 'A Systematic Review of Blockchain for Consent Management' (2021) 9(2) Healthcare (Basel) 137.

100 Joseph Lee and Vere-Marie Khan, 'Blockchain and Smart Contract for Peer-to-Peer Energy Trading Platform: Legal Obstacles and Regulatory Solutions' (2023) 19(4) UIC Review of Intellectual Property Law 285.

101 Ibid.

102 Mohd Javaid and others, 'A Review of Blockchain Technology Applications for Financial Services' (2022) 2(3) Bench Council Transactions on Benchmarks, Standards and Evaluations 100073.

In application to open finance and open banking, blockchain can facilitate more enhanced and robust authentication and identity management solutions. These solutions can be achieved through the technology's decentralised and self-sovereign identity models, wherein users have autonomy over their identity information.[103] Therefore, this reduces the consumer's reliance on centralised identity repositories, which are susceptible to data breaches.[104] In addition to other aspects of blockchain technology, smart contract applications for automated security systems present the opportunity for a powerful management system to be implemented in aiding personalised financial data. Furthermore, this would allow the consumer to exert greater control over their own data and financial decisions. For example, smart contracts can be used to define and enforce access control policies where consumers can select specified entities and types of information to be shared; this would ensure that only authorised entities can access sensitive data or initiate transactions.[105]

In addition to smart contracts, the use of private, permissioned chains, with the specification that only the requisite stakeholders would possess access to select sensitive financial data, would also provide enhanced privacy protection for consumers and financial institutions operating within open banking and open finance ecosystems. Further to this, an additional potential blockchain-based security measure would be the incorporation of zero-knowledge proofs, which are cryptographic methods used to ensure the integrity of data by having a user prove knowledge of data without revealing the actual data,[106] or through selective disclosure mechanisms, which would allow stakeholders to enhance data privacy protection mechanisms in compliance with the requisite legislation.[107]

A key example of requisite legislation is the introduction of the Digital Operational Resilience Act (DORA), which would apply to over 22,000 financial entities and information and communication technology (ICT) service providers operating within the EU.[108] As such, the creation of specific guidelines for industries operating within

---

103 Eranga Bandara, Xueping Liang, Peter Foytik, Sachin Shetty, and Kasun De Zoysa, 'A Blockchain and Self-Sovereign Identity Empowered Digital Identity Platform' (International Conference on Computer Communications and Networks (ICCCN), Athens, Greece, 2021) 1–7 <10.1109/ICCCN52240.2021.9522184> accessed 10 March 2024.

104 Khaled A.M. Ahmed, Sabry F. Saraya, John F. Wanis, and Amr M.T. Ali-Eldin, 'A Blockchain Self-Sovereign Identity for Open Banking Secured by the Customer's Banking Cards' (2023) 15(6) Future Internet 208.

105 Joseph Lee and Vere-Marie Khan (n 100).

106 Benfano Soewito and Yonathan Marcellinus, 'IoT Security System with Modified Zero Knowledge Proof Algorithm for Authentication' (2021) 22(3) Egyptian Informatics Journal 269–276.

107 Zhuoliang Qiu and others, 'Novel Blockchain and Zero-Knowledge Proof Technology-Driven Car Insurance' (2023) 12(18) Electronics 3869.

108 PWC, 'How the Digital Operational Resilience Act helps your continuity' (*PwC*) <https://www.pwc.nl/en/industries/financiele-sector/risk-and-regulation/digital-operational-resilience-act/how-the-digital-operational-resilience-act-helps

digital markets ensures that there are further protections in place with which these entities must comply. These guidelines include regulations around ICT risk management and third-party risk management.[109]

The application of blockchain technology to the open banking and open finance space would assist with the efficiency of transactions as well as compliance with regulatory requirements. Furthermore, blockchain's decentralised architecture reduces the reliance on a single point of failure in open banking systems. Therefore, by avoiding the risk of relying on a central authority for security, multiple nodes operating on the blockchain network would collectively ensure the security and integrity of the system. In turn, this would create a more resilient system against cyber risks and attacks.

Finally, there is potential to create a standardised and uniform API system to operate upon the blockchain, which would facilitate immutable, transparent, and accountable collaboration between financial institutions and third-party service providers. However, despite the numerous benefits associated with implementing blockchain technology, there must be careful consideration given to the potential limitations, scalability issues, and problems with integration into existing systems.

C. Risks of blockchain technology in open banking and open finance

As discussed above, there are also risks associated with utilising blockchain technology in open banking and open finance. For example, the technology itself is reliant upon decentralisation, but this does not mitigate every potential cyberattack or threat. Smart contracts operating upon the blockchain, as well as the consensus mechanisms which assist with creating nodes on the chain, may become vulnerable to digital hacks or attacks. Furthermore, as the digital infrastructure increases in size and usage, there are always avenues of risk being created due to the increasing number of stakeholders, transactions, operators, and those with access to the information. Therefore, continuous protocols must be put in place to maintain and remain updated in real-time with the operations and mechanisms of the chains in use.

Another issue with the application of blockchain technology to open banking and open finance is scalability.[110] A common issue found with blockchain networks is that the blockchain is only as efficient as the operating nodes and the volume of transactions.[111] Therefore, an increase in the usage of the chain would result in potentially

-your-continuity.html#:~:text=DORA%20will%20bring%20into%20scope,crypto%20asset%20providers%2C%20data%20reporting> accessed 15 November 2023.

109 Ibid.

110 Stefan De Angelis, Gilberto Zanfino, Leonardo Aniello, Federico Lombardi, and Vladimiro Sassone, 'Blockchain and Cybersecurity: A Taxonomic Approach' (*EU Blockchain Observatory Forum*, 2019) <https://www.eublockchainforum.eu/sites/default/files/research-paper/wrks-main_1.pdf> accessed 7 January 2024.

111 Nejc Rozman, Marko Corn, Gasper Skulj, Tomaz Berlec, Janez Diaci, and Primoz Podrzaj, 'Exploring the Effects of Blockchain Scalability Limitations on Performance

slower transactions, processing times, and increased fees, as well as digital strain on the operations of the chain. Further to this, blockchain's decentralised and pseudonymous nature creates a challenge in regulatory compliance within the existing financial regulation landscape. Additionally, there is no standardised protocol governing blockchain technology and its application in current financial instruments and frameworks. Therefore, integration into open banking and open finance systems may prove complicated across various financial institutions and third-party systems.

D. Solutions to the risk of blockchain technology

In light of the aforementioned discussion on risks associated with the application of blockchain technology in open banking and open finance, potential solutions to this would be systematic and multifaceted in approach. This approach would require the combination of smart technologies, regulatory measures, and analysis, as well as industry adoption and collaboration. With respect to smart technologies, there are inherent cyber risks associated with smart contracts and verification in blockchain technology. Therefore, cybersecurity measures such as security protocols would enhance blockchain networks and would provide the necessary steps towards the implementation of blockchain technology in open finance and open banking. Moreover, the utilisation of encryption-based technology and more complex authentication methods would aid in the fortification of system networks against cyber threats and any additional potential vulnerabilities within the open banking system.[112]

Furthermore, the establishment of consistent security audits and regulatory guidelines for appropriate practices to mitigate cyber risks would bolster the overall resilience of blockchain-based networks. In addition, the issues of scalability would be mitigated through potential enhancements to consensus mechanisms such as sharding, proof-of-stake, or off-chain scaling solutions. These solutions would provide significant improvements to the overall operational security measures with respect to completing transactions on-chain as well as the reduction of network congestion and storage.[113] Additionally, another solution would be a layer-two scaling solution, which is similar to the application of the lightning network for Bitcoin; this would increase transaction speeds and reduce fees while operating on blockchain technology without compromising the decentralised nature of the network.[114]

With respect to regulatory issues, current regulatory frameworks require significant consultation and considerable time for integration. As seen with the debate and

---

and User Behavior in Blockchain-Based Shared Manufacturing Systems: An Experimental Approach' (2023) 13(7) Applied Sciences 4251.

112 International Monetary Fund Western Hemisphere Department, 'Cybersecurity and Financial Stability: Considerations for Chile' (*IMF Staff Country Reports A002*, 2024) <https://www.elibrary.imf.org/view/journals/002/2024/042/article-A002-en.xml> accessed 11 March 2024.

113 Muhammad Hassan Nasir and others, 'Scalable Blockchains — A Systematic Review' (2022) 126 Future Generation Computer Systems 136–162.

114 Ibid.

implementation of DORA and PSD2, it is necessary for collaboration and consultation between regulatory bodies, industry stakeholders, and smart technology specialists to develop adaptable and comprehensive policies around the regulatory practices of blockchain and other smart technologies. This is because there is an overarching need to balance compliance with regulation in the interest of consumer and business protection while ensuring innovation and competition can thrive in a regulated environment.

In light of this, future legislation must address the risks associated with blockchain technology, open banking and open finance through adequate anti-money laundering procedures and robust KYC guidelines in alignment with blockchain's decentralised nature. For example, self-sovereign identity solutions may assist in ensuring a balance is struck between legislation and regulatory requirements without compromising consumers' or stakeholders' privacy and considerations.[115]

Further to this, this balancing solution may also be addressed through the creation of standardised, uniform protocols and guidelines to govern data exchange and communication mechanisms between multiple blockchain networks and involved stakeholders.[116] As such, interoperability-focused initiatives would serve as solutions; for example, cross-chain communication protocols or specific blockchain platforms geared towards interoperable solutions would assist by facilitating seamless integration and data-sharing mechanisms amongst diverse blockchain systems. Furthermore, the application of these solutions formulates the foundation for mitigating risks associated with blockchain technology in the open banking and open finance application models.

However, these solutions would require integrated and significant collaborative efforts from all stakeholders, such as consumers, businesses, third-party service providers, policymakers, financial institutions, and technological specialists. Through these efforts, cooperation to integrate smart technology into digital financial instruments would pave the way for a more interconnected and consumer-centric banking model that embodies the overarching ethos of consumer autonomy, market competitiveness, and the potential for the universal modernisation of regulatory instruments.

E. DAO as a solution

First of all, what is a data DAO? It is a decentralised autonomous organisation embedded on the blockchain to facilitate and govern data exchanges. Blockchain is a distributed ledger technology (DLT) and is essentially a database that uses encryption

115 Khaled A.M. Ahmed, Sabry F. Saraya, John F. Wanis, and Amr M.T. Ali-Eldin (n 104).

116 Massimiliano Aschi, Susanna Bonura, Nicola Masi, Domenico Messina, and Davide Profeta, 'Cybersecurity and Fraud Detection in Financial Transactions' in John Soldatos and Dimosthenis Kyriazis (eds), *Big Data and Artificial Intelligence in Digital Finance* (Springer 2022).

technology to achieve decentralisation, transparency, and immutability. Each node has a copy of the complete database. There are different types of blockchain and different generations of blockchain developments with various functionalities and vulnerabilities. Bitcoin is based on the first generation of blockchain; however, more DAOs are built on Ethereum, the so-called Blockchain 2.0. The DAO was based on Ethereum, which has led to hacking and subsequent forking. A DAO is a blockchain application in governance whereby transactions can be (but don't need to be completely) automated by smart contracts with predetermined rules and processes. A data DAO is hence a blockchain application in governance for data exchanges and governance. The function of a data DAO is not simply to facilitate data exchanges, but also communications and decision processes among the stakeholders (i.e., the participants).

What is the function of a data DAO? Due to the blockchain's characteristics of decentralisation, transparency, immutability, and encryption, a data DAO is claimed to be able to increase data sharing in a more secure way and to empower data owners such as consumers. This is in line with the English Law Commission's proposal of creating a third category of property for 'data objects' which can give data owners proprietary rights in their data.

What is the relationship between data DAO and Open Finance? If a data DAO can increase data sharing in a more secure way, this can encourage data owners as well as financial institutions to share data. Hence, it can increase competition, boost consumer welfare, and protect individual data in a decentralised manner with no single point of failure, minimising the risk of data being compromised. By this logic, data DAO can be a cybersecurity solution in open finance. As managing cybersecurity risk is a legal and regulatory requirement in open finance, data DAO can be considered RegTech, a type of regulatory technology aimed at managing regulatory and compliance processes within financial institutions.

How do we regulate a data DAO? A data DAO can be seen as an organisation (entity), an API, a RegTech application, or a social system. We have seen the collapse of the DAO on Ethereum, which was caused by hacking and forking. The recent collapse of FTX is said to be due to internal governance. Therefore, regulating the internal governance is essential to prevent failure. For instance, can it be without a third-party organiser? If some transactions are to be automated according to the predetermined rules and processes by smart contracts, how can smart contracts be regulated to deliver optimality?

As data DAO will essentially replace the functionality of the current API, some of the risks identified in the previous discussionof API will need to be factored into the relevant risk assessment. However, because a data DAO is a blockchain application, there are risks that do not associate with the current API. For instance: 1) 51 percent vulnerability; 2) private key security; 3) criminal activity; 4) double spending; 5) transaction privacy leakage; 6) criminal smart contracts; 7) vulnerabilities in smart contracts; 8) under-optimised smart contract.

As an application of RegTech, the current regulatory sandbox is being used as a regulatory process. Would the current regulatory sandbox be sufficient, especially if a data DAO is to be considered as a new social system where stakeholders are to interact with miners, validators, network providers, financial institutions, private institutions, government agencies, and individual consumers? In this social system, the true public value will need to be expressed, and based on that, equity can be delivered. One way of delivering equity in a utilitarian way is to assess if social benefits outweigh social costs.

There are two major regulatory issues: jurisdiction and financial stability. These are the two areas where there has not been a lot of literature. How to manage jurisdictional risk? How would data DAO affect financial stability? In other words, would systemic risk emerge? So, what is the possible model? Would data DAO be built on several infrastructures: on-chain, off-chain, sidechain, and cross-chain systems?

Whatever the system to be built, from the regulator's perspective, the objectives of data DAO and open finance should be aligned. Data DAO aims to close the gap in open finance. The regulatory objectives of data DAO should also be aligned with those of open finance. It is likely that there will be conflicts of interest between the stakeholders in open finance and the stakeholders of data DAO. It is submitted that the role of regulation and law is to mediate their interests.

VI. Conclusion

In conclusion, as digital financial systems continue to evolve through the integration of smart technology, there is a growing need for adequate cybersecurity measures and protocols in tandem with relevant and appropriate regulatory instruments to aid in the transition towards an open data landscape. Open banking and open finance have emerged as forefront mediums and potential catalysts for more autonomous consumer practices within the digital finance discussions.

While this chapter thoroughly explores the potential for blockchain-based cybersecurity initiatives, there is a significant need for accompanying regulatory instruments and legislation. As discussed, many jurisdictions have outlined and brought into force several legislative measures to address any potential lacunas or regulatory deficits within existing statutory frameworks. These different frameworks also demonstrate the diversity of thought and approaches within specific jurisdictions to data governance and data-driven economic institutions. Therefore, due to the nature of all the converging technologies, it is a rapidly evolving landscape with demonstrated legal and financial complexities.

Furthermore, as a direct result of the rising adoption of open banking and open finance practices with diverse stakeholders, cybersecurity measures and practices will inevitably require enhanced prioritisation due to the inherent risks associated with data-sharing API practices. Therefore, there is a demonstrated necessity to explore the application of blockchain technology to aid in cybersecurity practices aimed at protecting the integrity of the overall operational infrastructure in open banking and open finance systems.

7

Capital markets regulation in the age of social media: an analysis of the GameStop incident under the EU Market Abuse Regulation

Philipp Maume

I. Introduction: a new problem and old regulation

A. Capital markets regulation and the market for information

The capital carkets have a reputation for being dynamic and very prone to adopting new technologies early on – algorithmic and high-frequency trading, robo-advisory, the application of blockchain, and Artificial Intelligence (AI), etc. However, the concept of how to regulate the capital markets is relatively old. Academics do not fully agree about the 'birth' of capital markets regulation.[1] While elements of what we know as capital markets regulation today can be traced back to the first joint stock companies (most prominently in England) or to the late medieval Italian cities,[2] regulation as we know it is still mostly based on the US Securities Act of 1933 and the US Securities and Markets Act 1934.[3] Despite updates and amendments, the key concepts have remained mostly unchanged. Today, the International Organization of Securities Commissions (IOSCO) sets out 38 principles that are seen as international best practice,[4] including a long methodology for their assessment and implementation.[5] Although details of

---

1 On nomenclature: Legal systems around the globe differ in the use of the terms 'capital markets regulation', 'securities regulation' and 'financial markets regulation'. At least for the purposes of this chapter, the potential differences are not relevant, and the terms will be used interchangeably.

2 For an overview, see Mathias M Siems, 'The Foundations of Securities Laws' (2009) 20 European Business Law Review 141–171.

3 On the inception and principles of the US 1930s legislation, see Louis Loss, Joel Seligman, and Troy Paredes, *Fundamentals of Securities Regulation, Part I* (Wolters Kluwer 2011) 57–73.

4 International Organization of Securities Commissions, 'Objectives and Principles of Securities Regulation' (*IOSCO*, May 2017), available at <https://www.iosco.org/library/pubdocs/pdf/IOSCOPD561.pdf> accessed 26.03.2024.

5 International Organization of Securities Commissions, 'Methodology for Assessing Implementation of the IOSCO Objectives and Principles of Securities Regulation'

national capital markets regulation might differ from country to country, the international architecture of securities markets is built on strong and well-established principles. However, we need to keep in mind that the core concepts of regulation are nearly 100 years old.

These concepts rest on the idea that capital markets are markets for information.[6] They are like sponges that absorb and display all information. All investors need information to make informed decisions. The need for informed markets relates to the efficiency of investment decisions and the overall market outcome. Accurate information improves investment decisions, the monitoring by stakeholders, and the accountability of management. This idea is reflected in the established system of capital markets regulation. Instead of banning certain investments based on their quality (or lack of quality), regulation focusses on disclosure.[7] Extensive disclosure obligations (initial, ongoing, and ad-hoc) are supposed to decrease the information asymmetries between investors and issuers. The ban on insider trading is based on the idea of giving all investors equal access to relevant information. Finally, the prohibition of market manipulation, which is most relevant for this paper,[8] safeguards the market mechanism, preventing inaccurate or misleading information from being the basis of investment decisions.

B. Social media as a new challenge

But times have changed. The amount of information available to investors is much larger than it was when disclosure-based regulation was first introduced nearly a century ago. It is not only the data itself that has exponentially grown, but the way information is distributed through different channels has changed. In the 1990s, the internet enabled investors to gather information on companies, markets, and securities from all over the world, resulting in a massive push for the globalisation of capital markets. The rise of the internet and mobile communication devices such as smartphones has also given birth to new ways of distributing information. This includes how the information is spread, including all forms of social media and messenger services, and who receives or can receive the information.

Any public information can, in theory, have an impact on the capital markets in general, and on specific issuers in particular. Some posts on social media are 'trending' or even go 'viral', which means that the algorithm distributes them particularly

(*IOSCO*, May 2017), available at <https://www.iosco.org/library/pubdocs/pdf/IOSCOPD562.pdf> accessed 26.03.2024.

6 See Paul Latimer and Philipp Maume, *Promoting Information in the Market for Financial Services* (Springer 2015) 5 with further references.

7 On the dichotomy of disclosure-based regulation and merit-based regulation, see Neal H Brockmeyer, 'Regulation of Securities Offerings in California: Is It Time for a Change After a Century of Merit Regulation?' (2020) 54(1) Loyola of Los Angeles Law Review 1; Hugh H Makens, 'Who Speaks for the Investor? An Evaluation of the Assault on Merit Regulation' (1984) 13(3) University of Baltimore Law Review 435.

8 See below Section III.

effectively and many other users are sharing these posts. Let us imagine such a post contains rumours about a listed company, which – if they were true – would influence the investment decisions of respective investors. This could be a side effect of a post made by a nutrition activist, criticising the dubious origins of ingredients in baby food. Or it could be a planned and concerted effort by prospective investors aiming to bring down the share price. Either way, this mechanism would have been unthinkable 25 years ago, and it raises serious questions for capital markets regulation and its enforcement.

C. This chapter

This chapter will attempt to highlight some of the resulting issues. It will do so with a hands-on approach to regulation. Instead of discussing general principles of regulation, it will use EU capital markets regulation as a template.[9] This template will be applied to one of the most intriguing capital market events of recent times, the so-called 'GameStop' incident. This will enable us to identify some of the pressing problems of the interface between social media and capital markets. This paper will not attempt to answer the questions raised but give a first overview of what these questions are.

In Section II, it will briefly lay out the 'GameStop' incident, explaining how discussions on social media (here: Reddit) resulted in a stock market bonanza. In Section III, first the current EU regime on market manipulation will be outlined and then applied to the GameStop case. It will show that we might have to rethink some of the core concepts of capital markets regulation when it is applied to social media. In Section IV, this chapter will outline a related problem – the supervision of social media by national regulators. Section V will summarise the findings and highlight the issues that require further research.

II. The GameStop incident in a nutshell

'GameStop' has become the synonym for a series of events that took place in 2020/2021.[10] GameStop is a US company listed on the New York Stock Exchange (NYSE). Its traditional business is the selling and renting out of computer games. Due to the improved bandwidth of internet connections and the possibility to buy and download games from online platforms, GameStop's profitability and future prospects became more

---

9 Given the level of standardisation, this could be done using capital markets regulation from most other jurisdictions; the issues would probably be similar.

10 There is plenty of academic literature outlining these events; see, e.g., Allan M Malz, 'The GameStop Episode: What Happened and What Does It Mean?' (2021) 41(3) Cato Journal 529; Jacob Gremillion, 'Diamond Hands and Regulatory Demands: GameStop and the Shortcoming of Current Securities Regulation' (2021) 33(2) Loyola Consumer Law Review 406, both with numerous further references. The following description of the GameStop incident is based on these sources.

and more questionable over the years. In 2020, short sellers (most of them managed funds) had built up massive short positions, equating to more than 140 per cent of the company shares available in free float. In other words, these market participants bet on the share price falling in the not-too-distant future.

In the second half of 2020, the financial analyst Keith Patrick Gill started to create a series of tweets and uploaded several videos on YouTube. Using the aliases 'Roaring Kitty' and 'DeepF*ckingValue', he highlighted the existence of GameStop short-positions and the potential for significant price increases in the case of a short squeeze. This sparked a vivid debate on the online discussion forum Reddit. In the subforum 'r/wallstreetbets', private users encouraged each other to buy GameStop shares and call options. The general gist of the debate was to 'defend' GameStop against an 'attack' from short sellers. This narrative of 'David against Goliath' or 'consumers against capital' was quickly picked up by the media.

Over the next few weeks, the share price increased significantly. This forced the involved funds to cover their positions, which means that they had to buy the respective shares to prevent further losses. This further decreased the number of GameStop shares available on the stock market and further fuelled the share price bonanza. After the price had bobbed up and down around USD 3 in early 2020, the share price increased from USD 19.94 on 11 January 2021 to USD 347.51 on 27 January 2021. The results were significant. Online brokers such as Robinhood temporarily stopped GameStop share orders on 28 January 2021. Several funds suffered catastrophic losses, with Melvin Capital even requiring a USD 2.8 billion bailout. However, the distribution of losses and profits is not as clear as it seems. Many retail investors also suffered severe losses because they purchased the share when it was near its peak. Some hedge funds had invested quite early in GameStop and subsequently made huge profits.

Surprisingly, little came out of this episode in terms of litigation. Court actions in the US focussed on Robinhood and other neo-brokers for halting trading on the GameStop share.[11] Keith Gill was also sued for securities fraud for misrepresenting himself as a retail investor and profiting from artificially inflating the share price,[12] but the lawsuit was dismissed in April 2022.[13] Gill's employer, the insurance company

11 Already in February 2021, journalists counted over 30 lawsuits filed against Robinhood. See Michael Kan, 'Robinhood Now Faces Over 30 Class-Action Lawsuits for Blocking Stock Buys' (*PCMag* UK, 2 February 2021), available at <https://uk.pcmag.com/old-personal-finance-apps/131458/robinhood-now-faces-over-30-class-action-lawsuits-for-blocking-stock-buys> accessed 26.03.2024.

12 Christian Berthelsen, '"Roaring Kitty" Sued for Securities Fraud over GameStop Rise' (*Bloomberg*, 17 February 2021) <https://www.bloomberg.com/news/articles/2021-02-17/-roaring-kitty-sued-for-securities-fraud-over-gamestop-rise> accessed 26.03.2024.

13 Michelle Price, 'A year on, GameStop champion Roaring Kitty is quiet – yet much richer' (*Reuters*, 2 February 2022) <https://www.reuters.com/technology/year-gamestop-champion-roaring-kitty-is-quiet-yet-much-richer-2022-02-02/> accessed

MassMutual, was fined USD 4.75 million by the Massachusetts regulator for failure to supervise their employee properly. In October 2021, the US Securities and Exchange Commission (SEC) published a detailed report on the events and mechanisms that led to the GameStop share bonanza.[14] It did not indicate that any market manipulation had occurred. Surprisingly, this only caused little debate in the US academic literature about potential shortcomings of US securities regulation.[15]

III. The (hypothetical) application of EU market abuse rules

A. Market manipulation regulation under EU law

Market manipulation is considered the oldest form of market abuse, while insider trading and the unlawful disclosure of inside information (Art. 14) are relatively new concepts.[16] In the EU, the rules on market manipulation are housed in Articles 12 and 15 of the Market Abuse Regulation (MAR).[17] The MAR is the backbone of the EU financial markets conduct rules (so-called Level 1 regulation).[18]

As a starting point, the MAR rules do not require the conduct in question to take place on a trading venue,[19] or even in the EU.[20] It is sufficient that the conduct has an impact

---

26.03.2024; Brad Witter, 'Dumb Money's Keith Gill Faced Lawsuits After His GameStop Profit' (*Bustle*, 20 February 2024) <https://www.bustle.com/entertainment/keith-gill-today-dumb-money-gamestop-profit-lawsuits> accessed 26.03.2024.

14 US Securities and Exchange Commission, 'Staff Report on Equity and Options Market Structure Conditions in Early 2021' (*SEC*, 14 October 2021) <https://www.sec.gov/files/staff-report-equity-options-market-struction-conditions-early-2021.pdf> accessed 26.03.2024.

15 One of the few examples is Henry David Gale, '"Buy GameStop!": The Need to Rethink the Approach to Market Manipulation in a WallStreetBets World' (2023) 108(4) Iowa Law Review 1923, focussing on the different approaches taken by different US Courts of Appeal; see also Gremillion (n 10), on issues of neo-brokering and payment for order flow.

16 Sebastian Mock, 'The Concept of Market Manipulation' in Marco Ventoruzzo and Sebastian Mock (eds), *Market Abuse Regulation* (2nd edn, OUP 2022) 29.

17 Council Regulation (EU) No 596/2014 of the European Parliament and of the Council of 16 April 2014 on market abuse (market abuse regulation) and repealing Directive 2003/6/EC of the European Parliament and of the Council and Commission Directives 2003/124/EC, 2003/125/EC and 2004/72/EC [2014] OJ L 173/1 of 12.06.2014 (MAR); for an overview, see Sebastian Mock, 'History, Application, Interpretation, and Legal Sources of the Market Abuse Regulation' in Marco Ventoruzzo and Sebastian Mock (eds), *Market Abuse Regulation* (2nd edn, OUP 2022) 3–13.

18 For the four-tiered (or three-tiered, depending on how this is counted) approach to EU financial markets regulation, see, e.g., Konstantinos Sergakis, *The Law of Capital Markets in the EU: Disclosure and Enforcement* (Palgrave 2018) 6.

19 See Art. 2(3) MAR.

20 See Art. 2(4) MAR.

on a financial instrument listed on a regulated market in the EU.[21] That means that, in principle, retail investor activism anywhere in the world could be subject to the MAR framework. However, the MAR rules did not apply to the GameStop incident because the company was not listed on a regulated market in the EU. However, for further analysis, we will assume that this had been the case. This is not just a theoretical thought experiment. It is quite possible that in the future, EU-listed companies might be the subject of short-seller attacks and subsequently of retail investor 'intervention'.

Three general forms of market manipulation are regulated in Article 12 MAR.[22] The arguably most well-known one is information-based manipulation in Article 12(1)(c).[23] Here the person releases false or misleading signals regarding financial instruments. The motivation is to influence the price to place an order to gain profits from this manipulation.[24] In the more specific case known as 'scalping' under Article 12(2)(d), a person with a perceived expertise publicly recommends the acquisition or sale of a financial instrument which he or she had previously acquired without disclosing it.[25]

The second form is transaction-based manipulation in Article 12(1)(a). Here a person enters into a transaction or places/cancels an order to influence the market price of the financial instruments.[26] Transaction-based manipulations typically concern huge transactions (in relation to the respective market size)[27] or a series of smaller transactions that, in combination have a discernible effect on the market development. Article 12(2) sets out some further examples of transaction-based manipulation, namely 'cornering the market' (Article 12(2)(a)), 'marking the close' (Article 12(2)(b)), and algorithmic manipulation practices (Article 12(2)(c)).

The third alternative in Article 12(1)(b) could be referred to as activity-based manipulation. It is designed as a catch-all provision[28] that applies to other forms of conduct that might affect the price of a financial instrument, for example, behaviour outside the market itself (other than spreading rumours or other misleading information, which would be a case of Article 12(1)(c)).

21 So-called 'impact principle', see Philipp Maume, 'Market Abuse' in Philipp Maume, Lena Maute, and Mathias Fromberger, *The Law of Crypto-Assets* (Beck Hart Nomos 2022), 317.

22 Sergakis (n 18) 173, 178 et seqq.; Rüdiger Veil, 'Market Manipulation' in Rüdiger Veil (ed), *European Capital Markets Law* (3rd edn, Hart 2022) 227 et seqq.

23 Henceforth, all references to statutory law without indicating the respective statute are references to MAR.

24 Mock (n 16) 32.

25 Mock (n 16) 35; Veil (n 22) 243.

26 For a comprehensive overview of manipulative practices covered by Art. 12(1)(a), see Carsten Gerner-Beuerle, 'Art. 12 MAR' in Matthias Lehmann and Christoph Kumpan (eds), *European Financial Services Law* (Beck Hart Nomos 2019) 735–747.

27 Mock (n 16) 33.

28 Mock (n 16) 35.

At first glance, the GameStop case might touch on two different forms of market manipulation: first, recommendations given on social media might be considered information-based manipulation, particularly in the form of scalping; second, a large group of private investors teaming up could be transaction-based manipulation in the form of cornering. These two approaches will be discussed in more detail now.

B. GameStop and scalping/information-based manipulation

1. General assumptions

The analysis will consider two slightly diverging case scenarios. Two statements will be made in analogy to the GameStop scenario in our fictitious case: first, that short sellers have built up significant short positions, which will lead to significant losses if the price increases ('statement 1'); importantly, the issuer of this statement has acquired shares or respective put options before making the statement. Second, that it would be a good idea to team up with other private investors and acquire huge numbers of the respective shares to the detriment of the short sellers ('statement 2'). Both statements are made on an openly available online forum in English.

2. Information-based manipulation and scalping

2.1 Application to conduct in social media

As stated above, Article 12(1)(c) requires, *inter alia*, 'disseminating information through the media, including the internet, or by any other means'. In the more specific case of scalping under Article 12(2)(d) MAR, the prohibited conduct is based on 'the taking advantage of occasional or regular access to the traditional or electronic media by voicing an opinion'. Article 12 expressly mentions the internet and electronic media. There is no doubt that this includes social media, such as in our fictitious case setting.

For the application of Article 12(1)(c), the information must also have been disseminated. This means that it must have been available to the relevant audience. This is the case for at least the more popular publicly available online forum; apparently, the r/wallstreetbet subforum on Reddit had about eight million followers.[29] The more specific Article 12(2)(d) requires 'occasional or regular access to the traditional or electronic media'. This requirement is also met since the term 'media' is not limited to edited newspapers, news websites, or tv channels, but includes any form of mass communication on the internet.[30] In short, this means that postings on social media platforms might be subject to Article 12(1)(c) and Article 12(2)(d).[31]

---

29 The Economist, see 'The Real Revolution on Wall Street' (6 February 2021), available at <https://www.economist.com/leaders/2021/02/06/the-real-revolution-on-wall-street> accessed 26.03.2024.

30 See also the Oxford English Dictionary: 'Media: The main means of mass communication, esp. newspapers, radio, and television, and (from the later 20th century) content accessed via the internet...'.

31 Aurelio Gurrea-Martinez and others, 'Inside Information, Insider Dealing, Unlawful Disclosure of Inside Information and Market Manipulation' in Marco Ventoruzzo

2.2 Article 12(1)(c)

Article 12(1)(c) requires the disseminated information to be either false, likely to give a misleading signal to the market, or likely to create an abnormal price level. Neither statement 1 nor statement 2 is false. Statement 1 is an accurate description of the market situation, while statement 2 is a mere opinion – which cannot be true or false. Information is misleading if (even if it is accurate) it creates, considering the whole situation, an incorrect overall impression of the supply, demand, or price of the financial instrument. This is also not the case because the statements are straightforward and do not paint the market situation in an inaccurate manner. As a result, it is not a case of information-based manipulation under Article 12(1)(c).

2.3 Article 12(2)(d)

Scalping under Article 12(2)(d) does not require the information to be false or misleading. Instead, the policy reason for punishment is the combination of influencing the share price by making statements in combination with the prior acquisition of positions without disclosing them to the audience.[32] As the provision requires an 'opinion', statement 1 must contain some kind of subjective assessment, and the target audience must be able to derive some sort of endorsement or suggestion from the statement. This depends on the exact wording of the social media postings. Merely disclosing the existence of numerous short-selling provisions is probably insufficient. However, as soon as the consequences of respective fact (here: the short-sellers' losses if the price increases) are highlighted or explained, this would probably be an opinion under Article 12(2)(d). The crucial point is if readers of the social media postings in question would likely act in the way desired by the creator of the posting. It is the author's view that this is the case for both statement 1 and statement 2. However, statement 2 does not concern the demand for, supply of, or price of the share in question.[33] Instead, it is an activist call to take action in the markets. Thus, only statement 1 can be a case of scalping.

2.4 Problem 1: anonymity

It is not important for the application of Article 12(2)(d) that the manipulator has some kind of prominent position or high level of influence in the community. Anyone can commit scalping if the statement has the potential to move the share price. However, the miscreant must have been 'profiting subsequently from the impact of the opinions'. In other words, the statement must have resulted in a move in the share price. If there was no effect but the effect would have been likely, then this is a case of an

---

and Sebastian Mock (eds), *Market Abuse Regulation* (2nd edn, OUP 2022) 420.

32 Such conduct might also meet the requirements of Art. 20(1), which prohibits (inter alia) investment recommendations without disclosing conflicts of interest. If the conflict of interest is based on own positions in the respective financial instruments, both provisions overlap. If the issue is payments or other allowances from third parties, only Art. 20(1) applies.

33 This is not set out in the wording of Art. 12(2)(d). However, it follows from the logic of Art. 12(1)(c) as the underlying rule.

attempted market manipulation, which is also covered by Article 15 ('or attempt to engage in market manipulation').

The big question is if regular investors would pay attention to these statements on social media and would find them credible enough to consider acting themselves. Only then is a result on the share price possible and Article 12(2)(d) would apply. Although scalping does not require a particular position of reputation in the market, the provision rests on the idea of a market analyst giving detailed analysis on TV or on some blog. The audience knows the analyst or blogger, his or her reputation is key to the impact of the statement. This is not the case in an anonymous environment such as Reddit. Users' real-life names, positions, and other backgrounds are unclear. It is possible that a statement has been made by an experienced professional with a high level of insight – but the opposite is also a possibility. A user would simply not know for certain.[34] It is a reasonable assumption that reasonable investors would rely on anonymous sources to a lower extent.[35] However, as will be discussed later, on (anonymous) social media platforms, the whole notion of the 'reasonable investor' is in question anyway.[36]

This potentially creates a new information asymmetry: not between an investor and the issuer and other insiders, but between investors and the information itself. The link between social media and the capital markets is highly relevant – a study from the US suggested that one-third of young investors rely on social media for investment advice[37] (although it is not clear to what extent these sources are anonymous). Anonymity leads to a lack of accountability,[38] not only by law but also by social standards (e.g., no threat of reputational losses caused by repeated inaccurate statements). This is a direct result of the anonymous nature of social media and Web 2.0.

2.5 Problem 2: is a 'Reddit' user a 'reasonable investor'?

This anonymity issue is part of a wider conceptual problem. The user base and the conversation culture of an online forum are quite different from what we are used to

---

34 Of course, readers can to a certain extent assess the quality and reliability of anonymous social media postings, but uncertainties remain.

35 This aligns with empirical research on the matter, see Travis Dyer and Eunjee Kim, 'Anonymous Equity Research' (2021) 59(2) Journal of Accounting Research 575, 578.

36 See below B.2.5).

37 Emily Graffeo, 'A third of young traders go to social media for investment advice - and 12% say they invest because it "feels like a game", survey finds' (*Business Insider India*, 23 August 2021). Available at <https://www.businessinsider.in/investment/news/a-third-of-young-traders-go-to-social-media-for-investment-advice-and-12-say-they-invest-because-it-feels-like-a-game-survey-finds/articleshow/85565866.cms> accessed 26.03.2024.

38 Elsa Massoc and Maximilian Lubda, 'Social Media, Polarization and Democracy: A Multi-Methods Analysis of Polarized Users' Interactions on Reddit's r/WallStreetBets' (2022) SAFE Working Paper No. 337, available at <https://papers.ssrn.com/sol3/papers.cfm?abstract_id=4006283> accessed 26.03.2024.

in the financial markets. The level of accuracy of anonymous information on social media is often dubious at best. To put it bluntly, the level of nonsense on these platforms is often breathtaking – but not always. It is difficult to filter information for accuracy. The tone is also different; users tend to behave in anonymous online environments differently from real-life settings. The tone can be rougher. We also need to keep in mind that many non-lawyers tend to think that social media is 'unregulated' and that statements made on these platforms have nothing or little to do with real life. For a lawyer, this assumption might sound absurd, but it is an important friction between the 'old' world of capital market conduct and social media.

These differences result in a conceptual problem. Legally speaking, the pivotal issue in capital markets regulation is the role and the nature of the 'reasonable investor'.[39] His (or her) potential understanding of the capital markets is the foundation for the assessment of statements and behaviour under capital market regulation.[40] The reasonable investor is not an invention of EU law but has its origins in US securities regulation, and it has become the basis of regulation in various countries, including Canada, Australia, and New Zealand.[41] It is a theoretical construct that allows (or better: is supposed to allow) a generalised assessment of certain behaviour without conducting thorough empirical research. In other words, instead of asking 1,000 potential investors 'how do you understand the following statement?', the concept of the reasonable investor raises the question 'how would a reasonable investor understand the statement in question?' This might appear speculative and can be criticised as an improper one-size-fits-all approach. However, it allows the even application of capital market rules and promotes predictability.

Generally speaking, a reasonable investor acts rationally and is driven by the will to make profits. He or she will consider all publicly available information and make it the basis of the investment decision.[42] A reasonable investor is neither an insider nor a market professional but has a better understanding of market mechanisms and the economic context than the average citizen. For example, we can assume that a reasonable investor is able to read and understand a balance sheet. Based on these

---

39 For the concept of 'reasonable investor', see Niamh Moloney, *EU Securities and Financial Markets Regulation* (3rd edn, OUP 2014) 722; John Coffey and Jonathan Overett-Somnier, 'The Market Abuse Directive – the First Use of the Lamfalussy Process' (2003) Journal of International Banking Law and Regulation 370.

40 See, e.g., MAR Rec. 14; Committee of European Securities Regulators, 'Market Abuse Directive: Level 3 – second set of CESR guidance and information on the common operation of the Directive to the market' (CESR/06-562b, July 2007), available at <https://www.esma.europa.eu/sites/default/files/library/2015/11/06_562b.pdf> accessed 26.03.2024.

41 For an overview, see Lars Klöhn, 'Artikel 7: Insiderinformationen' in Lars Klöhn and others (eds), *Marktmissbrauchsverordnung* (2nd edn, Beck 2023), Art. 7 para 265/266.

42 This is based on the efficient capital markets hypothesis (ECMH) as stipulated by Eugene F Fama, 'Efficient Capital Markets: A Review of Theory and Empirical Work' (1970) 25(2) Journal of Finance 383 – in its semi-strong form.

assumptions, courts and regulators can assess the effect of certain market behaviour (for example, statements in prospectuses). The question is: how would the reasonable investor understand the statement in question? The result is not perfect but allows a somewhat consistent application of capital markets laws.

However, it is very questionable if the same assumptions can be made for users on social media.[43] Their interests, experiences, and drivers can vary greatly. This can be aptly demonstrated in our case: rational, profit-driven investors would probably be triggered by statement 1 but dismiss statement 2. Conversely, an activist with a non-financial agenda would probably act based on statement 2 but not based on statement 1. This could also be observed in the GameStop scenario, where the 'defence' of the company against an 'attack' by capitalists was a major theme – and some of these activist investors suffered substantial losses. An aforementioned study suggests that one in eight investors say that young investors invest because it feels 'like a game'.[44] In the US literature, the GameStop incident has sparked a debate about the emergence of the 'retail investor' as a new concept for capital markets regulation,[45] and its limitations.[46] However, retail investors should not be confused with users on social media because the majority of retail investors are also informed and driven by the view for profit.[47]

There is no easy way to address this problem. We simply do not know how and to what extent anonymous online settings are different from the classical capital market settings. Without this knowledge, it is extremely difficult to apply regulation consistently. The required insights have to be derived not from the realm of law, but from disciplines such as behavioural psychology or sociology.[48] Maybe theoretical models and empirical research can at least give some clues. For example, Reddit can hardly be compared to Twitter and its successors because of the maximum length of postings. Video-based platforms (e.g., TikTok) and graphic-based platforms (e.g., Instagram) are different from LinkedIn, which is more text-based and mostly attracts business professionals. Obviously, the issue is complex.

Bringing the law into the fray, we also need to consider that discussions on social media are subject to the freedom of speech and expression, which at the EU level set out in Article 11 of the Charter of Fundamental Rights of the European Union (CFR).

---

43 Jill E Fisch, 'GameStop and the Reemergence of the Retail Investor' (2022) 102 Boston University Law Review 1799, 1852–1853.

44 Graffeo (n 37).

45 Jennifer J Schulp, 'GameStop and the Rise of Retail Trading' (2021) 41(3) Cato Journal 511 (focussing on retail investor protection and potential limitations to trading access).

46 Fisch (n 43), passim.

47 Fisch (n 43), 1853.

48 For issues of behavioural science in the context of capital markets and banking regulation, see Aline Darbellay, 'The Promise and Perils of Behaviourally Informed Bank Disclosure Regulation' in Joseph Lee and Aline Darbellay (eds), *A Research Agenda for Financial Law and Regulation* (Edward Elgar 2024).

This means that a statement that turns out to be misleading (and influences the stock market) cannot automatically result in punishment. It would be absurd if the free exchange of ideas and opinions on the internet was curtailed by capital markets regulation. On the other hand, manipulating the capital markets (maybe even for one's own profit) cannot be hidden behind the mantle of freedom of speech.

C. The swarm: cornering the market

1. *Abusive squeeze*

To this point, the analysis covered a typical form of market manipulation (scalping) in a new environment (social media). But the even less researched aspect of the GameStop case is what has been aptly referred to as 'swarm trading'.[49] This term describes aligned market behaviour of a vast number of investors, typically small or retail investors. The underlying idea is that these investors form a huge, blurred, and (from the outside) unpredictable mass that moves the stock market in a certain direction. This could be seen either as a desirable democratic expression of the people's will or as activists ganging up to manipulate the financial markets.

One key element of these swarms, at least in this context, is that they are not controlled by the initiator or another entity. It is the dynamics between users sharing information and views that trigger the swarm behaviour. While it can be caused originally by single users (in the GameStop case: 'Roaring Kitty', in our example: statement 2), the effects are usually caused by the pervasiveness of social media and some kind of herd-instinct.[50] These dynamics are currently left unconsidered by the existing EU financial markets regulation regime.

In the German literature, some commentators considered if the GameStop situation could be a case of Art. 12(2)(a).[51] This provision bans 'the conduct by a person, or persons acting in collaboration, to secure a dominant position over the supply of or demand for a financial instrument … which has, or is likely to have, the effect of fixing, directly or indirectly, purchase or sale prices or creates, or is likely to create, other unfair trading conditions'. This bulky definition refers to market practices that are known as 'cornering' or 'abusive squeeze'. In short, a market participant would enter into transactions that create a market environment that limits the trading options of

---

49 The term was originally coined by the Economist (n 29).

50 Interestingly, political polarisation did not play a role in the GameStop incident; see Massoc and Lubda (n 38), 10 et seqq.

51 For example, Kilian Wegner, 'Das „GameStop"-Phänomen nach deutschem Marktmissbrauchsrecht: Marktmanipulation oder legitimes Anlegerverhalten?' [2021] Zeitschrift für Bank- und Kapitalmarktrecht 181; Jannik Piepenburg and Moritz Schwarz, 'Shortseller-Attacken und das „Phänomen GameStop" im Kontext des Kapitalmarktstrafrechts' [2021] Zeitschrift für Bank- und Kapitalmarktrecht 2760; Maximilian Merwald and Pirmin Schauer, 'Marktmanipulation, Social Media und Noise Trader im Fall GameStop' [2021] Zeitschrift für Bank- und Kapitalmarktrecht 280.

other market participants (literally 'cornering' them), resulting in adversely affected transaction conditions. At first glance, this appears to be like the GameStop case: large quantities of purchases limited the supply of shares and increased the price. Depending on the underlying derivative contracts, short sellers would either incur losses if they must buy shares to meet their contractual obligations, or if they are netted against other positions. Thus, they have been cornered because they have no choice but to act subject to the altered market conditions, as was planned by the 'activists'.

However, Article 12(2)(a) is at its heart a provision from competition law.[52] This means that the term 'dominant position' has the same meaning as the identical phrasing in Article 102 of the Treaty on the Functioning of the European Union (TFEU). As a starting point, it is not clear what a dominant position in the context of capital markets might be. The first step would be to define the relevant product market. Already this is unclear: do investors assume that from their perspective shares can be replaced by bonds? Or derivatives or funds? Or is the product market the respective share only? And how is the geographical market defined – would investors limit their decision to shares (or other instruments?) on the NYSE, or would they take into consideration other trading platforms? To the knowledge of the author, this issue is under-researched (but will not be discussed in more detail at this point of the analysis).[53]

More importantly, a single investor does not have a dominant market position, and the 'swarm' does not have legal personality. Only if the other investors' actions and their respective effects could be attributed to a single investor, could this investor potentially be in breach of Article 12(2)(a). However, it is unclear what the dogmatic basis would be. The investors making up the 'swarm' do not know each other by name, they do not have any binding agreements, and there is no control exercised by single members. This would most likely not meet the requirements of a 'collaboration' as required in Article 12(2)(a) either.

2. *Market manipulation regulation vs. investor activism?*

As a result, unless a single entity (or a small number of entities) factually controls the swarm, the conduct in question (here: statement 2) would not be prohibited under EU financial markets regulation. This leads to several questions for further discussion and research.

The first issue is if this result is adequate through the lens of financial markets regulation. Unless someone has their own stake in the share in question, it seems legal to influence other users on social media – financial markets activism is allowed, even to the detriment of other investors. For many users on social media, this result might be

52 Veil (n 22) 242.

53 See, e.g., the discussion of a joint (or: separate) market for exchange-traded derivatives (ETD) and over-the-counter derivatives (OTC Derivatives) in General Court Case T-175/12 *Deutsche Börse AG v European Commission* [2015] ECLI:EU:T:2015:148 – leaving open many questions.

acceptable, in particular in light of certain political views. But it is at odds with the role and the importance of capital markets in a modern economy. The capital markets are not just a playing field for greedy funds (although there is little doubt that they also play a role). They are essential for issuers to raise funds for investments, for private investors to generate savings for retirement, for states to finance public spending, for public funds to stabilise the pension system, etc. It could have dire consequences if there were no mechanism to safeguard these markets from any type of activism.

The need for regulatory reform is not a legal, but a political issue. Much will depend on whether the GameStop incident remains a rather singular event or not. If we assume that a need for regulatory reform exists, the ensuing issue is – what would the responding regulatory concept look like? It would not only have to deviate from the idea of rational economic behaviour, but it would also need to draw a line between instigators and followers because not every person joining in such activism can be subjected to criminal liability – this would be regulatory overkill. Instead, neighbouring disciplines such as psychology and sociology will need to analyse how swarms can form, how they can be influenced, and how they can be prevented if the result is at odds with the aims of financial markets regulation. This is a huge task.

3. *A similar problem: bank runs and social media*

A similar problem has been observed in the neighbouring area of banking law.[54] In the downfall of Silicon Valley Bank (SVB) in 2023, social media played a crucial role,[55] not only contributing to the bank's problems[56] by fuelling rumours and finally resulting in a bank run.[57] In the case of SVB, social media amplified the severity of the episode for other banks. The simple reason is that social media increases communication during the run, amplifying it.[58] The effect is similar to the GameStop scenario, but the driver is different. Regarding SVB, the fear of losing money also played a role, which is usually a more irrational foundation than the intention to achieve a common goal. Thus, the behavioural background is not comparable. However, the coinciding question is how these events can be predicted or observed.

---

54 See from the German literature, Felix-Julius Konow and Jan Sehorz, 'Soziale Medien als Risikofaktor für Bank-Runs' [2024] Zeitschrift für Bank- und Kapitalmarktrecht 234.

55 For analysis, see J Anthony Cookson et al., 'Social Media as a Bank Run Catalyst' (2023) Université Paris-Dauphine Research Paper No. 4422754, available at <https://papers.ssrn.com/sol3/papers.cfm?abstract_id=4422754> accessed 26.03.2024; Bank for International Settlements, 'Report on the 2023 banking turmoil' (Basel Committee on Banking Supervision, October 2023), available at <https://www.bis.org/bcbs/publ/d555.pdf> accessed 26.03.2024.

56 Bank for International Settlements (n 55) 20.

57 A bank run describes a vast number of customers withdrawing their funds from a bank. This typically exceeds the bank's reserves, possibly resulting in insolvency.

58 Cookson et al. (n 55) 1 et seqq.

IV. The next frontier: supervision and enforcement

A. The theory

The GameStop incident also raises questions about supervision and enforcement. Their importance for the development of financial markets has been subject to a vivid debate in the 1990s and 2000s. In short, after a longer period of deregulation and political emphasis on market self-regulation in the 1980s and early 1990s, academics and regulators turned their attention to the role of enforcement. In short, there is a consensus these days that effective capital markets regulation requires effective enforcement of the rules. This is ideally achieved by a mix of private and public enforcement mechanisms.[59]

A second debate focussed on the ideal structure of a system of regulatory agencies for financial markets issues. In short, three models can be identified.[60] First, an array of smaller, but highly specialised agencies that oversee different issues of financial markets regulation. The US, with its 15–20 agencies (depending on the method of counting), is a good example of this approach. Second, all supervisory functions can be bundled in one universal regulator ('one size fits all'). An example would be Germany, where (like in many countries in Europe) the regulator is responsible for capital markets, banking, insurance, and financial advisers,[61] but also issues of anti-money laundering, oversight of accounting and auditing, and even to a certain extent consumer protection. Third, some countries have separated the regulatory functions into two regulatory agencies, one responsible for banking/insurance and one for capital markets conduct (Twin Peaks). This is, to different extents, applied in the UK, Australia, and in New Zealand.[62]

---

59 For an overview, see, e.g., Howell E Jackson and Mark J Roe, 'Public and Private Enforcement of Securities Laws: Resource-Based Evidence' (2009) 93(2) Journal of Financial Economics 207, 208; John C Coffee Jr, 'Law and the Market: The Impact of Enforcement' (2007) 156(2) University of Pennsylvania Law Review 229, 297; Philipp Maume and Gordon Walker, 'Enforcing Financial Markets Law in New Zealand' (2013) 2013(2) New Zealand Law Review, 263, 264; Rafael La Porta, Florencio Lopez-de-Silanes and Andrei Shleifer, 'What Works in Securities Laws?' (2006) 61(1) Journal of Finance 1.

60 See Charles A E Goodhart, 'The Organizational Structure of Banking Supervision' (2003) 31(1) Economic Notes 1, 8 et seqq.; Eddy Wymeersch, 'The Structure of Financial Supervision in Europe: About Single, Twin Peaks and Multiple Financial Supervisors' (2007) 8(2) European Business Organization Law Review 237, 252 et seqq.; Martin Cihak and Richard Podpiera, 'Integrated Financial Supervision: Which Model?' (2008) 19(2) North American Journal of Economics and Finance 135, 137 et seqq.

61 In Europe, a general move towards unified supervision could be observed in the late 1990s and early 2000s; see European Central Bank, 'Developments in National Supervisory Structures' (*ECB*, June 2003), available at <https://www.ecb.europa.eu/pub/pdf/other/supervisorystructureen.pdf> accessed 26.03.2024.

62 For a comprehensive overview, see Andrew Godwin and Andrew Schmulow (eds), *The Cambridge Handbook of Twin Peaks Regulation* (Cambridge 2021), passim.

B. The situation under EU financial regulation

However, despite all debates, harmonisation and (alleged) best practice, supervision and enforcement remain matters of national law. Again, the legal situation in the EU is an apt example. After the Global Financial Crisis of 2007/2008, EU financial markets regulation has undergone a massive transformation. Several new legislative acts closed perceived gaps in the regulatory quilt, such as legislative acts regarding derivatives trading and clearing, rating agencies, or short selling.[63]

But despite this undeniable thrust towards tighter regulation and a higher level of harmonisation, supervision and enforcement remained a matter of national laws. Through the lens of path dependency, this is a logical development. The 'first generation' of EU financial markets regulation relied on Directives that required transposition into member state (=national) law. In this setting, it is logical that supervision and enforcement are carried out by national agencies because the subject is national law. It is unclear why this was not changed when the respective Directives were replaced by Regulations. Obviously, the forces of inertia must be taken into account: such a massive restructuring project would be immensely complex and costly. It would, at least in the short run, lead to frictions and new issues in oversight practice. It is also without question that a national regulator with close ties to the markets also has its merits (although this could probably be achieved under an EU umbrella). And although it is very difficult to find this in writing, there is also politics at play. A national regulator ensures that the respective member state retains some level of influence and control. Several EU insiders have confirmed to the author that this is one of the main drivers of the regulatory structure between EU and member states remaining mostly untouched.

Thus, the current regime typically works as follows: In the primary legislative act (usually a Regulation, in some cases a Directive)[64] the law states what tasks and competences need to be assigned to the regulators under national laws.[65] On the secondary level, these legislative acts leave some questions open and give the European Commission the right to enact legislation that contains more prescriptive rules such as regulatory standards. These are usually drafted by European Agencies such as the European Securities and Markets Authority (ESMA) and become, upon adoption by the Commission, binding for the member state regulators. On the tertiary level, the EU agencies such as ESMA publish vast guidance and Q&A on various issues. These are not binding unless adopted by a national regulator.[66] In this system, the EU agencies typically play a role that is confined to issues of harmonisation and best practice while front-line regulation is carried out by national regulators.

---

63 Overview at Rüdiger Veil, 'History' in Rüdiger Veil (ed), *European Capital Markets Law* (2nd edn, Palgrave 2017), 15–20.

64 For the tiered system of EU capital markets regulation, see Sergakis (n 18).

65 In the case of the MAR: Art. 22.

66 These documents are still not 'binding' in the legal sense. But adoption by a national regulator creates a self-commitment that is de facto binding.

C. The problem

The resulting problem is obvious. EU financial markets regulation is becoming increasingly complex and difficult to handle. The focus on national supervision and enforcement (complemented by increased cooperation) leads to duplication of structures. In theory, every member state will need to take care of the authorisation of financial advisers, payment services, of banks, and so on. Each agency will have to watch out for market misconduct, will have to review prospectuses. Each country will have its own approach on how to interact with market participants, etc. The big problem is that smaller countries will find it extremely challenging to fund national regulators sufficiently to make them capable of carrying out all these tasks. This has already been discussed in the 2000s as the 'small country rationale',[67] being one of the main reasons why smaller countries favour unified regulators. Despite 15 years of constant regulatory reform, the EU and its member states have not addressed this issue. Even modern codifications such as the Regulation on Markets in Crypto-Assets (MiCAR) (the new, comprehensive regulation for DLT-based assets)[68] stick to the old system: An active role for ESMA and the European Banking Authority (EBA) is only foreseen for the supervision of certain stablecoins,[69] probably because they by their very nature affect the EU in its entirety.

The problem is that most countries will not have the resources to establish an adequate monitoring system for social media. For example, the German Federal Financial Supervisory Authority (BaFin) (a universal regulator) has about 2,700 employees,[70] and the French Financial Markets Authority (AMF) (responsible for capital markets only) has about 500.[71] Smaller countries like Austria have significantly smaller financial markets regulators (Austrian Finanzmarktaufsicht (FMA): about 450 employees; universal regulator).[72] Even the big EU countries will find it very difficult to muster sufficient resources for effective social media supervision; for small countries such as the Baltic States, this would be quite impossible. A solution on the EU level seems logical. The less obvious but arguably even more important question is whether financial

67 Michael Taylor and Alex Fleming, 'Integrated Financial Supervision: Lessons from The Northern European Experience' (1999) World Bank Policy Research Paper No 2223, 10, available at <https://elibrary.worldbank.org/doi/abs/10.1596/1813-9450-2223> accessed 26.03.2024.

68 Council, Regulation (EU) 2023/1114 of the European Parliament and of the Council of 31 May 2023 on markets in crypto-assets and amending Regulations (EU) No 1093/2010 and (EU) No 1095/2010 and Directives 2013/36/EU and (EU) 2019/1937 [2023] OJ L 150/40 of 09.06.2023 (MiCAR).

69 See MiCAR Title III (asset-referenced tokens) and Title IV (e-money tokens).

70 BaFin, 'Working at BaFin' (19 April 2023), available at <https://www.bafin.de/DE/DieBaFin/ArbeitenBaFin/arbeitenbafin_node.html> accessed 26.03.2024.

71 AMF, 'Our People' (11 December 2020), available at <https://www.amf-france.org/en/amf/our-people> accessed 26.03.2024.

72 Familie & Beruf, 'Österreichische Finanzmarktaufsicht' (undated), available at <https://www.familieundberuf.at/unternehmen/oesterreichische-finanzmarktaufsicht> accessed 26.03.2024.

markets regulators are even the appropriate regulatory body to monitor social media. They are probably not.[73]

V. Summary

There is no doubt that EU financial markets abuse law can – in principle – be applied to social media conduct. However, a closer look reveals several conceptual problems. First, the possible anonymity on social media makes it very difficult for users to assess the quality and reliability of a statement regarding financial instruments. Second, conversely, it is difficult to predict how users in general will react to that very statement. Third, social media users fit the theoretical concept of a 'reasonable investor' only to a certain extent because quite a few of them are not 'informed' or do not pursue profits as the guiding theme of their actions. Fourth, the phenomenon of 'swarm' falls through the cracks of current regulation because the latter rests on the idea of one person or a small group of persons jointly acting. Fifth, if lawmakers wanted to close this gap, significant research on the dynamics in social media must be conducted. Sixth, it is unclear how the persisting idea of national enforcement of financial markets laws can be brought in line with the international or global nature of social media. Seventh, policymakers need to consider if financial regulators are the best-placed entity to supervise conduct on social media. There is a lot of work to be done.

[73] Differently, Fisch (n 43) 1854, suggests that (in case of the US) the SEC should 'consider engaging directly with social media to monitor ongoing developments'.

8

Market abuse in the crypto-assets market: same risks, same activities, and same regulatory outcomes?

Joseph Lee and Lukas Schu

I. Introduction

Since their inception in 2008, cryptocurrencies have not only proliferated but also evolved into a market valued in the trillions. Amidst their volatility, developers have introduced "stablecoins", which are pegged to fiat currencies, assets, cryptocurrencies, or algorithms to maintain stable prices. This innovation has led to a burgeoning stablecoin market, with some offerings gaining national and others achieving global reach. However, the collapse of entities such as Terra and Celsius has shown the potential financial stability risks posed by such digital assets, highlighting the growing and concerning interconnectivity between the crypto and traditional financial sectors.

In response to the risks posed by the crypto-asset markets, international forums have advocated for swift and substantial regulatory responses, guided by the principle of "same risks, same activity, same regulation". The Financial Stability Board (FSB) has called for robust regulation and supervision at both national and international levels to mitigate the financial stability risks of crypto-assets. The Bank for International Settlements (BIS) has set prudential requirements for banks holding crypto-assets, while the Financial Action Task Force (FATF) urges national implementation of Anti-Money Laundering/Combating the Financing of Terrorism (AML/CFT) standards for virtual assets and service providers. Echoing these global calls, the EU Markets in Crypto-Assets Regulation (MiCA) aims to position itself as a leader in crypto-asset regulation, introducing regulations for asset-referenced tokens, utility tokens, and e-money tokens, and recognising digital currencies as potential competitors to traditional money.

The crypto-assets markets, much like their traditional counterparts, are not immune to manipulative practices that exploit regular investors. This chapter will explore various market abuse techniques within the crypto-assets markets, drawing parallels and distinctions with the traditional securities market to aid policymakers in mapping the risks and regulatory responses. We will assess how MiCA addresses these issues, identify regulatory gaps, and consider whether existing legislation can bridge these gaps.

Where current laws fall short, we propose targeted regulatory measures to enhance market integrity and protect investors.

II. Market abuse behaviours

A. Pump-and-dump

Pump-and-dump schemes, historically prevalent in financial markets, exploit regulatory gaps to manipulate asset prices for profit. These schemes have been effectively curtailed within regulated markets through stringent prohibitions, safeguarding investor interests.[1] However, the crypto-asset markets, characterised by a relative regulatory vacuum, have witnessed a proliferation of such schemes, showing the urgent need for regulatory oversight.[2]

These schemes operate on a two-phase mechanism: initially, manipulators acquire significant holdings of a chosen asset, followed by the dissemination of misleading information to artificially inflate the asset's price.[3] Once the price peaks, these holdings are liquidated at inflated prices, leading to substantial profits for the manipulators at the expense of uninformed investors, who are left with devalued assets following the inevitable market correction. Traditionally targeting low-market-cap securities such as penny stocks, pump-and-dump schemes leverage the limited regulatory scrutiny and information transparency of such assets to manipulate market prices.[4] In contrast, the crypto market's inherent liquidity and bullish tendencies have made it a fertile ground for similar manipulative practices, with thinly traded, relatively illiquid crypto-assets being particularly vulnerable.[5]

Research by Dhawan and Putniņš demonstrates that smaller, less liquid coins are more frequently targeted by these schemes, suggesting a strategic preference that minimises the risk for manipulators while maximising potential profits.[6] This insight highlights the need for enhanced regulatory frameworks that can adapt to the evolving tactics of market manipulators in the crypto-assets space, ensuring protection for all market participants.

---

1 Anirudh Dhawan and Tālis J Putniņš, 'A New Wolf in Town? Pump-and-Dump Manipulation in Cryptocurrency Markets' (2023) 27 Review of Finance 935.

2 Onkar Singh, 'What are Crypto Pump-and-Dump Groups? Are They Legal?' (*Cointelegraph*, 3 August 2022) <https://cointelegraph.com/news/what-are-crypto-pump-and-dump-groups-are-they-legal> accessed 03 June 2023.

3 SEC, 'Pump and Dump Schemes' (Investor.gov - *US Securities and Exchange Commission*) <https://www.investor.gov/introduction-investing/investing-basics/glossary/pump-and-dump-schemes> accessed 03 June 2023.

4 ING, 'Pump and Dump – Vorsicht vor Betrug' (*ING Wissen Geldanlage*, 14 June 2022) <https://www.ing.de/wissen/pump-and-dump/> accessed 03 June 2023.

5 Josh Kamps and Benett Kleinberg, 'To the Moon: Defining and Detecting Cryptocurrency Pump-and-Dumps' (2018) 7(18) Crime Science 1–18.

6 Dhawan and Putniņš (n 1).

The transition of pump-and-dump schemes from traditional to crypto markets reflects the adaptability of these manipulative practices and shows the need for regulating digital asset markets. It necessitates a regulatory approach based on the understanding of the unique characteristics of crypto-assets while drawing on the regulatory experiences of traditional financial markets to mitigate the risks posed to investors and the broader financial system.

In contrast to traditional markets where pump-and-dump schemes might span months, their counterparts in the crypto markets are notably brief, often concluding within minutes. This rapid pace again highlights the necessity of advanced knowledge and swift action for profitable involvement in such schemes.[7] Organised primarily through online forums and chatrooms, including Discord and Telegram, these schemes can attract tens of thousands of participants, some of whom are openly informed about the scheme's intent. The organisers of these schemes publicly announce their plans to inflate the price of a specific crypto-asset, inviting members to participate. This creates an environment where the typical informational asymmetry seen in traditional pump-and-dump schemes is bypassed, as participants willingly engage in the manipulation.

However, this dynamic leaves uninformed investors vulnerable to sudden price spikes, often unable to discern the manipulative forces at play. Those who buy in at peak prices, only to see values plummet post-dump, experience immediate financial losses. Moreover, the occurrence of pump-and-dump schemes can lead to significant price volatility within the targeted crypto-assets.[8] While the long-term impact on these assets may be minimal, with prices eventually stabilising, the repeated occurrence of such schemes erodes overall market integrity and investor confidence. The frequent execution of pump-and-dump schemes across various platforms contributes to a perception of instability within the crypto-assets markets, potentially deterring investment and hindering market development. The overall effect is a challenge to the credibility and growth of the crypto-assets markets.

B. Insider trading

Insider trading, the use of non-public information for personal gain, is a malpractice found in both traditional and crypto financial markets. Despite the fundamental similarities in the concept of insider trading across these markets, there are notable distinctions in their dynamics and implications.

In traditional markets, insider trading typically involves company employees, regulators, or legislators leveraging confidential information to influence stock performance. However, in the crypto space, a broader range of individuals, including

7 Kamps and Kleinberg (n 5).

8 Tao Li, Donghwa Shin, and Baolian Wang, 'Cryptocurrency Pump-and-Dump Schemes' ([2021]) <https://papers.ssrn.com/sol3/papers.cfm?abstract_id=3267041> accessed 03 June 2023.

exchange operators, may engage in insider trading.[9] A prominent instance is the case at Coinbase, where a former product manager exploited confidential data about forthcoming listings to inform trades that profited acquaintances and himself.[10] This incident shows the unique vulnerabilities within crypto exchanges to insider malpractices.

Moreover, the prevalence of insider trading is significantly higher in crypto-assets markets compared to their traditional counterparts. Research by Félez-Viñas, Johnson, and Putniņš indicates that insider trading could affect 10–25 per cent of cryptocurrency listings, with decentralised exchanges (DEXs) being particularly susceptible.[11] The anonymity facilitated by lower know-your-customer (KYC) standards on the DEXs provides a conducive environment for such illicit activities. The implications of widespread insider trading in crypto-assets markets extend beyond individual investor losses. It erodes public trust in the fairness and integrity of the market, impairing its ability to attract new investments and hindering overall market development.[12] When insiders exploit privileged information, it results in other investors overpaying for assets or receiving less than fair value during sales, directly harming their financial interests and undermining confidence in the market's equity.

Beyond the Coinbase incident, another case involved executives at a well-known crypto trading platform who were found to be using undisclosed information about token listings to execute profitable trades ahead of public announcements.

C. Stop-loss hunting

Similar to other market manipulation strategies previously discussed, stop-loss hunting is not a phenomenon unique to the crypto-assets markets. It has long been a prevalent manipulation technique in traditional markets, especially within the foreign exchange (Forex) sector before its adaptation to the dynamics of the crypto-assets markets.[13] Stop-loss hunting involves market participants with significant

---

9 Prashant Jha, 'Crypto Exchanges Tackle Insider Trading after Recent Convictions' (*Cointelegraph*, 07 February 2023) <https://cointelegraph.com/news/crypto-exchanges-tackle-insider-trading-after-recent-convictions> accessed 3 June 2023.

10 The United States Attorney's Office Southern District of New York, 'Former Coinbase Insider Pleads Guilty in First-Ever Cryptocurrency Insider Trading Case' (*United States Department of Justice Press Release*, 7 February 2023) <https://www.justice.gov/usao-sdny/pr/former-coinbase-insider-pleads-guilty-first-ever-cryptocurrency-insider-trading-case> accessed 03 June 2023.

11 Ester Félez-Viñas, Luke Johnson and Tālis J Putniņš, 'Insider Trading in Cryptocurrency Markets' (8 August 2022) <https://papers.ssrn.com/sol3/papers.cfm?abstract_id=4184367> accessed 03 June 2023.

12 Knowledge at Wharton Staff, 'Why Insider Trading is Hard to Define, Prove and Prevent' (*Wharton School of the University of Pennsylvania*, 11 November 2009) <https://knowledge.wharton.upenn.edu/article/why-insider-trading-is-hard-to-define-prove-and-prevent/> accessed 03 June 2023.

13 Nick Goold, 'Why Professional Forex Traders Hunt for Stop Orders' (*Titanfx*, 24 February 2023) <https://titanfx.com/news/why-professional-forex-traders-hunt-for

holdings—often referred to as "whales", which can include brokers, hedge funds, or banks—utilising their substantial market influence to manipulate asset prices through large volume trades.[14] The goal is to drive the price to a level where it triggers a wave of stop-loss orders, enabling these manipulators to buy back the asset at a lower price, thereby increasing their holdings at the expense of smaller investors forced out of their positions.

This technique leverages the analysis of order flow or market depth data to determine the price ranges where a significant number of stop-loss orders are likely placed. By triggering these orders, the asset's price is further driven down, increasing liquidity at the lower price point, which the manipulators then absorb.

In the crypto-assets markets, the impact of stop-loss hunting can be magnified due to the typically lower liquidity of many coins.[15] This reduced liquidity means that even smaller entities or individuals with substantial holdings can significantly influence market prices. Consequently, the crypto-assets markets present a broader field for potential "whales" to engage in stop-loss hunting, complicating oversight and regulation efforts.

The adaptation of stop-loss hunting to crypto-asset markets shows the need for vigilant market monitoring and regulatory frameworks capable of addressing these manipulative practices. The inherent volatility and liquidity profiles of crypto-assets amplify the challenges of safeguarding investor interests against such tactics, highlighting the importance of both market education and enhanced regulatory measures to combat manipulation.

Stop-loss hunting can have severe negative impacts on investors as well as market stability. For individual traders who were not prepared for the artificial price movement and lost their positions because the stop-loss orders were triggered, this technique can cause significant losses.[16] They were forced to sell their assets at an artificially low price just before the market prices usually recover to their initial level and may even keep increasing in the way the investor anticipated.[17]

Another risk, potentially even a systemic risk, may lie in the combination of unpredicted price movements and the use of algorithms. The intention of stop-loss hunting

-stop-orders#:~:text=Stop%20hunting%20is%20a%20forex,move%20quickly%20in%20one%20direction> accessed 03 June 2023.

14 Agustinus Noertjahyana et al., 'Stop Hunt Detection Using Indicators and Expert Advisors in the Forex Market' (2020) 1502 Journal of Physics Conference Series 1.

15 Caleb & Brown, 'What is Crypto Liquidity?' (*Caleb & Brown*, 02 March 2024) <https://calebandbrown.com/blog/crypto-liquidity/> accessed 27 April 2024.

16 Goold (n 13).

17 Nic Puckrin, 'Stop-Loss Hunting: How Crypto Whales are Making a Killing' (*Coinbureau*, 30 March 2023) <https://www.coinbureau.com/analysis/stop-loss-hunting-crypto-whales/> accessed 03 June 2023.

to trigger stop-loss orders to create more liquidity may also trigger algorithms to interact in an unintended way and create flash crashes. In crypto-assets markets, it is comparatively easy for ordinary investors to use algorithmic trading techniques. There are many services online that provide software for crypto traders to start algorithmic trading on crypto exchanges.[18] Hence, one can expect that there are quite a few algorithms in place on crypto exchanges. Sudden artificial price declines that trigger stop-loss orders may also trigger sell orders of these algorithms. The algorithms may interact with each other and lead to a mass sell-off. Such flash crashes are not unknown to crypto markets. In 2017, the cryptocurrency Ether experienced a severe flash crash with a price drop from 319 US dollars to about 10 cents caused by one big sell that triggered multiple algorithms to sell too.[19] This fact, in combination with a lack of security mechanisms such as circuit breakers on crypto exchanges and a continuously increasing market capitalisation of crypto-assets,[20] could threaten the stability of the crypto-assets market. Due to a growing interconnectedness between crypto markets and the traditional financial system, significant crashes on crypto markets could pose a risk to overall financial stability.[21]

D. Front running

The last manipulation technique we wish to illustrate in this chapter is front running. In traditional markets, front running is known as a special kind of insider trading.[22] The key part of front running is the use of prior (confidential) knowledge to trade ahead of other market participants. An example of front running is brokers who execute big orders of their clients only after they have traded the same security on their own account first, thereby getting ahead of the orders coming from the client.[23] In this case, the broker uses the confidential information that their client will execute a significant order in a certain security—which might have an influence on the price—to trade before their client and benefit from potential price changes.

---

18 Maxim Roslyakov, 'Risks of Automated Trading and How to Manage Them' (*tradesanta*, 2019) <https://tradesanta.com/blog/risks-of-automated-trading-and-how-to-manage-them> accessed 03 June 2023.

19 Amexcited Guide, 'Flash Crash: Blitzeinschlag an der Börse' (*American Express*, 15 November 2022) <https://www.americanexpress.com/de-de/kampagnen/guide/geldanlagen/boerse/flash-crash-1664> accessed 03 June 2023.

20 Deloitte, 'Market Manipulation in Digital Assets' (*Deloitte*, March 2021) <https://www2.deloitte.com/content/dam/Deloitte/global/Documents/Financial-Services/gx-design-market-manipulation-in-digital-assets-whitepaper-v2-1.pdf> accessed 03 June 2023.

21 Lieven Hermans et al., 'Decrypting Financial Stability Risks in Crypto-Asset Markets' (*European Central Bank*, May 2022) <https://www.ecb.europa.eu/pub/financial-stability/fsr/special/html/ecb.fsrart202205_02~1cc6b111b4.en.html> accessed 15 May 2023.

22 Börse Frankfurt Börsenlexikon, 'Front Running' (Deutsche Börse Group) <https://www.boerse-frankfurt.de/wissen/lexikon/front-running> accessed 03 June 2023.

23 Ibid.

While in regular markets, it is important to obtain insider knowledge to be able to trade ahead of others, in crypto-assets markets, the necessary information to trade ahead of others can be obtained rather easily.[24]

A common way of front running in crypto-asset markets is to scan the blockchain for pending transactions and then get ahead of the trades.[25] Especially in decentralised networks, due to their transparent ledgers, smart algorithms can detect orders initiated by regular investors that are waiting on the blockchain to be executed.[26] If the manipulator discovers a trade that, in their opinion, will affect the market price, they react in milliseconds and pay a higher gas fee to the miner so that their own trade gets executed before the one they detected.[27] By getting ahead of the other trade, they can participate in any potential price variation caused by the trade. Besides just getting ahead of a trade waiting to be executed, there are plenty of different front running strategies operated by manipulators.[28]

The negative effects of front running are twofold: manipulators can reduce the profits of ordinary investors because they manage to get ahead of them and take a part of the gains away from the investor and profit themselves.[29] Furthermore, just like insider trading, front running can undermine confidence in the whole market. If investors have to fear that manipulators are regularly getting ahead of their trades, they have to fear that all of their trades could be flawed from the moment they are initialised.[30]

III. Markets in Crypto-assets Regulation (MiCA)

A. Introduction to MiCA

Law can address market efficiency, financial stability, market integrity, and investor protection issues. However, the rules applied to the traditional securities markets may not be suitable for the crypto-assets market due to both the definitional issue as well as the more decentralised and disintermediated nature of the crypto-assets markets.

---

24 Jeffrey Craig, 'What is Front Running and How Crypto Orders are Ripe for the Picking' (*phemex*, 22 September 2021) <https://phemex.com/academy/what-is-front-running> accessed 03 June 2023.

25 Nikolay Kaloyanov, 'Detect and Avoid Front Running in Crypto and NFT Trading' (*hi Foundation*, 24 October 2022) <https://resources.hi.com/how-to-detect-and-avoid-front-running-in-crypto-and-nft-trading/> accessed 03 June 2023.

26 Craig (n 24).

27 Nikolay Kaloyanov, 'How to Detect and Avoid Front Running in Crypto and NFT Trading' (*hi Foundation*, 24 October 2022) <https://resources.hi.com/how-to-detect-and-avoid-front-running-in-crypto-and-nft-trading/> accessed 03 June 2023.

28 Ibid.

29 Ibid.

30 Ibid.

The EU Markets in Crypto-assets Regulation (MiCA)[31] represents a significant stride toward the comprehensive regulation of the crypto-assets markets within the EU.[32] Introduced as part of the EU's digital finance package alongside the Digital Operational Resilience Act (DORA) and the Distributed Ledger Technology (DLT) Pilot Regime Regulation,[33] MiCA demonstrates the EU's commitment to fostering innovation while ensuring market stability, integrity, and investor protection.

MiCA was developed in response to the rapid evolution and growing adoption of crypto-assets, which, despite their potential to revolutionise finance,[34] have raised concerns regarding market integrity, investor protection, and financial stability, as discussed in Section II.[35] The regulation aims to address these concerns by establishing a harmonised regulatory framework across EU member states, thus eliminating regulatory fragmentation and enhancing legal certainty for market participants.

MiCA covers aspects from issuer compliance and the operation of service providers to consumer protection and measures against market abuse. By setting a clear set of rules and standards, MiCA aims to enhance the operational resilience of the crypto-assets markets, safeguard against financial crimes,[36] and ensure the protection of investors and consumers, beyond investor warning and education.

The inclusion of stablecoins within MiCA's regulatory scope also highlights the EU's awareness of their growing prominence and potential systemic risks. By subjecting stablecoins to stricter requirements, MiCA seeks to mitigate risks related to financial stability, ensuring that innovations in the digital finance space do not undermine the integrity of the financial system.

---

31 Council Regulation (EU) 2023/1114 of the European Parliament and of the Council of 31 May 2023 on markets in crypto-assets and amending Regulations (EU) No 1093/2010 and (EU) No 1095/2010 and Directives 2013/36/EU and (EU) 2019/1937 [2023] OJ L 150/40 of 09.06.2023 (hereafter MiCA).

32 Ryan Browne, 'EU Lawmakers Approve World's First Comprehensive Framework for Crypto Regulation' (*CNBC*, 20 April 2023) <https://www.cnbc.com/2023/04/20/eu-lawmakers-approve-worlds-first-comprehensive-crypto-regulation.html> accessed 03 June 2023.

33 Benjamin Beck, Marcel Hörauf and Patrick Scholl, 'EU Markets in Crypto-Assets (MiCA) Regulation Expected to Enter into Force in Early 2023' (*Mayer Brown*, 14 December 2022) <https://www.mayerbrown.com/en/perspectives-events/publications/2022/12/eu-markets-in-crypto-assets-mica-regulation-expected-to-enter-into-force-in-early-2023> accessed 03 June 2023.

34 Reasoning (2) of MiCA.

35 Reasoning (5) of MiCA.

36 Reasoning (4) of MiCA.

The passage of MiCA by the European Parliament in April 2023,[37] followed by its adoption by the European Council in May 2023,[38] marks a moment in the regulation of digital finance. Parts of MiCA coming into effect in June 2023, with full application by December 2024, signify a proactive step towards aligning the dynamic space of crypto-assets with the EU's broader financial regulatory framework, rather than treating it as a gaming and gambling space.

B. Regulatory approach

Regulatory approaches and objectives can determine the success of the financial market. Some regulations are anti-innovation, over-prescriptive, and unclear, which can all increase costs for the market participants. MiCA is a pioneering regulatory framework aimed at harmonising the approach to crypto-assets across EU member states.[39] Its development reflects an understanding of the balance between fostering innovation and ensuring market stability, investor protection, and environmental sustainability. By adopting a technologically neutral stance, MiCA aspires to support the growth and competitiveness of the European crypto-assets markets while remaining open to international developments.[40] The approach is pro-innovation, rather than aiming to regulate the activities out of existence.

MiCA's approach contrasts with more traditional regulatory strategies that may inadvertently stifle innovation or be overly prescriptive. Unlike regulations that may apply a one-size-fits-all approach to diverse financial sectors, MiCA is crafted specifically for the crypto-assets markets, addressing their unique challenges such as blockchain-based market space, and opportunities such as stablecoins as a means of payment to reduce costs related to cross-border transactions, while delivering the same regulatory outcomes, such as market integrity, investor protection, and financial stability. This specificity is intended to mitigate risks without curbing the potential for technological advancements and market growth, as blockchain technologies and other AI-based applications may be used in this market space to bring about financial inclusion.

Comparatively, regulatory approaches in other jurisdictions, such as the United States, differ significantly. In the US, regulatory bodies such as the Securities and Exchange Commission (SEC) and the Commodity Futures Trading Commission (CFTC) have primarily relied on existing financial market regulations to address issues within the

---

37 European Parliament, 'Proposal for a regulation of the European Parliament and of the Council on markets in crypto-assets in "A Europe Fit for the Digital Age"' (*European Parliament Legislative Train Schedule*, 20 April 2023) <https://www.europarl.europa.eu/legislative-train/theme-a-europe-fit-for-the-digital-age/file-crypto-assets-1> accessed 03 June 2023.

38 Council of the EU, 'Digital Finance: Council Adopts New Rules on Markets in Crypto-Assets (MiCA)' (*European Council Press release*, 16 May 2023) <https://www.consilium.europa.eu/en/press/press-releases/2023/05/16/digital-finance-council-adopts-new-rules-on-markets-in-crypto-assets-mica/> accessed 21 May 2023.

39 Reasoning (6) of MiCA.

40 Reasoning (7) of MiCA.

crypto-assets markets. This "same regulation" approach has often led to legal uncertainties and has placed the onus on courts to clarify the legal status of crypto-assets.[41] The evolving landscape in the US signals a growing demand for legislative clarity and a more defined regulatory framework for crypto-assets, similar to the clarity MiCA aims to provide within the EU.[42]

By establishing a dedicated framework for crypto-assets, MiCA represents a forward-thinking regulatory approach that not only aims to protect investors and ensure market integrity but also supports innovation and addresses environmental concerns. This approach highlights the EU's commitment to creating a regulatory environment that is adaptive, inclusive, and sustainable, setting a precedent for how jurisdictions can respond to the rapidly evolving crypto-asset market.

C. Scope

MiCA aims to address the risks of the crypto-assets markets that are not covered by the existing legislative frameworks applying to traditional securities markets. By clearly delineating the securities markets, which includes the securities tokens market, the law recognises the novelties that the crypto-assets market brings. This is not only due to the underlying technologies, such as the DLTs that require new regulatory responses, such as scanning the blockchain to obtain information on orders placed, but also because of the new participants such as miners and transaction validators, and the new business models that necessitate a new separate regulatory framework. By not applying the existing securities market rules to the crypto-assets markets, it also recognises the benefits that this whole new market can bring to the economy and society.

MiCA's scope is deliberately broad, encompassing a wide range of digital assets, yet it specifically excludes assets already regulated under existing EU legislative acts on financial services.[43] This approach acknowledges the new challenges as well as opportunities presented by crypto-assets, including new technologies, market participants, and business models that differ fundamentally from traditional financial systems.

MiCA's broad definition of crypto-assets as digital representations of value or rights using distributed ledger technology or similar technologies shows the EU's intent to create a regulatory framework flexible enough to accommodate future innovations. This definition harmonises the term crypto-asset among all European countries and ends varying definitions in each member state with a different focus, for example, the German solo run with the definition of crypto-assets in its Governance Banking

41 Richard Rosenthal and Roy Ben Hur, 'Navigating the Crypto Regulatory Landscape: Insights to Shape Your Digital Assets Strategy' (*Deloitte*, 16 November 2022) <https://www2.deloitte.com/us/en/pages/advisory/articles/crypto-policy-regulation.html> accessed 03 June 2023.

42 Ibid.

43 Reasoning (9) of MiCA.

Act (Kreditwesengesetz), which was primarily focused on capturing currency tokens such as Bitcoin.[44] However, the exclusion of certain assets, such as security tokens that qualify as financial instruments under Markets in Financial Instruments Directive (MiFID) II,[45] and services provided in a fully decentralised manner, such as complete peer-to-peer transactions without centralised intermediaries, alongside non-fungible tokens (NFTs),[46] from MiCA's purview has elicited some critique.

Besides already regulated crypto-assets, such crypto-asset services that are provided in a fully decentralised manner are also not regulated by MiCA. Furthermore, MiCA does not apply to non-fungible crypto-assets because the EU considers their financial use, as well as the risks they might pose to investors and to the financial system, to be limited.[47]

D. Categories

MICA reveals certain limitations in its scope of coverage. Notably, MiCA does not encompass all types of crypto-assets, leaving out specific categories such as NFTs. This exclusion raises concerns about potential regulatory evasion, where manipulative practices involving NFTs could undermine the integrity of both the broader crypto-assets market and the NFT market specifically.

MiCA categorises crypto-assets into three distinct groups based on their inherent characteristics and associated risks,[48] with particular emphasis on how these assets achieve value stability.[49] The first type of crypto-assets are *electronic money or e-money tokens*. They are defined as crypto-assets intended to maintain stable value by referencing a single official currency. These tokens are designed to offer a digital alternative to fiat currencies, facilitating stable and secure transactions.[50] The second type MiCA established under Art 3 (6) is *asset-referenced tokens*. These are crypto-assets that aim to stabilise their value by referencing a basket of values, which could include one or more fiat currencies, other assets, or a combination thereof. This category

44 Tobias Bauerfeind, Cornelius Hille and Detmar Loff, 'Aufsichtregime nach MiCAR aus Instituts- und Produktperspektive – Widerstreit oder Homogenität' (2023) 2 Recht der Finanzinstrumente 84.

45 Joseph Lee and Doreen Geidel, 'Mapping an Investor Protection Framework for the Security Token Offering Market: A Comparative Analysis of UK and German Law' (2021) 316 Taiwan Law Review; Council Directive 2014/65/EU of the European Parliament and of the Council of 15 May 2014 on markets in financial instruments and amending Directive 2002/92/EC and Directive 2011/61/EU [2014] OJ L 173 of 12.06.2014.

46 Reasoning (10) of MiCA.

47 Alireza Siadat, 'MiCAR – Regulierte Finanzinstrumente mit Schwerpunktsetzung auf NFT' (2023) Recht der Finanzinstrumente 4.

48 Reasoning (18) of MiCA.

49 Ibid.

50 Art. 3 (7) of MiCA.

broadens the scope of stablecoins,[51] addressing the diverse mechanisms employed to achieve value stability. The final type of crypto-asset covered by MiCA can be seen as a "catch-all category" for all other assets which are not classified as e-money tokens or asset-referenced tokens.[52] MiCA refers to these tokens as "Crypto-assets, other than asset-referenced tokens or e-money tokens".

E. Addressees of the Regulation

MiCA mainly addresses those entities that intend to offer to the public or seek admission to the trading of crypto-assets in the EU as well as the crypto-asset service providers.

In addition, the term "offer to the public" has a broad definition in Article 3 (12) MiCA and captures essentially any communication which presents sufficient information on the terms of the offer and the crypto-asset to enable holders to decide whether to purchase the crypto-asset. Hence, MiCA applies if this 'offer to the public' is made within the EU. This means that MiCA applies regardless of where the undertaking that makes the offer is established, if the communication to persons that represent the offer to the public happens in the Union.

The definition of a crypto-asset service provider, on the other hand, captures any undertaking whose business is the provision of crypto-asset services to clients on a professional basis in the EU.[53] Thereby, in accordance with Article 3 (16) MiCA, crypto-asset services are, for example, 1) the operation of a trading platform, 2) the exchange of crypto-assets for funds/other crypto-assets, or 3) the execution of orders for crypto-assets on behalf of clients. The definitions used in MiCA for the regulated crypto-asset services essentially correspond to the familiar definitions from MiFID II, which are already part of the legislation of the member states, for example, in Germany in section 1 of the Governance Banking Act (Kreditwesengesetz).[54] The crypto-asset services have to be provided within the EU as well in order for MiCA to apply. Crypto-asset services provided by a third-country firm on the own initiative of a person established in the Union are not deemed to be provided in the Union.[55] However, where a third-country firm solicits clients or prospective clients in the EU or promotes or advertises crypto-asset services or activities in the EU, its services should not be deemed to be crypto-asset services provided on the own initiative of the client.[56] In this case, the requirements established by MiCA apply to the third-country firm.

51 Beck, Hörauf and Scholl (n 33).
52 Ibid.
53 Art. 3 (15) of MiCA.
54 David John and Anika Patz, 'Verordnung über Märkte für Kryptowerte (MiCA) - Überblick über das neue EU-Regime für Kryptowerte und Kryptowerte-Dienstleister' (2023) 33 Der Betrieb 1906.
55 Art. 61 (1) of MiCA.
56 Reasoning (75) of MiCA.

To provide more regulatory certainty on this issue, under Article 61 (3) MiCA the European Securities and Markets Authority (ESMA) shall issue guidelines to specify the situations in which a third-country firm is deemed to solicit clients in the Union.

F. Requirements established by MiCA

Depending on the addressee and in accordance with the different risk assessments for the individual types of crypto-assets, MiCA provides a specified regulatory framework.

G. For offerors and undertakings seeking admission to trading of cryptoassets

MiCA mandates the creation of a white paper for every type of crypto-asset. This document must provide comprehensive details about the issuer, the crypto-asset-referenced tokens and e-money tokens, the white paper must include additional disclosures, such as detailed risk assessments and information on asset reserves. These enhanced requirements reflect the potentially higher risk profile of these assets compared to other crypto-assets.[57]

Issuers are held accountable for the accuracy and completeness of the information provided in the white paper.[58] Should the document contain incomplete, unclear, misleading, or false information, the issuer is liable for any losses incurred by investors as a result of these discrepancies. This provision aims to uphold market integrity and protect investor interests by ensuring transparency and accountability.

1. *Crypto-assets other than asset-referenced tokens or e-money tokens*

For offering a crypto-asset to the public within the EU or for its admission to the trading on a platform, when the asset is neither an asset-referenced token nor an e-money token, the primary requirement under MiCA is straightforward. The issuer must be a legally recognised entity that has submitted the necessary white paper for the crypto-asset to the appropriate regulatory authority and made this document accessible to the public, as stipulated in Article 4 of MiCA.[59]

Further, Article 14 of MiCA imposes additional obligations on issuers and those seeking to list such crypto-assets for trading. These parties are required to adhere to specified behavioural standards. This includes the obligation to identify, manage, and fully disclose any potential conflicts of interest that may arise during the course of their operations. Additionally, they must ensure that their operational systems are fully

---

57 For crypto assets other than asset-referenced tokens or e-money tokens, see Art. 6 of MiCA; for asset-referenced tokens, see Art. 19 of MiCA.

58 Philipp Maume, 'The Regulation on Markets in Crypto-Assets (MiCAR): Landmark Codification, or First Step of Many, or Both?' (2023) 20(2) European Company and Financial Law Review 243.

59 Oliver Read, 'Inkrafttreten der MiCA-Verordnung: Harmonisierte EU-Regulierung von Krypto-Assets?' (2023) 14(9–10) Corporate Finance 211.

compliant with established Union standards, emphasising the importance of transparency and integrity in their dealings.

2. *Asset-referenced tokens*

MiCA introduces a stringent regulatory framework for the issuance, public offering, and trading of asset-referenced tokens within the EU. To engage in these activities, entities must adhere to the following requirements.

Only the issuer of the asset-referenced token, who must be a legally recognised entity or undertaking established within the EU, is permitted to offer these tokens to the public or seek their admission to trading. This entity must have received authorisation from the competent regulatory authority or be a credit institution that meets specific criteria.[60]

There are additional obligations for issuers of asset-referenced tokens. Issuers are obligated to report on tokens with an issuance value exceeding 100 million EUR.[61] Robust governance structures are required under Article 34 of MiCA, including clear organisational responsibilities, risk management processes, and internal control mechanisms. Furthermore, issuers must maintain a specified amount of own funds and asset reserves under Article 35 of MiCA. These reserves must be legally separated from the issuer's own assets and other reserves (Article 37), ensuring that creditors cannot claim them (Article 35). Token holders are guaranteed the right to redeem their tokens from the issuer, reinforcing investor protection (Article 39). Finally, the European Banking Authority (EBA) has the authority to classify certain asset-referenced tokens as significant based on predefined criteria, subjecting these tokens to additional regulatory obligations (Article 45).

3. *E-money tokens*

To offer an e-money token to the public or for its admission to trading within the EU, entities must secure authorisation either as a credit institution or as an electronic money institution. They are also required to submit a crypto-asset white paper to the competent regulatory authority and ensure its publication, as mandated by Article 48 of MiCA.

MiCA aligns its regulatory framework for e-money tokens with the pre-existing Directive 2009/110/EC,[62] introducing specific additional requirements to address the unique aspects of e-money tokens within the crypto-assets markets. These supplementary mandates include, but are not limited to, provisions similar to those for

---

60 Ibid.

61 Art. 22 of MiCA.

62 Council Directive 2009/110/EC of the European Parliament and of the Council of 16 September 2009 on the taking up, pursuit and prudential supervision of the business of electronic money institutions amending Directives 2005/60/EC and 2006/48/EC and repealing Directive 2000/46/EC [2009] OJ L 267/7 of 10.10.2009.

asset-referenced tokens, particularly concerning the classification of e-money tokens as significant by the EBA. This classification, based on certain criteria detailed in Article 56 of MiCA, subjects e-money tokens to heightened scrutiny and regulatory obligations, reflecting a detailed approach to ensuring financial stability and consumer protection in the evolving digital assets landscape.

H. For crypto-asset service providers

Under MiCA, entities seeking to offer crypto-asset services within the EU must obtain prior authorisation as outlined in Article 59. This prerequisite ensures that all crypto-asset service providers operate within a regulated framework, enhancing the security and integrity of the digital assets markets. Specifically, financial institutions already authorised under existing legislative frameworks are subject to tailored requirements under Article 60 of MiCA, facilitating their entry into the crypto-asset services market.

The authorisation process demands detailed disclosures from applicants to the competent regulatory authority. This includes details on the legal structure of the company, its governance documents, and information about significant shareholders, ensuring a transparent evaluation of the entity's suitability to provide crypto-assets services. Additionally, Article 62(2) of MiCA mandates that applicants provide specific information relevant to the nature of the services they intend to offer. For instance, entities aiming to operate a trading platform must submit a detailed account of the platform's operational rules, while those looking to execute orders on behalf of clients are required to describe their execution policies.

Entities seeking to offer crypto-asset services within the EU must obtain prior authorisation as outlined in Article 59. This prerequisite ensures that all crypto-asset service providers operate within a regulated framework, enhancing the security and integrity of the digital assets market. Specifically, financial institutions already authorised under existing legislative frameworks are subject to tailored requirements under Article 60 of MiCA, facilitating their entry into the crypto-asset services market.[63]

The authorisation process demands detailed disclosures from applicants to the competent regulatory authority. This includes details on the legal structure of the company, its governance documents, and information about significant shareholders, ensuring a transparent evaluation of the entity's suitability to provide crypto-asset services. Additionally, Article 62(2) of MiCA mandates that applicants provide specific information relevant to the nature of the services they intend to offer. For instance, entities aiming to operate a trading platform must submit a detailed account of the platform's operational rules, while those looking to execute orders on behalf of clients are required to describe their execution policies.

---

63 John and Patz (n 54).

In their interactions with clients, crypto-asset service providers are mandated by Article 66 (1) of MiCA to conduct their business with honesty, fairness, and professionalism, at all times prioritising the best interests of their clients and potential clients.[64] This overarching principle is further delineated into specific obligations, such as the duty to provide clients with transparent and equitable information and to adequately inform them of the risks associated with their transactions.

Furthermore, Article 67 of MiCA imposes a requirement on all crypto-asset service providers to maintain adequate prudential safeguards. These financial safeguards, essential for ensuring the providers' operational resilience and client protection, may consist of either the providers' own funds, a comprehensive insurance policy that covers the entirety of the EU, or an equivalent guarantee.

Article 68 of MiCA elaborates on the requisite governance structures for these service providers. It highlights the importance of maintaining a management body and shareholders of good repute, implementing effective compliance mechanisms, and conducting thorough risk assessments. These governance arrangements are crucial for fostering a trustworthy and secure environment for the provision of crypto-asset services, ensuring that the operations of these providers are conducted in a manner that upholds regulatory standards and protects the interests of their clients.

Article 70 of MiCA mandates that crypto-asset service providers safeguard the ownership rights of their clients when holding crypto-assets on their behalf. This provision ensures that service providers have robust mechanisms in place to prevent the misuse of client assets for their own benefit. Specifically, it requires the establishment of arrangements that prohibit the use of clients' funds for the service provider's own transactions.

This regulatory requirement aims to avert scenarios similar to the collapse of FTX, where the platform misappropriated customer deposits for unauthorised purposes, including extending credit to related entities without proper disclosure. By enforcing strict custody and handling rules, MiCA seeks to protect investors and maintain trust in the digital asset ecosystem, ensuring that the assets held by service providers are managed with transparency and integrity.[65]

I. Prevention of market abuse

MiCA introduces a broad set of rules aimed at curbing market abuse within the crypto-assets space. These regulations extend to any activities related to crypto-assets that are

---

64 Bauerfeind, Hille and Loff (n 44).

65 Angus Berwick, John Shiffman and Koh Gui Qing, 'Exclusive: How a Secret Software Change Allowed FTX to Use Client Money' (*Reuters*, 14 December 2022) <https://www.reuters.com/technology/how-secret-software-change-allowed-ftx-use-client-money-2022-12-13/#:~:text=A%20digital%20dashboard%20used%20by,that%20Reuters%20has%20previously%20reported> accessed 03 June 2023.

either already admitted to trading or have been proposed for admission within the EU, as specified in Article 86 (1) of MiCA. Importantly, the jurisdiction of these rules is not limited to actions taking place on trading platforms or within the EU; instead, they apply universally to any abuse involving crypto-assets traded in the EU.

MiCA tackles insider dealing through Articles 87 and the subsequent articles. Article 87 outlines a wide-ranging definition of inside information, mandating its timely disclosure to mitigate the risk of informational asymmetries,[66] as outlined in Article 88. Moreover, Article 89 explicitly prohibits the misuse of such inside information for trading activities related to the implicated crypto-assets. This prohibition extends beyond personal gain, also criminalising the unauthorised sharing of inside information, as per Article 90.

This framework represents a significant step towards ensuring transparency and fairness in the crypto-assets market, addressing potential forums for market manipulation and insider trading. By setting these standards, MiCA aims to protect investors and maintain the integrity of the financial market within the context of the rapidly evolving digital assets space.

Article 91(1) of MiCA establishes a broad prohibition against market manipulation within the crypto-assets sector. To clarify this overarching prohibition, paragraph 2 of Article 91 details a comprehensive list of actions deemed as market manipulation.

Specifically, MiCA outlaws any actions that create false or misleading impressions regarding the supply, demand, or price of a crypto-asset. This includes practices aimed at artificially maintaining the price of one or several crypto-assets at a non-genuine level (Article 91(2)a). Furthermore, the regulation strictly prohibits the dissemination of information through any medium if such information is designed to mislead market participants about the supply, demand, or price of a crypto-asset, especially when the disseminator is aware or should be aware of the misleading nature of the information (Article 91(2)c).

These provisions target manipulative behaviours exemplified by pump-and-dump schemes, wherein perpetrators coordinate to inflate a crypto-asset's price through the spread of false or misleading information before selling off their holdings at the inflated price, thereby profiting at the expense of uninformed investors. By outlining these prohibitions, MiCA aims to safeguard the integrity of the crypto-asset market and protect investors from fraudulent practices.

Article 92 of MiCA is dedicated to the prevention and detection of market abuse, mandating that individuals and entities involved in arranging or executing crypto-asset

---

66 Watson Law, 'MiCA – Market Abuse Prevention under MiCA' (*Watson Law*, 01 February 2023) <https://watsonlaw.nl/en/mica-market-abuse-prevention-under-mica/> accessed 03 February 2024.

transactions implement robust mechanisms for this purpose. The scope of this provision has sparked considerable debate, particularly concerning its implications for maximal extractable value (MEV) activities within the cryptocurrency markets.[67] MEV represents the profit that miners or network participants can achieve by prioritising, including, or excluding specific transactions in the blocks they mine or validate.[68] A key point of discussion is whether MEV practices fall under the purview of Article 92, given that those who engage in MEV do not directly arrange or execute transactions in the traditional sense. Instead, they select transactions for inclusion in a block, influencing the order based on potential profit outcomes.[69] This nuanced distinction raises questions about the applicability of Article 92's requirements to MEV activities.

The resolution to this debate is anticipated to come from ESMA, which is expected to publish regulatory technical standards clarifying the application of Article 92 to MEV and similar practices. Should ESMA determine that MEV activities constitute a form of market abuse or have the potential to disrupt market integrity, Article 92 could necessitate the adoption of specific measures to mitigate such risks, aligning the operation of blockchain validators and miners with MiCA's overarching goal of ensuring a fair and abuse-free crypto market environment.

In addition to banning behaviours that improperly influence crypto-asset prices, create unfair trading conditions, or disseminate false or misleading signals, MiCA specifically prohibits exploiting media access to affect a crypto-asset's valuation. Under Article 91(3)c of MiCA, it is unlawful for any individual to express opinions about a crypto-asset in the media when they have previously taken positions in that asset and stand to gain from the market's reaction to their statements, without disclosing this conflict of interest. This provision is designed to prevent market manipulation through the use of public platforms or media influence, ensuring transparency and fairness in the promotion and discussion of crypto-assets.

IV. Gaps and recommendations

While MiCA introduces regulations to enhance investor protection within the under-regulated crypto-assets markets, it overlooks certain complexities, notably algorithmic trading's risks. MiCA's scope, although broad, leaves gaps in addressing the

67 Dalmas Ngetich, 'EU's MiCA Rules Could Prohibit MEV Activities on Ethereum' (*crypto.news*, 31 July 2023) <https://crypto.news/eus-mica-rules-could-prohibit-mev-activities-on-ethereum/> accessed 3 February 2024. Plexus, 'What is Maximal Extractable Value (MEV) in Crypto?' (Plexus, 3 January 2024) accessed 3 February 2024.

68 Ibid.

69 Jonathan Galea, 'Does MEV Fall Within Scope of MiCA's Market Abuse Provisions?' (*BCAS*, 04 September 2023) <https://blog.bcas.io/does-mev-fall-within-scope-of-micas-market-abuse-provisions> accessed 3 February 2024.

dynamics of algorithmic trading, which, due to its accessibility online, attracts a wide spectrum of traders—from individual investors to large institutions. This oversight could pose significant risks to market stability and integrity.

The potential for algorithms to interact in unforeseen ways, particularly during volatile market conditions or due to inherent flaws in the algorithms themselves, highlights a critical area for regulatory actions. Unlike MiFID II, which tackles algorithmic trading with detailed provisions for market participants and trading venues,[70] MiCA offers only foundational guidelines for crypto-asset service providers. This discrepancy suggests a need for a more enhanced regulatory framework within the crypto-assets sector to mitigate risks associated with advanced trading technologies.

The accessibility of algorithmic trading amplifies concerns, as it democratises the use of complex strategies previously reserved for sophisticated investors,[71] thus broadening the potential impact of inadequately regulated algorithmic activities. As the crypto-asset markets continue to evolve, aligning MiCA's provisions with the depth and specificity of MiFID II's approach to algorithmic trading could prove essential in safeguarding market stability and ensuring fair trading practices across all investor classes.[72]

MiFID II tackles the challenges posed by algorithmic trading through a dual-regulatory approach. First, it mandates direct market interventions, requiring trading platforms to implement systems capable of halting trading activities during periods of extreme market volatility.[73] Secondly, it requires entities engaged in algorithmic trading to adopt detailed internal risk management procedures. This includes pre-market testing of algorithms and implementing pre-trade controls such as price collars to mitigate undue market disturbances.[74] ESMA further supports this by detailing these requirements in Regulatory Technical Standard (RTS) 6, providing a framework for pre-trade controls among investment firms deploying algorithmic trading.[75]

Contrastingly, MiCA primarily sets forth guidelines for crypto-asset service providers, particularly those operating trading platforms for crypto-assets. Article 76 (7) of MiCA outlines essential operational requirements for these trading systems, showing

70 Joseph Lee and Lukas Schu, 'Regulation of Algorithmic Trading: Frameworks of Human Supervision and Direct Market Interventions' [2022] European Business Law Review 193.

71 Roslyakov (n 18).

72 For a detailed account of the risks associated with algorithmic trading, see: Lee and Schu (n 70).

73 Lee and Schu (n 70).

74 Ibid.

75 Commission Delegated Regulation (EU) 2017/589 of 19 July 2016 supplementing Directive 2014/65/EU of the European Parliament and of the Council with regard to regulatory technical standards specifying the organisational requirements of investment firms engaged in algorithmic trading [2016] OJ L 87/417 of 31.03.2017.

the need for resilience, capacity to manage peak volumes, and the capability to maintain orderly trading even under stress. Additionally, it requires systems to reject orders that surpass predefined thresholds or are erroneous, alongside mechanisms to prevent and detect market abuse. These stipulations aim to address the complexities introduced by algorithmic trading, ensuring trading platforms have the necessary safeguards.

However, MiCA's focus is narrower compared to MiFID II, primarily targeting platform operators rather than the broader market participants engaged in algorithmic trading. This limitation highlights a potential gap in addressing the full spectrum of risks that algorithmic trading may introduce to the crypto-assets market, especially regarding the direct responsibilities of traders employing these techniques. The specific requirements for trading platforms to test their systems and enforce order parameters, while crucial, may not fully encapsulate the proactive risk management strategies seen in MiFID II, further highlighting a need for potential regulatory enhancements in MiCA to more comprehensively cover the nuances of algorithmic trading within the crypto sector.

In addressing the risks of algorithmic trading within the crypto-assets sector, MiCA assigns significant responsibilities to crypto-asset service providers, particularly those operating trading platforms. These providers are tasked with ensuring that their systems are robust enough to manage heightened order volumes and mitigate associated risks. However, MiCA stops short of imposing specific requirements on individuals or entities using algorithmic trading strategies on these platforms, a gap that contrasts with the detailed pre-trade control measures and internal risk management procedures mandated for investment firms under MiFID II and its RTS 6.

This omission raises concerns about the efficacy of trading systems in isolating and mitigating risks inherent to algorithmic trading. The challenge extends beyond filtering clearly erroneous orders or those breaching pre-set thresholds. Detecting orders intended for market manipulation or understanding the unintended consequences of algorithmic interactions requires insights into the algorithms' underlying logic—insights that MiCA's current provisions do not directly address.

Since even individuals can apply algorithmic trading methods in the crypto-assets market, and therefore the scope of potential addressees and potential regulatory subjects of internal risk management procedures as established by MiFID II would be immense, this approach may not be successful in the crypto-assets market. Future research has to find a solution to assure that the algorithms applied can be trusted and do not cause manipulations or interfere with financial stability, either by making individual traders more responsible for the algorithms they apply (and finding a proper way to enforce this) or by establishing trustworthy pre-trade checks enforced by crypto-asset service providers.

Moreover, the applicability of MiFID II's rigorous regulatory framework hinges on whether a crypto-asset is classified as a financial instrument under its definitions.[76] MiCA provides a broad definition of crypto-assets, aiming to encompass all digital instruments not covered elsewhere. To help distinguish crypto-assets that qualify as financial instruments, MiCA suggests that ESMA will issue guidelines outlining specific conditions and criteria. This distinction is crucial, as it determines whether the comprehensive regulatory regime of MiFID II applies, thereby subjecting certain crypto-assets to a more stringent set of regulations compared to those solely governed by MiCA.

Another critical area requiring further regulatory clarity under MiCA involves crypto buy-back programmes. Similar to strategies employed by publicly traded companies, these programmes are used within the crypto-assets markets for token stabilisation. However, MiCA's current framework leaves ambiguity regarding the regulatory standing of these buy-back initiatives. Unlike the Market Abuse Regulation (MAR),[77] which permits buy-back programmes under specified conditions for financial instruments, MiCA has yet to adopt a similar exemption. This lack of clarity poses a challenge for market participants seeking to ensure the legality of their stabilisation efforts.

Since market stability should be an important regulatory outcome of crypto-asset regulation, a sound regulatory framework for crypto buy-back programmes, which takes the special requirements of crypto-assets into account, should be investigated and developed by future researchers to provide the crypto-asset markets with a reliable legal framework to stabilise their tokens.

As a German Federal Financial Supervisory Authority (BaFin) executive put it, "MiCA is an important step and is ground-breaking by international standards. However, there is still a regulatory need to close certain gaps and fully implement the principle of 'same business, same risks, same rules'."[78]

V. Conclusion

In this chapter, we explore the dynamics of market behaviour within the crypto-assets markets, highlighting the unique risks introduced by technologies, especially blockchain and algorithmic trading. These emerging risks are not adequately addressed by

---

76 Bauerfeind, Hille and Loff (n 44).

77 Council Regulation (EU) No 596/2014 of the European Parliament and of the Council of 16 April 2014 on market abuse (market abuse regulation) and repealing Directive 2003/6/EC of the European Parliament and of the Council and Commission Directives 2003/124/EC, 2003/125/EC and 2004/72/EC (2014) OJ L 173/1 of 12.06.2014.

78 Rupert Schaefer (BaFin Executive Director for Strategy, Policy and Controlling), 'MiCA ist ein wichtiger Schritt' (*BaFin Journal*, 17 May 2023) <https://www.bafin.de/SharedDocs/Veroeffentlichungen/DE/Fachartikel/2023/fa_bj_2305_Mica_Interview_EDSPS.html> accessed 15 February 2024.

traditional securities market regulations, although existing frameworks offer a partial foundation for crafting new legal approaches. The enactment of the EU's Markets in Crypto-Assets Regulation (MiCA) aims at mitigating market abuse risks inherent to the crypto-assets markets. Nonetheless, significant gaps remain, necessitating the development of additional regulatory measures to bridge them. While certain rules governing securities markets might be adapted to the crypto-assets context, the decentralised nature of crypto-assets trading—characterised by a predominance of peer-to-peer transactions—presents distinct challenges. These differences call for a more in-depth examination of new patterns and risks emerging from this novel trading environment. Consequently, regulatory innovation is imperative to effectively manage and mitigate these newly identified risks while delivering the same regulatory outcomes.

9

A European anti-money laundering supervisory authority: perspectives and challenges

Katia Villard

I. Introduction

Money is a prime motivation for crime.[1] Money in itself, however, is of no use.[2] It has value only if it can be used as a means of trade,[3] that is, (re)integrated into the legal economy. To this end, criminals must conceal the illicit origin of the money. Although the scale of this phenomenon is undoubtedly difficult to measure, the estimation of the United Nations Office on Drugs and Crime (UNODC) is from 2 to 5 per cent of global gross domestic product (GDP), in other words, 800 billion to 2 trillion dollars per year.[4]

Bearing this in mind, a meaningful social response to a criminal behaviour must not solely include the privation of the financial gain that was the "why" of the offence, that is, the confiscation of the proceeds from crime. It must also address the problem of the concealment of the ill-gotten gains into the legal economy, as this behaviour enables the offenders to benefit from the fruits of their crime by preventing the authorities from tracing the assets of criminal origin. This is where the anti-money laundering (AML) regime comes in. Over the years, combating money laundering has become a major concern of the international agenda.[5]

1 James W Coleman, 'Crime and Money: Motivation and Opportunity in a Monetarized Economy' (1992) 35 American Behavioural Scientist 827, 830; Stefan D Cassella, 'Nature and Basic Problems of Non-Conviction-Based Confiscation in the United States' (2019) 90(2) International Review of Penal Law 195, 196.

2 William C Gilmore, *Dirty Money - The Evolution of International Measures to Counter Money Laundering and the Financing of Terrorism* (4th edn, Conseil de l'Europe 2011) 31; see also Coleman (n 1) 830.

3 Gilmore (n 2) 31.

4 United Nations Office on Drugs and Crime, 'Money Laundering' (United Nations Office on Drugs and Crime, Overview) <https://www.unodc.org/unodc/en/money-laundering/overview.html> accessed 10 July 2023.

5 Benjamin Vogel, 'Introduction' in Benjamin Vogel and Jean-Baptiste Maillart (eds), *National and International Anti-Money Laundering Law: Developing the Architecture*

The architecture of the AML framework is based on two pillars: repression and prevention. The repressive policy aims at incriminating the phenomenon of money laundering, that is, conduct that seeks to conceal the link between an asset and the offence from which it derives,[6] through the (re)integration of the illicit proceeds into the legal economic system. The preventive policy aims at preventing and detecting the introduction of ill-gotten gains into the legal economy by imposing specific duties on financial institutions and certain other non-financial activities that are considered to be vulnerable to money laundering. As the preventive aspects of the AML regime impose a heavy burden on the private sector, they are much more debated than the repressive ones, including among civil society.

The AML regime is not only tasked with addressing the underlying crime. The objective is also – and maybe even in the first place, as regards the preventive aspect of the AML framework – the protection of the reputation and the stability of the financial sector.[7]

---

of Criminal Justice, Regulation and Data Protection (Intersentia 2020) 1; see also Commission, 'Communication from the Commission to the European Parliament and the Council towards Better Implementation of the EU's Anti-Money Laundering and Countering the Financing of Terrorism Framework' (Communication) COM(2019) 360 final, 1 (Commission, Implementation AML framework).

6 Ursula Cassani, 'L'internationalisation du droit pénal économique et la politique criminelle de la Suisse : la lutte contre le blanchiment d'argent' (2008) 2 Revue de droit suisse 227, 233.

7 Valsamis Mitsilegas, 'Countering the Chameleon Threat of Dirty Money: "Hard" and "Soft" Law in the Emergence of a Global Regime Against Money Laundering and Terrorist Finance' in Adam Edwards and Peter Gill (eds), *Transnational Organised Crime: Perspectives on Global Security* (Routledge 2003) 195, 197; John A E Vervaele, 'Fondements et objectifs des incriminations et des peines en droit pénal international et en droit pénal européen en matière de blanchiment' in Diane Bernard, Damien Scalia, Christine Guillain and Michel van de Kerchove (eds), *Fondements et objectifs des incriminations et des peines en droit européen et international* (Anthemis 2013) 217, 242; see also Verena Zoppei, *Anti-money Laundering Law: Socio-legal Perspectives on the Effectiveness of German Practices* (Springer 2017) 47; Recital 1 of the Council Directive (EEC) 91/308 of 10 June 1991 on the prevention of the use of the financial system for the purpose of money laundering [1991] OJ L 166/77 of 28.06.1991 (1st AML Directive); Recital 1 of the Directive (EU) 2015/849 of the European Parliament and of the Council of 20 May 2015 on the prevention of the use of the financial system for the purposes of money laundering or terrorist financing, amending Regulation (EU) No 648/2012 of the European Parliament and of the Council, and repealing Directive 2005/60/EC of the European Parliament and of the Council and Commission Directive 2006/70/EC [2015] OJ L 141/73 of 05.06.2015 (4th AML Directive). Vogel points out, however, that the meaning of the objective "protection of the financial sector" is not clear: Vogel (n 5) 3 f., and similarly, Benjamin Vogel, 'Conclusions and Recommendations' in Benjamin Vogel and Jean-Baptiste Maillart (eds), *National and International Anti-Money Laundering Law: Developing the Architecture of Criminal Justice, Regulation and Data Protection* (Intersentia 2020) 883 f.

Given the often cross-border dimension of money laundering, the fight against the phenomenon cannot be addressed solely with national – and thus disparate – answers.[8] It called for the creation of a supranational AML framework, which dates back about 35 years. Initially aimed at tackling the proceeds of drug trafficking and subsequently those derived from organised crime, the AML system currently applies to any offence or at least any serious offence that generated gains[9] (depending on the countries). In addition, the terrorist attacks of 9/11 and the growing concern about terrorism led to the emergence of the fight against the financing of terrorism through money laundering policies.[10] Thus, the AML regime has become the AML and countering the financing of terrorism (CFT) regime.[11]

The evolution of the legal framework is not only characterised by the constant expansion of the repressive aspect – in particular, the extension of the list of underlying crimes – but also by the ever-increasing "densification" of the preventive one. The texts establishing the duties imposed on the addressees of preventive AML requirements – in the first instance, the financial sector – have been continuously amended, updated, or replaced, setting ever more-exacting standards.[12] What we can probably call "a normative frenzy" continues today in an exponential way. The content of the AML obligations is now well established and the current preoccupations revolve around the effective implementation of the preventive regime by the institutions concerned. In particular, national disparities in the enforcement of the AML framework are highlighted.[13] This led to the topic of this chapter, namely the establishment of a European AML supervisory authority among other measures. To this end, we will first briefly present the evolution of the AML supranational framework that relates

---

8 Cassani (n 6) 234.

9 For instance, in Switzerland, money laundering implies the commission of a felony as defined by art. 10 § 2 of the Swiss Criminal Code (SCC) or an aggravated tax misdemeanour (art. 305bis (1) and (1bis) SCC). By contrast, the German Criminal Code (GCC) follows an all-crimes approach (§ 261 GCC).

10 Ursula Cassani and Katia Villard, 'The Changing Faces of Money Laundering Regimes' (2019) 90(2) International Review of Penal Law 159, 164.

11 For ease of reading, the acronym "AML" (and not "AML/CFT") will be used in this chapter.

12 Cassani and Villard (n 10) 162.

13 See Commission, 'Communication from the Commission to the European Parliament, The European Council, the Council, the European Central Bank, the Economic and Social Committee and the Committee of the Regions, Strengthening the Union framework for prudential and anti-money laundering supervision for financial institutions', (Communication) COM(2018) 645 final (Commission, Strengthening AML supervision) 3; Commission, Implementation AML framework (n 5) 5; Commission Staff Working Document, 'Impact assessment accompanying the Anti-money laundering package', SWD(2021) 190 final, 35 (Commission staff working document, Impact assessment); European Banking Authority, 'Opinion of the European Banking Authority on the future AML/CFT framework in the EU' EBA/OP/2020/14 of 10.09.2020 § 6 f and its annex European Banking Authority (EBA), 'EBA Report on the future *AML/CFT* framework in the *EU*', EBA/OP/2020/25, § 99 f.

to the preventive aspects of the fight against money laundering, that is, the one of the Financial Action Task Force (FATF) on money laundering and the one of the European Union. We will then focus on the (planned) tasks and organisation of this new agency (Section III) and will question the merits of the future institution and the challenges it faces (Section IV). This chapter will present a macro view (i.e., the objectives assigned to the authority) and will not enter into more specific issues[14] such as, *inter alia*, the criteria for the selection of the directly supervised entities[15] or the tasks and organisation of the Joint Supervisory Teams responsible for monitoring the selected entities.[16]

II. Overview of the evolution of the supranational preventive framework

The FATF was established in 1989 to "develop measures to combat money laundering".[17] In 1990, it published the first version of its 40 Recommendations, which were revised three times respectively in 1996, 2003, and 2012.[18] Furthermore the FATF Recommendations are amended on specific points on a regular basis.[19]

At the European level, the first instrument for combating money laundering was the Council Directive/91/308/EEC of 10 June 1991 on the prevention of the use of the financial system for the purpose of money laundering, commonly known as the first AML Directive. The second AML Directive[20] which amends the first one, dates from 2001. In 2005, a third AML Directive replaced the first two.[21] In 2015, a fourth AML Directive

14 See Silvia Allegrezza, *The Proposed Anti-Money Laundering Authority, FIU Cooperation, Powers and Exchanges of Information: A Critical Assessment* (Policy Department for Economic, Scientific and Quality of Life Policies Directorate, European Parliament, 30.06.2022) for an overview of the potential problematics.

15 See Allegrezza (n 14) 23 ff; regarding the publication of the list of the directly supervised entities in relation to the criteria used to select these entities, refer also to European Central Bank (ECB), 'Opinion of the European Central Bank of 16 February 2022 on a proposal for a regulation establishing the Authority for Anti-Money Laundering and Countering the Financing of Terrorism', (CON/2022/4) OJ C 210/5 of 25.05.2022, 4.

16 See Allegrezza (n 14) 29 ff.

17 The Financial Task Force, 'History of the Financial Action Task Force (FATF)' (FATF) <https://www.fatf-gafi.org/en/the-fatf/history-of-the-fatf.html> accessed 12 February 2024.

18 Aside from its Recommendations, the FATF also publishes other documents such as reports or guidance on specific topics.

19 The most recent one regarding the confiscation of assets dates back to November 2023.

20 Council Directive 2001/97/EC of the European Parliament and of the Council of 4 December 2001 amending Council Directive 91/308/EEC on prevention of the use of the financial system for the purpose of money laundering [2001] OJ L 344/76 of 28.12.2001 (2nd AML Directive).

21 Council Directive 2005/60/EC of the European Parliament and of the Council of 26 October 2005 on the prevention of the use of the financial system for the purpose of

was adopted.[22] Only a year later, in response to the terrorist attacks in Europe,[23] the fourth AML Directive was amended by the fifth AML Directive, adopted on 30 May 2018, with a deadline for transposition into national law by January 2020.[24]

The EU AML system is therefore currently as follows: the AML preventive obligations of the private sector are set up in a directive, which is a text addressed to the Member States that have some leeway in the implementation into domestic legislation.[25] Monitoring compliance with these obligations remains the role of national authorities.[26]

Less than four months after the adoption of the fifth AML Directive, the European Commission published a "communication"[27] addressed to the European Parliament, the European Council, the Council, the European Central Bank, the Economic and

money laundering and terrorist financing [2005] OJ L 309/15 of 25.11.2005 (3rd AML Directive).

22 4th AML Directive (n 7).

23 Commission, 'Action Plan for strengthening the fight against terrorist financing' (Communication) COM (2016) 50 final; Council Directive (EU) 2018/843 of the European Parliament and of the Council of 30 May 2018 amending Directive (EU) 2015/849 on the prevention of the use of the financial system for the purposes of money laundering or terrorist financing, and amending Directives 2009/138/EC and 2013/36/EU, [2018] OJ L 156/43 of 19.06.2018, Recital (2) (5th AML Directive).

24 Art. 4 5th AML Directive (n 23). In order to avoid possible confusion, one can moreover specify that a Directive regarding the repressive regime and sometimes (incorrectly) referred to as the "6th AML Directive" was also adopted in 2018 (Council Directive (EU) 2018/1673 of the European Parliament and of the Council of 23 October 2018 on combating money laundering by criminal law, [2018] OJ L 284/22 of 12.11.2018).

25 Art. 288 § 3 of the Consolidated Version of the Treaty on the Functioning of the European Union (TFEU).

26 See the 4th AML Directive (n 7) Art. 48; for details on the tasks of the supervisory authorities, see Dominik D Schlarb, 'Rethinking Anti-money Laundering Supervision: The Single Supervisory Mechanism - a Model for a European Anti-money Laundering Supervisor?' (2022) 13(1) New Journal of European Criminal Law 69, 70; Joint committee of the European Supervisory Authorities, 'Joint Guidelines on the characteristics of a risk-based approach to anti-money laundering and terrorist financing supervision, and the steps to be taken when conducting supervision on a risk-sensitive basis: The Risk-Bases Supervision Guidelines' (ESAs 2016 72, 16 November 2016) 3. These guidelines have been amended in December 2021, see EBA, 'Final Report: Guidelines on the characteristics of a risk-based approach to anti-money laundering and terrorist financing supervision, and the steps to be taken when conducting supervision on a risk-sensitive basis under Article 48(10) of Directive (EU) 2015/849 (amending the Joint Guidelines ESAs 2016 72) – The Risk Based Supervision Guidelines' (EBA/GL/2021/16, 16 December 2021).

27 The Communication is based on a Reflection Paper established by a joint working group on 31 August 2018, '*Reflection Paper on Possible Elements of a Roadmap for Seamless Cooperation Between Anti Money Laundering and Prudential Supervisors in the European Union*' (Reflection paper cooperation, 31 August 2018), <https://sven

Social Committee, and the Committee of the Regions entitled "Strengthening the Union framework for prudential and anti-money laundering supervision for financial institutions".[28] The document observes that although the fourth and the fifth AML Directives "strengthened [the] legislative framework, several recent cases of money laundering in European banks have given rise to concerns that gaps remain in the Union's supervisory framework".[29]

This statement led in 2019 to the granting of certain definite[30] supervisory powers to the EU prudential supervisor, that is, the European Banking Authority (EBA). Such powers pertained to the AML preventive framework applicable to financial entities.[31] The document concludes by evoking the possibility of "conferring specific AML supervisory tasks to a Union body".[32]

On 24 July 2019, the European Commission published a set of reports relating to the EU legal framework for preventing money laundering and terrorist financing and its implementation. A Communication to the European Parliament and the Council on the same day summarised these texts. It found that whilst much has been achieved these past years to improve the legislative framework, the major problem lies in the divergences in the application of the rules, leading to a structural issue in the EU's capacity to prevent the use of the financial system for illegitimate purposes.[33] The

-giegold.de/wp-content/uploads/2018/09/COM-Reflection-paper-on-elements-of-a-Roadmap-for-seamless-cooperation_Sept-2018.pdf> accessed 14 July 2023.

28 Commission, Strengthening AML supervision (n 13).

29 Commission, Strengthening AML supervision (n 13) 2.

30 Needless to say, the EBA already contributed in a general way to the monitoring of AML requirements in the field of its prudential supervision (see Commission, Strengthening AML supervision (n 13) 4 and 6; Reflection paper cooperation (n 27) 2 ff; Harry Huizinga, *The Supervisory Approach to Anti-money Laundering: an Analysis of the Joint Working Group's Reflection Paper* (European Parliament Economic Governance Support Unit, PE 624.424 November 2018) 7 f.).

31 Art. 9a and 9b Council Regulation (EU) 2019/2175 of the European Parliament and of the Council of 18 December 2019 amending Regulation (EU) No 1093/2010 establishing a European Supervisory Authority (European Banking Authority), Regulation (EU) No 1094/2010 establishing a European Supervisory Authority (European Insurance and Occupational Pensions Authority), Regulation (EU) No 1095/2010 establishing a European Supervisory Authority (European Securities and Markets Authority), Regulation (EU) No 600/2014 on markets in financial instruments, Regulation (EU) 2016/1011 on indices used as benchmarks in financial instruments and financial contracts or to measure the performance of investment funds, and Regulation (EU) 2015/847 on information accompanying transfers of funds [2019] OJ L 334/1 of 27.12.2019; see also for details, Gianni Lo Schiavo, 'The Single Supervisory Mechanism (SSM) and the EU Anti-Money Laundering Framework Compared: Governance, Rules, Challenges and Opportunities' (2022) 23(1) Journal of Banking Regulation 91, 97 f.

32 Commission, Strengthening AML supervision (n 13) 11.

33 Commission, Implementation AML framework (n 5) 5.

Commission therefore reiterated the idea of harmonising specific AML supervisory tasks at the Union level among other measures.[34] Following the reports of July 2019, the European Commission established on 13 May 2020 an Action Plan for a comprehensive Union policy on preventing money laundering and terrorist financing.[35] The Action Plan is based on six pillars: 1) ensuring the effective implementation of the existing EU AML framework; 2) establishing an EU single rule book on AML; 3) bringing about EU-level AML supervision; 4) establishing a support and cooperation mechanism for financial intelligence units (FIUs); 5) enforcing Union-level criminal law provisions and information exchange; 6) strengthening the international dimension of the EU AML framework.

Following the Action Plan, the European Commission presented on 20 July 2021 a legislative package[36] aimed at strengthening the EU AML regime and containing four proposals: 1) a regulation establishing a new AML authority;[37] 2) a regulation on AML rules that will be directly applicable to the private sector;[38] 3) a 6th AML Directive replacing the 4th one and containing provisions on areas in which Member States need some leeway, such as rules on national supervisors and FIUs;[39] 4) the revision of the 2015 Regulation on Transfers of Funds to trace transfers of crypto-assets.[40] The creation of the EU-level AML supervisory authority is announced as the masterpiece

34 Commission, Implementation AML framework (n 5) 5.

35 Commission, 'Action Plan for a comprehensive Union policy on preventing money laundering and terrorist financing (2020/C 164/06)' (Communication) C/2020/2800, OJ C 164/21 of 13.05.2020 (Commission, Action plan ML).

36 The legislative proposals are based on Art. 114 of the TFEU.

37 Commission, 'Proposal for a regulation of the European Parliament and of the Council establishing the Authority for Anti-Money Laundering and Countering the Financing of Terrorism and amending Regulations (EU) No 1093/2010, (EU) No 1094/2010, (EU) No 1095/2010' COM (2021) 421 final.

38 Commission, 'Proposal for a Regulation of the European Parliament and of the Council on the prevention of the use of the financial system for the purposes of money laundering or terrorist financing' COM (2021) 420 final (AML Regulation Proposal).

39 Commission, 'Proposal for a directive of the European Parliament and of the Council on the mechanisms to be put in place by the Member States for the prevention of the use of the financial system for the purposes of money laundering or terrorist financing and repealing Directive (EU) 2015/849' COM (2021) 423 final.

40 Commission, 'Proposal for a Regulation of the European Parliament and of the Council on information accompanying transfers of funds and certain crypto-assets (recast)' COM (2021) 422 final.

of the proposed measures.[41] This new European "watchdog" has been described as "a game changer" in the fight against money laundering.[42]

The Council adopted its position on the proposal in June 2022 (with the exception of the location of the new AMLA).[43] In March 2023, the joint competent committee of the European Parliament voted on a draft report amending the Commission proposal.[44] Interinstitutional negotiations between the European Parliament and the Council – with the support of the Commission[45] – followed shortly after.[46] In December 2023,

41 Refer to the following page of the Commission's website about a Proposal for a Directive on Anti-Money Laundering and Countering the Financing of Terrorism legislative package (Directorate-General for Financial Stability, Financial Services and Capital Markets Union, 20 July 2021) <https://finance.ec.europa.eu/publications/anti-money-laundering-and-countering-financing-terrorism-legislative-package_en> accessed 14 July 2023; see also Frank Meyer, 'A New EU Anti-Money Laundering Tsar' in Yvan Jeanneret and Bernhard Sträuli (eds), *Empreinte d'une pionnière sur le droit pénal: Mélanges en l'honneur de Ursula Cassani* (Schulthess 2021) 281, 283.

42 Refer to the quotes of Eva Maria Poptcheva, member of the European Parliament and co-rapporteur, on behalf of the Economic and Monetary Affairs Committee on a Regulation establishing the Anti-Money Laundering Authority, available at <https://multimedia.europarl.europa.eu/en/video/EP148202> accessed 10 July 2023 and to the quotes of Mairead McGuinness, Commissioner for Financial Services, Financial Stability and Capital Markets Union at the European Commission, 'Commission welcomes political agreement on the Regulation to establish the new Anti-Money Laundering Authority (AMLA)' available at <https://finance.ec.europa.eu/news/commission-welcomes-political-agreement-regulation-establish-new-anti-money-laundering-authority-2023-12-13> accessed 13 February 2024.

43 Commission, 'Proposal for a Regulation of the European Parliament and of the Council establishing the Authority for Anti-Money Laundering and Countering the Financing of Terrorism and amending Regulations (EU) No 1093/2010, (EU) No 1094/2010, (EU) No 1095/2010', COM (2021) 421 final (AML Authority Proposal), available at <https://www.consilium.europa.eu/en/press/press-releases/2022/06/29/new-eu-authority-for-anti-money-laundering-council-agrees-its-partial-position/> accessed 14 July 2023.

44 European Parliament Committee on Economic and Monetary Affairs and Committee on Civil Liberties, Justice and Home Affairs, 'Report on the proposal for a regulation of the European Parliament and of the Council establishing the Authority for Anti-Money Laundering and Countering the Financing of Terrorism and amending Regulations (EU) No 1093/2010, (EU) No 1094/2010, (EU) No 1095/2010' [2023] A9-0128/2023 of 05.04.2023 (joint committee draught report).

45 See Rule 74 § 2 of the Rules of Procedure of the European Parliament <https://www.europarl.europa.eu/olp/en/interinstitutional-negotiations> accessed 14 July 2023.

46 European Parliament, 'Stopping the flow of dirty money: Parliament ready for negotiations' (Press Release, 19.04.2023), <https://www.europarl.europa.eu/news/en/press-room/20230414IPR80123/stopping-the-flow-of-dirty-money-parliament-ready-for-negotiations> accessed 14 July 2023.

the Parliament and the Council reached a provisional agreement.[47] On 22 February 2024, the Council and the Parliament decided that the new AMLA will be based in Frankfurt, will have over 400 staff members, and will be operational mid-2025.[48] The text was formally adopted on 31 May 2024.[49]

One remark should be made at this point. While the first EU directives were implementing the FATF standards, and the FATF is traditionally considered as the global AML standard-setter, one can say that, in recent years, the EU took the lead. The EU wants its standards to go beyond those of the FATF and is willing to take on the key role in the fight against money laundering,[50] as demonstrated by the constant and ever more frequent amendments of the AML EU regulations. EU rules are primarily of concern for Member States; however, they nonetheless cannot be ignored by third countries for three main reasons. First, some EU provisions deal with the relations between EU institutions and third-country entities, obliging *de facto* these institutions to have equivalent standards.[51] Second, EU-based branches of companies situated in third countries are subject to EU legislation.[52] Third, the FATF may be guided by the EU regime while amending or revising its recommendations.

III. The new anti-money laundering supervisory authority

A. The tasks of the new anti-money laundering supervisory authority

The new EU AML supervisory authority (hereafter: EU AMLA) will have three tasks which aim at a more efficient and harmonised implementation of AML regulations:

---

47 Council of the European Union, 'Anti-money laundering: Council and Parliament agree to create new authority' (Press Release, 13.12.2023), <https://www.consilium.europa.eu/en/press/press-releases/2023/12/13/anti-money-laundering-council-and-parliament-agree-to-create-new-authority/> accessed 12 February 2024; Commission, 'Proposal for a Regulation of the European Parliament and of the Council establishing the Authority for Anti-Money Laundering and Countering the Financing of Terrorism and amending Regulations (EU) No 1093/2010, (EU) No 1094/2010, (EU) No 1095/2010' COM (2021) 421 final 2021/0240 (COD) – Confirmation of the final compromise text with a view to agreement of 12.02.2024.

48 Council of the European Union, 'Frankfurt to host the EU's new anti-money laundering authority (AMLA)' (Press Release, 22 February 2024) <https://www.consilium.europa.eu/fr/press/press-releases/2024/02/22/frankfurt-to-host-the-eus-new-anti-money-laundering-authority-amla/> accessed 23 February 2024.

49 Regulation (EU) 2024/1620 of the European Parliament and of the Council of 31 May 2024 establishing the Authority for Anti-Money Laundering and Countering the Financing of Terrorism and amending Regulations (EU) No 1093/2010, (EU) No 1094/2010 and (EU) No 1095/2010 (hereafter: the Regulation).

50 Commission, Action plan ML (n 35) 1.

51 See, for instance, Art. 12 § 3 or 18bis 4th AML Directive (n 7).

52 Art. 3 (2) (f) 4th AML Directive (n 7).

1) direct supervision of selected financial sector obligated entities; 2) indirect supervision of non-selected obliged entities and non-financial obliged entities; 3) coordination and support for FIUs.

1. *Direct supervision of selected financial sector obliged entities*

According to Article 5 (2) of the Regulation, "direct supervision" means: a) ensuring compliance of the selected entities with anti-money laundering and financing of terrorism (ML/FT) requirements, including obligations related to the implementation of targeted financial sanctions; b) verifying compliance on a risk-based approach and, if appropriate, imposing specific requirements, administrative measures, and pecuniary sanctions; c) participating in group-wide supervision, in particular in colleges of supervisors; d) developing and maintaining a system to assess the risks and vulnerabilities of the selected entities.

The selection of the directly supervised entities is based on two cumulative factors: the ML/FT risk profile and the provision of services in at least six Member States (Article 12, recital 20 and 26). The risk profile will be assessed at the level of the group (Article 12 § 3 and recital 26). The methodology and criteria to select the entities will be detailed in regulatory technical standards developed by the EU AMLA and adopted by the Commission (Article 12 § 3, Article 49, recital 22, and Art. 290 of the Treaty on the Functioning of the European Union (TFEU)).[53] The work carried out by the European Banking Authority should constitute a starting point for the development of the methodology and criteria (recital 22). In an initial selection process, the text provides for the direct supervision of 40 entities (Article 13 § 2 *a contrario* and recital 26). This first selection process is scheduled for July 2027 (Article 13 § 4). In addition, in order to ensure complete coverage of the internal market in the long term, the EU AMLA could then supervise: 1) more than 40 entities if a greater number of entities qualify for direct supervision; and 2) at least one entity per Member State (Article 13 § 2, 3 and recital 26) in the context of subsequent selection processes. Selection processes should occur every three years (Article 13 § 4).

A second category of entities could be subject to direct supervision, but – in principle – for a maximum period of three years: it concerns entities that seriously or systematically violate the AML requirements if the appropriate measures are not implemented at the national level or information of the steps taken is not provided to the EU AMLA (Article 32 recitals 19 and 36 ff).

Article 16 of the Regulation stipulates the creation of a Joint Supervisory Team for each selected entity. Each team shall be composed of staff from the EU AMLA and from each financial regulator responsible for the supervision of the entity at the national

---

53 The idea of such a selection process is to leave no discretion to the EU AMLA or the national supervisors in deciding the list of the directly supervised entities, with the objective of warranting a level playing field among the selected companies: recital 18 of the Regulation (n 49).

level. The access to the relevant information by the EU AMLA is regulated in Articles 17 ff of the Regulation.

As supervision must be paired with enforcement mechanisms, the EU AMLA is vested with the power to take measures and pecuniary sanctions in case of breaches of AML requirements (Articles 21 ff).[54] A temporary ban from exercising managerial functions in obliged entities can be pronounced against natural persons (Article 21 § 3 let. (e)).

2. *Indirect supervision of non-selected obliged entities and non-financial obliged entities*

With regard to indirect supervision, the tasks of the EU AMLA will mainly revolve around the performance of periodic assessments of the activities of the financial supervisors (Article 5 § 3 let. (b) and Article 30), respectively the conduct of peer reviews of the activities of supervisory authorities in the non-financial sector (Article 5 § 4 let. (b) to (d) and Article 35), as well as a role of supporter, coordinator, and arbitrator among the national supervisors (Article 5 § 3 let. (d) to (h), Articles 5 § 4 let. (e) to (9), 31, 33 and 36).

Moreover, financial supervisors will have to notify the EU AMLA when the situation of any non-selected obliged entity regarding its compliance with AML requirements and its exposure to money laundering and terrorism financing risks deteriorates significantly. This concerns particularly the case where the deterioration occurs in such a way that it may negatively impact several Member States or the Union as a whole (Article 32 § 1).

If a violation by a non-selected entity of its AML requirements occurs, the EU AMLA could invite the national supervisor to act in relation to the company involved. If the national supervisor does not respond, the EU AMLA may ask the Commission to grant permission to supervise the entity for a limited period (Article 32 § 5 ff). A request for direct supervision of non-compliant entities by the EU AMLA can also come from the national supervisor (recital 19 and Article 5 § 3 let. (c)). Furthermore, the Regulation provides a procedure in case of systematic failures of supervision (Article 34), which can lead to the issuing of a "formal opinion" by the Commission requiring the supervisor to comply with Union law (Article 34 § 6 and recital 35).

With respect to the supervisory authorities in the non-financial sector, the EU AMLA may investigate possible breaches of the AML regulations by non-financial supervisors (Article 32). If the supervisory authority fails to comply, this can lead to a warning detailing the breaches and identifying measures to be implemented (Article 37 § 4).

54 On the sanctioning powers of the Authority, see Laura Katharina Sophia Neumann, 'Das Sanktionenrecht der vorgeschlagenen EU-Agentur für die Bekämpfung von Geldwäsche und Terrorismusfinanzierung (AMLA)' (2021) 12 Neue Zeitschrift für Wirtschafts-, Steuer- u. Unternehmensstrafrecht 449.

The warning is addressed to the counterpart supervisors in other Member States or, where the supervisor is a self-regulatory body, to its public authority (Article 37 § 4).

3. *Coordination and support for financial intelligence units*

The function of FIUs is to receive suspicious transaction reports from obliged entities, to conduct their own analysis about the suspicious nature of the reported case and, where appropriate, to disseminate the results to the competent authorities (e.g., the criminal authorities).[55] FIUs thus play a filter and transmission belt role between obliged entities and criminal authorities.[56] In order to fulfil their tasks, FIUs may collect data, notably from obliged entities; however, they are not intended to have any supervisory or law enforcement powers.[57] FIUs may be part of another authority; however, given that they must be operationally independent, their core functions must be distinct from those of the other authority.[58] They may be considered the information hub.

The European Commission considered the option of creating an EU-level FIU.[59] It did not pursue it, due to the fact that such an option: 1) would require actions in areas going beyond the legal framework of the proposed reform; 2) would be counterproductive since the efficiency of FIUs is based on their access to information at the national level; 3) would be very expensive; and 4) did not have the support of the Member States.[60]

The simpler option of enhancing the efficiency of the national FIUs was therefore preferred. In this respect, the four main tasks of the EU AMLA are as follows: 1) when needed, the conduct of joint analysis with one or several national FIUs (Article 5 § 5 let. (d) and Article 40);[61] 2) the organisation and facilitation of some activities such as training programmes, personnel exchange programmes, expertise sharing, and development of IT tools and services to enhance the analysis methods of FIUs (Article 45 § 1) the hosting, management, maintenance, and development of a common database: the FIU.net (which is currently hosted by the Commission) (Article 47); 4) the conduct of peer reviews regarding the fulfilment by FIUs of their mission (Article 48). Moreover, an individual request for assistance may be submitted by a national FIU (Article 45 § 2) and the EU AMLA may act as a mediator in case of disagreement between FIUs (Article 46).

---

55 See Art. 29 of the FATF Recommendations and Interpretative Note; General Glossary of the FATF, Definition of "competent authorities".

56 Cassani Ursula, *Droit pénal économique* (Helbing Lichtenhahn 2020) 267.

57 See Art. 29 of the FATF Recommendation and Interpretative Note.

58 See section E.8 f. of the Interpretative Note of Art. 29 of the FATF Recommendations; see also Art. 39 § 3 of the Regulation, which provides, "where necessary", for an organisational separation within the EU AMLA for the tasks related to the FIUs mechanism.

59 Commission staff working document, Impact assessment (n 13) 35.

60 Commission staff working document, Impact assessment (n 13) 47 and 78.

61 The principle of the joint analyses has been established in the 4th AML Directive (n 7) (Recital 55 and Art. 51).

The communication between FIUs and the EU AMLA will be assumed by the delegation of one or several staff members of the FIUs to the EU AMLA, who will be located at the seat of the EU AMLA (Article 44).

B. The architecture of the new anti-money laundering supervisory authority

As part of its reflection on the creation of an EU-level AML supervisory authority, the European Commission considered the option of extending the mandate of the EBA, which currently already has some indirect supervisory powers in the area of AML regulations,[62] to direct supervisory powers.[63] It abandoned the idea in light of the differences in the tasks that EU AML supervision would require compared to the actual functions of the EBA.[64]

The EU AMLA will be composed of five bodies: 1) a General Board; 2) an Executive Board; 3) a Chair of the EU AMLA; 4) an Executive Director; 5) an Administrative Board of Review (Article 56).

The General Board will be two-headed: it will have a supervisory composition and an FIU composition (Article 57 § 1). In relation to the former, the General Board will be composed of the Chair of the EU AMLA (with a right to vote), the heads of the supervisory authorities of the obliged entities in each Member State (with a right to vote), and one representative of the Commission (without a right to vote) (Article 57 § 2). The functions of the General Board mainly revolve around the development of cooperation and mutual assistance between the EU AMLA and national supervisors (Article 60 § 1 *cum* Articles 7 to 10) and the adoption of draughts of technical standards,[65] recommendations, guidelines, and so on (Article 60 § 4). As to the FIU side, the General Board will be composed of the Chair of the EU AMLA (with a right to vote), the heads of the FIUs (with a right to vote), and one representative of the Commission (without a right to vote) (Article 57 § 3). It will perform the tasks of coordination and support to the national FIUs as summarised under Section A.3 (Article 60 § 3).

The Executive Board will be composed of the Chair of the EU AMLA, five full-time members (including the Vice-Chair), and, in relation to some of its tasks, a representative of the Commission (Article 63). The Executive Board is especially responsible for the execution of the functions of the EU AMLA as summarised under Sections A.1 and 2 (Article 64 § 1).

The Chair of the EU AMLA represents the institution and must prepare the work of the General Board and the Executive Board (Article 69).

---

62 See Section II and note 31.

63 Commission staff working document, Impact assessment (n 13) 77.

64 Commission staff working document, Impact assessment (n 13) 77 f.

65 The formal adoption of the standards falls within the competence of the Commission, see Art. 49 and 53 of the Regulation (n 49).

The Executive Director is in charge of the day-to-day management of the EU AMLA (Article 71 § 1). He/she is notably responsible for implementing the decisions adopted by the Executive Board (Article 71 § 1 let. (a)), the EU AMLA's budget (Article 79 § 1 let. (i)), and the annual work programme[66] of the EU AMLA under the control of the Executive Board (Article 79 § 1 let. (k)). The text underlines the independence of the function (Article 70 § 2).

The Administrative Board of Review will be established for the purpose of carrying out an internal administrative review of the supervisory and sanctioning decisions taken by the Executive Board against the selected obliged entities, and the decisions regarding the fees due by the entities (Articles 72 § 1 and 74 § 1) that are a source of funding for the EU AMLA (Article 77). It should be composed of five people and take its decisions based on a simple majority (Article 72 § 2 and 3). The decisions of the Administrative Board of Review regarding the measures and sanctions pronounced against selected obliged entities should be subject to appeal by the European Court of Justice (recital 67 and Article 28).

IV. Perspectives

The creation of an EU AML supervisory authority follows the current trend towards an EU-centralised supervision for the implementation of Union law.[67] Scholars drew the parallel with the prudential supervision of the single supervisory mechanism (SSM) applicable to the banking sector.[68]

The future EU AMLA was born out of one finding and one hypothesis: the observation that there were severe deficiencies in the implementation of AML requirements by the obliged entities and the assumption that the sole national authorities are not able to remedy the situation.

In relation to the (presumed) shortcomings in applying the AML regime, it is very difficult to measure the scale of the phenomenon given the lack of data.[69] It seems,

---

66 According to Art. 65 of the Regulation (n 49), the annual work programme should comprise detailed objectives and expected results including performance indicators; it shall also contain a description of the actions to be financed and an indication of the financial and human resources allocated to each action in accordance with the principles of activity-based budgeting and management.

67 See Georgios Pavlidis, 'The Birth of the New Anti-Money Laundering Authority: Harnessing the Power of EU-Wide Supervision' (2023) 30 Journal of Financial Crime 3.

68 See Schlarb (n 26); Schiavo (n 31).

69 See Vogel (n 7) 893; Allegrezza (n 14) 14; Joshua Kirschenbaum and Nicolas Véron, 'A better European Union architecture to fight money laundering' (2018) 19 Bruegel Policy Contribution, 14; Commission staff working document, Impact assessment (n 13) 60.

however, that there are enough recent known cases which reveal the deficiencies in implementing the AML duties[70] and therefore demonstrate the need to improve the effective application of the law.

Regarding the (presumed) inadequacies of a national response, several issues were raised. First of all, national disparities in the implementation of the AML regime were highlighted. The potential regulator's lenience towards domestic banks was evoked.[71] There is a recurring and ongoing problem of cooperation between the various actors (national supervisors, FIUs, prudential supervisors, criminal authorities).[72]

In our view, the argument of the uneven implementation of the AML framework has not been correctly formulated: the underlying issue is that the supervision of some national regulators (for various reasons, notably lack of human resources)[73] is not sufficiently effective.[74] More than the question of the different applications of common standards, the issue is the failed application of these standards. One point should be emphasised at this stage. The lack of clarity of the EU current framework and the degree of discretion of the Member States in transposing the AML directive have been identified as causes for the shortcomings in the implementation of the AML regime.[75] This will lead to the transformation of the AML directives into a regulation. This step appears to be coherent with the general evolution of the EU AML regime and resolves the problem of the (non)transposition of the directives.[76] It is, however, our assumption that the main problem lies in the non-implementation of the existing rules. If these rules were observed – following a bona fide interpretation where applicable – then only a "residue" of issues would remain.[77] It seems to us that the argument of a lack of clarity is regularly used to "justify" the non-application of norms whose essence is not so difficult to comprehend. Nonetheless, the hypothesis of the EU AML revision is that a supranational EU Authority will be better positioned to implement the EU AML regime than (at least some) national supervisors.

70 See, in particular, Commission, 'Report from the Commission to the European Parliament and the Council on the assessment of recent alleged money laundering cases involving EU credit institutions' COM (2019) 373 final.

71 See Huizinga (30) 9; Schlarb (n 26) 76 f.

72 See Commission, Implementation AML framework (n 5) 4 f.; Commission, Action plan ML (n 35) 4 and 8. EBA, Report on the future *AML/CFT* framework in the EU, EBA/OP/2020/25, § 68 ff. One of the objectives of the 5th AML Directive was precisely to enhance cooperation between all relevant authorities (Commission, Strengthening AML supervision (n 13) 1 f., fn. 7); EBA, 'Report on competent authorities' approaches to the supervision of banks with respect to anti-money laundering and Countering the Financing of terrorism (round 3–2022)' EBA/REP/2023/20, 38 ff (EBA Report 2023).

73 See Commission staff working document, Impact assessment (n 13) 19.

74 See also, for the shortcomings observed, EBA Report 2023 (n 72).

75 See Commission staff working document, Impact assessment (n 13) 3 and 8.

76 See Commission staff working document, Impact assessment (n 13) 73; Allegrezza (n 14) 20.

77 In the same direction, Allegrezza (14).

Regarding the issue of the preferential treatment of domestic institutions – should this prove to be the case – it seems a priori clear that a supranational authority appears more likely to guarantee its independence than the national regulators.

As for the shortcomings identified in the cooperation between the authorities involved in the AML regime, it is assumed that the direct supervision of some worldwide entities will solve the difficulties linked to the necessary coordination of the various national regulators in charge of the supervision of these companies. Moreover, the hypothesis is that a centralised AML supervisory system will promote an "efficient cooperation between all relevant competent authorities".[78] Concerning the cooperation between FIUs, it is precisely one of the objectives of the EU AMLA to play the role of coordinator between these units.

V. Challenges

The challenge faced by the EU AMLA clearly is to accomplish the ambitions it has been assigned. This will first depend on the allocated resources and political aspects that influence the organisation and the operation of the institution during and after the legislative process.[79] Aside from these "general" elements, the functioning of the supranational supervisory system will most likely rely on the cooperation and sharing of information with the national authorities. In particular, we think of the types of channels that could be used for this collaboration, considering the need for promptness that is essential for successful collaboration. In this regard, a challenge will be to determine the means for effective cooperation while at the same time respecting the requirements pertaining to fundamental rights of the persons involved – for example, data protection and procedural guarantees in proceedings.

Regarding direct supervision, more importantly than a single cooperation, what should take place is a real understanding within the Joint Supervisory Team and, more broadly, among other people involved in the supervision of the selected entity. It would be counterproductive to have a hierarchical relation between the staff from the Authority and the staff from the national supervisor. Depending on the (effective) functioning of the national supervision, more or less leeway should be provided to the national supervisor to take some (informal) decisions or, at least, make the relevant propositions.

One could moreover argue that mutual trust between the supervised entity and the regulator is an essential prerequisite to effective supervision (whether in the area of prudential supervision or AML supervision) and that such trust exists between the national supervisor and the institution.[80] In our view, however, an (overly) close

78 Recital 16 of the Regulation (n 49); see also Recital 79.
79 See Pavlidis (n 67) 6.
80 See Vogel (n 7) 1012.

relationship between the regulator and the entity can lead to lenience, which was one of the criticisms associated with national supervision. Nevertheless, it provides an additional argument in favour of leaving some flexibility to the (representatives of) the national authority in order to keep the dialogue open with the supervised entity.[81]

Concerns were also raised about the creation of a new authority, due to the geographical distance which complicates communication between the domestic authorities instead of facilitating it.[82] In our opinion, the problem of geographical distance should, however, be put in perspective considering the current means of communication. Moreover, national supervisors could remain the channel of information between the directly obliged entities and the EU AMLA. Concerning cooperation with foreign counterparts, the establishment of a supranational authority does not make collaboration more difficult *per se*. It will be precisely one of the challenges of the new institution, notably through its organisation and structure, to effectively enhance collaboration between the various actors and not represent an obstacle to it.

In relation to the (basic) EU AMLA's tasks pertaining to the supervision of non-financial institutions, it seems to us that it will, in any case, serve to contribute to raising awareness of vulnerable sectors that do not feel adequately involved in the fight against money laundering.

Finally, it seems quite clear that an effective coordination and support mechanism for FIUs, combined with a good database, contributed to the provision of interconnected information that is the "raisons d'être" of FIUs. Nevertheless, FIUs are facing fundamental problems regarding their real objective and, consequently, what happens to the information gathered,[83] excessive information sorting[84] and so on. These issues need to be addressed independently of the creation of the new EU AMLA (even if the development of IT tools will obviously help with information sorting).

---

81 Refer also to the comments of Ms Danièle Nouy, Chair of the ECB Supervisory Board from 2014 to 2018, regarding the supranational supervisory mechanism over banks: "the very close cooperation with national authorities helped the system to benefit from the best of both worlds – to have the experience of national supervisors, while also keeping some distance from individual banks in the Supervisory Board" (General Secretariat of the Council, 'Partial summary record of the meeting of the Committee on Economic and Monetary Affairs (ECON) of the European Parliament, held in Brussels on 3 and 4 November 2014', p. 3 available at <http://data.consilium.europa.eu/doc/document/ST-15376-2014-INIT/en/pdf> accessed 31 July 2023).

82 Vogel (n 7) 1011 f.; see also the opinion of the ECB (n 15) § 3.1.

83 See Vogel (n 7) 935 ff.

84 See Katia Villard, 'Art. 9' in Ursula Cassani, Christian Bovet, and Katia Villard (eds), *Commentaire romand: Loi sur le blanchiment d'argent* (Helbing Lichtenhahn 2022) 406 f.

VI. Conclusion

The new European authority has been qualified as a "game changer" in the fight against money laundering. We are a little less optimistic. The failures of the AML supranational policy[85] will not be resolved simply by the establishment of such a new institution, even if it meets all its objectives. It does not mean, however, that the creation of this EU AMLA is not worthwhile.

The EU is already trialling supranational supervision notably with the European Central Bank (ECB) and its direct prudential supervision over some banks. An AML supranational supervision can be inspired by the experience of prudential supranational supervision.[86] To the best of our knowledge, the powers conferred to the ECB are not called into question.

The scale of the phenomenon of money laundering and its cross-border dimension requires a coordinated and supranational fight. It seems that the addition of the "national forces" is not sufficient not only to establish the legislative framework but also to enforce it. It is not insignificant that some representatives of the civil society have also asked for a supranational authority.[87] The creation of such an institution appears to be the logical development of the integrated single financial market in which the laundering of illicit funds takes place[88] and the necessary internationalisation of the fight against money laundering.

---

85 For a list of failures, refer to Javier Doz Orrit and Benjamin Rizzo, Opinion of the European Economic and Social Committee on 'Proposal for a Regulation of the European Parliament and of the Council on the prevention of the use of the financial system for the purposes of money laundering or terrorist financing' [2021] OJ C 152/89 of 06.04.2022, § 3.6; for the detailed outcomes of an in-depth analysis, see also Vogel (n 7) 881–1025.

86 Refer also to the comparison of Schlarb (n 26) between the two regimes.

87 See Bloomberg Opinion Editorial Board, 'A Latvian Bank Shows the ECB Needs New Powers', *Bloomberg* (19 March 2018) <https://www.bloomberg.com/opinion/articles/2018-03-19/latvia-s-ablv-bank-has-a-lesson-for-the-ecb> accessed 16 July 2024; Roula Khalaf, 'The EU is Losing its Battle Against Money Laundering' *Financial Times* (London, 5 July 2018) <https://www.ft.com/content/92e131da-8047-11e8-bc55-50daf11b720d> accessed 16 July 2024.

88 Refer also to the reasoning of Kirschenbaum and Véron (n 69) 14 ff.

10 Traceability of crypto-asset transfers under the new EU AML/CFT regime: the crypto travel rule between challenges and open issues

Nadia Pocher

I. Introduction

In 2022, more than USD 31 billion flowed from illicit crypto-asset addresses to services such as crypto-asset exchanges.[1] The year after, the illicit crypto-asset flow amounted to about USD 22 billion, partially mirroring the overall drop in crypto-asset transaction volume following the 2022–23 Crypto Winter.[2] In this timeframe, the crash of Terra-Luna led to the bankruptcy of several leading actors in the decentralised finance space, as well as banks with significant crypto-asset exposures.[3] Following the collapse of the second largest crypto-asset exchange, FTX, in November 2022, the co-founder and former CEO Sam Bankman-Fried was found guilty of several counts of fraud and conspiracy.[4] Meanwhile, in February 2024, the US government fined the

---

1 Chainalysis, 'The Chainalysis 2024 Crypto Crime Report' (2024) 23 <https://go.chainalysis.com/crypto-crime-2024.html> accessed 10 November 2024.

2 ibid. Douglas W Arner and others, 'The Financialization of Crypto: Lessons from FTX and the Crypto Winter of 2022–2023' (2023) University of Hong Kong Faculty of Law Research Paper No. 2023/19 <https://papers.ssrn.com/sol3/papers.cfm?abstract_id=4372516> accessed 10 November 2024.

3 A primary case is that of Silicon Valley Bank. Dirk A Zetzsche and others, 'Remaining Regulatory Challenges in Digital Finance and Crypto-assets after MICA' (Committee on Economic and Monetary Affairs (ECON), Policy Department for Economic, Scientific and Quality of Life Policies, European Parliament, May 2023) 31 <https://www.europarl.europa.eu/RegData/etudes/STUD/2023/740083/IPOL_STU(2023)740083_EN.pdf> accessed 10 November 2024.

4 Luc Cohen and Jody Godoy, 'Sam Bankman-Fried Convicted of Multi-billion Dollar FTX Fraud' (*Reuters*, New York, 3 November 2023) <https://www.reuters.com/legal/ftx-founder-sam-bankman-fried-thought-rules-did-not-apply-him-prosecutor-says-2023-11-02/> accessed 10 November 2024.

largest crypto-asset exchange, Binance, USD 4.3 billion for money laundering,[5] amidst other charges that included market manipulation.[6] The co-founder and former CEO Changpeng Zhao had to step down and pay a personal fine of USD 50 million.[7] As it becomes relatively common for crypto-asset exchanges to face charges for failure to comply with laws and regulations, this poses an existential concern for the framework to prevent the misuse of financial systems for purposes of money laundering and terrorist financing (AML/CFT).

The vulnerability of crypto-assets to financial turmoil is far from new. From the events of the Silk Road darknet marketplace and the Mt. Gox exchange in the 2010s, to the alleged involvement of Tornado Cash in the laundering of USD 1 billion in 2023,[8] the perception of crypto-assets as a means to achieve unaccountability in value transfers keeps generating concerns. Meanwhile, alongside advances in crypto-asset analytics, the techniques deployed to engage in illicit activities become increasingly sophisticated.[9] In 2023, USD 743.8 million were sent from illicit addresses primarily linked to ransomware attacks to cross-chain bridge protocols,[10] compared to only USD 312.2 million in 2022.[11] Further, not only has the crypto-asset space overall emerged as not as decentralised as advertised,[12] but this holds true also for illicit activities: in 2023, more than two-thirds of all illicit funds sent to off-ramping services (i.e., services that allow one to "cash out" crypto-assets) were sent to five services.[13]

5 Jonathan Stempel, 'Judge Approves Binance $4.3 Billion Guilty Plea as US Seeks to Modify Founder Zhao's Bond' (*Reuters*, New York, 23 February 2024) <https://www.reuters.com/technology/judge-approves-binance-43-billion-guilty-plea-us-seeks-modify-founder-zhaos-bond-2024-02-23/> accessed 10 November 2024.

6 U.S. Securities and Exchange Commission, 'SEC Files 13 Charges Against Binance Entities and Founder Changpeng Zhao' (SEC Press Release, Washington DC, 5 June 2023) <https://www.sec.gov/news/press-release/2023-101> accessed 10 November 2024.

7 Chris Prentice, David Lawder, and Jonathan Stempel, 'Binance's Zhao Pleads Guilty, Steps Down to Settle US Illicit Finance Probe' *Reuters* (New York, 22 November 2023) <https://www.reuters.com/markets/us/us-authorities-set-unveil-settlement-with-binance-source-2023-11-21/> accessed 10 November 2024.

8 Southern District of New York, 'Tornado Cash Founders Charged With Money Laundering and Sanctions Violations' (U.S. Attorney's Office Press Release, New York, 23 August 2023) <https://www.justice.gov/usao-sdny/pr/tornado-cash-founders-charged-money-laundering-and-sanctions-violations> accessed 10 November 2024.

9 Nadia Pocher and others, 'Detecting Anomalous Cryptocurrency Transactions: An AML/CFT Application of Machine Learning-Based Forensics' (2023) 33 Electronic Markets 37.

10 For more insights into cross-chain bridges: Sung-Shine Lee and others, 'SoK: Not Quite Water Under the Bridge: Review of Cross-Chain Bridge Hacks' (2023, IEEE International Conference on Blockchain and Cryptocurrency).

11 Chainalysis (n 1) 25, 32.

12 Tom Barbereau and others, 'Decentralised Finance's Timocratic Governance: The Distribution and Exercise of Tokenised Voting Rights' (2023) 73 Technology in Society.

13 Chainalysis (n 1) 26.

The international AML/CFT regime has long fought against the circulation of illicit money through transfers of funds, as it significantly threatens financial integrity and stability. Well before the advent of crypto-assets, strategies to "follow the money" have been deployed to constrain the activities of criminal groups by targeting their economic resources.[14] Various forensic techniques are deployed to monitor and investigate financial transactions, and constantly evolve to account for emerging technologies and decentralisation.[15] Despite the advancements in transaction analytics, however, one of the backbones of the efforts to ensure accountability in the financial space is that of securing the traceability of transactions.

This chapter explores the obligations laid out by the "(crypto) travel rule" both at an international and EU level, with specific reference to the new measures introduced by the EU AML Package. It does so by considering the broader expansion of the AML/CFT measures to the crypto-asset field, as well as pinpointing major challenges to their effective implementation.

II. Crypto-asset service providers and the AML/CFT framework

The measures to prevent and repress money laundering and terrorist financing comprise criminal sanctions as well as compliance duties qualified in several ways (e.g., civil, administrative) depending on the legal system. As a field where regulatory action often intertwines with the socio-economic context – for example, organised crime-related factors, tax crimes such as tax evasion, and fiscal policies – the fight against financial crime tends to be in the political limelight and exposed to territorial fragmentation. The gist of AML/CFT measures, however, tends towards global coherence in the form of compliance with the standards laid out by the Financial Action Task Force (FATF), an international organisation established in 1989. Although the FATF Standards, known as Recommendations, are instruments of soft law, participating jurisdictions are committed to transposing them into national law through individual regulatory and operational initiatives.[16] In this regard, the FATF cooperates closely with regional bodies and organisations such as the International Monetary Fund (IMF), the World Bank, and the United Nations (UN).[17]

---

14 William F Wechsler, 'Follow the Money' (2001) 80(4) Foreign Affairs 40.

15 Nick Furneaux, *Investigating Cryptocurrencies: Understanding, Extracting, and Analyzing Blockchain Evidence* (Wiley 2018); Pocher and others (n 9).

16 Iwona Karasek-Wojciechowicz, 'Reconciliation of Anti-Money Laundering Instruments and European Data Protection Requirements in Permissionless Blockchain Spaces' (2021) 7(1) Journal of Cybersecurity 2 <https://academic.oup.com/cybersecurity/article/doi/10.1093/cybsec/tyab004/6166133>.

17 FATF, 'International Standards on Combating Money Laundering and the Financing of Terrorism & Proliferation: The FATF Recommendations' (*FATF*, 2012) 8 <https://www.fatf-gafi.org/en/publications/Fatfrecommendations/Fatf-recommendations.html> accessed 10 November 2024.

The final goal of AML/CFT measures is to prevent criminals from enjoying the profit of illicit activities, thwarting their capacity to disguise the origin of funds and provide them with a legitimate appearance. For this reason, at the origins of the framework in the 1970s and 1980s, the focus was on proceeds of organised criminal activities with substantial returns – for example, trafficking in drugs and illegal firearms and corruption.[18] The crimes that generate proceeds whose laundering is considered by law as money laundering are known as "predicate offences", and they have broadened over time. According to FATF, money laundering must be interpreted to include the widest range of predicate offences.[19] In terms of money laundering activities – that is, what is done with the proceeds generated from the predicate offence – the EU AML Regulation refers to converting or transferring property derived from criminal activity, concealing or disguising qualities of said property (e.g., source, location, ownership), possessing or using said property, including any participation and attempt to facilitate these actions.[20]

A. The AML/CFT regime between FATF's standards and EU law

The FATF Recommendations require participating countries to establish authorities that regulate, monitor, supervise, and handle the licensing of various actors in different sectors, as well as impose disciplinary and financial sanctions.[21] The regimes established in different jurisdictions rely on a set of "regulated entities", also labelled "obliged entities", required to actively cooperate with the authorities, chiefly in terms of monitoring financial transactions and value exchanges.[22] Their selection is grounded on their (purported) oversight capacity, which is in practice often debated. The risk-based approach (RBA) sits at the core of the regime, and compliance and supervision measures are tuned to the principle of proportionality. To do so, regulated entities and authorities must consider risk factors identified by the FATF, such as the "red flag indicators", but also by the AML Regulation, national regulation, and supervisory authorities – that is, stricter if risk factors are higher and vice versa. The end goal is to draw the attention of competent authorities in case of suspicions of illicit

18 Liliya Gelemerova, 'On the Frontline against Money-Laundering: The Regulatory Minefield' (2009) 52(1) Crime, Law and Social Change 33, 34, 36.

19 FATF (n 17). FATF Recommendation 3.

20 The AML Regulation is Regulation (EU) 2024/1624 of the European Parliament and of the Council of 31 May 2024 on the prevention of the use of the financial system for the purposes of money laundering or terrorist financing [2024] OJ L 2024/1624of 19.6.2024. Its Article 2(1) directly refers to the definition of money laundering as per Article 3(1–5) of Directive (EU) 2018/1673 of the European Parliament and of the Council of 23 October 2018 on combating money laundering by criminal law [2018] OJ L 284/22 of 12.11.2018.

21 FATF (n 17) 7. Recommendation 26; Carol R Goforth, 'Crypto Assets: A Fintech Forecast' (2021) 37 Banking & Finance Law Review 5, 10; Chris Brummer, *Soft Law and the Global Financial System: Rule Making in the 21st Century* (2nd edn, Cambridge University Press 2015) 88, 89.

22 For FATF, regulated entities encompass financial institutions and designated non-financial businesses and professions.

activities. At the receiving end, there are national Financial Intelligence Units (FIUs), who receive, assess, and share financial information (e.g., suspicious transaction reports, other data relevant for analysis) with other national authorities or other FIUs.

At the EU level, a key part of AML/CFT activities consists of incorporating FATF Standards into Union law, where EU law operates as a legalisation means whereby soft law is transformed into embedded rules.[23] From 1991 onwards, the EU has drafted legislation to harmonise Member States' responses in the AML/CFT sphere. The actions have so far taken the form of directives of minimum harmonisation, where considerable discretion is left to national transposition. The alternative of maximum harmonisation would be incompatible with the RBA.[24] Article 5 of the Treaty on European Union (TEU) requires EU actions to comply with subsidiarity and proportionality, and the inherent cross-border nature of AML/CFT problems makes it impossible to achieve results through individual Member State actions. It is in this context that, in 2021, the Commission put forward a set of proposals known as the "AML Package". The goal was not to transform the content of the framework, still anchored to the FATF's approaches and methods, but rather to ensure the implementation of the regime by overcoming national fragmentation originated by the transposition of directives, while narrowing the gap with the new Regulation (EU) 2023/1114 on Markets in Crypto-Assets, known as MiCA Regulation.[25]

The AML Package contained four legislative proposals that were adopted between 2023 and 2024. In the first place, the AML Regulation establishes an AML/CFT single rulebook. Although the regulation does not disrupt the regime in terms of content, as a regulation it is directly binding on Member States, individuals, and organisations in its entirety. The main changes include the expansion of regulated entities to crypto-asset service providers (CASPs), the clarification of risk indicators, the strengthening of measures to mitigate the misuse of bearer instruments, and the establishment of a limit to the use of cash for large transactions. Parallelly, the so-called Sixth AML Directive focusses on FIUs.[26]

---

23 Abraham Newman and David Bach, 'The European Union as Hardening Agent: Soft Law and the Diffusion of Global Financial Regulation' (2014) 21(3) Journal of European Public Policy 430, 430–432.

24 Commission, 'Proposal for a Regulation of the European Parliament and of the Council on the prevention of the use of the financial system for the purposes of money laundering or terrorist financing' COM (2021) 420 final, 5. For EU requirements laid out by directives, with "minimum harmonisation" a directive sets minimum standards and Member States retain the right of setting higher ones, while with "maximum harmonisation" they cannot introduce stricter rules.

25 Regulation (EU) 2023/1114 of the European Parliament and of the Council of 31 May 2023 on markets in crypto-assets, and amending Regulations (EU) No 1093/2010 and (EU) No 1095/2010 and Directives 2013/36/EU and (EU) 2019/1937 [2023] OJ L 150/40 of 09.06.2023.

26 Directive (EU) 2024/1640 of the European Parliament and of the Council of 31 May 2024 on the mechanisms to be put in place by Member States for the prevention of the use of the financial system for the purposes of money laundering or terrorist

Further, the Regulation establishing the EU Anti-Money Laundering Authority (AMLA) introduces EU-level supervision of selected entities, assistance to financial supervisors, and coordination of information exchange.[27] As agreed in February 2024, AMLA will be located in Frankfurt, Germany.[28] The new Authority will adopt regulatory technical standards, guidelines, or recommendations for regulated entities, supervisors, or FIUs. Fourthly, Regulation (EU) 2023/1113 was adopted to recast Regulation (EU) 2015/847 – known as the Fund Transfer Regulation (FTR). The goal was to expand beyond wire transfer traceability obligations, according to which financial institutions and payment service providers (PSPs) exchange certain information. As outlined below, the new framework introduces the obligation to collect and share data on originators and beneficiaries of crypto-asset transfers.

B. The application to the crypto-asset space

Over the years, the AML/CFT regime was adjusted to the novel ways of transmitting value online. The FATF started to address crypto-asset risks in 2014–15, issuing background notions on virtual currencies,[29] and a first guidance.[30] These documents did not address crypto-assets comprehensively and focussed exclusively on the on- and off-ramps to the traditional financial system. In 2018, the FATF clarified the application of the Standards to virtual assets, and the amended Recommendation 15 included virtual asset service providers (VASPs) into the standards' scope. The development of new products, services, and providers led the FATF to specify in 2021 that the Standards apply "to both virtual-to-virtual and virtual-to-fiat transactions and interactions involving virtual assets".[31]

financing, amending Directive (EU) 2019/1937, and amending and repealing Directive (EU) 2015/849 [2024] OJ L, 2024/1640 of 19.6.2024.

27 Regulation (EU) 2024/1620 of the European Parliament and of the Council of 31 May 2024 establishing the Authority for Anti-Money Laundering and Countering the Financing of Terrorism and amending Regulations (EU) No 1093/2010, (EU) No 1094/2010 and (EU) No 1095/2010 [2024] OJ L, 2024/1620 of 19.6.2024.

28 European Commission, 'Commission Welcomes the Selection of Frankfurt as the Seat for the Authority for Anti-Money Laundering and Countering the Financing of Terrorism' (European Commission Press Release, Brussels, 22 February 2024) <https://ec.europa.eu/commission/presscorner/detail/en/ip_24_972> accessed 10 November 2024.

29 FATF, 'Virtual Currencies – Key Definitions and Potential AML/CFT Risks' (FATF Report, June 2014) <https://www.fatf-gafi.org/media/fatf/documents/reports/Virtual-currency-key-definitions-and-potential-aml-cft-risks.pdf> accessed 10 November 2024.

30 FATF, 'Guidance for a Risk-Based Approach: Virtual Currencies' (June 2015) <https://www.fatf-gafi.org/content/dam/fatf-gafi/guidance/Guidance-RBA-Virtual-Currencies.pdf.coredownload.inline.pdf> accessed 10 November 2024.

31 FATF, 'Virtual Assets and Virtual Asset Service Providers - Updated Guidance for a Risk-Based Approach' (October 2021) 7, 8 <https://www.fatf-gafi.org/publications/fatfrecommendations/documents/guidance-rba-virtual-assets-2021.html> accessed 10 November 2024; Goforth (n 21) 10.

The most recent FATF definition of a virtual asset is "a digital representation of value that can be digitally traded, or transferred, and can be used for payment or investment purposes", excluding "digital representation of fiat currencies, securities, and other financial assets that are already covered elsewhere in the FATF Recommendations".[32] VASPs, in turn, comprise natural or legal persons that as a business conduct – for or on behalf of another natural or legal person – one or more activities among: exchange between virtual assets and fiat currencies, between one or more virtual assets, transfer of virtual assets from one address or account to another, safekeeping or administration of virtual assets or instruments enabling control over them, provision of financial services related to an offer and/or sale of virtual assets.[33] In 2019, the FATF adopted the Interpretative Note to Recommendation 15 to clarify the application of the RBA to virtual asset activities and issued the first related comprehensive Guidance.[34] This was revised in 2021, also concerning risks in peer-to-peer transactions and the "travel rule" implementation.[35] Meanwhile, after a surge in ransomware attacks,[36] the FATF published the "Virtual Assets Red Flag Indicators of Money Laundering and Terrorist Financing", with a section on anonymity.[37] In 2024, the FATF issued an overview of the status of implementation of Recommendation 15, including its member jurisdictions but also those with significant VASP activities.[38] The report further accounts for the implementation of the crypto travel rule, at least in the form of draft legislation.[39]

Within the previous EU framework, Article 2(1)(g) and (h) of the AML Directive included fiat-to-crypto exchanges and custodian wallet providers.[40] Yet, the AML

---

32 FATF (n 31) 109; FATF (n 17).

33 FATF (n 31) 109.

34 FATF, 'Guidance for a Risk-Based Approach: Virtual Assets and Virtual Asset Service Providers' (June 2019) <https://www.fatf-gafi.org/publications/fatfrecommendations/documents/guidance-rba-virtual-assets.html> accessed 10 November 2024; FATF (n 17); Goforth (n 21) 11; FATF (n 31) 4, 8.

35 FATF (n 31) 5, 6.

36 ibid 10.

37 FATF, 'Virtual Assets Red Flag Indicators of Money Laundering and Terrorist Financing' (September 2020) <https://www.fatf-gafi.org/media/fatf/documents/recommendations/Virtual-Assets-Red-Flag-Indicators.pdf> accessed 10 November 2024.

38 FATF, 'Status of Implementation of Recommendation 15 by FATF Members and Jurisdictions with Materially Important VASP Activity' (March 2024) <https://www.fatf-gafi.org/content/dam/fatf-gafi/publications/VACG-Table-Jurisdictions-2024.pdf> accessed 10 November 2024.

39 ibid 10.

40 The term "AML Directive" refers to the last consolidated version of Directive (EU) 2015/849 of the European Parliament and of the Council of 20 May 2015 on the prevention of the use of the financial system for the purposes of money laundering or terrorist financing, amending Regulation (EU) No 648/2012 of the European Parliament and of the Council, and repealing Directive 2005/60/EC of the European Parliament and of the Council and Commission Directive 2006/70/EC [2015] OJ L 141/73 of 05.06.2015 (Fourth AML Directive), as amended by Directive (EU) 2018/843 of the European

Regulation broadens the scope of application of the regime from virtual currencies to crypto-assets and refers to the MiCA Regulation for the definitions. As per Article 3(1)(5) of the MiCA Regulation, a crypto-asset is "a digital representation of a value or of a right that is able to be transferred and stored electronically using distributed ledger technology or similar technology".[41] A crypto-asset service provider (CASP) provides services such as custody and administration, trading, exchange (for funds or other crypto-assets), execution (or reception and transmission) of orders, placing, advice, portfolio management, and transfer services.[42] The provision of advice is the only case that does not fall within the scope of the AML Regulation.

III. The obligation to ensure traceability of fund flows

The traceability of money flows is crucial to prevent, detect, and investigate money laundering and terrorist financing.[43] As per FATF Recommendation 16 on "wire transfers",[44] financial institutions must "include required and accurate originator information, and required beneficiary information, on wire transfers and related messages". They must also ensure that such information remains with the transfer throughout the payment chain. This is the so-called "travel rule", which is designed to detect any attempt to move illicit funds by making sure to trace the relevant transactions and collect the necessary information to hold the perpetrators accountable. In practice, a set of data must accompany the funds throughout the payment chain. This is achieved through a duty on some regulated entities to collect and share certain information on originators and beneficiaries of all wire transfers and to make it available to the authorities – for example, FIUs and law enforcement agencies.[45] Further,

Parliament and of the Council of 30 May 2018 amending Directive (EU) 2015/849 on the prevention of the use of the financial system for the purposes of money laundering or terrorist financing, and amending Directives 2009/138/EC and 2013/36/EU [2018] OJ L 156/43 of 19.06.2018 (Fifth AML Directive). The AML Directive was repealed by Directive (EU) 2024/1640 (n 26).

41 The definition of crypto-assets in the MiCA Regulation corresponds to the definition of virtual assets set out in the revised FATF Recommendations. Further, the list of crypto-asset services and crypto-asset service providers covered in the MiCA Regulation encompasses the virtual asset service providers identified as such by FATF.

42 Regulation (EU) 2023/1114 (n 26) Article 3(1)(15–16).

43 Regulation (EU) 2023/1113 of the European Parliament and of the Council of 31 May 2023 on information accompanying transfers of funds and certain crypto-assets and amending Directive (EU) 2015/849 [2023] OJ L 150/1 of 09.06.2023, Recital 16.

44 A "wire transfer" is any electronic transaction on the originator's behalf through a financial institution to make funds available to a beneficiary at a beneficiary financial institution. Glossary of FATF Recommendation 16.

45 The originator is the "account holder who allows the wire transfer from that account, or where there is no account, the natural or legal person that places the order with the ordering financial institution to perform the wire transfer". The beneficiary is the "natural or legal person or legal arrangement who is identified by the originator as the receiver of the requested wire transfer". Glossary of FATF Recommendation 16.

they must monitor the transfers to detect the absence of this required information and take appropriate measures, as well as take freezing actions and prohibit transactions with sanctioned persons or entities.[46]

The Interpretative Note to FATF Recommendation 16 lays out different rules imposed on ordering, intermediary, and beneficiary financial institutions and money or value transfer services (MVTSs).[47] The travel rule was implemented in the EU in 2015, when the adoption of the Fourth AML Directive was accompanied by that of Regulation (EU) 2015/847 on information accompanying transfers of funds (FTR) sent or received by a PSP or intermediary PSP established in the Union.[48] Within that regime, funds are defined as "banknotes and coins, scriptural money and electronic money",[49] and "transfer of funds" refers to transactions performed by electronic means, including credit transfers, direct debits, money remittances, and transfers via payment cards, e-money, and mobile phones.[50]

Recommendation 16 and its Interpretative Note are undergoing a revision process that includes a public consultation. FATF, 'Public Consultation on Recommendation 16 on Payment Transparency' (*FATF*, 26 February 2024) <https://www.fatf-gafi.org/en/publications/Fatfrecommendations/R16-public-consultation-Feb24.html> accessed 10 November 2024.

46 FATF (n 17) FATF Recommendation 16.

47 MVTS are "financial services that involve the acceptance of cash, cheques, other monetary instruments or other stores of value and the payment of a corresponding sum in cash or other form to a beneficiary by means of a communication, message, transfer, or through a clearing network to which the MVTS provider belongs". This can involve intermediaries and any new payment methods – e.g., hawala, hundi, fei-chen. ibid 132.

48 Regulation (EU) 2015/847 of the European Parliament and of the Council of 20 May 2015 on information accompanying transfers of funds and repealing Regulation (EC) No 1781/2006 [2015] OJ L 141/1 of 05.06.2015, Article 2(1); Article 2(4) excludes PSP-to-PSP fund transfers from the regime.

49 By reference to Article 4(15) of Directive 2007/64/EC of the European Parliament and of the Council of 13 November 2007 on payment services in the internal market amending Directives 97/7/EC, 2002/65/EC, 2005/60/EC, and 2006/48/EC and repealing Directive 97/5/EC [2007] OJ L 319 of 05.12.2007 (PSD) replaced by Article 4(25) of Directive 2015/2366 of the European Parliament and of the Council of 25 November 2015 on payment services in the internal market, amending Directives 2002/65/EC, 2009/110/EC, and 2013/36/EU and Regulation (EU) No 1093/2010, and repealing Directive 2007/64/EC [2015] OJ L 337/35 of 23.12.2015 (PSD2). The definition of "funds" refers to Directive 2009/110/EC of the European Parliament and of the Council of 16 September 2009 on the taking up, pursuit, and prudential supervision of the business of electronic money institutions amending Directives 2005/60/EC and 2006/48/EC and repealing Directive 2000/46/EC [2009] OJ L 267/7 of 10.10.2009 (EMD2), where e-money is "electronically, including magnetically, stored monetary value as represented by a claim on the issuer which is issued on receipt of funds for the purpose of making payment transactions as defined in point 5 of Article 4 of PSD, and which is accepted by a natural or legal person other than the electronic money issuer" (Article 2(2)).

50 Regulation (EU) 2015/847 (n 50) Article 3(9).

A. The crypto travel rule

The crypto travel rule expands the scope of obligations for information sharing to the crypto-asset space. In 2018, the revision of the Interpretative Note to FATF Recommendation 15 on "new technologies" addressed the application of FATF Recommendation 16 to virtual asset transfers. Countries were asked to introduce new rules for financial institutions and VASPs, whereby (i) originators obtain and hold required and accurate originator information and required beneficiary information on virtual asset transfers, submit it (directly or indirectly – that is, not necessarily attached to the transfer) to the beneficiary (if any) immediately and securely, and on request make it available to the competent authorities; (ii) beneficiaries obtain and hold required originator information and required and accurate beneficiary information on transfers of virtual assets, and on request make it available to the competent authorities. The scope of application of other rules laid out by FATF Recommendation 16 was extended accordingly – for example, data monitoring, freezing actions, prohibiting transactions with designated persons.[51]

Consistently, the EU AML Package included a proposal to recast the FTR and introduce the crypto travel rule. The new regime was adopted as Regulation (EU) 2023/1113 and establishes the obligation to collect and make accessible specific data on originators and beneficiaries of crypto-asset transfers to the authorities.[52] In doing so, the reform explicitly targets crypto-asset anonymity, as "the global reach, the speed at which transactions can be carried out and the possible anonymity offered by their transfer, particularly expose crypto assets to the risk of criminal misuse against jurisdictions".[53] The regime applies to those transfers of crypto-assets, including by means of crypto-ATMs,[54] where the CASP of the originator or beneficiary, or the intermediary CASP,[55] has its registered office in the EU.[56]

A transfer of crypto-assets is defined as any transaction that aims to move crypto-assets from one distributed ledger address, crypto-asset account, or other storage device to another one.[57] It is carried out by at least one CASP on behalf of an originator or a beneficiary, regardless of whether the originator and beneficiary are the

---

51 FATF (n 17) Revised Interpretative Note to FATF Recommendation 15.

52 Article 3(14) and (15) of Regulation (EU) 2023/1113 (n 45) refer to MiCA's definition of crypto-assets and CASPs, respectively. In the United Kingdom, the crypto travel rule was enacted in the new Part 7A of The Money Laundering, Terrorist Financing and Transfer of Funds (Information on the Payer) Regulations 2017 (SI 2017/692). Part 7A was inserted by SI 2022/860.

53 Regulation (EU) 2023/1113 (n 45).

54 A crypto-ATM is a physical or online electronic terminal enabling CASPs to transfer crypto-assets; ibid, Article 3(17).

55 Intermediary CASPs are those CASPs (other than that of the originator or beneficiary) that receive and transmit crypto-asset transfers on behalf of the CASP of the originator or of the beneficiary, or of another intermediary CASP. ibid, Article 3(16).

56 ibid, Article 2(1).

57 ibid, Article 3(10).

same person and whether the CASPs of the originator and the beneficiary are the same one.[58] All regulated entities that offer crypto-asset services within the meaning defined above, such as banks, fall within the scope of application of the crypto travel rule.[59] The regime does not apply when both the originator and beneficiary are CASPs acting on their own behalf. Likewise, as further discussed below, it does not apply to person-to-person transfers without the involvement of a CASP.[60] In line with the RBA, the original version of the recast proposal distinguished between crypto-asset transfers of more than EUR 1,000 – that is, individual transfers exceeding the threshold or multiple transfers seemingly linked – and those below this threshold. The latter were subject to a more lenient regime. This approach was rejected during the legislative process, and crypto-asset transfers are now subject to the same requirements regardless of their amount and their domestic or cross-border features. This is not only due to their borderless nature, but also to the fact that they facilitate the structuring of large transactions into smaller transfers, in a context where calculating linked transactions is disrupted by high volatility.[61]

Hence, no matter the transferred value, the CASP of the originator is required to: (i) obtain and hold for five years accurate – that is, verified for accuracy – information on the *payer*: name, distributed ledger address and/or crypto-asset account number, address, official ID number, customer ID number or date and place of birth, current Legal Entity Identifier (LEI) or equivalent (if applicable);[62] (ii) obtain and hold for five years certain accurate information on the *beneficiary*: name and distributed ledger address and/or crypto-asset account number, current LEI or equivalent (if applicable);[63] (iii) securely submit *all of the above* to the beneficiary entity in advance of, simultaneously, or concurrently with the transfer.[64] The CASP of the beneficiary is required to: (i) monitor that the required data is included in the transfer or follows it; (ii) before making the assets available to the payee, verify the accuracy of the data using reliable and independent sources.[65] The intermediary CASP is required to ensure all data is relayed with the transfer and to comply with data retention obligations.[66]

---

58 ibid, Article 3(10).

59 Regulation (EU) 2023/1114 (n 25), Articles 59 and 60.

60 Regulation (EU) 2023/1113 (n 45), Article 2(4).

61 ibid, Recitals 27 and 30.

62 ibid, Article 14(1). Article 14(6–7) provides criteria for accuracy verification. Data retention duties are laid out by Article 26. The LEI is "a unique alphanumeric reference code based on ISO 17442 standard assigned to a legal entity" (Article 3(23)).

63 ibid, Article 14(2).

64 As per ibid. Article 14(4), the data as per Article 14(1–2) does not need to be attached directly to or included in the transfer. Further, as per Article 15(1), in case of a batch file transfer from one originator, Article 14(1) shall not apply to the individual transfers, provided the batch file contains the information as per Article 14(1–3), verified as per Article 14(5–6), and the individual transfers contain the originator distributed ledger address, crypto-asset account number, or individual identifier.

65 ibid, Article 16(1) and (3).

66 ibid, Article 19.

Upon request, all the information must be shared with the authorities. The dynamics of these exchanges are depicted in Figure 10.1.

For some transfers, a "distributed ledger address" – defined as "an alphanumeric code that identifies an address on a network using distributed ledger technology or similar technology where crypto-assets can be sent or received" – and/or a "crypto-asset account number" – that is, the number of an account held by a CASP "in the name of one or more natural or legal persons which can be used for the execution of transfers of crypto-assets" – may not exist.[67] Accordingly, in terms of data to collect, reference to a "distributed ledger address" is limited to cases in which the transfer is "registered on a network using distributed ledger technology or similar technology", and reference to an "account number" is limited to cases in which "such an account exists and is used to process the transaction".[68] When this is not the case, the originating CASP must ensure the transfer is accompanied by a "unique transaction identifier" that allows traceability of the transfer back to the originator and the beneficiary.[69]

It is prohibited for originating CASPs to execute any transfer before they can ensure full compliance with the above, and beneficiary CASPs must establish procedures to apply when the required data is lacking – that is, to decide whether to execute, reject, or suspend the transfer, and to determine follow-up actions.[70] Notably, if the beneficiary or intermediary CASP becomes aware of missing or incomplete information, they must either reject the transfer or ask for the information before making the crypto-assets available to the beneficiary or before transmitting the transfer.[71] If a CASP repeatedly fails to provide the required data, the beneficiary or intermediary CASP must (a) take actions such as issuing warnings or setting deadlines before proceeding to reject the transfer, or restricting or terminating the business relationship with the CASP; (b) reject directly any future transfers from the CASP or restrict and terminate the business relationship with it;[72] (c) consider the missing/incomplete data when deciding on the suspiciousness of the transfer or related transactions to report them accordingly.[73] Intermediary CASPs that become aware of missing/incomplete information can decide whether to reject the transfer and return the transferred crypto-assets or to ask for the required data.[74]

67 ibid, Article 3(18) and (19).
68 ibid, Article 14(1)(b).
69 ibid, Articles 14(3) and 3(12); The "unique transaction identifier" is defined as a combination of letters, numbers, or symbols determined by a CASP, which permits the traceability of the transfer of crypto-assets back to the originator and the beneficiary.
70 ibid, Article 17(1).
71 ibid, Articles 17(1) and 21(1).
72 ibid, Articles 17(2) and 21.
73 ibid, Articles 18 and 22(2); suspicious transaction reports are to be submitted to the authorities as per the AML Regulation.
74 ibid, Article 21.

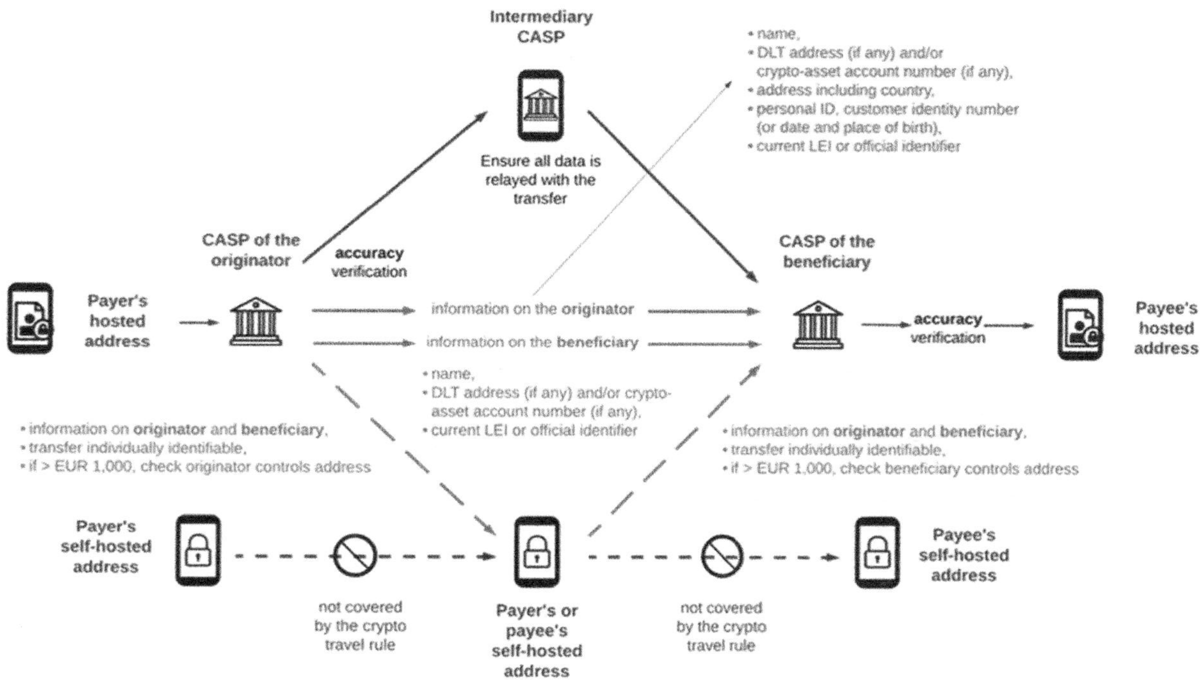

Source: Elaboration of the author.

Figure 10.1 Information exchange as per the crypto travel rule under Regulation (EU) 1113/2023

B. Anonymity-related risks and self-hosted addresses

Some crypto-asset transfers present high-risk factors for money laundering, terrorist financing, and other criminal activities, especially when they are related to "products, transactions, or technologies designed to enhance anonymity, including privacy wallets, mixers, or tumblers".[75] In compliance with the RBA, this must be taken into consideration by regulated entities. Accordingly, the European Banking Authority (EBA) is expected to clarify the risk factors to be considered by CASPs to ensure the traceability of these transfers, such as in the case of transactions with non-Union counterparties that are not regulated, registered, or licenced anywhere, or with self-hosted addresses. In particular, the EBA is expected to issue guidelines specifying which enhanced due diligence measures should be applied to mitigate such risks – for example, the adoption of analytics tools to detect the origin or destination of crypto -assets.[76] Another example of a high-risk use case is that of transfers through "crypto-ATMs", as they allow users to perform transfers by depositing cash, often without customer identification and verification. Due to the possibility of using cash of unknown origin, they are deemed an ideal vehicle for illicit activities.[77]

Because the AML/CFT framework is fundamentally intermediary-based, it is not surprising that the recast of the FTR does not apply to "person-to-person transfers",[78] defined as transfers of crypto-assets without the use or involvement of any CASP.[79] This is also depicted at the bottom of Figure 10.1. One of the key points introduced by Regulation (EU) 2023/1113, however, explicitly covers the regime applicable to transfers involving self-hosted wallets, using the term "self-hosted addresses", defined as distributed ledger addresses not linked to a CASP nor to a similar entity established outside the EU.[80] Self-hosted wallets are also known as unhosted, private, non-custodial, or self-custody wallets. This means users are the sole holders of their private keys, and thus have full control of their crypto-assets. The alternative is keeping them in a third-party wallet offered by a provider of custody services such as a crypto-asset exchange.[81] Indeed, the crypto travel rule applies to crypto-asset transfers to or from a self-hosted address, if a CASP is involved. Acknowledging the complexity of this regulatory endeavour, the recast provided for further evaluation to be performed by the Commission.[82]

---

75 ibid, Recital 69.
76 ibid, Recital 17.
77 ibid, Recital 25.
78 ibid, Article 2(4).
79 ibid, Article 3(13).
80 ibid, Article 3(20).
81 Nadia Pocher, 'Self-Hosted Wallets: The Elephant in the Crypto Room?' *(KU Leuven CiTiP Blog*, 11 March 2021) <https://www.law.kuleuven.be/citip/blog/self-hosted-wallets/> accessed 10 November 2024.
82 Regulation (EU) 2023/1113 (n 45), Recital 38. As per Recital 58, considering the high risks associated with self-hosted addresses and corresponding complexities (e.g., verification of ownership data), by 1 July 2026, the Commission will assess the need for additional risk mitigation measures, including possible restrictions. The Commission

Meanwhile, Regulation (EU) 2023/1113 already provides important specifications concerning self-hosted addresses in the form of specific duties placed on originating and beneficiary CASPs. As per Articles 14(5) and 16(2), in the case of transfers of crypto-assets made to or from a self-hosted address, the CASP of the originator and of the beneficiary, respectively, must obtain and hold the information mentioned above and ensure the crypto-asset transfer can be individually identified. In addition, in the case of transfer of more than EUR 1,000 to or from a self-hosted address, the CASP of the originator and of the beneficiary must take adequate measures to verify that the address is owned or controlled by the originator or beneficiary, respectively. As clarified in the recitals, the CASP usually collects this information from its client, considering the lack of counterparties. In this respect, the verification of the accuracy of the information provided by the clients can be challenging. The industry has been relying on several general methods to collect proof of ownership of self-hosted addresses, including visual proof (the user sends the CASP a screenshot of the wallet displaying the withdrawal address), the Satoshi test (the user sends a trivial amount to the CASP, thereby proving control of the address), and manual signing (the user must sign a message using the key associated with the specific address, thereby proving control).[83] Further, proprietary solutions have emerged for holders of self-hosted addresses to reliably provide their status within transaction monitoring and/or know your customer (KYC) applications already in use by the service provider – for example, the Address Ownership Proof Protocol (AOPP).[84]

Besides the risk mitigation and verification measures, when the entity becomes aware that the provided information is inaccurate or encounters suspicious patterns, it must perform enhanced due diligence and, if needed, submit a suspicious transaction report to the authorities.[85] In this context, one should not forget that the use of self-hosted wallets to move crypto-asset funds across borders is listed among the FATF's red flags concerning anonymity,[86] and thereby frequently requires close scrutiny.

IV. Techno-legal challenges and open issues

Even if the scope of AML/CFT measures has expanded over time to include (a part of) the crypto-asset space, the underlying approach remains largely intermediary-based and relies on the cooperation of regulated entities. There was no major alteration of the fundamentals of the regime to tailor it to crypto-asset specificities. On the one

will assess the effectiveness and proportionality of the mechanisms to verify the accuracy of the ownership information.

83 21 Analytics, 'Self-Hosted Wallet Verification Methods: An Overview' (*21 Analytics*, 30 March 2023) <https://www.21analytics.ch/blog/unhosted-wallet-verification-methods-an-overview/> accessed 10 November 2024.

84 21 Analytics, 'AOPP Explained' (*21 Analytics*) <https://www.21analytics.ch/what-is-aopp/> accessed 10 November 2024.

85 Regulation (EU) 2023/1113 (n 45), Recitals 39 and 45.

86 FATF (n 37) 10.

hand, risk-based procedures and policies were adapted to the crypto-asset space, and most jurisdictions made considerable progress in responding to emerging risks. On the other hand, these efforts still appear insufficient to address comprehensively the problems associated with the crypto-asset sphere without thrusting significant burdens on the industry. Compliance with the crypto travel rule is one of the most topical examples.[87] The controversy comprises technical issues interwoven with policy decisions and business incentives, mirroring the tension between the increasing sophistication of the crypto-asset space (including related misuses for criminal purposes) and the needs of an AML/CFT regime that is inherently intermediary-based and explicitly not applicable to person-to-person transfers that are not linked to any activity of a service provider.

Increasingly, crypto-asset regulation aligns with the principle of "same activities, same risks, same rules".[88] Accordingly, activities involving crypto-assets are expected to receive regulatory treatment that resembles in its rationale the one targeting traditional financial assets. With regard to risks of anonymity, for instance, the regulatory approach resembles the one applicable to physical cash and bearer instruments, currently subject to a series of monitoring and restrictive rules. A primary example is the introduction of an EU-wide limitation of EUR 10,000 for large cash payments in exchange for goods or services, which applies to transactions carried out in a single operation and to several operations that are seemingly linked and does not apply to payments between natural persons not acting in a professional capacity.[89] However, the specifics of the crypto-asset space bring about their share of challenges when subject to functionally similar compliance requirements – for example, difficulty in identifying linked transactions.[90] This emphasises the importance of implementation measures such as the EBA's "Travel Rule Guidelines", currently subject to a consultation procedure.[91] The role of the EBA in this field will be increasingly shared with, and later transferred to, the AMLA.

At the time of writing, at least four problematic angles have emerged on a general level: the impact of the rule on self-hosted to hosted wallet transactions and the legitimacy of restrictions; the challenge of linking crypto-asset activities to the respective actors, at least in terms of attribution to real-world identities to be identified as originators

---

87 Goforth (n 21) 11.

88 Regulation (EU) 2023/1114 (n 25), Recital 9. The approach resembles that of the United States Securities and Exchange Commission in applying functional tests to define crypto-asset exchanges and apply securities law (e.g., Howey test). FATF (n 38).

89 Regulation (EU) 2024/1624 (n 20), Article 80(1) and (4).

90 ibid, Recital 160.

91 EBA, 'Consultation Paper on the Draught Guidelines on Preventing the Abuse of Funds and Certain Crypto-Assets Transfers for Money Laundering and Terrorist Financing Purposes under Regulation (EU) 2023/1113 ("The Travel Rule Guidelines")' (*EBA*, 2023) <https://www.eba.europa.eu/publications-and-media/press-releases/eba-consults-guidelines-preventing-abuse-funds-and-certain> accessed 10 November 2024.

and beneficiaries; the absence of global standards and technical solutions to underpin affordable compliance; and compliance with data protection requirements.

A. The challenge of attribution

The first two issues can be interpreted as a challenge of attribution of crypto-asset activities, under the perspectives of who is to be (and can be) regulated under the AML/CFT scheme – for example, entities that qualify as CASPs – but also who the real-world identities involved in the transaction as payer/originator and payee/beneficiary are. In other words, both viewpoints relate to accountability. The third problem is denounced by the industry, and it is an underlying issue that assumes a regulated entity is identified but lacks a Regulatory Technology (RegTech) solution to comply with the requirements.[92]

As the AML/CFT regime is traditionally based on the role of intermediaries in the detection of suspicious transactions, also the revision of the FTR pivots on CASPs. In the crypto-asset sphere, however, this approach fails to comprehensively account for its technical and structural peculiarities.[93] Focussing on self-hosted wallet/address activities, the two noteworthy scenarios, depicted in Figure 10.2, generate a two-fold issue of regulatory compliance. On the one hand, in the case of self-hosted to self-hosted wallet transactions, the fact that there is no regulated entity involved eludes the crypto travel rule and cash-related restrictions. While this encouraged regulators to consider restrictions, in terms of bans or often threshold limits, the issue generated a heated debate. Questions of legitimacy arose, and advocacy groups argue that it could give way to total surveillance – at odds with fundamental liberties such as privacy and autonomy, and with financial inclusion. It could also possibly generate a displacement of a considerable portion of activities towards unsupervised areas.[94] On the other hand, in the case of self-hosted to hosted wallet transfers, when regulated entities receive a transfer, they are required to obtain originator data but have no (regulated) counterparty entity to interact with, and are required to put a series of risk mitigation measures in place. Hence, self-hosted wallet holders could eventually be unable to transact with regulated PSPs if they are unable or unwilling to provide the necessary information. This would also be the case if the PSP adopts a de-risking approach and refuses to accept any transaction to/from self-hosted wallets in light of their real or perceived risk.

---

92 Doron Goldbarsht and Louis De Koker, 'From Paper Money to Digital Assets: Financial Technology and the Risks of Criminal Abuse' in Doron Goldbarsht and Louis De Koker (eds), *Financial Technology and the Law: Combating Financial Crime* (Springer International Publishing 2022) 309.

93 Valentina Covolo, 'The EU Response to Criminal Misuse of Cryptocurrencies: The Young, Already Outdated 5th Anti-Money Laundering Directive' (2020) 28 European Journal of Crime, Criminal Law and Criminal Justice 217, 247.

94 Miller Whitehouse-Levine and Lindsey Kelleher, 'Self-Hosted Wallets and the Future of Free Societies. A Guide for Policymakers' (*Blockchain Association*, November 2020) <https://theblockchainassociation.org/wp-content/uploads/2020/11/Self-Hosted-Wallets-and-the-Future-of-Free-Societies.pdf> accessed 10 November 2024.

Source: Elaboration of the author.

Figure 10.2 Depiction of self-hosted-to-hosted and self-hosted-to-self-hosted address transfers

Meanwhile, decentralised finance shows that even if the development of innovative services is influenced by regulation, part of the crypto-asset space is still leveraging technology to stay outside the border of compliance. These new schemes generate a challenge of attributing activities to a regulatable entity. The crypto travel rule is a prime example of how AML/CFT regulation is still dependent on the model of centralised exchanges (CEXs) and has not captured decentralised exchanges (DEXs) yet.[95] In this context, doubts have arisen about the nature of peer-to-peer trading platforms and DEXs, as – strictly speaking – these entities do not provide a service of exchange or conversion. Indeed, peer-to-peer exchanges provide users with a marketplace, handled by software, that aids in the connection between prospective buyers and sellers.[96] The scope of the issue narrows when considering the understanding of CASP provided by the MiCA Regulation. Indeed, this includes as a "crypto-asset service" also the operation of a trading platform defined as a multilateral system bringing together or facilitating "the bringing together of multiple third-party purchasing and selling interests in crypto-assets, in the system and in accordance with its rules, in a way that results in a contract, either by exchanging crypto-assets for funds or by the exchange of crypto-assets for other crypto-assets",[97] the execution of orders on behalf of third parties, placing activities, and order reception and transmission on behalf of third parties. But even when a peer-to-peer platform falls within the scope of a given AML/CFT framework, it is often problematic to identify the entity.[98] It is worth mentioning that not only is the share of crypto-asset activity performed through DEXs not trivial, but the CEX-centric nature of compliance can generate a substantial shift of liquidity to DEXs.[99] While the definition of the MiCA Regulation can mitigate the formal exclusion from the regime, it cannot solve the technical conundrum that makes it hard to thrust cooperation duties on them. This is highly problematic in consideration of the overall increase in decentralised finance (DeFi) laundering-related misuse starting from 2021,[100] while data reveal the preferred choice of malware operators to receive

---

95 Syren Johnstone, *Rethinking the Regulation of Cryptoassets: Cryptographic Consensus Technology and the New Prospect* (Edward Elgar Publishing 2021) 125.

96 Covolo (n 95) 235–236.

97 Regulation (EU) 2023/1114 (n 25), Article 3(1)(16) and (18).

98 Jai Massari and Christian Catalini, 'DeFi, Disintermediation, and the Regulatory Path Ahead' (*The Regulatory Review*, 10 May 2021) <https://www.theregreview.org/2021/05/10/massari-catalini-defi-disintermediation-regulatory-path-ahead/> accessed 10 November 2024.

99 Johnstone (n 97) 125; Massari and Catalini (n 100).

100 The Spartan Protocol hack is a prime example of the use of DeFi for laundering. After over 300 million USD worth of crypto-assets was stolen, the hackers converted the funds into anyETH and anyBTC (Ethereum and Bitcoin composites built on separate blockchains to the originals), then swapped some anyBTC for Bitcoin. Two chain-hopping protocols were used to convert funds into Ethereum and renBTC, then sent to a DEX and swapped for new Ethereum and wrapped Ethereum. The use of these platforms makes investigations significantly more complex. The funds were lastly sent to Tornado Cash; Chainalysis, 'The 2022 Crypto Crime Report' (2022) 7, 12 <https://go.chainalysis.com/2022-Crypto-Crime-Report.html> accessed 09 April 2024.

payments on self-hosted addresses, with the second choice being to receive them to addresses hosted by high-risk exchanges with low or non-existent compliance.[101]

B. The challenge of interoperability

While it is not easy to mitigate the risk of abuses without displacing illicit activities to peer-to-peer transfers, one wonders whether restricting self-hosted wallets unduly affects the freedom of economic activity, and/or whether the degree of enforceability of such limitations should bear any weight in the relevant policy-making.[102] Indeed, under the current regime, it seems impossible to enforce restrictions outside the scope of regulatable entities,[103] while CASPs denounce the lack of affordable compliance tools, and experts outline that the application of compliance requirements is over-burdening the industry. For the purposes of technology neutrality, Regulation (EU) 2023/1113 does not require CASPs to make use of a specific technology to exchange the information. The EU co-legislators explicitly welcome as critical "standard-setting initiatives involving or led by the crypto-asset industry" to design interoperable solutions based on international or EU standards.[104]

Ever since the crypto-asset space started familiarising with the crypto travel rule, the industry has indeed commenced an exploration of various compliance technology solutions and RegTech tools. Relevant protocols are typically built to enable the secure exchange of originator and beneficiary information, and most of the solutions are commercial – for example, TRISA, VerifyVASP.[105] One open-source protocol emerged with the Travel Rule Protocol (TRP), developed in mid-2020 by an industry working group and merged with the OpenVASP association in late 2021. TRP is fully decentralised and free of charge.[106] However, overall, crypto travel rule compliance solutions have shown limited use. Unlike what happens for fiat money with the Society for Worldwide Interbank Financial Telecommunications (SWIFT), which serves as a dominant secure messaging network for financial institutions to exchange information about financial transactions and has become the industry syntax standard,[107]

---

101 ibid, 61, 74.

102 Pocher (n 83).

103 Nadia Pocher, 'Crypto-Wallets and the New EU AML Package: Where Are the Battle Lines Drawn?' (*KU Leuven CiTiP Blog*, 28 May 2023) <https://lirias.kuleuven.be/4070348?limo=0> accessed 10 November 2024.

104 Regulation (EU) 2023/1113 (n 45) Recital 50.

105 Magdalena Boškić, 'How RegTech Tools Enable Regulatory Compliance for Cryptoassets: A Case Study for Cryptoasset Transaction Monitoring' (2023) 8(2) Journal of Digital Banking 176, 184; For a brief overview of travel rule solutions: Chaehyeon Lee and others, 'Design of Blockchain-Based Travel Rule Compliance System' (*IEEE*, 2022) <https://arxiv.org/abs/2204.13508> accessed 10 November 2024.

106 Boškić (n 107) 184. OpenVASP Association, 'What Is the Travel Rule Protocol (TRP)?' (*OpenVASP*, 1 May 2022) <https://www.openvasp.org/blog/what-is-the-travel-rule-protocol-trp> accessed 10 November 2024.

107 Susan V Scott and Markos Zachariadis, *The Society for Worldwide Interbank Financial Telecommunication (SWIFT)* (Routledge 2013).

in the crypto-asset space there is no equivalent global standard for the exchange of information.[108] The different protocols under development are also not interoperable, except for the consensus reached regarding a single data messaging format – the InterVASP Messaging Standard (IVMS 101) – which established a common language for communication. The lack of unified compliance technology solutions is challenging according to the FATF.[109]

Further, the problem of (affordable) compliance is worsened by the divergent approaches across jurisdictions, both in the implementation of the crypto travel rule and in the specific requirements (e.g., de minimis threshold). The different pace of implementation of the crypto travel rule across jurisdictions causes both an unlevel playing field and difficulties for the entities that must comply earlier than their counterparts, known as the "sunrise issue".[110]

C. The challenge of data protection

While the regime to be applied to transfers involving self-hosted addresses generates one of the key controversies surrounding the FTR recast, another topical aspect concerns the interplay between the travel rule and data protection. Indeed, issues arise in terms of data protection and compliance with the General Data Protection Regulation (EU) 2016/679 (GDPR). The processing of personal data under the new FTR is subject to the GDPR and can be performed exclusively for AML/CFT prevention purposes, with specific prohibition of any commercial exploitation.[111] AML/CFT purposes are deemed an important public interest ground, but the transfer of personal data to a third country must be performed in accordance with Chapter V of the GDPR, which lays out rules for the transfers of personal data to third countries or international organisations. PSPs and CASPs that operate in multiple jurisdictions, with branches or subsidiaries outside the EU, should not be prevented from sharing data about suspicious transactions within their organisation, but they must apply adequate safeguards and have appropriate technical and organisational measures in place to protect personal data against accidental loss, alteration, or unauthorised disclosure or access.[112]

However, crypto-assets are inherently cross-border, and they can be transferred to a provider that is registered in a jurisdiction with different rules on data protection and its enforcement, or even to one that is not registered in a jurisdiction. In the first case, the CASP of the originator should assess the ability of the CASP of the beneficiary to receive and retain the data in compliance with the GDPR. Yet, the European Data

108 Boškić (n 107) 185.

109 ibid; FATF, 'Second 12-Month Review of the Revised FATF Standards on Virtual Assets and Virtual Asset Service Providers' (July 2021) <https://www.fatf-gafi.org/content/dam/fatf-gafi/guidance/Second-12-Month-Review-Revised-FATF-Standards-Virtual-Assets-VASPS.pdf> accessed 10 November 2024.

110 Boškić (n 107) 179.

111 Regulation (EU) 2023/1113 (n 45) Article 25(1–2).

112 ibid, Recital 19.

Protection Board (EDPB), in consultation with the EBA, will issue guidelines on the practical implementation of data protection requirements for transfers of personal data to third countries in the context of transfers of crypto-assets. For those situations in which personal data cannot be sent because the requirements of the GDPR cannot be fulfilled, the EBA is expected to provide guidelines on the procedures to follow to assess whether to execute, reject, or suspend the transfer.[113]

For a travel rule system to comply with the GDPR, overarching requirements are those laid out by Article 25 of the GDPR regarding "privacy by design" and "privacy by default". They relate, respectively, to ensuring data protection through technology design and to processing personal data only when necessary for a specific purpose and in a transparent fashion vis-à-vis the individuals involved.[114] The debate underlines the need to design the interplay between the AML/CFT sphere and privacy and data protection safeguards in the regulatory framework. Likewise, the specific crypto travel rule context requires appropriate design of RegTech/compliance technology solutions, able to embed the presence of various regulatory requirements such as AML/CFT and data protection.[115]

V. Conclusions

In recent years, the obligation to ensure the traceability of crypto-asset transfers has emerged as a key measure to prevent, detect, and investigate money laundering and terrorist financing. At a global level, this has been at the core of the FATF Recommendations since 2018. In the EU, the crypto travel rule was introduced by Regulation (EU) 2023/1113. The efforts to fight the lack of accountability in the crypto-asset space respond directly to the exposure and permeability of the traditional financial system to crypto-asset-related risks, showcased by the Crypto Winter 2022–23. At the same time, the application of traceability requirements poses major challenges for AML/CFT regulated entities involved in crypto-asset transfers. This occurrence is a primary example of the difficulty of applying an intermediary-based framework to the crypto-asset sphere, where the regime designed for self-hosted wallets arguably falls short in accounting for the difficulty of collecting the necessary information and, perhaps most importantly, verifying it according to the required accuracy and reliability.

---

113 ibid, Recital 34.

114 Ross P Buckley, Douglas W Arner, and Dirk A Zetzsche, *FinTech: Finance, Technology and Regulation* (Cambridge University Press 2023) 154.

115 Nadia Pocher and Andreas Veneris, 'Privacy and Transparency in CBDCs: A Regulation-by-Design AML/CFT Scheme' (2022) 19(2) IEEE Transactions on Network and Service Management 1776; Panagiotis Michalopoulos and others, 'Compliance Design Options for Offline CBDCs: Balancing Privacy and AML/CFT' (2024) IEEE International Conference on Blockchain and Cryptocurrency (ICBC).

The crypto travel rule debate also testifies to the importance of carefully assessing how to implement the "same activities, same risk, same rules" principle when the activities are performed in a context that features a range of stakeholders who differ starkly from the traditional financial system. At the EU level, much remains to be seen after the adoption of the implementing measures, guidelines, and risk assessments required from various actors by the new Regulation (EU) 2023/1113. These will foreseeably continue to rely on industry standardisation initiatives, usually privately led. One can speculate that a key point will be the start of the activities of AMLA, the new EU-level supervisor. Hopefully, the new institutional set-up will enable a stronger EU effort in leading the development of effective crypto travel rule solutions based on sound techno-legal collaboration. This will be crucial to efficiently handle the need to concurrently ensure data protection safeguards as required by the GDPR.

Acknowledgement

Parts of this chapter build upon research originally conducted for the author's doctoral thesis: Nadia Pocher, 'Distributed Ledger Technologies Between Anonymity and Transparency: AML/CFT Regulation of Cryptocurrency Ecosystems in the EU' (PhD Thesis, Katholieke Universiteit Leuven, Alma Mater Studiorum Università di Bologna 2023). The additional research for this book chapter was funded by the Luxembourg National Research Fund (FNR), grant reference NCER22/IS/16570468/NCER-FT [CryptoReg], as well as by FNR-PayPal, PEARL grant reference 13342933/Gilbert Fridgen. For open access purposes, and in fulfilment of the obligations arising from the grant agreement, the author applied a Creative Commons Attribution 4.0 International (CC BY 4.0) licence to any Author Accepted Manuscript version arising from this submission.

11 Regulation of payment systems from the perspectives of consumer protection and fraud prevention

Christopher Chao-Hung Chen

I. Introduction

This chapter examines regulations of Payment Services Providers (PSPs) from the perspectives of consumer protection and fraud prevention. This chapter considers contractual terms and regulatory rules that are relevant to maintaining the integrity of payment services, focussing on the following three issues: (1) manner and efficiency of processing a payment instruction, (2) safeguarding customers' money in a payment account, and (3) prevention of fraud. In the digital era, it is essential to maintain the integrity of electronic payment services. It is also important to ensure the final completion of a payment instruction and to reduce the chance of fraud in order to create and maintain a functional, efficient, and trustworthy electronic payment system. The lack of strong integrity in the market not only affects the quality of payment services but also destroys the trust of end users of payment services. Without such trust, the payment services market would not operate efficiently.

Drawing mainly from existing regulations in Singapore, Hong Kong, and Taiwan, this chapter considers contractual and regulatory regimes that have the effect of protecting the payment system and end users against fraud. This chapter generally argues that private ordering is probably not an effective instrument to regulate the conduct of PSPs. Therefore, a certain degree of regulation may be necessary to improve a PSP's conduct standards (in terms of payment processing) and to prevent fraud, though contracts may complement Payment Services Regulation (PSR) to offer a more complete package.

From the broader historical perspective, there have been a variety of payment instruments available to market participants.[1] Many still co-exist even in developed countries. Traditionally, the most common form of payment is through delivery of cash in

1 Christopher Chen, *The Evolution of Law against Payment Frauds* (Routledge 2023) 23–45.

the form of coins or notes. Then, merchants developed ways to make remote payments with negotiable instruments (e.g., draughts, bills of exchange, or cheques). From the 1960s, there has been a growing use of credit cards,[2] ushering in an era of card-based payments connected to the existing banking network. Moreover, people may also send money from one bank account to another. Entering into the 21st century, there are more technology-based payment services such as stored-value cards (e.g., London's Oyster Card) and electronic wallets (such as China's WeChat Pay or Kenya's M-Pesa) by which people may send or receive money through a QR-code-based payment system or electronic transfer of monetary value between two accounts. With the arrival of bitcoins and blockchain, it is also possible to transfer money value with cryptocurrencies rather than cash or money deposited in a bank or e-wallet account.

From an end user's perspective, a PSP must be able to ensure that a payment or payment instruction is completed successfully and efficiently and that monetary value placed in a payment account (e.g., value stored in an e-wallet) is safe and secure. In other words, for an end user, it is essential that a payment has reached an intended payee with the correct amount within the time acceptable to the parties. For a stored-value card or an e-wallet, it is essential that the customers' money in the account does not disappear. In addition, it is also essential to counter fraudulent activities plaguing a PSP or the payment system.[3] From this perspective, there could be concerns over the conduct of PSPs (in relation to handling cash flows and payment instructions) and some prudential issues (regarding monetary value kept in a payment account) in terms of processing payments, safeguarding customers' money, and preventing fraud. Those are the three main issues that this chapter will explore.

Traditionally, payment services are largely governed by banking regulations. Before the arrival of modern electronic payment services, banks handled most payment services, including the distribution of cash, the clearing of cheques, and the issuance of credit cards. However, in recent years, we have seen a flurry of non-bank PSPs around the world offering customers other ways to move money from one place to another. Some of these new payment services could be linked to the traditional banking network (e.g., using a credit card in an e-wallet). Some could operate relatively on their own (e.g., paying by transferring cryptocurrencies through a crypto-exchange). However, the variety of new electronic PSPs presents challenges to the regulation of payment services.

PSRs have hence undergone various reforms in several countries in the past decade. For instance, in Singapore, the Parliament has passed the Payment Services Act 2019 (PSA 2019)[4] as a standalone and uniform legislation governing payment services as a whole in Singapore. The PSA 2019 classifies payment services into seven categories,

---

2 See generally David L Stearns, *Electronic Value Exchange: Origins of the VISA Electronic Payment System* (Springer 2011).

3 Chen (n 1) 49–50.

4 Singapore Payment Services Act No. 2 of 2019 (PSA 2019). Most parts of PSA 2019 came into effect in 2020.

including account issuance service, domestic money transfer service, cross-border transfer service, merchant acquisition service, e-money issuance service, digital payment token services, and money-changing service.[5] A PSP may be licensed for one or multiple categories of services.[6] Through these licences, the Monetary Authority of Singapore (MAS), Singapore's sole financial regulator, regulates different aspects of payment services from retail monetary transfer and money-changing (for foreign exchanges) to wholesale level services (e.g., merchant acquisition) and new forms of payment services (such as e-money issuance and digital payment token services). Singapore's PSA 2019 represents a move to consolidate pieces of PSRs into one single piece of legislation. This approach provides a platform for the further development of the payment services market. Based on the PSA 2019, the MAS has issued further regulatory rules and guidelines for PSPs.

In Hong Kong, the Payment Services and Stored Value Facilities Ordinance (PSSVFO)[7] is the primary source of legislation governing payment services for the Hong Kong Monetary Authority (HKMA). The PSSVFO was first promulgated in 2004 under the title of "Clearing and Settlement Ordinance", which was changed to its current title in November 2018. Traditionally, the PSSVFO focusses on operators of payment clearing and settlement services (e.g., Visa). This still forms a significant part of PSSVFO. However, since 2015, the PSSVFO was revised and extended to operators or issuers of "stored value facilities" (SVFs), which means a facility that may be used for storing the value of an amount of money that can be paid into the facility from time to time and may be used as a means of making payments.[8] An SVF may include a facility in physical or electronic form (but other than cash).[9] Therefore, the PSSVFO not only regulates traditional payment services operators (e.g., credit card systems) but it also regulates some new forms of electronic payment services.

In Taiwan, PSRs also evolved over time. In addition to banking laws, there have been special laws authorising the Financial Services Commission (FSC), the financial regulator, to regulate electronic payment services. In and before 2021, there were two separate legislations governing electronic payments – one for stored value cards (SVCs) and the other for non-bank electronic PSPs – before their merger in January 2022. The Act Governing Issuance of Electronic Stored Value Cards (ESVC Act) was first issued in 2009 (and significantly revised in 2015) to regulate the issuance of SVCs, such as the EasyCard used for the mass rapid transport (MRT) system in Taipei. The ESVC Act focusses on issuers and the issuance of SVCs, which appear in physical form or in electronical format.[10] The Act Governing Electronic Payment Institutions (EPI Act) was first promulgated in 2015 and later significantly revised in 2020 to regulate electronic

5 PSA 2019 First Schedule para 1 (Singapore).

6 PSA 2019 s 5(1) (Singapore).

7 Hong Kong Payment Services and Stored Value Facilities Ordinance (PSSVFO), Cap 584.

8 PSSVFO s 2A(1).

9 PSSVFO s 2A(6).

10 Act Governing Issuance of Electronic Stored Value Cards (ESVC Act) Art. 3(1).

PSPs. The EPI Act broadened the scope of regulation from SVCs to other kinds of electronic PSPs, including e-wallet operators or even small currency exchanges.[11] The ESVC Act and EPI Act empower the FSC to regulate issuers of SVCs and electronic PSPs if they fall within the ambit of respective laws. Thus, for a few years, there were two laws co-existing. However, the two legislations also have some degree of overlap since some SVC issuers also offer e-wallet services (e.g., Taipei's EasyCard offering Easy Wallet services). Hence, on 27 January 2022, the government decided to abolish the ESVC Act and instead use the EPI Act as the main legislation to regulate non-bank PSPs.

The regulatory framework certainly affects the comparability of regulations in different markets. For instance, Singapore's PSA 2019 also regulates physical money exchangers, but this is not the case for Taiwan's EPI Act and Hong Kong's PSSVFO. In all three markets, there has been a growing number of regulations governing non-bank PSPs in the past decade alongside traditional banking regulations. This development reflects the growth of the payment services market with more technology-based PSPs and non-bank service providers entering the market. This chapter will undertake a more holistic approach to payment services laws and regulations. Maintaining the integrity of payment services involves not only public regulations of PSPs but also contractual arrangements. Together, they form a more complete package to regulate the conduct of PSPs and to maintain the integrity of payment services and the payment system.

In the remainder of this chapter, Section II discusses the angle of private ordering by examining samples of user agreements between a PSP and customers. This analysis lays the foundation for the contractual relationship between a customer and a PSP at the service and transaction levels. Section III then considers relevant rules under PSRs in Singapore, Hong Kong, and Taiwan. The goal is to illustrate conduct of business and prudential rules that help ensure the integrity of payment services and prevent fraud. Section IV will conclude this chapter by reflecting upon private ordering and regulatory rules to maintain the integrity of payment services and prevent fraud.

This chapter will focus on laws and regulations in Taiwan, Hong Kong, and Singapore for illustration. For clarification, this chapter does not conduct a full comparative law study in the three markets. This chapter focusses on electronic and digital payment services such as electronic wallets (e-wallets) or other forms of digital payment rather than traditional bank transfers (which may be conducted online) or credit card payments, though they may share some common issues.

11 Taiwan Act Governing Electronic Payment Institutions (EPI Act) Art. 4.

II. Private ordering approach

Some consumer protection issues could be addressed by contractual terms. For their own interests, PSPs should have incentives to strengthen and maintain the safety of the system and to prevent fraud from happening. Hence, PSPs may use contractual terms to impose obligations on customers to achieve the goal.[12] The legal instrument that a PSP may adopt is the user agreement between a PSP and its customers. User agreements provide the foundation to analyse the rights and obligations of a PSP and a customer. In theory, a PSP and a customer may be able to bargain for contractual terms regarding the allocation of losses if something goes wrong with the payment services (e.g., an account being hacked). However, given that a PSP has to face many customers, in practice, user agreements should tend to be standard forms. In other words, customers most likely have no choice but to accept the terms offered by a PSP.

This section analyses some contractual terms from several electronic PSPs as case studies in Taiwan, Singapore, and Hong Kong. The purpose is to understand contractual arrangements to ensure the integrity of payment services and the allocation of losses. This chapter focusses on terms stating a PSP's obligation regarding the processing of payment instructions and the prevention of fraud. This chapter uses a sample of user agreements from e-wallet services associated with stored-value cards for the mass transport system in Singapore and Hong Kong, including the EZ-Link Wallet[13] in Singapore, Octopus Online Payment Service (for Octopus Wallet)[14] in Hong Kong, and Taiwan's EasyWallet (by the EasyCard).[15] For clarification, this chapter does not offer a comprehensive and exhaustive study of all PSPs and contractual terms in the three markets.

First, regarding the manner and efficiency of payment services, a user agreement often does not state a PSP's general conduct obligation directly. In contrast, a PSP might include terms that otherwise exempt a PSP from potential liability for delays or disruption of services. For instance, Singapore's EZ-Link Wallet provides that it does not warrant that the e-wallet service will be available and uninterrupted at all times.[16] The agreement also makes it clear that the firm is not liable for the losses incurred when an end user is not able to use the services.[17] In another example, the Octopus in Hong Kong states in the user agreement that "[i]n the absence of manifest error, the record

---

12 See Chen (n 1) 152–155.

13 EZ-Link Wallet, 'EZ-Link Terms and Conditions' <https://www.ezlink.com.sg/terms/#ezlink-wallet> accessed 20 October 2023.

14 Octopus Payment Service, 'Terms & Conditions for Octopus Online Payment Service' <https://www.octopus.com.hk/en/document/online_payment_terms.pdf> accessed 20 October 2023.

15 EasyWallet, 'User Agreement' (May 2020 Version) <https://www.easycard.com.tw/_upload/files/easywallet-law-20200615.pdf> accessed 20 October 2023.

16 EZ-Link Wallet Agreement, Clause 6; Octopus Agreement, Clause 7(e).

17 EZ-Link Wallet Agreement, Clause 6; Octopus Agreement, Clause 7(f).

kept by the Octopus is final, conclusive and binding on" a customer.[18] This also has the effect of clarifying a PSP's obligation about the finality of payment.

In contrast, the EasyWallet in Taiwan provides that the firm should "immediately transfer monetary value from one account to another".[19] The user agreements of EZ-Link Wallet in Singapore and Octopus Wallet in Hong Kong do not have a similar term. The term in the EasyWallet agreement comes from the contractual template for electronic payment institutions (EPIs) issued by Taiwan's financial regulator.[20] Hence, this should become a standardised term for electronic PSPs operated in Taiwan.

Second, it is common to see PSPs impose some conduct obligations on customers. One such obligation is to require a customer to check his account balance after each transaction.[21] In Taiwan, the EasyWallet further requires that the PSP ask a customer to confirm a transaction before the final processing of a payment instruction.[22] This is not only to confirm the proper processing of a payment instruction from the customer's end, but it may also help the customer and the PSP identify fraud or transaction errors as early as possible.

Another important obligation is to ensure the security of the payment system and customers' payment accounts. Therefore, it is necessary to reduce the chance that a payment account is hacked or misused by a fraudster. There are two dimensions of using contractual terms to enhance security. On the one hand, recognising the fact that unauthorised use of a payment account often comes from a customer leaking his account information somewhere, a PSP may impose a general obligation on a customer to safeguard account information and password properly.[23] Similarly, user agreements may specifically require a customer not to allow a third party to use his account.[24] To strengthen the PSP's position in the case of unauthorised use of a payment account, Hong Kong's Octopus also states that it is not liable to a customer for losses arising from or in connection with any unauthorised use of a payment account.[25]

On the other hand, it is also the PSP's obligation to ensure that the system has proper security measures in place to detect and prevent potential hacking or data breach.[26] Of course, robust security measures should be the baseline requirement for any PSP. A PSP does not necessarily have to make it a contractual obligation. However, from the

18 Octopus Agreement, Clause 3.2(f).
19 EasyWallet Agreement, Clause 6(2).
20 Clause 5(3) of the Template for Standard Form for Electronic Payment Institutions, <https://www.ey.gov.tw/Page/AABD2F12D8A6D561/2a2776f4-d8d6-4e1a-8104-aa37cfeabc1a> accessed 20 October 2023.
21 Octopus Agreement, Clause 3.2(g).
22 EasyWallet Agreement, Clause 8(1).
23 E.g., EasyWallet Agreement, Clause 10(1).
24 E.g., EZ-Link Agreement, Clause 14.
25 Octopus Agreement, Clause 7(g).
26 E.g., EasyWallet Agreement, Clause 11.

perspective of a customer, having a contractual obligation to maintain proper security for the payment system could make it easier for a customer to seek remedies if his account is hacked due to a security failure of a PSP. Whether such failure could be attributed to the fault of a PSP is a separate issue.

Third, another way to curtail potential losses from fraud is to limit the amount of money that can be stored in an e-wallet or transferred in a transaction. For instance, the EZ-Link Wallet in Singapore only allows a customer to deposit a maximum amount of S$500 into the e-wallet.[27] In Taiwan, the EasyWallet allows a customer to transfer a maximum NT$50,000 for each individual transaction and a maximum NT$100,000 in aggregate for each day.[28] The maximum deposit or transaction limit naturally caps the losses that a customer can incur if a payment account is hacked by a fraudster. While it may cause inconvenience to some end users, it can serve as a simple way to protect consumers against unauthorised use of their payment account. Of course, the limit does not necessarily prevent fraud from happening for smaller amounts below the cap.

Last, a user agreement can also allow a PSP to stop payment for a suspicious transaction. For example, Hong Kong's Octopus Wallet states that the PSP can refuse to act on a payment instruction if it is doubtful of its legality or authenticity, and the PSP has no obligation to enquire.[29] This would allow a PSP to preemptively stop a fraudulent transaction *ex ante.*

In the end, one question is whether it is sufficient to count on user agreements to provide sufficient consumer protection mechanisms. There is no doubt that contracts would play a significant role in defining the relationship between a PSP and a customer. The private ordering approach does not replace other legal or regulatory mechanisms. If there is indeed fraud, criminal law would be applicable anyway. Instead, contracts would complement other legal tools to protect users of electronic payment services and to counter fraud.

However, this chapter also argues that there are limits to the private ordering approach to consumer protection and fraud prevention for electronic payment services. First, there seems to be no standard practice in the world regarding terms that should be stated in user agreements. There are, of course, some common terms. However, even by comparing the three user agreements from e-wallets in Singapore, Hong Kong, and Taiwan, this chapter finds that there is a variety of contractual arrangements. Thus, contractual solutions are far from uniform globally.

Second, user agreements are made by the PSP. Inevitably, they are standard forms. Hence, it is natural that PSPs would focus more on terms that regulate a user's conduct

---

27 EZ-Link Wallet Agreement, Clause 2.

28 EasyWallet Agreement, Clause 8(2).

29 Octopus Agreement, Clause 7(a).

and less on their own obligations without regulatory intervention (e.g., Taiwan's contractual template for EPIs). For instance, the EZ-Link Wallet in Singapore and the Octopus Wallet in Hong Kong both choose not to mention anything related to how they would process a payment instruction. In contrast, in Taiwan, due to the contractual template by the financial regulator, at least PSPs have to promise to process an instruction immediately. It is beyond the scope of this chapter to examine whether Taiwan's template approach is appropriate or whether the terms stated in the contractual template are reasonable. However, regulators probably could monitor the potential use of unfair terms (e.g., certain exclusion clauses) in user agreements for payment services.

III. Regulation of payment services providers

PSRs may step in to fill the gap and to strengthen the basis of consumer protection and fraud prevention if private ordering (in addition to criminal sanctions for wrongdoing) is not sufficient. As discussed in Section I above, the regulatory framework differs among the three markets. In Taiwan, the EPI Act is the primary source of regulations for electronic payment service providers. In Singapore, the PSA 2019 offers a broader regulatory mandate for all forms of PSPs (e.g., money exchangers) in the payment system. In Hong Kong, the PSSVFO, Cap 584, regulates the payment system and issuers of stored value cards. The discussion below will focus on electronic PSPs such as e-wallets. For clarification, this chapter will not engage in detailed discussions of banking regulations if it is a commercial bank that offers payment services.

In this part, this chapter will first introduce the background of payment service regulations in Singapore, Hong Kong, and Taiwan. The chapter then will consider general conduct obligations and prudential requirements that may have the effect of safeguarding a customer's money. Section IV will then reflect upon existing contractual and regulatory rules in the future.

A. General conduct obligation about the manner of fund transfer

Regulations could impose a general obligation on PSPs regarding the manner and/or speed of payment services. By the nature of payment services and pursuant to contracts, a PSP should duly execute a customer's payment instructions in principle. For instance, barring any exceptional situation, if an e-wallet operator receives an instruction from Customer X to transfer \$100 from X's account to Y's account in the same system, the e-wallet operator should complete the instruction by transferring monetary value worth \$100 from X's account to Y's. The following question is when such a transfer has to be completed. In other words, how efficiently must a payment instruction be processed and completed?

There are different regulatory wordings in statutes in the three markets. Regulations may generally require a PSP to process a payment instruction as soon as possible. For instance, Taiwan's EPI Act provides that an EPI "shall carry out the transfer of funds according to the payment instructions agreed by users in advance or *instantly without any delay*, and nor accept a request from a third party for the suspension of payment or remittance, or other similar requests"[30] (emphasis added). Hence, under Taiwan law, unless a PSP agrees with a customer (normally in the user agreement) about a specified timeframe, a PSP has to carry out a payment instruction "instantly without delay". There is no further guidance on how "instant" it should be. Perhaps it is not practical to expect that the transaction should always be completed within seconds. However, legislators likely do not contemplate "instantly without any delay" to be days or even hours unless there are system errors or problems with the internet.

Singapore prescribes a fixed maximum timeframe for a payment instruction. The PSA 2019 provides that an Activity B licensee (including domestic money transfer services) has to ensure a payee receives the money within three business days from the date the money is accepted for any domestic transfer service.[31] For an Activity C licensee (for cross-border transfer), the timeline is seven days.[32] The maximum timeframe obviously varies depending on the type of services. It is sensible and reasonable to set a longer timeframe for cross-border services and shorter for domestic transfers. In contrast, Taiwan's lawmakers probably did not consider the possibility of cross-border electronic payment services when making the EPI Act.

In contrast to Taiwan and Singapore, Hong Kong law makes no specific mention of the timeframe for processing a payment instruction other than generally prescribing a PSP (i.e., a stored value facility) to conduct its business in a safe and efficient manner.[33] Otherwise, there could be criminal penalties.[34] Regarding efficiency, the PSSVFO provides that "a reference to the efficiency of a stored value facility includes in particular any matter relating to the speed and efficiency with which operations relating to the facility are carried out".[35] The HKMA does not further define how efficient an SVF has to be in its regulatory guidelines other than a simple paragraph stating that an SVF "should provide efficient and reliable SVF payment services which are commensurate with the mode of operation of its SVF".[36]

Eventually, a policy question is how much delay in processing a payment instruction would be tolerable, assuming there is no *force majeure* or other external incident (e.g., large-scale power storage that causes service interruption) causing disruption or delay. There are pros and cons regarding whether regulators should set a deadline or a fixed period for a PSP to execute a payment instruction and complete the funds transfer. Taiwan's and Hong Kong's approaches (e.g., "without delay" in Taiwan or "operate

30 EPI Act, Art. 18(1).
31 MAS Notice on Conduct (PSN07) para 11.
32 PSN07, para 12.
33 PSSVFO s 8O(1).
34 PSSVFO s 8O(2).
35 PSSVFO s 8P(2).
36 Hong Kong Monetary Authority (HKMA) Guideline on Supervision of Stored Value Facility Licensees para 7.3.8.

efficiently" in Hong Kong) may offer more flexibility to accommodate a wide range of situations where payment services are affected.

In contrast, a clear deadline should give more clarity to consumers about when they would receive the funds in their accounts. It may offer PSPs some protection against short-term problems (e.g., power outages for a few hours in an area). However, whether a fixed period is feasible must depend on whether it is practical for a PSP to comply. In practice, Taiwan, Singapore, and Hong Kong all have some form of "real-time gross settlement" (RTGS) system.[37] Hence, for inter-bank transfers in the retail market, a payee of a small sum should be able to receive money in his bank account almost immediately if a transfer request is made when the system is operational. For a domestic transfer of a large sum, it may take a few hours to arrive depending on the technical standards of the relevant payment clearing system. For e-wallets, if a fund transfer is made between two accounts in the same e-wallet (e.g., from one SingTel Dash account to another SingTel Dash account), the transfer should in practice be completed within seconds or minutes at worst, barring any technical errors or connection issues. Hence, the three-day timeframe for domestic transfers under Singapore's PSA 2019 seems to be quite generous, providing the bottom line for a domestic electronic transfer service. Nevertheless, a normal customer probably could not wait for more than a few hours (let alone three days) for an electronic payment instruction to be processed and completed.

Furthermore, there could be situations where a PSP can legitimately refuse to execute a payment instruction. Both contractual agreements and regulatory rules may allow or sometimes require a PSP to stop a fund transfer. The most obvious legal impediment is to stop processing a payment due to reasons related to anti-money laundering and countering the financing of terrorism (AML/CFT) rules. There is a strong political and public policy context to the enforcement of AML/CFT rules to cut off the financing of criminals and terrorists. There is no exception for non-bank PSPs. Singapore, Hong Kong, and Taiwan all extend AML/CFT rules to electronic PSPs. For instance, in Singapore, the MAS has issued specific AML/CFT rules for non-bank PSPs and digital payment token services.[38] If a PSP suspects a payment instruction to be illegal or if an account may violate AML/CFT laws, then it is natural that a PSP should not allow an account holder to continue using his payment account.

B. Safeguarding customers' money with prudential requirements for payment service providers

In addition to a general conduct obligation about processing a payment, another important tool to protect customers is to impose some prudential requirements on

---

37 Chen (n 1) 33–36.

38 MAS, Notice on Prevention of Money Laundering and Countering the Financing of Terrorism – Specified Payment Services (PSN01) and Notice on Prevention of Money Laundering and Countering the Financing of Terrorism – Digital Payment Token Services (PSN02).

PSPs for the purpose of safeguarding their money or value stored in an e-wallet. The primary goal is clearly to ensure that a PSP has the funds and liquidity to meet customers' demands, though the prudential requirements for PSPs do not have to be as sophisticated as those for commercial banks. There could be several tools that a regulator may adopt.

First, there could be a minimum capital requirement to maintain the solvency and financial capacity of a PSP. For instance, in Taiwan, the EPI Act requires that an EPI needs to have at least NT$ 500 million of equity capital.[39] Moreover, the financial regulator may also impose a limitation on multiples between the balance of funds and the equity capital.[40] Similarly, in Singapore, the MAS sets the minimum base capital for a holder of a major payment institution licence to be S$250,000, and S$100,000 for the holder of a standard payment institution licence.[41] In Hong Kong, an SVF operator is required to have adequate financial resources and no less than HK$25 million of paid-up capital.[42]

Those requirements at least ensure that PSPs have some level of financial cushion to meet the demands of customers and creditors, though a requirement for minimum capital does not necessarily mean that a PSP is less likely to become insolvent. A further issue is whether regulators should develop more sophisticated methods to calculate and regulate a PSP's solvency and capital adequacy like banks and insurers. This chapter does not argue that electronic PSPs should be regulated like banks or insurers in terms of prudential regulation. After all, the business model of a PSP is a lot simpler than that of commercial banks and insurance companies. However, it may still require domestic and global regulators to monitor market development carefully when new non-bank PSPs in the financial technology era grow larger and attract more customers to place money in their e-wallets.

Second, regulators may also require PSPs to provide extra protection to customers' funds placed in an e-wallet to ensure that PSPs will be able to meet their obligations to customers. The extra protection could be in the form of a trust arrangement for customers' funds and/or in the form of a guarantee or performance bond. For instance, Taiwan's EPI Act requires an EPI to "declare trust in full or obtain *full guarantee* from a bank for the users' stored funds and for funds collected/paid as an agent" (emphasis added).[43] An EPI either has to create a trust (for the stored funds) with a bank (as the trustee) or acquire a performance bond from a bank.[44] The amount of guarantee or performance bond should be at least the full amount of stored funds or funds collected. In other words, an EPI needs to have a guarantee or performance bond to warrant a full refund to customers. In case an EPI fails to create a trust or

39 EPI Act, Art. 9(1).
40 EPI Act, Art. 24(1).
41 MAS Guidelines on Licensing for Payment Service Provider (PS-G01), para 3.1.5.
42 PSSVFO Schedule 2 Part 2 para 2
43 EPI Act, Art. 21(1).
44 EPI Act, Art. 21(3).

meet its obligation to acquire a performance bond/guarantee from a bank, Taiwan law also requires an EPI to prepare for a separate solvency fund.[45] The solvency fund will be used to return money to customers if an EPI becomes insolvent.[46] Moreover, under Taiwan law, an EPI has to deposit the funds it received from customers into a dedicated deposit account in the same currency with a bank, with proper recording of transactions and flow of funds.[47] An EPI cannot use funds in payment accounts other than meeting a customer's payment instruction or withdrawal of funds.[48]

In Singapore, a major payment institution has to place a sum of money in the form of a cash deposit or bank guarantee as security to the MAS.[49] The sum should be S$100,000 if the average total value of payment transactions in a month (over a calendar year) does not exceed S$6 million; otherwise, it is S$200,000 for all other cases.[50] However, there is no such deposit requirement for a standard payment institution.

In addition, a major payment institution (for domestic money transfer) must

> ensure that no later than the next business day after any relevant money is received from, or on account of, a customer, the whole or such part, as may be prescribed, of the relevant money, is safeguarded by an undertaking from a safeguarding institution to be fully liable to the customers, by a guarantee given by a safeguarding institution for the amount of money, by depositing money in a trust account, or otherwise in the manner prescribed by the regulator.[51]

By definition, a safeguarding institution has to be a bank or any financial institution prescribed by the MAS.[52] Hence, it literally it means that a major payment institution has to acquire a guarantee or an undertaking of a similar effect from a bank to ensure it will be able to meet their obligations to customers in the future.

While Singapore law seems to be similar to Taiwan law, there is a critical difference. First, under Taiwan law, acquiring a performance bond (or guarantee) and placing customers' money into a separate bank account are cumulative requirements. An EPI has to comply with both. In contrast, in Singapore, a major payment institution has an option. It can choose to acquire a bank guarantee or performance bond, but it may also decide to place customers' money into a trust account to ring-fence the funds. The difference should be reflected in compliance and operational costs. While the intention of Taiwan law is clearly to ensure that an EPI has sufficient funds to return

45 EPI Act, Art. 41(1).
46 EPI Act, Art. 41(2).
47 EPI Act, Art. 17(1).
48 EPI Act, Art. 22(1), exception in Art. 22(2) (e.g. deposit, certificate of deposit, or government bonds).
49 PSA 2019, s 22(1).
50 PS-G01, para 3.1.6.
51 PSA 2019, s 23(2). See subsection 4 for the requirement for e-money issuers.
52 PSA 2019, s 23(14).

to customers, the requirements for extra protection (i.e., trust, performance bond, and additional solvency fund) imply higher operational and compliance costs. It is probably not cheap to acquire a sufficient performance bond or guarantee from a bank if there is a large sum of stored funds held by an EPI. How those costs may affect the market remains to be seen. If the costs are too high, they may prohibit smaller PSPs from entering the market. This may be an issue that Taiwan's FSC has to consider carefully.

Second, Taiwan law only requires EPIs to place customers' money into a bank account. In contrast, in Singapore, a major payment institution satisfies the safeguarding requirement by placing customers' funds into a trust account with a safeguarding institution,[53] which should be a bank or finance company that is not the PSP.[54] Placing customers' money in a separate bank account simply means that customers' money does not mingle with the firm's own money (assuming the money is put in another bank account); but it does not mean customers' money is off the PSP's balance sheet. Compared with a trust account, it does not seem to offer better protection to customers if the money is placed in a separate bank account. This chapter does not venture further to examine in detail trust law. However, the subtle difference may have an impact on customers' rights to their money if a PSP unfortunately fails.

Hong Kong law seems to be vague compared with Singapore and Taiwan. On the one hand, the HKMA requires an operator of a stored value facility to have in place risk management policies and procedures to manage the float or deposit (i.e., customers' money stored in the facility) to ensure that "there will always be sufficient funds for the redemption of the stored value that remains on the facility".[55] The operator should also ensure that at all times the float or deposit is "kept separate from any other funds paid to or maintained or received by the [operator]" and is "adequately protected by the measures adopted by the applicable company for protecting the float or deposit".[56] On the other hand, Hong Kong law does not seem to require a PSP to park customers' money in a trust account like in Singapore.

C. Fraud risk management

Rampant fraud may threaten the viability of electronic payment services. Hence, similar to open banking,[57] cybersecurity and fraud risk management is of utmost importance for electronic PSPs. Not only would a customer suffer losses if his money deposited with an electronic PSP is gone due to a security breach, but the market

53 PSA 2019, s 23(5).
54 PSA 2019, s 23(10).
55 PSSVFO, Schedule 3 part 2 para 7(a).
56 PSSVFO, Schedule 3 part 2 para 7(c).
57 Joseph Lee and Vere-Marie Khan, 'Developing Cybersecurity in Open Banking and Open Finance: the Application of Blockchain Technology and Decentralised Autonomous Organisations' in Joseph Lee and Aline Darbellay (eds), *A Research Agenda for Financial Law and Regulation* (Edward Elgar 2024).

might lose faith in a particular PSP or the electronic payment services as a whole. Either way, it is not good for the development of the payment services market.

As discussed in Section II, PSPs can use contracts to impose an obligation on customers to safeguard their account information, passwords, or other security measures. For this purpose, similar to open banking, PSPs may have to establish procedures and systems to identify potential attacks, implement secure computer networks, and deal with the aftermath.[58] Regulators may also require PSPs to maintain proper cybersecurity protocols and have sound technology risk management practices in place to deter hacking or breaches of customers' accounts. For instance, Singapore requires PSPs to comply with technology risk management guidelines and cyber hygiene guidelines, including the use of two-factor verification and security measures to protect the system and administration accounts.[59]

In Hong Kong, the PSSVFO specifically provides that a PSP must ensure that "the operation of any stored value facility issued, or the issue of which is facilitated, under its licence is conducted in a safe and efficient manner calculated to minimise the likelihood of any disruption to the functioning of the facility".[60] Otherwise there could be criminal penalties.[61] The reference to "safety and efficiency" of a stored value facility includes the following aspects: reliability and robustness of the operation of the facility, asset control over the facility, the integrity of the information held, risk management and control procedures, soundness and integrity of the facility, and services provided by any infrastructure associated with the facility.[62]

Moreover, fraud risk management is also an important aspect of regulations for PSPs in addition to maintaining security measures. Fraud risk management should be an integral and essential part of a PSP's risk management practice and internal control system. A sound fraud risk management system might require a PSP to set up a monitoring mechanism to identify fraudulent activities and an internal governance regime to report and handle red flags for fraud.

In Hong Kong, for instance, the PSSVFO specifically requires that a PSP should come with effective means to detect fraud and attempted fraud.[63] In Singapore, while the PSA 2019 itself does not provide a specific requirement for fraud risk management, the MAS has issued technology risk management guidelines, which require a PSP to implement real-time fraud monitoring systems to identify and block suspicious or fraudulent online transactions.[64] There should also be a process to investigate

58 Ibid.
59 PS-G01, para 4.4.
60 PSSVFO s 8O(1).
61 PSSVFO s 8O(2).
62 PSSVFO s 8P(1).
63 PSSVFO, Schedule 2 part 2 para 5(1)(b).
64 MAS, Technology Risk Management Guidelines, para 14.3.1.

suspicious transactions to ensure issues are adequately and promptly addressed.[65] If a firm has identified a suspicious transaction, it should notify the customers.[66]

In contrast, in Taiwan, neither the EPI Act nor its subsidiary regulations by the FSC have a clear requirement for adequate fraud risk management. The FSC only requires that an EPI should suspend or terminate a payment account if the account has been used for fraudulent or illegal purposes[67] in addition to guidelines regarding cybersecurity.[68] It does not necessarily mean that an EPI does not need to have a sound fraud risk management practice in place. However, there is no solid legal requirement in the regulatory wording.

IV. Concluding remarks: comparison and reflection

In summary, this chapter briefly compares contracts and regulations in Singapore, Hong Kong, and Taiwan regarding electronic payment services, focussing on three main issues: general conduct obligations concerning payment processing, safeguarding a customer's money in an e-wallet, and fraud risk management and prevention. The ultimate goals are to protect end users of electronic payment services for efficient services and maintain the integrity of a payment system.

This chapter has the following general observations. First, PSPs may use contractual terms to regulate their own and customers' conduct. However, given that user agreements tend to be standard forms, we should not unrealistically expect PSPs to hold themselves to higher (if not the highest) standards in user agreements. Hence, regulations may have to fill in the gap if necessary.

This is duly reflected in rules governing the manner and efficiency of processing a payment instruction. As discussed in Sections II and III above, the two e-wallet agreements this chapter samples in Singapore and Hong Kong made no mention of any obligation regarding how fast the respective e-wallet should process a customer's payment instruction. Payment regulations offer some more guidance as Singapore provides a fixed number of days for a PSP to complete a transaction, and Hong Kong offers only general guidance on the efficiency of payment processing. In contrast, in Taiwan, both a user agreement (and the contractual template for electronic payment institutions) and the EPI Act specifically require a PSP to process a payment instruction "instantly with any delay". The experience in Taiwan may indicate that PSRs may affect contractual practices.

65 MAS, Technology Risk Management Guidelines, para 14.3.2.
66 MAS, Technology Risk Management Guidelines, para 14.3.3.
67 FSC, Rules Governing the Administration of Electronic Payment Business, Art. 28.
68 FSC, Regulations Governing the Standards for Information System and Security Management of Electronic Payment Institutions.

A further question is how far regulations should intervene to prescribe the manner and efficiency of the provision of payment services. As seen from the regulations in Singapore, Hong Kong, and Taiwan, there seems to be no universal solution. At the moment, e-wallet operators should be able to process a payment instruction within seconds or minutes except when there are other external problems (e.g., internet outage). Hence, there seems to be no strong need for further regulations at the moment. However, if one day payment services become more sophisticated than simply transferring monetary value from one account to another, more conduct obligations may be necessary.

Second, it is important to safeguard money stored in an e-wallet, similar to the need to protect deposit-holders and insureds for their money in bank accounts or insurance policies. However, PSRs are far less developed than banking and insurance regulations in this regard. By comparing rules in Singapore, Hong Kong, and Taiwan, this chapter observes that regulators in the three markets generally use three primary methods to safeguard customers' money: minimum capital requirement, third-party protection (e.g., performance bond or guarantee), and segregation of customers' money (into a separate bank account or a trust). At the moment, there is a wide range of electronic PSPs in the world, from large players to small ones. The regulatory tools mentioned above may be sufficient for smaller PSPs. However, if a PSP becomes much larger and more interconnected with banks and other financial institutions, regulators should perhaps ponder whether it is desirable to have more regulations on at least large PSPs to protect customers' money and the whole payment system.

Third and last, a sound payment system needs to tackle fraud tampering with a payment system or service. There are cybersecurity issues for electronic payment services. However, fraud risk management is more than just cybersecurity. In addition to setting up robust security measures for its system, a PSP should establish sound fraud risk detection and management systems (at least in Singapore and Hong Kong's regulations). As the payment services market grows more digitalised, PSPs and regulators should monitor the development of the market and types of fraudulent activities in order to implement proper contractual and legal regimes to prevent fraud from happening *ex ante* and cope with fraudulent activities when they happen.

In conclusion, with the rise of financial technology, payment services laws gradually grow out of the shadow of banking regulations. We have seen Singapore and Taiwan issuing standalone regulations to govern PSPs, with Hong Kong adapting from an old law. With the growing PSRs, it is also important to consider further prudential and conduct regulations for PSPs. This chapter seeks to offer a glimpse of potential contractual and regulatory issues for the purpose of protecting customers of e-wallets. While the market and payment technology are developing, there are bound to be more issues arising in the future that require legal solutions.

12 A research agenda for online dispute resolution for DLT finance

Pietro Ortolani

I. Introduction

Over the last decade, Distributed Ledger Technology (DLT) has enabled the rise of a wide range of unprecedented digital assets and financial instruments, triggering fascinating changes in the world of global finance.[1] Such a quick pace of innovation, however, has unavoidably brought about numerous disputes related to DLT finance: think, for instance, of claims related to the provision of inaccurate or incomplete information during the launch of a new coin or token, or the failure of custodians (e.g., cryptoasset exchange service providers) to protect their clients against hacks.[2] These developments, in turn, raise the question of how to prevent and resolve the disputes that inevitably arise in the new DLT financial arena. This chapter sketches out future lines of legal research, which may contribute to answering this question.

The remainder of the chapter proceeds as follows. Section II will consider "traditional" dispute resolution mechanisms (i.e., court litigation and arbitration) and illustrate some of the unanswered questions that currently exist. The chapter will also put forth suggestions as to how future research could contribute to answering those questions. Subsequently, Section III will zoom in on some new tools for the prevention and resolution of DLT finance disputes and describe the potential as well as the

1 Alexis Collomb and Klara Sok, 'Blockchain/Distributed Ledger Technology (DLT): What Impact on the Financial Sector?' (2016) 103(3) Digiworld Economic Journal 93; Ittay Eyal, 'Blockchain Technology: Transforming Libertarian Cryptocurrency Dreams to Finance and Banking Realities' (2017) 50 Computer 38; Alexander Bechtel and others, 'The Future of Payments in a DLT-based European Economy: A Roadmap' in Markus Heckel and Franz Waldenberger (eds), *The Future of Financial Systems in the Digital Age: Perspectives from Europe and Japan* (Springer 2022).

2 Gregory Chartier, 'Conflict of Laws and the Use of Distributed Ledger Technology in Derivatives Markets' in Andrea Bonomi, Matthias Lehmann, and Shaheeza Lalani (eds), *Blockchain and Private International Law* (Brill Nijhoff 2023); Elizabeth Chan, Nicole Tang, and Edward Taylor, 'Crypto Disputes: The Valuation Challenge' (2023) 17(1) Dispute Resolution International 21; Dirk Wiegandt, 'Blockchain and Smart Contracts and the Role of Arbitration' (2022) 39(5) Journal of International Arbitration 671.

limitations of the technology underlying those tools. Once again, particular attention will be devoted to the contours of a future research agenda in this field. Finally, Section IV will summarise the findings and draw some conclusions.

II. Distributed ledger technology-related financial disputes and traditional dispute resolution mechanisms

In order to sketch a comprehensive research agenda for online dispute resolution (ODR) with respect to DLT finance, it is necessary to start from the dispute resolution mechanisms that are most commonly used for the resolution of financial disputes, that is, court litigation and arbitration. While these mechanisms have already been extensively discussed in legal literature, that does not mean that all questions have been answered. To the contrary, DLT's peculiar characteristics raise questions with respect to both courts and arbitration, which have not been sufficiently scrutinised and answered yet. The following sub-sections will describe those questions, starting from courts, and then moving on to arbitration. Against this descriptive background, it will be possible to sketch a research agenda aimed at filling the current gaps in our understanding of the interplay between traditional dispute resolution avenues, on the one hand, and DLT finance, on the other hand.

A. Court litigation

Disputes concerning DLT-related financial transactions are routinely decided by national courts all over the world. Nevertheless, the framework of court litigation does not fit neatly with the reality of DLT finance, for a number of reasons. First, parties engaging in DLT-related financial transactions may do so while maintaining anonymity;[3] this, in turn, casts doubt not only on national courts' ability to provide relief where needed but also on the practical prospects for enforceability of any judgment rendered by those courts. Second, national courts typically determine the boundaries of their jurisdiction on the basis of territorial criteria, which have largely been developed before the emergence of DLT.[4] Those criteria are sometimes difficult to reconcile with the distributed and essentially delocalised nature of the ledgers that enable a wide range of alternative finance transactions. Third, even if two parties to a DLT-related financial transaction enter into a choice-of-court agreement, conferring jurisdiction upon a certain national court to the exclusion of all others, such a clause may fail to prevent complex jurisdictional problems whenever the cause of action is not contractual in nature.[5] Fourth, at a more practical level, the cost and

3 Nima Norouzi, 'The Sovereignty of Blockchain Dispute Resolution' (2021) 2(1) Journal of Private and Economic Law 1.

4 Dan Jerker B Svantesson and Symeon C Symeonides, 'Cross-border Internet Defamation Conflicts and What to Do About Them: Two Proposals' (2023) 19(2) Journal of Private International Law 137.

5 Pietro Ortolani, 'The Impact of Blockchain Technologies and Smart Contracts on Dispute Resolution: Arbitration and Court Litigation at the Crossroads' (2019) 24(2)

complexity of court litigation may constitute a significant deterrent for parties needing legal protection with regard to a DLT-related financial dispute. The following sub-sections will expound on these issues and set forth a research agenda for future further investigation.

1. *Anonymity and court litigation*

Recent practice demonstrates that some national courts have shown a willingness to hear claims brought against unknown defendants, in cases concerning DLT finance.[6] However, this trend is far from universal, and other legal systems prevent the filing of a civil lawsuit against defendants that cannot be precisely identified. Failing any court willingness to hear cases against anonymous defendants, the route of court litigation is likely precluded upfront for plaintiffs that have engaged in a DLT-related financial transaction with a prospective defendant but are unable to identify them. This, in itself, raises an interesting comparative law research question: to what extent do different national courts allow civil lawsuits against unknown defendants, and what is their rationale for accepting or refusing to do so? More comparative analysis on this topic would be very helpful in order to assess the consequences from an access to justice perspective, and potentially pave the way towards reform and harmonisation in this area.

Even in those legal systems where a lawsuit against an anonymous defendant is theoretically possible, further questions arise. What is the practical usefulness of a favourable judgment if the anonymity of the judgment debtor makes the coercive enforcement of the court decision practically impossible? This, once again, is a question that would deserve further comparative legal research. A possible hypothesis to be tested is that, in many of the cases where a DLT-related financial lawsuit is brought against an unknown defendant, the latter is only one of a number of defendants, and the other defendants have been identified. By way of example, a lawsuit could be brought against both an anonymous tortfeasor or counterparty to a financial transaction, and an identifiable or identified custodian (e.g., a cryptoasset exchange). If successful, the plaintiff could then seek enforcement against that custodian. Should this hypothesis indeed prove true, an argument could be put forth concerning the limitations of court litigation in this field. More specifically, even in legal systems where litigation against anonymous defendants is possible, its usefulness is limited to specific cases involving multiple parties (at least some of which have been identified by the plaintiff). For other types of disputes, instead, court litigation is an unviable option.

2. *Distributed ledgers and jurisdictional dilemmas*

In most legal systems, the jurisdiction of courts to deal with civil or commercial claims is determined by private international law rules (either statutory or jurisprudential) which were developed before the emergence of DLT and largely refer to physical

Uniform Law Review 430.

6 *Janesh s/o Rajkumar v Unknown Person ("CHEFPIERRE")* [2022] SGHC 264; *Fetch.ai Ltd v Persons Unknown* [2021] EWHC 2254 (Comm).

localisation criteria. Applying those rules to DLT-related financial disputes may prove challenging, if not outright impossible. As already mentioned, whenever the defendant is not identifiable, it may be impossible to establish jurisdiction based on rules that refer to the defendant's domicile (*actor sequitur forum rei*).[7] Furthermore, irrespective of whether the defendant can be geographically located, the distributed nature of the ledger supporting a financial transaction may hinder the identification of the place of performance of the contract, or (in case of a tortious cause of action) of the place where the harmful event allegedly occurred. In this context, a jurisdictional analysis will often require a complex factual evaluation, in order to determine whether a sufficient connection with the *forum* exists. By way of example, if the applicable private international law rules require the plaintiff to specify the geographical location of certain disputed cryptoassets, it may be important to evaluate whether those cryptoassets are being held through an intermediary or, if not, whether they are currently stored in a "hot" or a "cold" wallet, since these factual circumstances may affect the possibility of establishing the physical location of the assets at any given time.[8]

Looking at these dilemmas from the perspective of a future research agenda, many interesting possibilities arise. The most challenging and fascinating question is whether the rise of DLT finance, together with other developments brought about by digitalisation, requires an (at least partial) reconsideration of the geographical rootedness of private international law. While it is obviously challenging to apply to DLT finance jurisdictional rules that were created with "analogue" transactions in mind, it is equally challenging to imagine a radically alternative approach, which would allow a national court to assess its own jurisdiction while disregarding geographical localisation criteria altogether.[9]

Further interesting questions emerge when looking at these issues from a comparative law perspective. In recent times, certain courts have shown a willingness to accept jurisdiction over cases concerning DLT finance, even when the geographical connection between the transaction and the *forum* was tenuous at best.[10] It would

7 See, e.g., in case of defendants domiciled in a European Union (EU) Member State, Article 4 of the Council Regulation (EU) No. 1215/2012 of the European Parliament and of the Council of 12 December 2012 on jurisdiction and the recognition and enforcement of judgments in civil and commercial matters, [2012] OJ L 351/1 of 20.12.2012 (Brussels I *bis* Regulation).

8 Amy Held, 'Crypto Assets and Decentralised Ledgers: Does Situs Actually Matter?' in Andrea Bonomi, Matthias Lehmann, and Shaheeza Lalani (eds), *Blockchain and Private International Law* (Brill Nijhoff 2023).

9 Dan Jerker B Svantesson, *Solving the Internet Jurisdiction Puzzle* (Oxford University Press 2017).

10 In the aforementioned *Fetch.ai* case (n 6), for instance, the High Court of England and Wales held that, in the case of pure economic loss suffered as a consequence of a crypto-exchange hack, the place where the damage is suffered is the domicile of the victim. As pointed out by Matthias Lehmann, 'Hacked Crypto-Accounts and the Continued Importance of Rome II in the English Courts: Fetch.AI v Persons Unknown' (*EAPIL Blog*, 18 January 2022) <https://eapil.org/2022/01/18/hacked-crypto-accounts

be interesting to investigate whether the approaches of different national courts in this respect are progressively diverging, and (if yes) whether such divergence could be understood as a form of regulatory competition, with some legal systems purposefully stretching the boundaries of their jurisdictional rules with the goal of attracting DLT finance disputes.

3. *Limitations of choice-of-court agreements*

Apparently, a solution to the jurisdictional dilemmas outlined in the previous subsection would be to include in a DLT-related financial contract a choice-of-court clause, conferring exclusive jurisdiction upon a single national court. To be sure, this does often happen in practice: the general terms and conditions underlying an Initial Token Offering (ITO), for instance, routinely contain jurisdiction clauses.[11] These clauses, however, are likely unable to resolve all of the problems that can arise with respect to DLT financial disputes. First of all, a choice-of-court agreement typically defines its scope with respect to a certain contract, covering disputes that have a contractual cause of action. However, certain DLT financial disputes are likely to be tortious in nature; for instance, the provision of misleading information in a white paper, as well as the omission of relevant information, should probably qualified as a tortious "fraud to the market", along the lines of what happens in prospectus liability cases with respect to more traditional financial instruments.[12] It is often unclear to what extent a choice-of-court clause in a contract can cover those tortious claims.[13] Furthermore, even in cases where the wording of the clause is deemed broad enough to encompass tortious actions, further problems are likely to arise. Whenever

-and-the-continued-importance-of-rome-ii-in-the-english-courts-fetch-ai-v-persons-unknown/> accessed 20 December 2023, this conclusion would not be tenable in the courts of EU Member States, given the case law of the Court of Justice of the European Union in Case C-375/13 *Harald Kolassa v Barclays Bank plc* [2015] ECLI:EU:C:2015:37 and Case C-304/17 *Helga Löber v Barclays Bank plc* [2018] ECLI:EU:C:2018:701. See also Tobias Lutzi, 'The Tort Law Applicable to the Protection of Crypto Assets' in Andrea Bonomi, Matthias Lehmann, and Shaheeza Lalani, *Blockchain and Private International Law* (Brill Nijhoff 2023) 399.

11 For instance, in the *Tezos* case (In Re Tezos Securities Litigation [2017] Case No. 3:17-cv-06779-RS (N.D. Cal. 2017)), the choice in favour of the court of Zug (Switzerland) did not prevent the filing of a class action in the United States.

12 With reference to the issuance of different types of cryptoassets in the EU, the information to be included in the white paper is detailed in Annexes I-III to Council Regulation (EU) 2023/1114 of the European Parliament and of the Council of 31 May 2023 on markets in crypto-assets, and amending Regulations (EU) No 1093/2010 and (EU) No 1095/2010 and Directives 2013/36/EU and (EU) 2019/1937 (MiCA) [2023] OJ L 150/40 of 09.06.2023. See instead, with reference to prospectus liability, Matteo Gargantini, 'Competent Courts of Jurisdiction and Applicable Law' in Danny Busch, Guido Ferrarini, and Jean Paul Franx (eds), *Prospectus Regulation and Prospectus Liability* (OUP 2020) 459.

13 See e.g., with reference to the Council Regulation (EC) No 44/2001 of 22 December 2000 on jurisdiction and the recognition and enforcement of judgements in civil and commercial matters (Brussels I Regulation) [2001] OJ L 12/1 of 16.01.2001, Case

a plaintiff purchases cryptoassets on the secondary market and subsequently initiates litigation against the issuer of those assets, it is debatable to what extent a choice-of-court clause included by the issuer in its general terms and conditions can produce effects. Furthermore, if the plaintiff is not a professional investor, the applicability of a consumer-specific jurisdictional regime may be triggered. As a consequence, the applicable private international law regime may exclude or limit the opposability of a choice-of-court agreement to the plaintiff.

Observing these issues from a research agenda angle, the most pressing question is whether private international law is in need of an update and, if yes, in what direction such a reform effort should take. On the one hand, choice-of-court agreements are a crucial tool in ensuring predictability and centralisation of litigation. As such, more clarity on the applicability of those clauses with respect to tortious actions and secondary market purchasers would likely bring about more predictability. On the other hand, the rationale traditionally underlying consumer-specific jurisdictional rules is applicable to many DLT financial transactions, where cryptoassets are purchased by inexperienced investors, who may have been unaware of the content and potential consequences of the issuer's terms and conditions. More research on this crucial tension is necessary before the legal framework applicable to choice-of-court clauses in DLT finance can be responsibly modernised.

4. *Access to justice constraints*

Court litigation inherently entails a certain complexity, duration, and cost. While certain legal systems strive to enhance access to justice, litigation comes with a degree of friction that can never be entirely eliminated. Therefore, it is debatable whether all disputes are suitable for litigation: certain types of low-value cases can be efficiently dealt with by courts if multiple claimants can collectively seek redress, but they can also be resolved out of court. DLT financial transactions may, depending on their size and characteristics, result in low-value disputes, for which litigation may not always be a realistic option. Given this background, a fascinating (and not yet fully answered) research question emerges: to what extent do plaintiffs in DLT finance disputes enjoy effective access to justice, and which factors influence their dispute resolution decisions? Some high-profile DLT finance cases, for instance, have resulted in class actions;[14] for other disputes, however, the affected parties may have opted for a different dispute resolution avenue, or even failed to take any action whatsoever. In order to get more clarity on the current reality of access to justice for DLT finance disputes, more empirical research is needed. A survey could help clarify the opinions and thinking patterns of those involved in this type of dispute. Complementarily,

---

C-352/13 *Cartel Damage Claims (CDC) Hydrogen Peroxide SA v Evonik Degussa GmbH and Others* [2015] ECLI:EU:C:2015:335, para. 31.

14 See e.g. In Re Tezos Securities Litigation (n 11). For an empirical analysis of the crypto-related cases litigated in US courts up until 2022, see Farshad Ghodoosi, 'Crypto Litigation: An Empirical View' (2022) 40 Yale Journal of Regulation 87.

interviews with different stakeholders could generate qualitative insights into the current DLT finance dispute resolution landscape.

B. International arbitration

At first sight, given the cross-border nature of many DLT finance disputes, international arbitration is ideally suited as a dispute resolution mechanism. As a procedure, arbitration strikes a balance among different legal traditions and can thus provide a neutral dispute resolution forum for parties that may be reluctant to litigate in a foreign court. Furthermore, arbitral awards are entitled to international recognition and enforcement under the 1958 New York Convention, which significantly enhances the attractiveness of arbitration vis-à-vis court litigation. However, when delving deeper into the topic, a more nuanced reality comes to light. Arbitration has certain limitations that may curtail its attractiveness for certain types of DLT finance disputes. The following sub-sections will expound on two examples and sketch a research agenda for further investigation on these topics.

1. *The limitations of arbitration's consensual framework*

First of all, many of the shortcomings discussed above with regard to choice-of-court agreements may affect arbitration agreements as well. For instance, secondary market purchasers may not always be bound by arbitration clauses in the terms and conditions published by the issuer of a given cryptoasset. Furthermore, an arbitration clause may not be opposable to investors that qualify as consumers, depending on the applicable law.[15] As a consequence, even if an agreement to arbitrate exists, it may be unable to capture all disputes that potentially arise with respect to a certain DLT financial transaction. In terms of a future research agenda, these shortcomings raise the question of whether consent is still an adequate cornerstone for arbitration. Some authors have argued that, at least for business-to-business international commercial contracts, arbitration should become the default dispute resolution mechanism, to be used even in the absence of an agreement of the parties, as long as the latter have not opted out of it.[16] It would be interesting to test the practical tenability of such an argument in favour of "default arbitration", with specific respect to DLT finance.

2. *Suitability of arbitration for crypto-related disputes*

DLT-related disputes are multifaceted in nature and, therefore, not always suitable for arbitration. First of all, the value in dispute is an important factor influencing the viability of arbitration: for relatively low values, recourse to arbitration is likely

---

15 *Amir Soleymani v Nifty Gateway LLC and The Competition and Markets Authority* [2022] EWCA Civ 1297.

16 Gilles Cuniberti, 'Beyond Contract – The Case for Default Arbitration in International Commercial Disputes' (2008) 32(2) Fordham International Law Journal 417; Gary B Born, 'BITS, BATS and Buts: Reflections on International Dispute Resolution' (2013) 10(38) Revista Brasileira De Arbitragem 138; Gilles Cuniberti, *Rethinking International Commercial Arbitration: Towards Default Arbitration* (Edward Elgar 2017).

unwarranted, unless multiple claims can be bundled up in a mass arbitration.[17] Furthermore, as already mentioned, arbitration may not be available when the claims are non-contractual in nature, and/or where the prospective plaintiff and respondent are not privy to the same arbitration clause (e.g. because the plaintiff purchased the assets giving rise to the dispute on the secondary market). In addition, the availability of arbitration may vary, depending on the applicable law, in situations where one of the disputing parties has been declared insolvent.[18]

By contrast, arbitration may be particularly well-suited to resolve certain types of DLT financial disputes, where the amount in dispute is relatively high, and the cause of action is contractual. For instance, as a consequence of the aforementioned "crypto-winter" (i.e., the loss of value of a wide range of cryptoassets starting from 2022), a high number of disputes are emerging with regard to mergers between or acquisitions of crypto-related companies. Further research is necessary to assess the suitability of arbitration to resolve this specific subset of M&A disputes. Along similar lines, cryptoassets are routinely used in the context of secured loans,[19] and arbitration could be used to resolve disputes related to defaults on those loans.[20] In sum, future research should allow for a more granular understanding of what "crypto-arbitration" is, and what types of disputes it is suitable for.

3. *Anonymity in arbitration*

Anonymity may constitute an obstacle against arbitration for DLT finance disputes. Depending on the *lex arbitri*, an arbitral tribunal may be prevented from hearing a case unless all parties to it have been identified. Among the many concerns that anonymity raises in this context, identifying the parties may be essential for the arbitrators to evaluate whether the dispute is genuine or a sham arbitration, as well as to rule out violations of anti-money laundering legislation, public policy, or other mandatory law in the public interest.[21] Apart from the law of the seat of arbitration, similar

---

17 See, e.g., the mass American Arbitration Association (AAA) arbitration against Genesis Global Capital, Digital Currency Group (DCG), and Genesis Global Trading: Monika Ghosh, 'Gemini Earn Users Launch Class Arbitration against Genesis, DCG' (*Cryptoslate*, 3 January 2023) <https://cryptoslate.com/gemini-earn-users-launch-class-arbitration-against-genesis-dcg/> accessed 20 December 2023.

18 Edward Taylor and Helen Wang, 'Crypto Winter Disputes: Navigating the Intersection of Crypto, Arbitration and Insolvency' (*International Bar Association*, 21 October 2022) <www.ibanet.org/crypto-winter-disputes> accessed 20 December 2023.

19 Matthias Haentjens and Matthias Lehmann, 'The Law Governing Secured Transactions in Digital Assets' in Andrea Bonomi, Matthias Lehmann, and Shaheeza Lalani, *Blockchain and Private International Law* (Brill Nijhoff 2023) 456.

20 See *GGC International Limited v Ver* [2023] 1:2023cv01560 (S.D.N.Y.); *Janesh s/o Rajkumar* (n 6).

21 Anne-Grace Kleczewski, 'The Good, the Bad and the Ugly: The Private International Law, the Crypto Transactions and the Pseudonyms' in Andrea Bonomi, Matthias Lehmann, and Shaheeza Lalani (eds), *Blockchain and Private International Law* (Brill Nijhoff 2023).

constraints against anonymous arbitration may derive from the law of the place of likely enforcement of any future arbitral award.

Given these limitations, further research is necessary to investigate whether the use of arbitration for DLT finance disputes could be reconciled with some degree of anonymity of the parties. For instance, it is unclear whether an arbitral tribunal could give a third party (e.g., an arbitral institution or a cryptoasset custodian) the mandate to identify the disputants and then hold the proceedings pseudonymously, with the disputants not revealing their identities to the arbitrators or to each other. Interestingly, comparable arrangements are routinely used in arbitration, albeit for admittedly different purposes. For instance, under Article 3(8) of the 2020 International Bar Association (IBA) Rules on the Taking of Evidence in International Arbitration, an arbitral tribunal may, after consultation with the parties, appoint a third-party expert entrusted with the task of reviewing a piece of documentary evidence and reporting on an objection made by one of the parties as to the production of that piece of evidence. This way, the Tribunal can rule on the objection without being directly exposed to the contents of the document.

III. DLT financial disputes and new avenues of online dispute prevention and resolution

Court litigation and arbitration are by no means the only mechanisms that can be used for the resolution of DLT financial disputes. Next to them, new instruments of dispute prevention and resolution are emerging, leveraging the potential of DLT in an attempt to enhance speed and minimise costs. This section will zoom in on some of the most important developments in this field, considering in particular the potential for future scientific investigations. The first sub-section will discuss the dispute-prevention potential of smart contracts. Subsequently, the following sub-sections will scrutinise the emergence of new, self-enforcing ODR mechanisms, such as Kleros, and the attempts to bridge the gap between these new forms of ODR and the legal framework traditionally governing the enforcement of judgments and arbitral awards.

A. The dispute-prevention function of smart contracts

Over the past decade, a vast debate has been developing about the nature of smart contracts, their potential, and their limitations.[22] For the purposes of this chapter, it is not necessary to discuss whether and under what circumstances a smart contract

---

22 See Zibin Zheng and others, 'An Overview on Smart Contracts: Challenges, Advances and Platforms' (2020) 105 Future Generation Computer Systems 475; Merit Kõlvart, Margus Poola, and Addi Rull, 'Smart Contracts' in Tanel Kerikmäe and Addi Rull (eds), *The Future of Law and eTechnologies* (Springer 2016) 133; Max Raskin, 'The Law and Legality of Smart Contracts' (2016) 1(2) Georgetown Law Technology Review 305; Primavera De Filippi, Chris Wray, and Giovanni Sileno, 'Smart Contracts' (2021) 10(2) Internet Policy Review.

could be legally qualified as a contract, and what the consequences of that qualification may be. To the contrary, it will suffice to consider certain claims that have been made with respect to smart contracts and their dispute-avoidance potential. In a broad sense, smart contracts can be used to automate the execution of an agreement, thus ruling out or minimising the risk of non-performance. Taken at face value, the automation that smart contracts bring about seems to be able to exclude the need for dispute resolution altogether. Indeed, if technology can ensure the automatic performance of an agreement, there would not be any need for the resolution of disputes arising out of a breach of contract.[23] Reality, however, is more nuanced than the aforementioned claims would suggest, and technical as well as practical obstacles stand in the way of the complete automation of contractual relationships in the field of DLT finance. First of all, smart contracts are written in programming language and must therefore follow a deterministic logic. Such an if-then logic is adequate to automate certain types of contractual clauses, which do not require any particular case-by-case analysis for their application. However, any non-trivial financial agreement will also contain other clauses, which do not embody such a strict binary logic.[24] For instance, any reference to good faith or best efforts will require a contextual analysis of the circumstances of the case before any assessment can be made as to whether an agreement has been breached. Therefore, most DLT financial contracts cannot be fully translated into code, and their enforcement cannot be entirely automated. In certain scenarios, a smart contract might be able to refer to an external oracle, which in turn will provide the necessary contextual evaluation; in other circumstances, however, it will not be possible to completely exclude the risk of a dispute through the automatic performance of the underlying contractual relationship. Furthermore, at a practical level, the automatic performance of a contractual clause might require the storage of a significant amount of funds in escrow, which in turn might frustrate the very purpose of an agreement.[25] To give a practical example, a lender might extend a loan to be repaid in instalments, unless certain predetermined events of default occur and allow the lender to accelerate or terminate the loan agreement. It might be technically possible for a smart contract to detect the occurrence of an event of default and, in that case, trigger the immediate repayment of the loan in full, upon the instruction of the lender. However, in order for this type of smart contract to be successfully deployed, it would be necessary for the entire sum to be stored in escrow throughout the entire duration of the loan agreement, so that the smart contract will have access to sufficient funds in case of acceleration or termination. This, in turn, would make those funds unavailable for the borrower, thus frustrating the entire purpose of the loan agreement.

---

23 Riikka Koulu, 'Blockchains and Online Dispute Resolution: Smart Contracts as an Alternative to Enforcement' (2016) 13(1) SCRIPTed 40.

24 Eliza Mik, 'Smart Contracts: Terminology, Technical Limitations and Real World Complexity' (2017) 9 Law, Innovation & Technology 269; Eliza Mik, 'Contracts in Code?' (2021) 13 Law, Innovation & Technology 478.

25 Pietro Ortolani, 'Self-Enforcing Online Dispute Resolution: Lessons from Bitcoin' (2015) 36(3) Oxford Journal of Legal Studies 595.

From the point of view of a future research agenda, the observations sketched above show the need for a more nuanced investigation of what smart contracts can do in practice, and conversely, what they *cannot* do. Too often, during the last decade, legal literature has portrayed an overly optimistic picture of smart contracts, without contextualising it in light of the technological limitations of this tool, as well as the practical and economic reality of the financial transactions that are supposed to make use of this technology.

B. Self-enforcing online dispute resolution

The rise of DLT has triggered the emergence of new forms of ODR, which do not correspond to any of the procedures that we traditionally associate with the resolution of financial disputes. As already mentioned, smart contracts can receive instructions from external oracles and perform actions accordingly. This technology can be used for dispute resolution purposes; by way of example, an oracle can communicate to a smart contract the outcome of a given dispute concerning a financial contract and instruct the smart contract to transfer certain disputed assets (e.g., a Non-Fungible Token (NFT), or some cryptocurrency) to the prevailing disputant. At its core, this technique enables new forms of technology-mediated enforcement, whereby the outcome of a dispute resolution procedure can be implemented without relying on the voluntary compliance of the losing party, or the coercive enforcement of public authorities (e.g., bailiffs).[26]

In recent years, the self-enforcing potential of DLT has been harnessed by ODR procedures that leverage the wisdom of the crowd in order to find the correct resolution

26 Pietro Ortolani, 'The Three Challenges of Stateless Justice' (2016) 7 Journal of International Dispute Settlement 596.

of a legal dispute.[27] A good example of this development is Kleros.[28] If two parties agree to use Kleros with reference to a given financial contract, either of them will be able to initiate a procedure against the other in the case of disagreement. The parties will normally be able to present their arguments in writing and upload evidence. Subsequently, other Kleros users are allowed to cast a vote and express their opinion on how the dispute should be resolved, based on the basis of the arguments and evidence that the disputants have submitted. The users cast their votes through a special token, and at the end of a predetermined dispute resolution, the case is resolved in favour of the party that received the majority of the votes. Thanks to a smart contract, Kleros decisions are self-enforcing, and the prevailing party will automatically receive the disputed assets. The users that voted with the majority will receive their tokens back, plus a percentage of the tokens cast by the minority. The users in the minority, conversely, will lose their tokens. This system is supposed to create an economic incentive for the users to decide the case fairly, trying to predict the most reasonable and acceptable outcome of the dispute.

Procedures such as Kleros do not resemble traditional arbitration from multiple points of view.[29] The procedure is remarkably fast, and the possibility for the parties to present their evidence and put forth defences is limited to the affordances that the Kleros system allows (for instance, there is normally no possibility of an oral hearing). The dispute is not decided by one or three arbitrators chosen by the parties or by an appointing authority; on the contrary, it is voted upon by a "swarm" of users

27 Alesia Zhuk, 'Applying Blockchain to the Modern Legal System: Kleros as a Decentralised Dispute Resolution System' (2023) 4 International Cybersecurity Law Review 1; Yannick Gabuthy, 'Blockchain-Based Dispute Resolution: Insights and Challenges' (2023) 14(3) Games 34; Matthew Dylag and Harrison Smith, 'From Cryptocurrencies to Cryptocourts: Blockchain and the Financialization of Dispute Resolution Platforms' (2023) 26(2) Information, Communication & Society 372; Luis Bergolla, Karen Seif, and Can Eken, 'Kleros: A Socio-Legal Case Study of Decentralized Justice & Blockchain Arbitration' (2022) 37 Ohio State Journal on Dispute Resolution 55; Bronwyn E Howell and Petrus H Potgieter, 'Uncertainty and Dispute Resolution for Blockchain and Smart Contract Institutions' (2021) 17(4) Journal of Institutional Economics 545; Yann Aouidef, Federico Ast, and Bruno Deffains, 'Decentralized Justice: A Comparative Analysis of Blockchain Online Dispute Resolution Projects' (2021) 4 Frontiers in Blockchain 3; Matija Kontak, 'Modern Tools to Lower the Costs of Disputes: Digitalisation and the New Venues of Online Dispute Resolution' (2021) Harmonius: Journal of Legal & Social Studies South East Europe 113; Aleksei Gudkov, 'Crowd Arbitration: Blockchain Dispute Resolution' (2020) Legal Issues in the Digital Age 59; Cemre C Kadıoğlu Kumtepe, 'A Brief Introduction to Blockchain Dispute Resolution' (2020) 14(2) John Marshall Law Journal 138.

28 Kleros, 'The Justice Protocol: Kleros is a decentralized arbitration service for the disputes of the new economy' <https://kleros.io/> accessed 20 December 2023.

29 For a more extended overview of these reasons, see Pietro Ortolani, 'Digital Dispute Resolution: Blurring the Boundaries of ADR' in Michel Cannarsa and others (eds), *The Cambridge Handbook of Lawyering in the Digital Age* (Cambridge Law Handbooks, Cambridge University Press 2021) 140.

whose number and identity are neither predictable in advance nor entirely disclosed afterwards. The remedies that can be sought by the parties are also rudimentary: the disputants can mainly seek the transfer of certain cryptoassets which must have been previously stored in escrow, for the purpose of ensuring the self-enforcement of the decision. In addition, while arbitrators must be impartial and independent, and therefore lack any economic incentive to decide a dispute in one way or another, Kleros users face a strong economic incentive to gain or lose tokens, depending on how they decide the case. These are only some of the reasons why procedures such as Kleros may well not legally qualify as arbitration. The unique nature of these new forms of ODR, in turn, raises fascinating research questions, which are not fully answered yet. More research is necessary to clarify the legal nature of these procedures, and the way in which they can fit within national legal systems. In addition to these more dogmatic lines of research, empirical investigation would be highly beneficial to learn more about the reality of these procedures. From a quantitative standpoint, the public nature of permissionless blockchains would allow gathering information on the usage rate of these procedures, as well as the average value in disputes and other recurring characteristics. Complementarily, qualitative investigation could help understand the viewpoints and expectations of those who use those procedures, either as disputants or as jurors. In particular, a study of the *ex ante* and *ex post* expectations of disputants could help clarify whether these new forms of ODR can indeed afford users a cost-effective procedure, which delivers what the disputants want.

C. Bridging the gap between on-chain dispute resolution and off-chain enforcement through consent awards

While the self-enforcement potential of blockchain-based ODR is significant, it is far from unlimited. As already mentioned, in procedures such as Kleros, the outcome is only automatically enforceable if it consists in the transfer of disputed cryptoassets which have been previously stored in escrow. To the contrary, whenever a dispute resolution outcome requires the performance of actions which cannot take place on a blockchain, the possibility of technology-mediated self-enforcement is excluded. Because of this, attempts have been recently made to bridge the gap, ensuring that a dispute resolution outcome is both self-enforcing on the blockchain and enforceable as a legal title off-chain. For instance, in at least one known case, two parties to a contract have agreed to use Kleros for the resolution of a dispute, and then have entrusted a sole arbitrator with the task of issuing an award on agreed terms, transposing the terms of the Kleros decision into an arbitral award.[30] As such, this technique is far from new and is routinely used to record the terms of a settlement agreement into an

[30] Mauricio Virues Carrera, 'Accommodating Kleros as a Decentralized Dispute Resolution Tool for Civil Justice Systems: Theoretical Model and Case of Application' <https://ipfs.kleros.io/ipfs/QmfNrgSVE9bb17KzEVF0Gf4KKA1Ekaht7i0LjYzheZ6prE/Accommodating%20Kleros%20as%20a%20Decentralized%20Dispute%20Resolution%20Tool%20for%20Civil%20Justice%20Systems%20-%20Theoretical%20Model%20and%20Case%20of%20Application%20-%20Mauricio%20Virues%20-%20Kleros%20Fellowship%20of%20Justice.pdf> accessed 20 December 2023.

award, so as to ensure enforceability. In this case, however, the content of the award on agreed terms was determined not by the parties themselves, but by the Kleros jurors through their decision. More research is necessary to assess the availability of this technique in different legal systems, as well as (in cases where the law of the seat allows the issuance of such an award by consent) the international enforceability of this type of award. Furthermore, at a normative level, more reflection is needed as to whether this use of the award by consent is desirable. On the one hand, arbitration is a creature of consent, and the aforementioned arrangement is entirely based on the parties' contractual freedom. On the other hand, however, the parties consent to a decision whose contents they are not aware of; as a consequence, doubts may arise as to whether party autonomy needs to be somehow limited in this scenario.

IV. Conclusions

This chapter has shown that DLT finance can give rise to a variety of disputes. As a consequence, it would not be wise to try to resolve them all through a single procedure: while high-value disputes may be suitable for international arbitration, for instance, financial contracts with a relatively low value may be best suited for the new and rapidly emerging forms of ODR, which this chapter has described. Furthermore, the chapter has highlighted the tortious nature of some DLT financial disputes, as well as the potential qualification of investors as consumers. These factors, depending on the applicable law, may have a significant impact on the parties' possibility to devise a predictable dispute resolution policy by means of arbitration or choice of court agreements.

In light of the variety of possible DLT finance disputes, as well as the many factors influencing their resolution, the chapter has sketched a future research agenda in this field, formulating dogmatic, normative, and empirical research questions that currently lack a sufficient answer. Given the fast pace at which DLT finance evolves, the relevance of these questions may vary in the future, and further questions are likely to arise. This, however, should not discourage legal researchers from engaging in this field; on the contrary, precisely because of how fluid and multifaceted DLT finance is, their contribution is particularly needed.

Index

abusive squeeze (cornering) 150–51
Account Information Service Providers (AISPs) 95, 101, 102–3, 115
Address Ownership Proof Protocol (AOPP) 211
after-the-fact determination, bank disclosure regulation 19
Ahmed, K. 131, 134
AI *see* artificial intelligence
Alexander, K. 7, 10
algorithmic trading's risks 161–2, 174–7
Allegrezza, S. 182, 192, 193
alternative compliance mechanisms, crypto environment, self-regulation 55–6, 57
anonymity
  capital markets regulation, EU Market Abuse Regulation (MAR), GameStop analogy 146–8
  distributed ledger technology (DLT) and future research, court litigation 238, 239, 240
  distributed ledger technology (DLT) and future research, international arbitration 244–5
  European anti-money laundering (AML), traceability of crypto-asset transfers 206, 210–11, 212
anti-money laundering (AML)
  consumer protection and fraud prevention, and Payment Services Providers (PSPs) 230
  crypto-assets and market abuse 157
  cybersecurity in open banking and finance, blockchain technology 134
  EU *see* European anti-money laundering (AML) supervisory authority (AMLA)
  see also fraud prevention
Application Programming Interfaces (APIs)
  cybersecurity in open banking and finance, blockchain technology 135
  cybersecurity in open banking and finance, cybersecurity risks 129
  cybersecurity in open banking and finance, open banking 114, 115–16, 117, 119, 120
  Open Finance and Open Banking, EU and UK comparison 88, 101, 105, 107
arbitration, distributed ledger technology (DLT) *see* distributed ledger technology (DLT) and future research, international arbitration
Arner, D. 84, 89, 90, 91, 92, 93, 94, 98, 103, 108, 110, 115, 197
artificial intelligence (AI), sustainable finance 23–37
  AI definition 29
  AI principles and rules, proposals for 32–5, 33–4, 35
  AI principles and rules, proposals for, hard-law regulation implementation 34, 36
  blockchain 30
  bond markets 25
  change implementation and new sense of responsibility 36–7
  COVID-19 pandemic effects 25
  cybersecurity and privacy concerns 34, 36
  economic sectors using AI and impact indexes 31
  EU AI Act 33–4
  exchange-traded funds (ETF) 25
  external oversight and verification mechanisms, need for 36
  extra-financial reporting as labour intensive 27–8
  finance, impact on 29–32
  finance, impact on, AI applications 30–31

finance, impact on, data gathering cost reduction 30–31
global spending on AI systems 29–30
greenwashing issues 25, 26–7, 36
Internet of Things (IoT) 30–31
OECD 'Recommendation' on AI 32–3
potential and pitfalls 24–8
risk factors 28, 33–4, 35
third party involvement 27
universal metrics, lack of 26
asset, crypto *see* crypto-asset headings
asset pool and maturity mismatch risk, China 75
asset-backed securities business, China 74–5
association, decentralized autonomous organizations (DAOs) 48, 49–51
attribution challenge, European anti-money laundering (AML), traceability of crypto-asset transfers 213–16
Australia 148, 153
Austria 155
authority-to-authority and business-to-business data-sharing, open finance 121
Awrey, D. 84, 92, 93, 121, 124

Baisch, R. 56, 59
bank disclosure regulation 5–22
adverse (unfavourable) information, revealing 20–21
after-the-fact determination 19
bank runs 6, 11, 12–13, 14, 21
Basel Committee on Banking Supervision (BCBS) 10
behavioural biases 15–16
bubbles, issues with 11–12, 19, 20
conduct-of-business rules 6, 19
corporate governance 7–8, 9
credit ratings, regulatory over-reliance on 20
design challenges 13–16
emergency liquidity assistance 10–11, 21
fair markets promotion 11
financial crisis effects 9, 12
financial innovation challenges 15
Financial Instability Hypothesis 12
financial stability objective 9–11, 14
herd behaviour issues 12–13, 20–22
information overload concerns 17
information transmission mode 18
and intermediaries 18
investor involvement 6–7, 11–13, 14, 17, 18, 21
key investor information document (KIID) 17
liquidity shock effects 10–11, 21
managerial decision-making 7, 8
mandatory disclosure paradigm 5–6, 7, 13–19
market discipline approach 10–11
market efficiency theory 15–16
market failures 7, 9, 14, 16
public enforcement 19
public good, information as 9
reputational risks 12–13, 21
risk management 6, 8, 9, 10–11, 12–13, 20–22
securities regulation model 7, 8, 13, 14, 15, 19, 20
shareholder interests 8, 19
stakeholder orientation 7–9
strike-suit theory and opportunism 19
sustainability objectives 9
trust factors 6, 11, 12–13
Twin Peaks model 13–14
voluntary disclosure issues 14
Bank for International Settlements (BIS) 157
bank runs 6, 11, 12–13, 14, 21, 152
banking, open *see* cybersecurity in open banking and finance
Banking and Insurance Regulatory Commission (CBIRC), China 72, 76–7, 79
Bao, Y. 63–82
Bar-Gill, O. 14, 15, 16
Basel Committee on Banking Supervision (BCBS) 10
Bauerfeind, T. 167, 172, 177
Beck, B. 164, 168
Beck, T. 85–6, 106
Binance 198
Bitcoin 133, 135, 167
blockchain
artificial intelligence (AI), sustainable finance 30
crypto environment 48, 53
crypto-assets and market abuse 163, 165, 166
cybersecurity in open banking *see* cybersecurity in open banking and finance, blockchain technology
distributed ledger technology (DLT) 249
see also on-chain mechanisms
bond markets, artificial intelligence (AI), sustainable finance 25
bonds, guarantee or performance bonds 231–3
Boškić, M. 55–6, 216, 217
Brinckmann, H. 7, 15
bubbles, issues with, bank disclosure regulation 11–12, 19, 20

business models and potential risks, China 71–6
buy-back programmes, EU Markets in Crypto-assets Regulation (MiCA) 177

capital markets regulation and social media 139–56
  bank runs and Silicon Valley Bank (SVB) 152
  EU financial regulation 154–6
  EU financial regulation, complexity issues 155
  EU financial regulation, financial crisis effect 154
  information disclosure 140, 144, 145–6
  shares 141–3, 146, 147
  social media challenge 140–41
capital markets regulation and social media, EU Market Abuse Regulation (MAR) 143–52
  activity-based manipulation 144
  global coverage 143–4
  information-based manipulation 144
  'scalping' 166
  transaction-based manipulation 144
capital markets regulation and social media, EU Market Abuse Regulation (MAR), GameStop analogy 141–3, 145–56
  dominant position consideration 150, 151
  freedom of speech and expression considerations 149–50
  information dissemination, misleading 145–6
  market manipulation regulation vs. investor activism 151–2
  'reasonable investor' consideration 148–9
  Reddit 142, 145, 147–8, 149
  regulatory reform consideration 152
  'retail investor' issues 149
  scalping and anonymity 146–8
  scalping and share price influence 146, 147
  share sales 141–3
  share sales, supervision and enforcement issues 153–6
  'swarm trading' 150–52
  'swarm trading', abusive squeeze (cornering) 150–51
  user credibility assumptions 149
Cassani, U. 180, 181, 190
Central Bank Digital Currencies (CBDCs) 43
certification of protocols, crypto environment, self-regulation 54–5
Chen, C. 221–36
Chen, H.-Y. 64, 76
China, peer-to-peer (P2P) lending platforms 63–82
  asset pool and maturity mismatch risk 75
  asset-backed securities business 74–5
  asset-backed securities business, fund pool model 75
  Banking and Insurance Regulatory Commission (CBIRC) 72, 76–7, 79
  business models and potential risks 71–6
  comprehensive wealth management platform suggestion 81
  as credit intermediary 65, 69, 71, 73–4, 79, 81
  creditors' rights 66, 67, 75
  enforcement 78–80
  entry criteria and return rate 65–6, 70
  Ezubao 74
  Five-Year Plan, 13th 77
  future direction 80–81
  historical development phases 68–70
  hybrid mode 65
  illegal fundraising and fraud 69, 70, 72, 74, 75, 80
  information disclosure policies 65, 66, 67, 70, 71, 72–3
  Internet Finance Association 69, 77
  investor confidence issues 76, 79
  licensed lending institution suggestion 80–81
  loan assistance institution suggestion 80–81
  local regulatory and rectification rules 71–2
  macro-economic downturn effect 69
  maturities' duration 70, 75
  'one method and three guidelines' principle 77–8
  Pai Pai Dai (Xinye Technology) 64–5, 68, 72–3, 81
  per capita loan amounts 70
  Plan for Rectification of P2P Online Lending Risks 69
  pure online mode 64–5, 72–3
  regulatory frameworks 76–80
  risk potential 75–6, 80
  third party involvement 72, 74
  UK and US experiences 66–8
  US Lending Club comparison 66–7, 74, 75
choice-of-court agreements
  distributed ledger technology (DLT), court litigation 238, 241–2
  distributed ledger technology (DLT), international arbitration 243
co-regulatory approach, crypto environment, self-regulation 55, 56

Coffee, J. 7, 18, 153
Coinbase 160
company law and crypto environment 42–4
competition
cybersecurity in open banking and finance 114, 115, 116, 119, 123, 125
Open Finance and Open Banking, EU and UK comparison 92, 93, 94, 96
conduct-of-business rules, bank disclosure regulation 6, 19
consumer protection
cybersecurity, open banking 114, 114–15, 118, 120
cybersecurity, open finance 122, 123
consumer protection and fraud prevention, and Payment Services Providers (PSPs) 221–36
anti-money laundering and countering financing of terrorism (AML/CFT) rules 230
conduct obligations 226
contractual agreements 225, 226–8, 230, 234
e-wallets 222, 224, 225, 227, 228, 230, 231–2
fraud risk management and cybersecurity 233–5
future direction 235–6
guarantee or performance bonds 231–3
minimum capital requirement 231
money storage limits 227
monitoring of market development 231
payment instruction refusals 230
private ordering approach 225–8
prudential requirements for safeguarding money 230–33
PSP reforms and categories 222–3
"real-time gross settlement" (RTGS) system 230
regulation of PSPs 228–35
regulation of PSPs, processing delays 229–30
security of payment system, ensuring 226–7
solvency fund 232
suspicious transactions, dealing with 227, 235
and terrorism 230
third party involvement 226, 229, 236
user agreements 225–6, 227–8
consumer protection and fraud prevention, and Payment Services Providers (PSPs), Hong Kong
AML/CFT rules 230
Hong Kong Monetary Authority (HKMA) 223, 229, 233
Octopus 225–6
Payment Services and Stored Value Facilities Ordinance (PSSVFO) 223, 224, 228, 229, 231, 234
"real-time gross settlement" (RTGS) system 230
consumer protection and fraud prevention, and Payment Services Providers (PSPs), Singapore
AML/CFT rules 230
EZ-Link Wallet 225, 227, 228
fund transfer and general conduct obligation 228–30
Monetary Authority of Singapore (MAS) 223, 224, 230, 231, 232, 233, 234–5
Payment Services Act (PSA) 222–3, 224, 228, 229
"real-time gross settlement" (RTGS) system 230
consumer protection and fraud prevention, and Payment Services Providers (PSPs), Taiwan
AML/CFT rules 230
EasyWallet 226, 227
Electronic Payment Institutions (EPI) Act 223–4, 228–9, 231, 232–3, 235
"real-time gross settlement" (RTGS) system 230
contract place of performance identification, distributed ledger technology (DLT) 240–41
contracts, smart *see* smart contracts
contractual agreements, Payment Services Providers (PSPs) 225, 226–8, 230, 234
cooperative, decentralized autonomous organizations (DAOs) 47–8
cornering (abusive squeeze) 150–51
cost factors
data gathering cost reduction and AI 30–31
distributed ledger technology (DLT), court litigation 238–9
Countering/Combating the Financing of Terrorism (CFT) *see* terrorism
court litigation, distributed ledger technology (DLT) *see* distributed ledger technology (DLT) and future research, court litigation
COVID-19 pandemic effects, and (AI) 25
credit intermediary, China 65, 69, 71, 73–4, 79, 81
credit ratings, banks' regulatory over-reliance on 20
creditors' rights, China 66, 67, 75

crypto environment, traditional to decentralized governance 39–61
alternative regulatory designs 43
company law and financial market regulation, impact on 42–4
cyberattacks 40
decentralized finance (DeFi) business models 39, 42, 60–61
distributed ledger technology (DLT) 39, 40, 42, 45
fragmentation issues 43–4
future direction 60–61
future research 44
intermediaries, vanishing role of 39, 43, 44
legal framework consequences 43–4
on-chain mechanisms 42, 43, 50, 51
organizational rules and corporate structure 39
peer-to-peer organizations 49–50
smart contracts as transactional mechanisms 41–2
standardization considerations 43
technical design of decentralized environment 40–44
technical design of decentralized environment, network structures and clusters (subnetworks) 40–41
crypto environment, traditional to decentralized governance, decentralized autonomous organizations (DAOs) 39, 40–43, 60
association 48, 49–51
blockchain activities 48
cooperative 47–8
legal personality criterion 45–6
limited liability company 46–7, 51, 60
numerus clausus of available legal forms 45–8, 51
principal-agent problem, absence of 45
self-determination characteristic of smart contracts 45
smart contract programs 44–5, 47
stock corporation, unsuitability of 46
crypto environment, traditional to decentralized governance, governmental regulation 56–61
data security measures 58
decentralized autonomous organizations (DAOs) 57–8, 59
decentralized finance (DeFi) business models 57, 58, 59, 60
e-wallet addresses and tracking 60
extended regulatory regime 58
hard law and soft law, distinction between 56
intra-systemic risks 58
licensing considerations 59, 60
non-action letters 60
prohibition regulation 59
safe harbor rules 57–8, 61
sandbox and experimental regulation 56–7, 61
service providers performing on- and off-ramp procedures 59
supervision and enforcement 60
technology-neutral regulation 58
traditional instruments, analogous application 59
crypto environment, traditional to decentralized governance, new regulatory framework for decentralized finance 52–60
decentralized applications (DApps) 52, 53, 54–6, 58, 59
decentralized finance (DeFi) business models 52–3, 54
distributed ledger technology (DLT) 52
technological and legal challenges 52–3
value chain issues 52
crypto environment, traditional to decentralized governance, new regulatory framework for decentralized finance, self-regulation 53–6, 60–61
alternative compliance mechanisms 55–6, 57
and blockchain 53
certification of protocols 54–5
co-regulatory approach 55, 56
involved network participants 54
technical protocol standards and governance 53–4
transparency requirements 54
crypto "travel rule", European anti-money laundering (AML) 204, 206–9, 212, 215, 216, 218
Crypto Winter effects 197, 244
crypto-asset transfers, traceability of crypto-asset transfers, European anti-money laundering (AML) *see* European anti-money laundering (AML), traceability of crypto-asset transfers and AML/CFT
crypto-assets and market abuse 157–78
Anti-Money Laundering/Combating the Financing of Terrorism (AML/CFT) standards 157
blockchain scanning 163
front running technique 162–3
front running technique, market confidence issues 163

"same risks, same activity, same regulation" principle 157
stablecoins 157
crypto-assets and market abuse, EU Markets in Crypto-assets Regulation (MiCA) 163–74
algorithmic trading's risks 174–7
asset-referenced tokens 167–8, 169, 170
blockchain 165, 166
crypto buy-back programmes 177
crypto-asset definition 166–7
crypto-asset service provider requirements 168, 171–2, 175–6
crypto-assets other than asset-referenced tokens or e-money tokens 168, 169–70
distributed ledger technology (DLT) 166
e-money tokens 167, 168, 169–71
exclusions 167
gaps and recommendations 174–7
information dissemination restrictions 173
market abuse prevention 172–4
market risk factors, addressing 166
maximal extractable value (MEV) activities 174
media access restrictions 174
non-fungible tokens (NFTs) exclusion 167
offerors and undertakings seeking trading admission 168, 169–71
pro-innovation approach 165
pump-and-dump schemes, protection against 173
regulation addressees 168–9
regulatory approach 165–6
scope 166–7
stablecoins 164, 165, 168
transparency and fairness goal 173
US regulatory approach comparison 165–6
crypto-assets and market abuse, insider trading 159–60, 173
Coinbase case 160
decentralised exchanges (DEXs), susceptibility of 160
and know-your-customer (KYC) standards 160
public trust and integrity issues 160
crypto-assets and market abuse, pump-and-dump schemes 158–9, 173
dissemination of misleading information 158
and low-market-cap securities 158
and price volatility 159
swift action issues and online forums and chatrooms 159
uninformed investors, vulnerability of 159
crypto-assets and market abuse, stop-loss hunting and asset price manipulation 160–62
algorithm use as systemic risk 161–2
Ether flash crash 162
investor losses 161
market monitoring, need for 161
crypto-ATMs, European anti-money laundering (AML) 210
customer identity and access management (CIAM) system, open banking 115
cyberattacks
crypto environment, traditional to decentralized governance 40
cybersecurity in open banking and finance 120, 128–9, 132
cybersecurity, consumer protection and fraud prevention 233–5
cybersecurity in open banking and finance 113–37
cybersecurity in open banking and finance, blockchain technology 130–36
anti-money laundering procedures 134
Application Programming Interfaces (APIs) 135
Bitcoin 133, 135
cyberattacks 120, 128–9, 132
decentralized autonomous organizations (DAOs) 134–6
distributed ledger technology (DLT) 134–6
encryption-based technology 133, 134–5
Ethereum 135
EU Digital Operational Resilience Act (DORA) 131–2, 134
FTX collapse 135, 172
future research 137
interoperability-focused initiatives 134
jurisdiction and financial stability issues 136
know your customer (KYC) guidelines 134
layer-two scaling solution 133
private, permissioned chains 131
regulatory compliance issues 133
regulatory issues 133–4, 135–6
risk factors and solutions 132–6
sandbox regulatory process 136
scalability issues 132–3
security audits and regulatory guidelines 133
smart contract applications 131, 132, 133
third party involvement 132, 133, 134, 135
transaction efficiency 132
users' autonomy over identity information 131

cybersecurity in open banking and finance, cybersecurity risks 128–30
Application Programming Interfaces (APIs) 129
cyberattacks 128–9
EU Second Payment Services Directive (PSD2) 129–30
Trojan viruses, malware, or phishing attacks 129
cybersecurity in open banking and finance, open banking 113–21, 124–30
Account Information Service Providers (AISP) licence 115
Account Information Services (AISs) 115–16
Application Programming Interfaces (APIs) 114, 115–16, 117, 119, 120
benefits 117–19
challenges 119–21
competition 114, 115, 116, 119
consumer control and informed financial decisions 118
consumer and institutional trust, need for 114, 114–15, 120
customer identity and access management (CIAM) system 115
cyberattacks or malfunctions, dealing with 120
data loss prevention policies 119, 120, 125
distributed denial-of-service (DDoS) attacks 127
e-commerce integration facilities 118–19
encryption use 125, 126, 127
EU General Data Protection Regulation (GDPR) 127
EU Second Payment Services Directive (PSD2) 115, 116, 128, 134
firewalls, detection systems 125–6, 127
fraud prevention 120, 127
Host-Based Intrusion Detection Systems (HIDS) 125
identity and access management (IAM) systems 115
infrastructure monitoring, need for 120–21
innovation opportunities 118, 119
Intrusion Detection Systems (IDS) 125
Know Your Customer (KYC) requirements 115
loan and mortgage applications 119
Multi-Factor Authentication (MFA) security practices 126
network breaches 125, 127
operations 114–17
Payment Card Industry (PCI) Data Security Standard (DSS) (PCI DSS) 126
Payment Initiation Service (PIS) 115, 116
safeguarding financial data 124–5
Security Information and Event Management Systems 126–7
singular personal finance assistance application 117, 118
"store, process, or transmit" sensitive authentication data 128
strong customer authentication (SCA) 115
technological challenges 120–21
third party involvement 113–14, 115–16, 117, 118–19, 120–21, 125, 128, 129, 130
UK Account Servicing Payment Service Providers (ASPSPs) 116, 117
UK Competition and Markets Authority (CMA) study 116, 117
UK Open Banking Implementation Entity (OBIE) 116
UK Payment System Regulations (PSR) 116
cybersecurity in open banking and finance, open finance 121–4
authority-to-authority and business-to-business data-sharing 121
automated and standardised data-sharing protocols 123
benefits 122–3
challenges 123–4
consumer consent and data portability 122, 123
EU Data Strategy 121
financial inclusion concept 122–3
fraud prevention mechanisms and security measures 123
industry fragmentation and coordination issues 124
innovation and competition 123, 125
loans, savings, and investment products, access to 123
marginalised or unbanked individuals 123
Regulatory Technology (RegTech) 121, 123, 135, 136
sharing of financial data and information with other products and services 122
Supervisory Technology (SupTech) 121
third party involvement 122, 123

Darbellay, A. 5–22, 149
data gathering, finance, impact on, data gathering cost reduction, artificial intelligence (AI), sustainable finance 30–31

data loss prevention policies, cybersecurity in open banking and finance, open banking 119, 120, 125
data protection
challenge, European anti-money laundering (AML), traceability of crypto-asset transfers and AML/CFT 217–18
crypto environment, governmental regulation 58
cybersecurity in open banking and finance, open banking 124–5
cybersecurity in open banking and finance, open finance 121, 122, 123
European anti-money laundering (AML) supervisory authority (AMLA) 194
Open Finance and Open Banking, EU and UK comparison 88, 90–92, 101, 102
De Filippi, P. 41, 54, 245
decentralised exchanges (DEXs) 160, 215–16
decentralized applications (DApps) 52, 53, 54–6, 58, 59
decentralized autonomous organizations (DAOs) *see* crypto environment, traditional to decentralized governance, decentralized autonomous organizations (DAOs)
decentralized autonomous organizations (DAOs), cybersecurity in open banking and finance, blockchain technology 134–6
Diamond, D. 12, 20
"distributed ledger address", European anti-money laundering (AML), traceability of crypto-asset transfers and AML/CFT 208
distributed ledger technology (DLT)
crypto environment 39, 40, 42, 45
crypto environment, new regulatory framework for decentralized finance 52
cybersecurity in open banking and finance, blockchain technology 134–6
EU Markets in Crypto-assets Regulation (MiCA) 166
distributed ledger technology (DLT) and future research 237–50
financial disputes and traditional dispute resolution mechanisms 238–45
distributed ledger technology (DLT) and future research, court litigation 238–43
access to justice constraints 242–3
anonymity issues 238, 239, 240
choice-of-court agreement 238, 241–2
contract place of performance identification 240–41
cost factors 238–9
Initial Token Offering (ITO) 241
jurisdictional dilemmas 239–40
national courts and territorial criteria 238
distributed ledger technology (DLT) and future research, international arbitration 243–5
arbitration suitability 243–4
arbitration suitability, and anonymity 244–5
choice-of-court agreements 243
Crypto Winter effects 244
limitations 243
and mergers and acquisitions (M&A) 244
and New York Convention 243
and secured loans 244
distributed ledger technology (DLT) and future research, online dispute prevention and resolution, new avenues 245–50
consent awards 249–50
cryptocurrency 247
Kleros system 248–50
Non-Fungible Token (NFT) 247
on-chain dispute resolution 249–50
and permissionless blockchains 249
self-enforcing resolution 247–50
smart contracts 245–7
smart contracts, and programming language issues 246
dominant position consideration, EU Market Abuse Regulation (MAR), GameStop analogy 150, 151
Dünser, T. 52, 58
Dybvig, P. 12, 20

e-commerce integration facilities, open banking 118–19
e-money tokens, EU Markets in Crypto-assets Regulation (MiCA) 167, 168, 169–71
e-wallets
consumer protection and fraud prevention 222, 224, 225, 227, 228, 230, 231–2
crypto environment, governmental regulation 60
emergency liquidity assistance, bank disclosure regulation 10–11, 21
encryption use
cybersecurity in open banking and finance, blockchain technology 133, 134–5

cybersecurity in open banking and finance, open banking 125, 126, 127
enforcement
China, peer-to-peer (P2P) lending platforms 78–80
crypto environment, governmental regulation 60
GameStop incident and share sales 153–6
Enriques, L. 6, 9, 11, 17, 18
entry criteria and return rate, China, lending platforms 65–6, 70
Ethereum 135, 162
EU
AI Act 33–4
Anti-Money Laundering Authority (AMLA) 202
Capital Markets Union 109
Charter of Fundamental Rights 149
comprehensive crowdfunding regulation 82
Corporate Sustainability Reporting Directive (CSRD) 28
Crypto-Assets Regulation (MiCAR) 52–3, 56, 215
Data Strategy 121
Digital Operational Resilience Act (DORA) 131–2, 134, 164
Distributed Ledger Technology (DLT) Pilot Regime Regulation 164
Financial Data Access (FIDA) framework 85, 86, 90, 96, 99, 101, 104, 106, 107, 108, 109, 110
financial regulation 154–6
General Data Protection Regulation (GDPR) 34, 95, 103–4, 107, 127, 217, 218
Green Deal 25
Market Abuse Regulation (MAR) 20, 177
Market Abuse Regulation (MAR), and capital markets regulation *see* capital markets regulation and social media, EU Market Abuse Regulation (MAR)
Markets in Crypto-Assets (MiCA) Regulation 155, 157, 201, 204
Markets in Crypto-Assets (MiCA) Regulation, and market abuse *see* crypto-assets and market abuse, EU Markets in Crypto-assets Regulation (MiCA)
Markets in Financial Instruments Directive (MiFID) II 167, 168, 175, 176, 177
Open Banking framework 99, 100, 101, 102–3, 105, 108
Open Finance framework 101–2, 103–4, 105, 106, 107–10
Payment Services (PSR) 96, 107
Second Payment Services Directive (PSD2) 90, 94–5, 96, 101–2, 103, 108, 115, 116, 128, 129–30, 134
EU, cases
Cartel Damage Claims (CDC) Hydrogen Peroxide SA v Evonik Degussa 242
Deutsche Börse AG v European Commission 151
Harald Kolassa v Barclays Bank plc 241
Helga Löber v Barclays Bank plc 241
Marcus Geltl v Daimler 14
Spector Photo Group v CGFA 14
European anti-money laundering (AML) supervisory authority (AMLA) 179–96
Action Plan for preventing money laundering and terrorist financing 184–5
AML Directives 182–4, 187
AMLA tasks 187–91
challenges 194–5
and countering the financing of terrorism (CFT) 181
data protection and procedural guarantees 194
direct supervision of selected financial sector obliged entities 188–9, 191, 194
EU institutions and third-country entities, relations between 187
European Banking Authority (EBA) powers 184, 188, 191
Financial Action Task Force (FATF) Recommendations 182, 187
financial intelligence units (FIUs), coordination and support 190–91, 195
geographical distance issues 195
indirect supervision of non-selected obliged entities and non-financial obliged entities 189–90
Joint Supervisory Team 188–9, 194
money laundering and financing of terrorism (ML/FT) risk profile 188
national implementation disparities 193–4
organizational structure 191–2
preventive framework 182–7
sanctions 188, 189, 192, 199, 200, 205
shortcomings 192–3
single supervisory mechanism (SSM) 192
suspicious transactions, dealing with 190
trust factors 194–5

European anti-money laundering (AML), traceability of crypto-asset transfers and AML/CFT 197–219
  Address Ownership Proof Protocol (AOPP) 211
  AML Directive 203–4
  AML Package 201, 206
  anonymity-related risks 210–11, 212–13
  attribution challenge 213–16
  crypto "travel rule" 204, 206–9, 212, 215, 216, 218
  crypto-asset anonymity issues 206
  crypto-asset service providers (CASPs) 199–204, 206–8, 210–11, 213, 215, 216, 217–18
  crypto-asset space allocation 202–4
  "crypto-ATMs" 210
  data protection challenge 217–18
  decentralised exchanges (DEXs) 215–16
  "distributed ledger address" 208
  EU Anti-Money Laundering Authority (AMLA) 202
  EU Markets in Crypto-Assets (MiCA) Regulation 201, 204, 215
  and European Banking Authority (EBA) 210, 212, 218
  Financial Action Task Force (FATF) 199, 200–202, 203, 204, 205, 206, 217
  financial intelligence units (FIUs) 201, 211
  "follow the money" strategies and traceability of transactions 199
  freezing actions 205, 206
  Fund Transfer Regulation (FTR) 202, 206, 213, 217
  harmonisation measures 201
  interoperability challenge 216–17
  Legal Entity Identifier (LEI) 207
  money or value transfer services (MVTSs) 205
  Payment Service Providers (PSPs) 205, 213, 217
  peer-to-peer transactions 203, 215, 216
  "person-to-person transfers" 210
  ransomware attacks 203
  Regulatory Technology (RegTech) tools 213, 216
  risk-based approach (RBA) 200–201, 203, 207, 210–11
  "same activities, same risks, same rules" principle 212
  self-hosted wallets 210–11, 212–13
  Society for Worldwide Interbank Financial Telecommunications (SWIFT) 216
  subsidiarity and proportionality compliance 201
  suspicious transactions, dealing with 211, 213, 217
  techno-legal challenges 211–18
  third party involvement 210, 215
  traceability of fund flows, obligation to ensure 204–11
  transfer of crypto-assets 206–8
  virtual asset service providers (VASPs) 202–3, 206, 216, 217
  Virtual Assets Red Flag Indicators 203
European Banking Authority (EBA) 155, 170, 171, 184, 188, 191, 210, 212, 218
European Cooperative Society (SCE) 48
European Data Protection Board (EDPB) 217–18
European Securities and Markets Authority (ESMA) 154, 155, 169, 174, 175, 177
European Supervisory Authorities (ESAs) 98–9
exchange-traded funds (ETF) 25
Ezubao, China 74

Financial Action Task Force (FATF) 157, 182, 187, 199, 200–202, 203, 204, 205, 206, 217
financial crisis effects 9, 12, 154
financial inclusion concept 92, 115, 122–3, 165, 213
financial information service providers (FISPs) 101, 104
Financial Instability Hypothesis, bank disclosure regulation 12
financial intelligence units (FIUs) 190–91, 195, 201, 211
Financial Stability Board (FSB) 157
financial stability objective, bank disclosure regulation 9–11, 14
FinTech 56, 60, 62–3, 64, 87, 88, 92, 119, 123
firewalls, open banking 125–6, 127
Fisch, J. 149, 157
"follow the money" strategies and traceability of transactions, European anti-money laundering (AML) 199
France 155
fraud prevention
  China 69, 70, 72, 74, 75, 80
  consumer protection *see* consumer protection and fraud prevention, and Payment Services Providers (PSPs)
  open banking 120, 127
  open finance 123
  see also anti-money laundering (AML)

freedom of speech and expression considerations, GameStop analogy 149–50
freezing actions, European anti-money laundering (AML) 205, 206
front running technique, crypto-assets and market abuse 162–3
FTX 135, 172, 197
fund pool model, China 75
Fund Transfer Regulation (FTR), European anti-money laundering (AML) 202, 206, 213, 217
future research
  crypto environment 44
  cybersecurity in open banking and finance, blockchain technology 137
  distributed ledger technology (DLT) *see* distributed ledger technology (DLT) and future research

Gamestop analogy, capital markets regulation *see* capital markets regulation and social media, EU Market Abuse Regulation (MAR), GameStop analogy
geographical distance issues, European anti-money laundering (AML) 195
Gerding, E. 12, 15–16, 19, 21
Germany 153, 155, 166–7, 168, 177
Gilotta, S. 6, 9, 11, 17, 18
Global Mangrove Trust 31
global spending on AI systems 29–30
Goforth, C. 200, 202, 203, 212
Gounari, M. 115, 116, 124, 130
governance, crypto environment *see* crypto environment, traditional to decentralized governance
Grameen Bank 63
greenwashing issues, artificial intelligence (AI) 25, 26–7, 36
guarantee or performance bonds, consumer protection and fraud prevention 231–3

He, Q. 69, 72, 74
herd behaviour issues, bank disclosure regulation 12–13, 20–22
Hong Kong, consumer protection *see* consumer protection and fraud prevention, and Payment Services Providers (PSPs), Hong Kong
Host-Based Intrusion Detection Systems (HIDS), open banking 125
Hu, H. 9, 15, 18
Huang, R. 64, 65, 66, 69, 75, 77
Huizinga, H. 184, 193

identity and access management (IAM) systems, open banking 115
information disclosure
  bank disclosure regulation *see* bank disclosure regulation
  capital markets regulation and social media 140, 144, 145–6
  China 65, 66, 67, 70, 71, 72–3
  crypto-assets and market abuse, pump-and-dump schemes 158
  EU Markets in Crypto-assets Regulation (MiCA) 173
infrastructure monitoring, need for, open banking 120–21
Initial Token Offering (ITO), distributed ledger technology (DLT) 241
innovation 15, 118, 119, 123, 165
insider trading, and crypto-assets *see* crypto-assets and market abuse, insider trading
intermediaries
  and bank disclosure regulation 18
  China, credit intermediary 69, 71, 73–4, 79, 81
  China, information intermediary 65, 66, 67, 71, 72–3
  crypto environment 39, 43, 44
international arbitration, distributed ledger technology (DLT) *see* distributed ledger technology (DLT) and future research, international arbitration
International Organization of Securities Commissions (IOSCO) 139–40
Internet of Things (IoT) 30–31
interoperability
  cybersecurity in open banking and finance, blockchain technology 134
  European anti-money laundering (AML) 216–17
Intrusion Detection Systems (IDS), open banking 125
investor involvement
  bank disclosure regulation 6–7, 11–13, 14, 17, 18, 21
  China, peer-to-peer (P2P) lending platforms 76, 79
  crypto-assets and market abuse, pump-and-dump schemes 159
  crypto-assets and market abuse, stop-loss hunting 161
  EU Market Abuse Regulation (MAR), GameStop analogy 149
  market manipulation regulation vs. investor activism, GameStop analogy 151–2

Jackson, H. 88, 153

key investor information document (KIID), bank disclosure regulation 17
Khan, V.-M. 93, 113–37, 233
Kleros system, distributed ledger technology (DLT) 248–50
know your customer (KYC) guidelines 115, 134
know-your-customer (KYC) guidelines 160

Lee, J. 63–82, 93, 113–37, 157–78, 233
Legal Entity Identifier (LEI), European anti-money laundering (AML) 207
legal personality criterion, crypto environment, decentralized autonomous organizations (DAOs) 45–6, 49, 51
Lehmann, M. 240–41, 244
Leisinger, B. 55, 58, 59
Li, X. 69, 72, 74
licensing considerations, crypto environment, governmental regulation 59, 60
limited liability company, crypto environment, decentralized autonomous organizations (DAOs) 46–7, 51, 60
liquidity shock effects, bank disclosure regulation 10–11, 21
Littlejohn, G. 85, 92, 94, 98, 103, 107, 109
Liu, J. 68, 73
loans
  lending platforms, China *see* China, peer-to-peer (P2P) lending platforms
  open banking 119
  open finance 123
Loss, L. 7, 139
low-market-cap securities, pump-and-dump schemes 158
Lubda, M. 147, 150

Macey, J 84, 92, 93, 121, 124
macro-economic downturn effect, China 69
managerial decision-making, bank disclosure regulation 7, 8
mandatory disclosure paradigm, bank disclosure regulation 5–6, 7, 13–19
marginalised or unbanked individuals, open finance 123
market abuse, crypto-assets *see* crypto-assets and market abuse
market discipline approach, bank disclosure regulation 10–11
market efficiency theory, bank disclosure regulation 15–16
market failures, bank disclosure regulation 7, 9, 14, 16
market manipulation regulation vs. investor activism, GameStop analogy 151–2
market monitoring, consumer protection and fraud prevention 231
Martins Pereira, C. 83–112
Massoc, E. 147, 150
maturities' duration, China 70, 75
Maume, P. 139–56, 169
Maurenbrecher, B. 55, 58, 59
maximal extractable value (MEV) activities, EU Markets in Crypto-assets Regulation (MiCA) 174
media access restrictions, EU Markets in Crypto-assets Regulation (MiCA) 174
Meirich, D. 42, 54, 55, 56, 57, 58, 59
mergers and acquisitions (M&A), and distributed ledger technology (DLT) 244
Meyer, S. 45, 47, 48
Mienert, B. 44, 45
Mock, S. 143, 144
money storage limits, consumer protection and fraud prevention 227
money or value transfer services (MVTSs), European anti-money laundering (AML) 205
Morvan, A.-S. 103, 106
Muçi, E. 101, 104, 108
Multi-Factor Authentication (MFA) security practices, open banking 126

national courts and territorial criteria, distributed ledger technology (DLT) 238
national implementation disparities, European anti-money laundering (AML) 193–4
networks
  breaches, open banking 125, 127
  crypto environment, traditional to decentralized governance 40–41
  crypto environment, traditional to decentralized governance, self-regulation 54
New York Convention 243
New Zealand 153
Noble, E. 93, 104
non-action letters, crypto environment, governmental regulation 60
non-fungible tokens (NFTs) 167, 247

numerus clausus of available legal forms, decentralized autonomous organizations (DAOs) 45–8, 51

OECD, 'Recommendation' on AI 32–3
offerors and undertakings seeking trading admission, EU Markets in Crypto-assets Regulation (MiCA) 168, 169–71
on-chain mechanisms
  crypto environment, traditional to decentralized governance 42, 43, 50, 51
  distributed ledger technology (DLT) 249–50
  see also blockchain
'one method and three guidelines' principle, China 77–8
online dispute prevention, distributed ledger technology (DLT) *see* distributed ledger technology (DLT) and future research, online dispute prevention and resolution, new avenues
open banking and finance, cybersecurity *see* cybersecurity in open banking and finance
Open Finance and Open Banking, EU and UK comparison 83–112
  account information service providers (AISPs) 95, 101, 102–3
  Application Programming Interface (API) 88, 101, 105, 107
  changing financial system 87
  and competition considerations 92, 93, 94, 96
  convergence and divergence in process 98–100
  convergence and divergence in process, development lead 98–9
  convergence and divergence in substance 100–105
  data sharing 88, 90–92, 101, 102
  data sharing, compulsory approaches 91–2, 93–4, 100
  data sharing, hybrid approaches 92, 93–4, 99–100
  data sharing, market-led approaches 92
  differences between 83–4
  EU Capital Markets Union 109
  EU Financial Data Access (FIDA) framework 85, 86, 90, 96, 99, 101, 104, 106, 107, 108, 109, 110
  EU General Data Protection Regulation (GDPR) 95, 103–4, 107
  EU Open Banking framework 99, 100, 101, 102–3, 105, 108
  EU Open Finance framework 101–2, 103–4, 105, 106, 107–10
  EU Payment Services (PSR) 96, 107
  EU Second Payment Services Directive (PSD2) 90, 94–5, 96, 101–2, 103, 108
  European Supervisory Authorities (ESAs) 98–9
  financial information service providers (FISPs) 101, 104
  and FinTech 87, 88, 92
  future direction 87–90
  mutual lessons 105–10
  Open Baning as aspect of Open Finance 89–90
  Open Banking definition 87–8
  Open Data framework 89, 90
  payment initiation service providers (PISPs) 95, 101, 102–3
  policy concerns 93
  regulatory approaches 90–94
  regulatory approaches, compulsory 96–7, 100
  similarities and differences 94–8
  SME banking data 88, 89, 100, 101
  standardisation requirements 86, 93, 102, 103, 105, 107, 109
  third-party involvement 87–8, 90, 92, 93, 95, 96, 101, 102
  timing of transition to Open Finance 99–100, 107
  UK, Brexit effects 96, 97, 106
  UK Competition and Markets Authority (CMA) 94–5, 98, 101, 102, 108, 110
  UK Financial Conduct Authority (FCA) 97, 98, 100, 104–5, 107–8, 109, 110
  UK Joint Regulatory Oversight Committee (JROC) 98, 99
  UK Open Banking framework 96, 97, 99, 100–101, 105, 108, 109
  UK Open Banking Implementation Entity (OBIE) 95, 98, 101, 102
  UK Open Finance framework 104–5, 106, 107–8, 109–10
opportunism, bank disclosure regulation 19
Ortolani, P. 237–50

Pai Pai Dai (Xinye Technology), China 64–5, 68, 72–3, 81
Paredes, T. 14, 17
Partnoy, F. 11, 20
Pavlidis, G. 23–37, 190, 194
Payment Card Industry (PCI) Data Security Standard (DSS) (PCI DSS), open banking 126

Payment Initiation Service (PIS), open banking 115, 116
payment initiation service providers (PISPs), Open Finance and Open Banking, EU and UK comparison 95, 101, 102–3
payment instruction refusals, consumer protection and fraud prevention 230
Payment Services Providers (PSPs)
consumer protection *see* consumer protection and fraud prevention, and Payment Services Providers (PSPs)
European anti-money laundering (AML) 205, 213, 217
peer-to-peer (P2P) transactions
China *see* China, peer-to-peer (P2P) lending platforms
crypto environment, traditional to decentralized governance 49–50
European anti-money laundering (AML), traceability of crypto-asset transfers and AML/CFT 203, 215, 216
person-to-person transfers, European anti-money laundering (AML) 210
Petit, A. 85–6, 106
Pocher, N. 197–219
price volatility, crypto-assets and market abuse, pump-and-dump schemes 159
private ordering approach, consumer protection and fraud prevention 225–8
prohibition regulation, crypto environment, governmental regulation 59
prudential requirements for safeguarding money, consumer protection and fraud prevention 230–33
public enforcement, bank disclosure regulation 19
pump-and-dump schemes *see* crypto-assets and market abuse, pump-and-dump schemespure online mode, China 64–5, 72–3

ransomware attacks, European anti-money laundering (AML) 203
Raskin, M. 41, 245
real-time gross settlement (RTGS) system, consumer protection and fraud prevention 230
'reasonable investor' consideration, GameStop analogy 148–9
Reddit, capital markets regulation and social media, EU Market Abuse Regulation (MAR), GameStop analogy 142, 145, 147–8, 149
Regulatory Technology (RegTech), open finance 121, 123, 135, 136
Remolina, N. 84, 88, 91, 93, 97, 98, 106
reputational risks, bank disclosure regulation 12–13, 21
'retail investor' issues, GameStop analogy 149
return rate, and entry criteria, China 65–6, 70
risk factors
artificial intelligence (AI), sustainable finance 28, 33–4, 35
bank disclosure regulation 6, 8, 9, 10–11, 12–13, 20–22
China, peer-to-peer (P2P) lending platforms 71–6, 80
crypto environment, traditional to decentralized governance, governmental regulation 58
crypto-assets and market abuse, EU Markets in Crypto-assets Regulation (MiCA) 166, 174–7
crypto-assets and market abuse, stop-loss hunting and asset price manipulation 161–2
cybersecurity in open banking *see* cybersecurity in open banking and finance, cybersecurity riskscybersecurity in open banking and finance, blockchain technology 132–6
cybersecurity in open banking and finance, open banking 120, 127
European anti-money laundering (AML) 200–201, 203, 207, 210–11
Roslyakov, M. 162, 175

safe harbor rules, crypto environment, governmental regulation 57–8, 61
"same activities, same risks, same rules" principle 157, 212
sanctions, European anti-money laundering (AML) supervisory authority (AMLA) 188, 189, 192, 199, 200, 205
sandbox process 56–7, 61, 136
scaling 132–3
scalping 146–8, 166
Schiavo, G. 184, 192
Schlarb, D. 183, 192, 193, 196
Schu, L. 157–78
secured loans, and distributed ledger technology (DLT) and future research, international arbitration 244
securities
bank disclosure regulation 7, 8, 13, 14, 15, 19, 20
China 74–5

European Securities and Markets Authority (ESMA) 154, 155, 169, 174, 175, 177
International Organization of Securities Commissions (IOSCO) 139–40
US Securities and Exchange Commission (SEC) 20, 67, 143, 148, 165–6
security
consumer protection and fraud prevention, and Payment Services Providers (PSPs) 226–7
cybersecurity *see* cybersecurity in open banking and finance
self-determination characteristic of smart contracts 45
self-enforcing resolution, distributed ledger technology (DLT) 247–50
self-hosted addresses, European anti-money laundering (AML) 210–11, 212–13
self-regulation, crypto environment *see* crypto environment, traditional to decentralized governance, new regulatory framework for decentralized finance, self-regulation
Serdaris, K. 6, 17
Sergakis, K. 143, 144, 154
shares
bank disclosure regulation 8, 19
capital markets regulation and social media 141–3, 146, 147
Singapore
consumer protection *see* consumer protection and fraud prevention, and Payment Services Providers (PSPs), Singapore
Janesh s/o Rajkumar v Unknown Person ("CHEFPIERRE") 239, 244
single supervisory mechanism (SSM), European anti-money laundering (AML) 192
singular personal finance assistance application, open banking 117, 118
smart contracts
crypto environment 41–2
crypto environment, decentralized autonomous organizations (DAOs) 44–5, 47
cybersecurity in open banking and finance, blockchain technology 131, 132, 133
distributed ledger technology (DLT) 245–7
SME banking data, Open Finance and Open Banking, EU and UK comparison 88, 89, 100, 101
social media, and capital markets regulation *see* capital markets regulation and social media
Society for Worldwide Interbank Financial Telecommunications (SWIFT) 216
stablecoins
crypto-assets and market abuse 157
EU Markets in Crypto-assets Regulation (MiCA) 164, 165, 168
standardisation considerations
crypto environment 43
Open Finance and Open Banking, EU and UK comparison 86, 93, 102, 103, 105, 107, 109
stock corporation, crypto environment, decentralized autonomous organizations (DAOs) 46
stop-loss hunting *see* crypto-assets and market abuse, stop-loss hunting and asset price manipulation
"store, process, or transmit" sensitive authentication data, open banking 128
strike-suit theory and opportunism, bank disclosure regulation 19
strong customer authentication (SCA), open banking 115
subsidiarity and proportionality compliance, European anti-money laundering (AML) 201
Sunstein, C. 8, 9, 16, 19
supervision
crypto environment, governmental regulation 60
GameStop incident and share sales 153–6
Supervisory Technology (SupTech) 121
suspicious transactions, dealing with
consumer protection and fraud prevention, and Payment Services Providers (PSPs) 227, 235
European anti-money laundering (AML) supervisory authority (AMLA) 190
European anti-money laundering (AML), traceability of crypto-asset transfers and AML/CFT 211, 213, 217
sustainability objectives, bank disclosure regulation 9
sustainable finance, and AI *see* artificial intelligence (AI), sustainable finance and ESG investing
swarm trading, EU Market Abuse Regulation (MAR), GameStop analogy 150–52
swift action issues and online forums and chatrooms, pump-and-dump schemes 159

Switzerland 11, 45, 46, 48, 51, 56, 60

Taiwan, consumer protection *see* consumer protection and fraud prevention, and Payment Services Providers (PSPs), Taiwan
Tariq, U. 125, 129
technical design, crypto environment 40–44
technical protocol standards, crypto environment, self-regulation 53–4
techno-legal challenges, European anti-money laundering (AML) 211–18
technological challenges, open banking 120–21
technology-neutral regulation, crypto environment, governmental regulation 58
Teichman, D. 15, 17, 20, 21
Terra-Luna 197
terrorism
  consumer protection and fraud prevention, and Payment Services Providers (PSPs) 230
  European anti-money laundering (AML) supervisory authority (AMLA) 181, 184–5, 188
  traceability of crypto-asset transfers and AML/CFT *see* European anti-money laundering (AML), traceability of crypto-asset transfers and AML/CFT
third party involvement
  artificial intelligence (AI), sustainable finance 27
  blockchain technology 132, 133, 134, 135
  China 72, 74
  consumer protection and fraud prevention 226, 229, 236
  cybersecurity in open banking and finance, open finance 122, 123
  European anti-money laundering (AML) 210, 215
  open banking 113–14, 115–16, 117, 118–19, 120–21, 125, 128, 129, 130
  Open Finance and Open Banking, EU and UK comparison 87–8, 90, 92, 93, 95, 96, 101, 102
timing of transition to Open Finance 99–100, 107
too-big-to-fail (TBTF) banks 8
traceability of crypto-asset transfers *see* European anti-money laundering (AML), traceability of crypto-asset transfers and AML/CFT
transfer of crypto-assets, European anti-money laundering (AML) 206–8
"travel rule", crypto, European anti-money laundering (AML) 204, 206–9, 212, 215, 216, 218
Trojan viruses, malware, or phishing attacks, cybersecurity in open banking and finance 129
trust factors
  bank disclosure regulation 6, 11, 12–13
  crypto-assets and market abuse, insider trading 160
  European anti-money laundering (AML) 194–5
  open banking 114, 114–15, 120
  open finance 123
Tsai, C.-H. 64, 76
Twin Peaks model, bank disclosure regulation 13–14

UK
  Account Servicing Payment Service Providers (ASPSPs) 116, 117
  Bank of England (BoE) and discount window facility (DWF) drawings 11
  Brexit effects 96, 97, 106
  capital market regulation 153
  and China, peer-to-peer (P2P) lending platforms 66–8
  Competition and Markets Authority (CMA) 94–5, 98, 101, 102, 108, 110, 116, 117
  Financial Conduct Authority (FCA) 97, 98, 100, 104–5, 107–8, 109, 110
  HSBC advertising campaign 27
  Joint Regulatory Oversight Committee (JROC) 98, 99
  National AI Strategy 35
  Open Banking framework 96, 97, 99, 100–101, 105, 108, 109
  Open Banking Implementation Entity (OBIE) 95, 98, 101, 102, 116
  Open Finance framework 104–5, 106, 107–8, 109–10
  Payment System Regulations (PSR), open banking 116
  Zopa P2P lending platform 66
UK, cases
  Amir Soleymani v Nifty Gateway LLC and The Competition and Markets Authority 243
  Fetch . ai Ltd v Persons Unknown 239, 240
UN Office on Drugs and Crime (UNODC) 179
UN Sustainable Development Goals 28

unbanked or marginalised individuals, open finance 123
uninformed investors, vulnerability of, pump-and-dump schemes 159
universal metrics, lack of, artificial intelligence (AI), sustainable finance 26
US
  bank runs and Silicon Valley Bank (SVB) 152
  and China, peer-to-peer (P2P) lending platforms 66–8
  Commodity Futures Trading Commission (CFTC) 165–6
  crypto-assets and market abuse 165–6
  Delaware, OpenLaw 46
  Lending Club P2P lending platform 66–7, 74, 75
  National Artificial Intelligence Initiative Act 34–5
  Securities and Exchange Commission (SEC) 20, 67, 143, 148, 165–6
  Vermont, Blockchain-Based Limited Liability Company 46
  Wyoming, DAO Limited Liability Company (LLC) 46–7
US, cases
  GGC International Limited v Ver 244
  In Re Tezos Securities Litigation 241, 242
user agreements, consumer protection and fraud prevention 225–6, 227–8
user credibility assumptions, GameStop analogy 149

value chain issues, crypto environment, new regulatory framework for decentralized finance 52
Veil, R. 144, 151, 154
Villard, K. 179–96
virtual asset service providers (VASPs), European anti-money laundering (AML) 202–3, 206, 216, 217
Virtual Assets Red Flag Indicators, European anti-money laundering (AML) 203
Vogel, B. 179–80, 192, 194, 195
Volkswagen 'Dieselgate' scandal 26
voluntary disclosure issues, bank disclosure regulation 14

wallets *see* e-wallets
wealth management, China 81
Weber, R. 39–61
Wright, A. 41, 45, 54

Zachariadis, M. 114, 216
Zamir, E. 15, 17, 20, 21
Zetzsche, D. 52, 56, 57, 58, 59, 98, 197

Printed and bound by CPI Group (UK) Ltd, Croydon, CR0 4YY
17/06/2026
14902646-0003